National Parks:
conservation or cosmetics?

The Resource Management Series

Editors: Richard Munton and Judith Rees

1   *Water planning in Britain*
    Dennis Parker and Edmund C. Penning-Rowsell

2   *The countryside: planning and change*
    Mark Blacksell and Andrew Gilg

3   *Countryside conservation*
    Bryn Green

4   *Coal in Britain: an uncertain future*
    Gerald Manners

5   *National parks: conservation or cosmetics?*
    Ann and Malcolm MacEwen

National Parks:
conservation or cosmetics?

Ann and Malcolm MacEwen
Bartlett School of Architecture and Planning,
University College London

London
GEORGE ALLEN & UNWIN
Boston   Sydney

George Allen & Unwin (Publishers) Ltd,
40 Museum Street, London WC1A 1LU, UK

George Allen & Unwin (Publishers) Ltd,
Park Lane, Hemel Hempstead, Herts HP2 4TE, UK

Allen & Unwin Inc.,
9 Winchester Terrace, Winchester, Mass 01890, USA

George Allen & Unwin Australia Pty Ltd,
8 Napier Street, North Sydney, NSW 2060, Australia

First published in 1982

British Library Cataloguing in Publication Data

MacEwen, Ann
  National Parks. – (The Resource management
series; 5)
1. National parks and reserves – England
I. Title   II. MacEwen, Malcolm
719′.32′0942   SB484.G7
ISBN 0-04-719003-5
    0-04-719004-3 pbk

Library of Congress Cataloging in Publication Data

MacEwen, Ann.
  National parks, conservation or cosmetics?
(The Resource management series; 5)
Bibliograpy: p.
Includes index.
1. National parks and reserves – Great Britain.
2. National parks and reserves – Government policy –
Great Britain. 3. Conservation of natural resources –
Great Britain. I. MacEwen, Malcolm, 1911-
II. Title. III. Series.
SB484.G7M23   333.78′3′0941   81-12673
ISBN 0-04-719003-5   AACR2
ISBN 0-04-719004-3 (pbk.)

Set in 10 on 12 point Times by Red Lion Setters, London
and printed in Great Britain
by Mackays of Chatham

We each dedicate this book to the other, without whom it could not have been written.

Foreword

The Resource Management Series reflects the view that academic research should play a crucial role in developing informed policies on resource use. In particular, research is required to establish the objective need for resource developments and to assess their physical and socio-economic implications. Without it, society may continue to choose those resource-use options that have easily definable, short-term political or economic advantages but which fail to take account of their longer term environmental and economic consequences. By the same token, academic investigation must be based on a sound understanding of the legal, administrative, economic and political contexts within which resource management decisions are made. Otherwise, research results will remain unread by policy-makers and will not be incorporated into their decision making processes.

The *Series* has been planned as an interdisciplinary vehicle for major contributions from scholars and practitioners with a wide variety of academic backgrounds. Each book reflects the individual views and experiences of the authors: no attempt has been made to impose a standard series style or length, such matters being more properly determined by the subject matter and the authors. All the books are, however, bound together by a common concern to improve our understanding of resource management policies, and all are based on substantial research or practical management experience.

All the requirements laid out in the first paragraph are met by this book. In their contribution to the *Series*, Ann and Malcolm MacEwen present the most searching and far-reaching inquiry into the national park system of England and Wales for many years. Substantive studies of the parks are few and official reports have proved dull reading, reiterating established thinking. By contrast, this book challenges conventional wisdom arguing that the national parks have been examined as if in a vacuum and thus apart from the economic forces that are moulding the rest of the countryside. This is patently untrue, the limited powers of the national park authorities being quite inadequate to nullify the effects of agricultural mechanisation, to control afforestation or mineral extraction, or to protect the living countryside and the welfare of its local population. What is needed in the long run, the authors argue, is not so much a strengthening of the powers wielded by the authorities so that they can maintain the last bastions of semi-wild countryside, as a changed perspective – to one that is less exploitative and more conscious of the need to sustain the natural and cultural attributes of the countryside.

To substantiate their position the authors have spent three years research-ing into the history, resources and administration of the national parks, and Malcolm MacEwen has just ended eight years on the Exmoor National Park Committee as an appointed member. They examine in detail the present system and call for its amendment. They applaud the statutory requirement of the authorities to produce management plans, note the plans' dependence on countryside management and then go on to demonstrate how the manage-ment approach is hindered by a lack of staff and money and, in particular, the absence of back-up enforcement powers. This situation will not be radically altered by the imminent Wildlife and Countryside Act. The authors, in an extremely important section of the book, draw attention to the ways in which *national* policies for agriculture, mineral extraction, defence and forestry all inhibit the achievement of the statutory amenity and conservation aims of *national* parks, by encouraging the substitution of capital for labour leading to a reduced work force on the land and further rural depopulation in the remoter areas of the parks.

A review of the park system was promised by government for 1981. This promise has been rescinded, but in one way we should be grateful. This thought-provoking book is the review *locum tenens* and must now provide the starting point for any official discussion on the future of the parks.

RICHARD MUNTON and JUDITH REES
April 1981

Preface

This book was conceived in 1977, when the controversy over the reclamation of Exmoor raised some questions about the national park system for England and Wales that went far beyond the local issues. In our submission to University College London and to our financial sponsors we said that there were two concerns about the performance of the system that called for fresh examination. The first, expressed by conservationists and recreational groups, was that it failed to satisfy the national interest in the protection of nature and landscape and their enjoyment by the public. The second, expressed by some residents and local authorities, was that it failed to satisfy the social and economic needs of those who lived and worked in the national parks. The conflicts of interest reflected by these concerns had led to a tug-of-war for nearly 30 years between the county councils and the conservation or recreation interests over the desirability or otherwise of amending the 1949 National Parks and Access to the Countryside Act. The national parks lobby (with which we were associated) seemed to us to be suffering from what the Americans call 'mindset'. Repeated failures to achieve the traditional remedies prescribed by the thinking of the 1940s had dimmed its perception of their limited relevance to the forces that were operating in the late 1970s. We questioned whether a simple shift of responsibility from the county councils to more centralised or autonomous national park authorities (NPAs) could satisfy either sets of interests, or resolve the problems on the ground.

Even if the demands of the national parks lobby were achieved in full – and of that there was little or no prospect – the basic difficulties would remain. The national park authorities would still be unable to change the mutually conflicting policies for the primary industries of agriculture, forestry, mineral extraction and water management. They would still be faced with the fact that the land-use planning system gave them little control over the use of either publicly or privately owned land in the countryside. Much play was being made in national park and Countryside Commission circles about the new doctrine of 'management', that was intended to fill the gaps in the land-use planning system and resolve conflicts of interest in the countryside, but what did it amount to in reality? We asked whether the conservation of natural beauty and the promotion of its enjoyment by the public (the two statutory national park purposes) were not too narrow in themselves. Could they be realised in a man-made or a man-managed landscape unless they were an integral part of social and economic policies designed to sustain the activities that gave the landscape much of its form and recreational potential? Why, we asked, had Britain been one of the few countries, if not the only one, to split the unity of nature, by entrusting the protection of scenery or 'natural beauty' (to use the statutory term taken from Wordsworth) to the Countryside Commission and the protection of wildlife or 'nature' to the Nature Conservancy Council?

Our objective, therefore, was to study whether, given the complexity of the national and local interests and their interactions, the national park system makes it possible to reconcile them, or to establish priorities. We began by posing the question whether the designation of national parks was the best or only means of achieving the aims of conservation and recreation. We had the advantage of knowing one national park authority from the inside throughout a critical period. But this insiders' view could be amplified and corrected from 1977 onwards by the mass of new information that began to emerge with the publication of the first national park plans and their innumerable supporting papers. The draft county structure plans, reports of survey and local plans that were being prepared at the same time were additional sources of information. Against a background of extensive reading, we visited each of the national parks in England and Wales a number of times. Although Scotland is not the subject of our study, we visited Scotland and studied the very different Scottish system of countryside management, mainly for the light this might throw on the situation south of the border. For much the same reason we visited national parks in France, Western Germany, the Rocky Mountains of Canada and the United States and regional parks in France (parcs naturels et régionaux). One of us also took part in a conference of European mountain farmers in the Pyrenees.

In the course of these visits we spent a considerable amount of time in the field and in the office with National Park Officers and their staffs, with wardens (or rangers as they now tend to be called), farmers, landowners, officers of the National Trust, the Ministry of Agriculture and the Forestry Commission and experts in various aspects of conservation and recreation. In addition to these informal discussions and interviews, we set up a number of more specific studies. In each national park we conducted structured interviews lasting anything from two to four hours, with eight people or 80 people in all. The cross-section of interviewees was designed to expose us to the views and experiences of people with a broad range of interests and knowledge. Those interviewed included the chairman (or vice-chairman in one case) of the NPA, the National Park Officer, a county council member of the NPA and a ministerial appointee, a district councillor who was not as a rule on the NPA, and people associated with farming or landowning interests, conservation or recreation and local employment. We sent a postal questionnaire to all 272 members of NPAs and obtained a 72% response which enabled us to draw a clear picture of the composition and characteristics of the committees and boards administering the national parks.

To test the view put to us by many farmers that the rundown of agricultural manpower might be reducing the labour force in the uplands below the levels required to maintain the 'traditional' landscape, we commissioned a study of landscape conservation in the White Peak from Rachel Berger, and published it separately (Berger & MacEwen 1979). Carys Swanwick, an ecologist with valuable field experience, prepared a paper for us on Nature Conservation and Landscape Conservation (Swanwick 1980) to clarify the relationship between the two functions, its history and the way it is changing. Geoffrey Sinclair, who was simultaneously studying the relationship of agriculture and landscape in the uplands for the Countryside Commission, advised us on the characteristics and management of semi-natural vegetation and provided the vegetation maps. We have drawn heavily on the information provided by these consultants and owe a great deal to the stimulus they provided. However, we alone are responsible for the use made of the information and for the opinions expressed in the book. We visited the New Forest and the Broads, on which working papers were prepared. We also tried to elucidate the arcane mysteries of local government finance and the National Park Supplementary Grant, with considerable help from the staff of the Treasurer of Somerset County Council, who is also the Treasurer of the Association of County Councils.

The form of the book reflects the pattern of the work and the way in which we have come to think about national parks (in the peculiarly British sense of the term) in relation to the economic and social life and to the rest of the countryside. Part 1 provides the historical background. Part 2 describes the physical, social and economic characteristics of the national parks and the ways in which people enjoy them. In Part 3 we discuss the national park system in theory and practice, using a number of case studies of which one, that of Exmoor, takes the whole of Chapter 8. Part 4 is concerned with the impact of government policies, which clearly have a central role in determining or influencing the decisions taken on the ground by public and private owners or managers of land. Finally, in Part 5 we reach some conclusions, first for the national park system itself and then for the countryside as a whole.

The study has been complicated by the fact that life does not stand still while authors describe it. As we write this Preface, the fate of the government's pitifully weak Wildlife and Countryside Bill hangs in the balance, an all-party amendment to provide legal powers to protect sites of special scientific interest (SSSIs) having been defeated by only nine votes in the House of Lords – 109 to 100. During the three years that this book has been in preparation, the perspectives for Britain's economic and political future have been altered dramatically. Partly for this reason, and partly because our own ideas have been evolving as the work has proceeded, we have become more flexible in our ideas than we were at the outset. We have had to face difficult issues that we had avoided, or evaded, in the past. It has not been easy to resolve the differences between two authors who, despite sharing a common outlook on the world (not to speak of marriage) are separated by differences in temperament, styles of work and professional experience. The tension thereby created has been, at times, extremely painful, but without it we could not have thought our way through the issues.

We have probably not been completely successful in avoiding facile generalisations, and the last thing we would claim for this book is that it provides definitive answers to the questions we and others have asked. Our aim has been more modest. It has been, first of all, to escape from the intellectual framework provided under very different conditions by the founding fathers of the national park movement in the 1930s and 1940s; and to initiate a new debate about national parks related to the political, economic, social and cultural conditions of the 1980s. Thinking about conservation, in particular, has begun to undergo a revolution in recent years and we have been carried along by this process as the book was being researched and written. We are not only older than we were three years ago but wiser. We hope that the wider diffusion of the learning experience which we have been through will contribute to a better understanding of the national parks and the countryside.

Ann MacEwen
Malcolm MacEwen
University College London
March 1981

Acknowledgements

It is not possible to thank or even to name individually all those people and organisations whose help and co-operation were extended to us. We are specially grateful to those family farmers who gave hours they could ill spare from lambing or haymaking, and to those councillors, officers, housewives and others whose interviews far out-ran the allotted time. In the Preface we refer to the studies undertaken by our consultants, Rachel Berger, Geoffrey Sinclair and Carys Swanwick, to whose skill and knowledge we are deeply indebted. We also wish to place on record our gratitude to the following for their help and co-operation.

University College London, the Bartlett School of Architecture and Planning and Professors Gerald Smart and John Musgrove, for making this study possible and providing us with the invaluable facilities and stimulus of a university environment; The Ernest Cook Trust for making the initial grant that got the study off the ground, and the Nuffield Foundation for providing the greater part of our funds; the National Park Officers in all ten national parks, their officers and wardens or rangers, who were infinitely helpful in providing information and ideas and showing us the situation on the ground; Michael Dower, Geoffrey Sinclair, Gerald Smart and Gerald Wibberley for acting as an informal advisory group, and as individuals for criticizing some papers and chapters; Mike Edwards, Barry Goldsmith, Philip Lowe and Andrew Warren of University College London for criticizing various papers and chapters; Francis Ritchie for reading the historical chapter; John Dunning, farmer and Countryside Commissioner; Reg Hookway, director of the Countryside Commission, John Foster, director of the Countryside Commission for Scotland, John Mackie, the former chairman of the Forestry Commission and Alan Leavett of the Department of the Environment; the Arkleton Trust, the Association of County Councils, the Country Landowners Association, the Council for National Parks, the Council for the Protection of Rural England, the Nature Conservancy Council, the Ministry of Agriculture, Fisheries and Food and officers of its Agricultural Development and Advisory Service, the National Farmers' Union (the county secretaries of which arranged many meetings with local farmers) and in particular David Hellard, the Cumbria secretary; Dennis Hancock of Somerset County Council Treasurer's Department; M. Guimet, of the Centre for Mountain Studies, Grenoble University, and officers of the Canadian, U.S., French and Bavarian national park services; Michael Hand, for preparing the working papers on the Broads and the New Forest; Nicola Frank and Jenny Hall, our research assistants at various times, particularly for their work on the membership study and local representation on national park authorities; Catherine Babbage in Minehead and Gitta Lunt in London, for typing and retyping the text several times, often under great pressure; and last, but very far from least, our editors, Richard Munton and Judith Rees, whose criticism and constructive suggestions enabled the authors to improve this book.

We acknowledge permission to reproduce copyright material from the following:

Association of County Councils, Countryside Commission for Scotland, Department of the Environment, Dartmoor National Park Committee, Exmoor National Park Committee, Her Majesty's Stationery Office, the Director, Second Land Utilisation Survey. Ordnance Survey material was used in the preparation of many of the maps: Crown copyright reserved.

Contents

Foreword   *page*   ix

Preface   xi

Acknowledgements   xv

List of tables   xx

List of figures   xx

Commonly used acronyms or abbreviations   xxi

PART 1   HISTORY

1   *THE HISTORY OF THE NATIONAL PARKS*   3

The national park idea   3
The 1949 Act: assumptions and consequences   9
1949–74: downhill (nearly) all the way   21

PART 2   THE NATIONAL PARKS

2   *NATURE, MAN AND CONSERVATION*   33

Nature   33
Man   64
Conservation   68

3   *ENJOYMENT*   73

Town, country and the national parks   73
National and regional roles   77
Accommodation   80
Interfering busybodies or ministering angels?   84
Cars and people   90
Elitism and democracy   93

4   *THE UPLAND PARADOX*   96

CONCLUSION TO PART 2   111

PART 3   THE SYSTEM AT WORK

Introduction   113

5   *NATIONAL PARK ADMINISTRATION*   115

Boards or committees?   115
Membership characteristics   121
Money and manpower   127

6 *PLANS AND POLICIES* 136

Two kinds of plan 136
Conservation policies 139
Recreation policies 143
Development control 149

7 *GETTING THINGS DONE* 156

Introduction 156
The management of public land 157
Practical projects 162
Management agreements 166

8 *CONFLICT IN EXMOOR* 173

The background 173
1962−8: the first round 174
1968−74: the lull before the storm 176
1974−7: war breaks out 177
1977: the Porchester Inquiry 181
1977−80: an uneasy peace 184
Management agreement guidelines 187

PART 4 THE IMPACT OF GOVERNMENT

9 *LIVES AND LIVESTOCK* 197

Hill farming policies 197
Living with the consequences 201
The neglect of the commons 205
The human resource 206

10 *THE WOODS AND THE TREES* 212

Forest policy 212
Impact on the national parks 216
Plans and controls 218
The 'consultative' procedure 219
A study in compromise 221
Questionable assumptions 225
Broadleaved woodlands 226
A new approach 228

11 *TWO EXPLOSIVE ISSUES* 231

Mineral working 232
Military training 238

PART 5 CHANGE OF DIRECTION
Introduction 247

12 *A PLACE FOR NATIONAL PARKS* 249

Lessons of a misunderstood system 249
Strengthening the system 252
A new deal for the uplands 265

13   *CONSERVATION AND THE COUNTRYSIDE*   268
     The official attitude   268
     An integrated approach   269
     Designation and control   273
     Bridging the divide   276
     The rights of landownership   278
     The politics of change   282

Postscript   284

Bibliography   287

Index   298

List of tables

1.1	National parks in England and Wales designated under the 1949 National Parks and Access to the Countryside Act.	*page*	14
5.1	Composition of national park authorities 1980–1.		116
5.2	Response to questionnaire.		123
5.3	Farmers and landowners.		124
5.4	Party political support on National Park Authorities 1964–74.		125
5.5	Who pays for the national parks? Sources of national parks finance 1979–80.		128
5.6	Changes in national park expenditure by function, 1973–4 and 1979–80.		129
5.7	National park expenditure 1979–80.		130
5.8	Expenditure on land acquisition and management agreements in national parks 1979–80.		132
5.9	National park staff 1980.		133
5.10	National park staff functions 1980.		133
6.1	Planning decisions in national parks 1972–80.		151
6.2	Planning decisions by national parks 1979–80.		151
7.1	Public and semi-public landownership in national parks 1980.		158
8.1	Moorland conservation in Exmoor, 31 December 1980.		188
10.1	Planting and restocking of conifers and broadleaved trees (1979–80) in hectares and as percentages of planted area.		214
10.2	Land acquired and planted (in hectares) in Great Britain in 1972 and 1980.		215
10.3	Land owned by Forestry Commission and private woodland under dedication schemes in national parks.		217
10.4	Government subventions for afforestation and hill farming: hypothetical case 1980–90.		224

List of figures

1.1	National parks, AONBs and the area of the Broads Authority.	15
2.1	Relief and rivers of England and Wales.	35
2.2–3	Northumberland national park, physical features and vegetation.	38–9
2.4–5	Yorkshire Dales, physical features and vegetation.	40–1
2.6–7	Peak District, physical features and vegetation.	42–3
2.8–9	Lake District, physical features and vegetation.	44–5
2.10–11	North York Moors, physical features and vegetation.	46–7
2.12–13	Snowdonia, physical features and vegetation.	48–9

2.14–15 Brecon Beacons, physical features and vegetation.   50–1
2.16–17 Pembrokeshire Coast, physical features and vegetation.   52–3
2.18–19 Exmoor, physical features and vegetation.   54–5
2.20–21 Dartmoor, physical features and vegetation.   56–7
2.22   The upland profile and plant succession.   61
3.1   National parks, national road networks and towns.   78
4.1   Assisted areas as defined by the Department of Industry 1980.   98
4.2   Cycle of intensification and decline.   100
4.3   Less Favoured Areas.   102
4.4   Age and sex structure by national parks, 1971.   106
4.5   Special Investment Areas, Development Commission 1978, and
         area of the Development Board for Rural Wales.   109
8.1   Exmoor moorland 1980.   179
11.1   Military training areas of Dartmoor.   241
12.1   Scotland's national scenic areas.   260

Commonly used acronyms or abbreviations

ACC   Association of County Councils
AONB   Area of Outstanding Natural Beauty
BBNPC   Brecon Beacons National Park Committee
CAP   Common Agricultural Policy
CAS   Centre for Agricultural Strategy (University of Reading)
CC   Countryside Commission
CCS   Countryside Commission for Scotland
CIS   Counter-Information Services
CLA   Country Landowners' Association
CNP   Council for National Parks
CoSIRA   Council for Small Industries in Rural Areas
CRC   Countryside Review Committee
DART   Dartington Amenity Research Trust
DNPC   Dartmoor National Park Committee
DOE   Department of the Environment
DOT   Department of Transport
EEC   European Economic Community
EFG   Economic Forestry Group Ltd
ENPC   Exmoor National Park Committee
ETB   English Tourist Board
FC   Forestry Commission
FW   Farmers' Weekly
HC   House of Commons (Official Report)
HL   House of Lords (Official Report)
ITE   Institute of Terrestrial Ecology
IUCN   International Union for the Conservation of Nature and Natural
           Resources

JAC	Joint Advisory Committee
LASDO	Landscape Special Development Order 1950
LDSPB	Lake District Special Planning Board
LFA	Less favoured area
MAFF	Ministry of Agriculture, Fisheries and Food
MLNR	Ministry of Land and Natural Resources (1964–6)
MOD	Ministry of Defence
NC	Nature Conservancy (1949–72)
NCC	Nature Conservancy Council (1972–)
NCVO	National Council of Voluntary Organisations
NDDC	North Devon District Council
NFU	National Farmers' Union
NNR	National Nature Reserve
NRIC	Nature Reserves Investigation Committee
NPA	National park authority
NPC	National Parks Commission (1949–68)
NPN	National Park News
NT	National Trust
NYCC	North Yorkshire County Council
NYMNPC	North York Moors National Park Committee
PCNPC	Pembrokeshire Coast National Park Committee
PFA	Public Finance and Accountancy
PPJPB	Peak Park Joint Planning Board
RA	Ramblers' Association
RAC	Regional Advisory Committee (of the Forestry Commission)
RSPB	Royal Society for the Protection of Birds
SDD	Scottish Development Department
SNPC	Snowdonia National Park Committee
SO	Scottish Office
SPNC	Society for the Promotion of Nature Conservation
SPNR	Society for the Promotion of Nature Reserves
SSSI	Site of Special Scientific Interest
TGO	Timber Growers' Organisation
UMEX	Upland Management Experiment
WMN	Western Morning News
WO	Welsh Office
WSC	Windermere Steering Committee
WTB	Wales Tourist Board
YHA	Youth Hostels Association

Part 1 *History*

1 *The history of national parks*

The national park idea

National parks can be seen as part of man's reaction to his own ruthless exploitation of nature. The 19th century saw the conquest and division of the globe by the advanced industrial nations of the West, and the use of industrial technology to exploit the natural resources of the world. The cornucopian view that the bounty of nature has no limits was almost universal, and nowhere was it held more strongly than in the United States of America where the very scale and character of the process of conquest produced its own, specifically American, reaction.

In 1864 George Perkins Marsh published '*Man and nature*', a statement of a new, ecological view that man must live with nature if he was not to endanger the sources of life. While the Civil War was in progress, Abraham Lincoln signed an Act of Congress in 1864 ceding the Yosemite Valley and the Mariposa Grove of giant sequoias to the State of California to be used as a public park on condition that it would be 'inalienable for all time'. In 1872 the first national park was established at Yellowstone. But what at first sight seems a simple desire to protect natural beauty becomes most complex when examined more closely. A recent study of the origins of the national parks in the US suggests that they originated in the search for a national identity and the glorification of the scenic wonders revealed by the exploration and conquest of the West (Runte 1979). The driving force behind the designation of Yosemite was 'monumentalism not environmentalism', and it was not until the 1930s that a part of the Florida Everglades was designated as the first 'wilderness' national park.

The American idea that a democratic government should preserve regions of scenic beauty for the enjoyment of all its citizens has been traced by Roper (1973) back to Jefferson in 1815 and Emerson in 1884. But Roper credits Frederick Law Olmsted, the father of landscape architecture and one of the least recognised geniuses of the USA, with being the first to formulate both a political philosophy and practical policies for national parks. In Olmsted's report to the Yosemite commissioners in 1865 on the measures needed to protect the character of Yosemite in perpetuity for the benefit of future generations he wrote:

It is the main duty of government, if it is not the sole duty of government, to provide means of protection for all its citizens in the pursuit of happiness against the obstacles, otherwise insurmountable, which the selfishness of individuals or combinations of individuals is liable to interpose to that pursuit (quoted in Roper 1973, p. 283).

Olmsted also rejected what Roper calls 'the ugly class philosophy of the old world', expounded by Wordsworth and others, which assumed that the greater part of the working population was incapable of enjoying beauty either in nature or in art. On the contrary, Olmsted attributed any weakness in their aesthetic faculties to the monopolisation of 'the choicest natural scenes in the country and the means of recreation in them' by a very few, very rich people whose number in the British Isles he put at less than one in 6000 of the population.

The central idea was therefore a democratic one. The state would keep out the freebooters of private (or public) enterprise, protecting the 'natural scenery' for the enjoyment of the public. But Olmsted, here as in many other matters, was ahead of his time and American words were not precisely matched by American actions. The Yosemite commissioners adopted some of his practical suggestions but suppressed his report with its radical philosophy. For many years, until the days of mass motoring, it proved to be not the common people but the 'carriage trade' – 'moneyed people of the old, established families and the upstart nouveaux riches, all able to go first class' (Haines 1977) – who patronised the new railroads that had opened up a burgeoning but elite tourist trade to the west.

Outside the protected areas the state and private enterprise were to continue the biblical mission of subduing the Earth. Congress acted on the principle that only 'worthless' land could be included in the designated areas, cutting them down to exclude any land that could be exploited for timber, water or minerals and destroying the possibility of preserving whole biological units (Runte *op. cit.*). It has at times obliged the lumber, mining or water interests by reducing the area of a park – on rare occasions *after* it has been established. But despite the conflicts of interest that have always been present, the ideas that Olmsted and other American pioneers developed have spread all over the world, and have undergone a long process of evolution.

The formal purposes of national parks have not undergone much change, as can be seen by looking at some definitions. The National Park Service Act of 25 August 1916 stated the objectives of the service to be 'to conserve the scenery and natural objects and the wild life therein, to provide for the enjoyment of the same, in such a manner and by such means as will leave them unimpaired for the enjoyment of future generations'. Responsibility for achieving these aims was entrusted to an agency of the federal government.

The definition adopted by the International Union for the Conservation of Nature and Natural Resources (IUCN) in 1969 reflects the development of ecological science, but is not fundamentally different:

A national park is a relatively large area (a) where one or several eco-systems are not materially altered by human exploitation and occupation, where plant and animal species, geomorphological sites and habitats are of special scientific, educative and recreative interest or which contain a natural landscape of great beauty and (b) where the highest competent authority of the country has taken steps to prevent or eliminate as soon as possible exploitation or occupation in the whole area and to enforce effec-tively the respect of ecological, geomorphological or aesthetic features which have led to its establishment and (c) where visitors are allowed to enter, under special conditions, for inspirational, cultural and recreative purposes (IUCN 1975).

The language is turgid but the meaning is inescapable. The protection of fauna, flora, habitats and landscapes is to be the direct responsibility of the state. The public's enjoyment must be consistent with the overriding purpose of conservation and the time-scale is implicitly 'for ever'. But the English-man or Welshman would be right to ask, when he reads this definition, whether the Lake District and Snowdonia are 'national parks' at all. Whatever they may be, our 'national parks' do not conform to the IUCN definition and for that reason are not included in the IUCN list of internationally recognised national parks, even though they appear to serve the same broad purposes. These are defined in Section 5(1) of the National Parks and Access to the Countryside Act 1949: 'The provisions of this Act shall have effect for the purpose of preserving and enhancing the natural beauty of the areas specified . . . and for the purpose of promoting their enjoyment by the public'.

This definition uses the term 'natural beauty' (to which we shall return) rather than the ecological language of the IUCN definition. But the essential difference between the American or international concepts and our own is that the national parks of England and Wales – there are none in Scotland, for reasons which become clear later – are areas that *have* been 'materially altered by human exploitation and occupation' for thousands of years and are now changing faster than ever before. They are farmed, afforested, criss-crossed by roads and power lines, worked for their resources of water and minerals, studded by hamlets, villages and even small towns, and are thronged at busy seasons by millions of tourists with their cars and coaches. They are for the most part privately owned and little of the land in public ownership (Table 7.1, p. 158) has been acquired for national park purposes. Most of it was acquired for military training, afforestation, water or electricity supply.

The reasons for the different British approach are obvious. Despite the term 'natural beauty', our landscape is to a high degree managed by man or, in the current jargon, it is a 'cultural landscape'. But the British attempt to achieve the twin national park purposes of conservation and recreation under such conditions raises many difficult questions, not all of which were understood by those who conceived the idea or drafted the legislation. There are elements in the British concept of protecting wilderness, or wildness, which exclude man. But there is also an element of returning to the earlier ideal of the inhabited, pastoral landscape as man's way of using nature to provide 'natural beauty'. The British experiment may be seen as an imaginative step that extended the idea of preservation from wilderness reserves to the countryside at large, in areas where the land remained in diverse ownerships and sustained a population through a diversity of uses. The regional parks (parcs naturels et régionaux) of France or the 'greenline' parks of the USA are adaptations or developments of the same idea, which the IUCN itself formally recognised in 1978 by creating a new category of 'protected landscape'. The paradox remains that in the United Kingdom the title 'national park' has misled visitors and natives alike for more than 30 years, arousing fears that have little justification and expectations that it has not satisfied.

The national park movement

The movement for the protection of the most beautiful scenery in England and Wales originated in the Lake District. Wordsworth published his *Guide to the Lakes* in 1810. He concluded by saying that he and other 'persons of pure taste ... deem the district a sort of national property, in which every man has a right and interest who has an eye to perceive and a heart to enjoy' (Wordsworth 1977, p. 92). But the movement had, from the beginning, the class tone that Olmsted had so vehemently criticized. Wordsworth combined a deep understanding of nature with a poetic vision of landscape. His famous rhetorical question

> Is then no nook of English ground secure
> From rash assault?

formed the opening lines of a sonnet objecting to the Kendal to Windermere Railway. He had a rooted belief that the landscape would be ruined if 'artisans, labourers and the humbler class of shopkeepers', whose 'common minds precluded pleasure from the sight of natural beauty', were tempted by the railway to 'ramble at a distance' (ibid., pp. 153–4).

The National Trust was founded in the Lake District in 1885, by much the same people as formed the Friends of the Lake District, the preservationist group from which the movement for national parks sprang in the 1930s. The Council for the Preservation (now Protection) of Rural England (CPRE) was formed in 1926 with the strong preservationist and rural bias its title implied. In 1929, Ramsay Macdonald's second Labour government appointed the Addison Committee to report on the feasibility of national parks and the improvement of facilities for countryside recreation. Its report (Addison 1931) recommended the establishment of National Reserves and Nature Sanctuaries, and the appointment of national authorities for England and Wales with limited powers to bring them into being. It relied for their realisation on regional planning schemes to be prepared by regional planning executives, but the 1932 Town and Country Planning Act placed such burdens of compensation on planning authorities that its provisions were, for most practical purposes, a dead letter.

The principal effect of the Addison report was to provide a platform around which a lobby was formed to exert pressure on government for national parks in particular. On the initiative of the Friends of the Lake District, the CPRE and the Ramblers' Association, the Joint Standing Committee for National Parks was set up in 1936, with the participation of nearly all the major open-air organisations. Under the chairmanship of Sir Norman Birkett KC, it rapidly became a formidable organisation. Its strength lay in its social and political breadth. It had bases in the countryside — where the CPRE and Friends of the Lake District had considerable influence among landowners and others — and in the towns where the Ramblers' Association had working class and Labour associations.

In *Freedom to roam* (1980) Howard Hill tells the story of the pre-war campaigns and demonstrations, in which men who confronted gamekeepers armed with cudgels and police on the northern grouse moors were fined and sent to prison. These confrontations ensured that a Labour government would be under strong pressure from its supporters to secure access to open country. From 1882 onwards, Parliament had rejected six Access to Mountains Bills. But paradoxically it was the eventual passage of the 1939 Access to Mountains Act that did most to strengthen the determination of the ramblers to get some effective legislation. For this Private Member's Bill introduced by Arthur Creech-Jones, later Colonial Secretary in the 1945 Labour government, was so thoroughly degutted in Committee that it became more a landowners' than a ramblers' charter. Trespassing on grouse moors during the shooting season was made a criminal offence and the system for establishing access was not merely so cumbersome as to be unworkable but was to be paid for by the ramblers! The Act was never implemented.

The Second World War was the decisive factor that made the politically unattainable politically possible. The demand for a 'better Britain', to replace the Britain of dole queues, means-tests and massive unemployment, exerted pressure on the coalition wartime government to demonstrate that it contemplated some decisive changes when the war was over. In his official history of *National parks and recreation in the countryside*, Gordon Cherry has described the promise of national parks as a cheap, easy and acceptable offering as part of the new postwar Britain — so much so that by the time war was over 'in the heady atmosphere of this period it was not practical politics to resist the promise' (Cherry 1975, p. 159).

Other factors helped to transform the aspirations of voluntary movements into government policy. Max Nicholson has attributed the immense advances made in the Second World War to the 'wartime suspension of the normal British mechanisms for ensuring inaction' (Nicholson 1972, p. 183). One aspect of this was the arrival in Whitehall of a multitude of temporary wartime civil servants unencumbered by the orthodoxies of the Civil Service. One of these was Nicholson himself; another was John Dower, an architect, an active member of the Ramblers' Association and one of the most prominent members of the Standing Committee on National Parks. From being an external lobbyist, drafting the Committee's policy statements, he became almost overnight the confidant of Lord Reith, the Minister of Town and Country Planning, who asked him to write a report on national parks. By a fortunate accident of timing, the Dower *Report on national parks in England and Wales* was published by the government in April 1945 (Cmnd 6378). The general election in July of the same year brought into office a Labour government which was more deeply committed to the national park idea than the Tory Party. Some of the new ministers had personal associations with the ramblers' movement – notably Lewis Silkin, the Minister of Town and Country Planning, and Hugh Dalton, the Chancellor of the Exchequer.

But national parks and access to open country were not the only aspects of conservation that the new ministers had to consider. The voluntary movement for the conservation of nature goes back to the Victorian campaigns for legislation to protect endangered species. The Society for the Promotion of Nature Reserves (SPNR) was formed in 1912 and during the Second World War the movement for nature conservation had been organising itself to secure postwar changes just as effectively, but far less obtrusively, than the national parks lobby. In 1941, the SPNR convened the 'Conference on Nature Preservation in Post-War Reconstruction' at which the County Councils' Association gave early warning of its hostility to the idea of an executive national parks authority. The seeds of division between landscape and nature conservation sown in earlier years bore fruit and the Conference decided to concentrate on the scientific aspects of nature conservation. At the government's request, the Conference established the Nature Reserves Investigation Committee (NRIC) in 1942. In March 1943 the British Ecological Society set up a special committee to review the whole question of nature conservation and ecological research. The work of these committees resulted in nature conservation becoming increasingly removed from the realms of land-use planning. It became instead a scientific matter to be administered by scientists, falling within the sphere of the Lord President of the Council, the minister then responsible for science in the Cabinet, who was advised by Max Nicholson.

Within days of taking office, Lewis Silkin appointed Sir Arthur Hobhouse, chairman of the County Councils' Association, as chairman of a Committee on National Parks in England and Wales, charged with making specific recommendations arising out of the Dower report. But the Committee had two offshoots. One was the Special Committee on Footpaths and Access to the Countryside, with Sir Arthur in the chair; the other was the Wildlife Special Conservation Committee, with Sir Julian Huxley FRS as chairman, which reported on the Conservation of Nature in England and Wales. All three committees reported in the same year (Hobhouse 1947a,b, Huxley 1947) and this led in turn to the passing of the National Parks and Access to the Countryside Act 1949. But the Act proved to be a grievous disappointment to the amenity lobby, while fulfilling the highest hopes of the scientists.

The 1949 Act: assumptions and consequences

Anybody who goes back today to the Dower and Hobhouse reports should be struck by the fact that neither of them examined the case for their concept of national parks, nor considered whether the aims of preservation and public enjoyment could be achieved by other means. Dower declared on the first page that there was no need to argue the case for national parks for that, he said, had already been made and won. All that remained was 'to fill in the details'. This was the report not of a civil servant weighing pros and cons, but of an articulate and perceptive partisan. Dower correctly anticipated that some of the most critical and difficult problems would arise from the desire of government and other public agencies to exploit the natural resources of the parks. He fully grasped the British characteristic that the landscape that was to be 'preserved' was 'the joint product of nature and human use over many generations; it cannot be preserved in anything like its present aspect unless that human use is kept going' (Dower 1945). But Dower and Hobhouse were locked into a set of shared assumptions which received little critical attention. These assumptions were spelt out in the Scott report (1942) on *Land utilisation in rural areas*, which was one of a trinity of reports that laid the basis of the postwar planning system. Two assumptions were of particular importance. One was the idea that the town and country planning system (which did not then exist except on paper) would reconcile private landownership and the exploitation of the natural resources of the parks with the public good and ensure a harmonious, well-ordered, well-designed countryside. The other was that a prosperous farming industry would preserve both the rural landscape and the rural communities.

The Dower and Hobhouse reports are commonly regarded as the foundation texts that laid the basis of the 1949 Act. But the Scott report was the seminal document. It broke entirely new ground by looking at the social, economic, aesthetic and ecological problems of the countryside as a whole. It was a passionate reaction against the disastrous depression years and the devastation that a depressed agriculture had had on farming, the rural communities and the landscape itself. Its aim was to resuscitate village life, to achieve parity of living conditions between town and country and to stop the drift from the land. It hoped to achieve these aims through prosperity on the farm and by providing modern services such as piped water, electricity, good housing, recreational facilities and village colleges (what we might now call community schools embracing adult education and recreation) and by fostering rural trades and crafts. Industry was to be steered to the towns, not the villages, because it could bring 'undesirable consequences', by which the Scott committee meant that wages could rise too rapidly beyond the level that farming would pay. Its centralist approach was rejected by Dower as too extreme, for it saw national parks, the footpath network and access to open country all fitting into a pattern of gradual but orderly change, directed by a central planning authority. But its essential thesis was that the rural community was an agricultural community, dependent on the continuance and revival of the traditional mixed character of British farming for its prosperity. It firmly declared that 'there is no antagonism between use and beauty', a doctrine repeated *ad nauseam* by the farmers' spokesmen ever since.

Herein lay the fatal contradiction of the Scott report, for it believed in having the best of all worlds – traditional mixed farming, rural living standards raised to urban levels and the 'traditional' landscape. It failed to anticipate the course of postwar farming and the consequences for the rural community, not because the signs were invisible but because it failed to recognise the evidence. In doing so it reflected a view commonly held at the time that 'the countryside as a whole would soon start to recover from the intensive cultivation of the war years' (Mabey 1980). But Professor S. R. Dennison, an economist, flatly challenged the basic assumptions of the committee in a dissenting report. He denied that the rural community was any longer agricultural. He anticipated the postwar trend by arguing that agricultural prosperity depended on efficiency, which could be achieved only by specialist farming and by reducing the number of workers. He looked to industry to provide the jobs that agriculture would lose and suggested that farmers could be paid to conserve landscape as 'landscape gardeners and not as agriculturalists'. Dennison clearly regarded as nonsense the famous Scott dictum that 'the cheapest, indeed the only way, of preserving the countryside in anything like its traditional aspect would be to farm it'. He regarded traditional farming as incompatible with prosperity and was happy to see it disappear.

The assumptions made by the Scott Committee had far-reaching consequences. National parks became part of the land-use planning system introduced by the 1947 Town and Country Planning Act. The system was completed by the New Towns Act 1948 and the National Parks and Access to the Countryside Act 1949. The 1947 Act introduced the principle that new development and changes in the use of land were to be subject to development control to ensure their conformity to development plans to be prepared by the local planning authorities. In rural areas these were the county councils. Speculation in land was to be discouraged by nationalising development values, at the bargain price of £300 million, and by imposing a development charge which was set initially at 100%. The charge was repealed by the Conservative government in 1953, and the system has undergone other changes since then. Development plans are being replaced by structure plans and local plans, but the essentials remain. The term 'national park authority' (NPA) is not to be found in any of the statutes, which refer invariably to the 'local planning authorities' for the national parks – that is to say to the county councils or to the two planning boards set up in the Lake District and the Peak. The NPAs were conceived in the legislation as planning not managerial bodies, and form part of the machinery of local, not central, government. Two-thirds of their members have always been appointed by the county councils and one-third by the secretaries of state – currently by the Secretaries of State for the Environment and for Wales.

The Scott report had insisted that traditional farming would look after both the landscape and the rural communities. The farming and landowning lobby used this argument to claim for themselves virtual exemption from development control, and the General Development Order defined the meaning of 'development' to exclude agricultural and forestry operations. This exemption has been modified over time, and the larger farm or forestry buildings are no longer exempt from control, but the basic philosophy behind the exemption has not greatly changed. Although farming, forestry and woodland operations take up 96% of the land surface of national parks (Anderson 1980), planning in the countryside is overwhelmingly concerned with built development. A Landscape Area Special Development Order was made in 1950, in anticipation of national parks designation, to bring the design and materials of farm buildings in parts of what are now the Lake District, the Peak and Snowdonia National Parks under a form of planning control. But this Order has never been extended to cover the siting of buildings or to all the national parks, despite the government's acceptance (DOE 1976b) of the recommendation by the National Park Policy Review Committee (Sandford 1974) that this should be done.

It is not easy today, when 'planning' and 'planners' have been made the scapegoats for nearly every failure in urban and rural society, to recall the confidence that the postwar thinkers placed in the planning system they introduced. As the public were to control development and the use of land and to take the profit from land speculation, landownership was seen by Dower and Hobhouse as having only limited relevance. The owners and users of land would have to behave in conformity with the public interest as laid down in the development plans. So great was Dower's faith in the capabilities of the new planning system that he saw no role for the National Trust to acquire land on any scale in national parks. However, he did regard public acquisition of land as an indispensable – if normally a reserve – weapon in the national park armoury, to be used unhesitatingly wherever control or financial assistance seemed likely to be inadequate or too expensive. He advocated a policy of steadily buying agricultural land, particularly hill farms or common land, for the purposes of improvement and securing public access. The Hobhouse report recommended that half of the capital budget of £10 million for the first 10 years should be spent on the acquisition and improvement of land. The money was to come from the National Land Fund of £50 million (equivalent in terms of land prices to perhaps £1500 million in 1980), announced by Hugh Dalton in his budget speech in April 1946, in anticipation of national parks legislation. It was to be a 'nest egg' to be spent over four or five years and replenished if it were exhausted 'to give the public permanent access to the national parks'. In fact, not a penny of it reached the national park authorities until the Fund acquired the Egremont Estate in the Lake District in 1979 in lieu of death duties.

By the time the National Parks Act of 1949 was passed, the political and economic climates had changed. The county councils, having become the planning authorities for the intended national park areas in 1947, declined to surrender power to a National Parks Commission. The new Chancellor of the Exchequer, Sir Stafford Cripps, insisted with cold logic that if the county councils were to run the parks, their administrative and day-to-day costs should be paid for out of the rates. Even capital expenditure was only to be grant-aided up to a maximum of 75%. In the atmosphere of 'austerity', rationing and shortages, the money dried up. When the next Conservative government cut the National Land Fund back to £10 million and the Treasury succeeded in imposing its view that all expenditure from the Fund was to be subject to the normal controls over current spending, any prospect of substantial expenditure on land acquisition finally disappeared. But the question of landownership did not. The more the weaknesses of development control and local authority administration became apparent, the more inevitable it was that the question of landownership would have to be reconsidered.

It is not without significance that in Scotland the movement for national parks failed to achieve legislation. The Ramsay committee, the counterpart of Hobhouse, in its reports on National Parks and the Conservation of Nature in Scotland (Ramsay 1945, 1947), had come near to the American concept of a national park 'owned or controlled by the Nation'. It firmly recommended that land required for national park purposes, including the open moorlands to be designated for free public access as of right, should be acquired outright, if possible by agreement but if not, compulsorily. National parks in Scotland foundered on the resistance of the landed interests to the radical proposals of the Ramsay report. Five areas proposed by the Ramsay report as national parks in Scotland lingered on as 'National Park Direction Areas', within which proposals for development were notified to the Secretary of State for Scotland, the title 'national park' serving only as a buoy to mark the scene of the wreck and to recall the ideas of the 1940s. A direction by the Secretary of State finally extinguished National Park Direction Areas in 1980. We return to the Scottish situation in Chapter 12.

The designated areas

The underlying assumptions helped to obscure the fundamental problems inherent in applying the national park concept to British conditions. Dower himself conceded that the term was confusing, for he and everybody else in the national park movement rejected the idea of turning entire areas like the Lake District into 'parks', in the normal meaning of that word, as a place to which the public resorts freely for open-air relaxation. The meaning in fact given to this word can be seen from the successive definitions of the term 'national park'. Here is Dower's:

> an extensive area of beautiful and relatively wild country in which, for the nation's benefit and by appropriate national decision and action, (a) the characteristic landscape beauty is strictly preserved, (b) access and facilities for open-air enjoyment are amply provided, (c) wild life and buildings and places of architectural and historic interest are suitably protected, while (d) established farming use is effectively maintained (Dower 1945, p. 6).

Above all, the national parks should be confined, he said, to relatively wild country, to mountains and moors with the associated farm lands of their valleys and fringes, heaths, rocky and infertile coastlines and the rougher parts of numerous downs, hills and forests. His definition was accepted by the Hobhouse Committee (1947a) which summarised the 'essential requirements' of a national park as 'great natural beauty, a high value for open-air recreation and substantial continuous extent'. Part 2 of the 1949 Act defined the areas to be designated as 'those extensive tracts of country in England and Wales as to which it appears to the [National Parks] Commission that by reason of

(a)   their natural beauty, and
(b)   the opportunities they afford for open-air recreation having regard to their character and to their position in relation to centres of population,

it is especially desirable that the necessary measures shall be taken for the purposes mentioned in the last foregoing subsection', i.e. for the preservation and enhancement of their natural beauty and the promotion of their enjoyment by the public. What is common to the successive definitions of a national park is that the areas to be designated include, however worded, extensive tracts of 'open country' defined in the 1949 Act as 'mountain, moor, heath, down, cliff or foreshore'. This definition was extended in 1968 to include woodlands, rivers and canals. Open country, so defined, has the park-like attribute that the public can have access to it. It is also likely to have an above-average scientific interest for nature conservation.

The ten national parks designated by the National Parks Commission and confirmed by the secretary of state between 1951 and 1957 are shown in figure 1.1 and listed in Table 1.1. Nine of the ten are in the uplands and include extensive tracts of open country. The one exception is the Pembrokeshire Coast National Park which also includes the upland area of the Preseli Hills. The definition ensured that the national parks would be located in the North and West. In practice, little or no regard was paid to the designation of areas 'in relation to centres of population', which has led to the legitimate complaint that the recreational needs of many of the conurbations have not been considered.

Nine of the first ten parks designated (all but the North York Moors) were in the list of ten proposed by Dower as a first instalment. All of them were in Hobhouse's list of 12. Dower included the Cornish coast in his ten, while Hobhouse also included the Broads and the South Downs. With minor changes, Hobhouse's boundaries were adopted. The subjective and aesthetic nature of the boundaries was described aptly by Hobhouse (op. cit. 1947a, p. 11). They were drawn following recognisable features on the ground and corresponding as nearly as possible to what seemed 'the proper limits of each area, judged on the basis of landscape quality and recreational value, qualified in some cases by other considerations'. One of the latter was to exclude large settlements and degraded landscapes such as the limestone quarries near Buxton and the slate quarries at Blaenau Ffestiniog in Snowdonia, but not the artillery ranges of Northumberland, Dartmoor and Pembrokeshire.

The reports and the legislation were, however, in far less accord about the vast remaining areas of beautiful countryside, whether open country or not, that they wished to protect. Dower proposed a reserve list of 12 potential

Table 1.1 National Parks in England and Wales designated under the 1949 National Parks and Access to the Countryside Act (from Countryside Commission *Annual Report* 1978–9, *Digest of Annual Statistics* 1979).

Park	Area designated (mile²)	(km²)	Date of confirmation	Population (1971)
Peak District	542	1404	1951	36 708
Lake District	866	2243	1951	44 050
Snowdonia	838	2171	1951	26 272
Dartmoor	365	945	1951	28 064
Pembrokeshire Coast	225	583	1952	20 553
North York Moors	553	1432	1952	21 800
Yorkshire Dales	680	1761	1954	18 189
Exmoor	265	686	1954	10 458
Northumberland (including Roman Wall)	398	1031	1956	3297
Brecon Beacons	519	1344	1957	29 372
Totals	5251	13 600		238 763

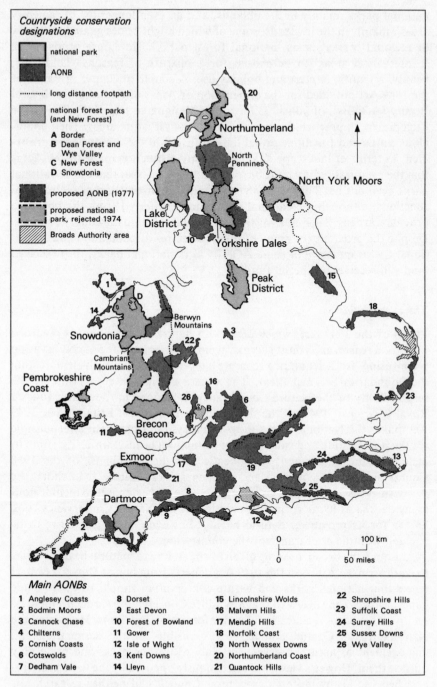

20

A

Northumberland

North Pennines

North York Moors

Lake District

10

Yorkshire Dales

Peak District

15

18

D

14

Berwyn Mountains

Snowdonia

3

22

Cambrian Mountains

Pembrokeshire Coast

16

26

B

6

7

23

Brecon Beacons

11

4

Exmoor

17

19

Dartmoor

21

24

13

8

25

9

C

12

2

5

| 0 | | 100 km |

| 0 | | 50 miles |

N

Main AONBs

1	Anglesey Coasts	8	Dorset	15	Lincolnshire Wolds	22 Shropshire Hills
2	Bodmin Moors	9	East Devon	16	Malvern Hills	23 Suffolk Coast
3	Cannock Chase	10	Forest of Bowland	17	Mendip Hills	24 Surrey Hills
4	Chilterns	11	Gower	18	Norfolk Coast	25 Sussex Downs
5	Cornish Coasts	12	Isle of Wight	19	North Wessex Downs	26 Wye Valley
6	Cotswolds	13	Kent Downs	20	Northumberland Coast	
7	Dedham Vale	14	Lleyn	21	Quantock Hills	

Figure 1.1 National parks, AONBs and the area of the Broads Authority. Crown copyright reserved.

national parks, mainly in the uplands, and an even longer list of 'amenity areas', mainly in the lowlands, some of which might be designated as county or regional 'parks' or as 'national forest parks'. Hobhouse proposed 52 'conservation areas' to be chosen for a mixture of reasons – landscape, beauty, scientific interest and holiday use. A couple of clauses in Part 6 of the 1949 Act provided for the designation of Areas of Outstanding Natural Beauty (AONBs), of which 33 have been designated (Fig. 1.1). They have been drawn, in practice, from Hobhouse's conservation areas. Their anomalous status and functions reveal the confusion in the minds of the draftsmen. In terms of landscape quality, the only distinction made by the Act is that their natural beauty must be 'outstanding', whereas that of the national parks need not be! They were given no nature conservation or recreational functions, although recreational use could be inferred from the power to provide wardens. Their administration was entrusted to the county councils. Despite the proximity of many of them to centres of population and recreational use as intensive in some AONBs as in national parks, they received (and still receive) no special funds.

The great divide

Part 3 of the 1949 Act, which dealt with nature conservation, is regarded with good reason as its most successful part. But its handling of conservation is confusing, for it set up two separate agencies without clearly demarcating the boundaries between them. The sphere of 'nature conservation', the responsibility of the Nature Conservancy, is defined in the Conservancy's Royal Charter of 1949 as 'the flora and fauna of Great Britain'. The 1949 Act makes the National Parks (now Countryside) Commission responsible for the preservation and enhancement of 'natural beauty' which it defines to include 'flora, fauna and' (as amended by the Section 21 of the 1968 Countryside Act) 'geological and physiographical features'. In short, the Act defines 'natural beauty' to embrace nature and extends it to include non-living as well as living forms. In practice, as the Nature Conservancy took nature for its province, 'natural beauty' has come more and more to be equated with the appearance of the countryside.

Although the broad meaning given by the statute to 'natural beauty' seems to embrace nature, in fact the 1949 Act departs from one of Dower's central tenets that national parks and nature conservation should be in the same hands. Dower had suggested that a Wildlife Conservation Council should be set up with advisory, educational and information functions. He wanted the National Parks Commission to be responsible for the designation and management of nature reserves, certainly within the parks and preferably outside them. Dower's views were strenuously opposed by the natural scientists, because his Wildlife Conservation Council had neither research nor management functions. These would have been the responsibility of a National Parks Commission that would have been unlikely, in the scientists' view, to have the necessary scientific expertise. The British Ecological Society argued vehemently that Dower failed to recognise that nobody was 'expert' enough to manage reserves for conservation unless there was a large accompanying research programme (Swanwick 1980). Dower was right in his perception that 'nature' should be separated neither from 'landscape' nor from human relations. But he misjudged the situation in two ways. Coming as he did from an amenity and recreation background, he underestimated the requirements of management and the importance of putting ecology on a strong scientific base through research. And his view that a national scientific authority for nature reserves could get through Whitehall and Westminster only as a pendant to national parks legislation was the reverse of the truth. The scientists saw national parks as a political millstone round the neck of nature conservation.

According to John Sheail (1976), Silkin initially accepted Dower's point of view, but other considerations prevailed and the Huxley Committee on nature conservation was asked to report separately. It was a scientific committee and it took the scientists' point of view. The Huxley report (*op. cit.*) recommended the establishment of a Wildlife Biological Service, later renamed the Nature Conservancy, to be responsible both for the management of reserves and for scientific research and for giving the proposed National Parks Commission the scientific guidance it would need to enable it to look after nature conservation in the national parks. The Hobhouse Committee agreed and envisaged that the National Parks Commission's staff would need to have expert knowledge ranging over fields as far apart as 'rural economy, land management, ecology and other natural sciences', allied to 'a high degree of aesthetic and architectural judgment'. Huxley and Hobhouse therefore envisaged two authoritative, expert, executive agencies complementing each other. What emerged was entirely different. The government accepted the Huxley report and set up the Nature Conservancy by Royal Charter in 1949, in advance of the national parks legislation. Whereas the recommendations on nature conservation were carried out virtually unchanged, those on national parks and access (Hobhouse 1947a,b) emerged from the 1949 Act as a pale shadow of their authors' intentions.

The National Parks Commission, whose functions and powers were defined in Part 1 of the 1949 Act, was given no executive, administrative, landowning or land managing functions. Apart from designating national parks and AONBs (subject to ministerial confirmation), its role was entirely advisory and supervisory. The Commission contained no full-time members and only its chairman and vice-chairman were paid. Its expenditure was met on the departmental vote, not by the grant-in-aid normally given to independent agencies such as the Nature Conservancy. Unlike the Conservancy, too, it was staffed by civil rather than public servants, in the choice of whom its freedom was severely restricted. (Legislation to give the Countryside Commission – successor to the National Parks Commission – the autonomy of a grant-aided body is being enacted by the Wildlife and Countryside Bill, introduced in November 1980.) It was given no local role or staff at all. The Act shifted responsibility from the centre, where Dower and Hobhouse had placed it, to the county councils as local planning authorities. One-third of the members of the national park boards or committees were appointed not by the Commission (as Dower and Hobhouse proposed) but by ministers. They were in no sense the representatives or nominees of the Commission, whose advice on these appointments was often disregarded.

The Nature Conservancy, on the other hand, was given an independent status, executive functions and appropriate powers. Its purposes were to provide scientific advice on the conservation of natural fauna and flora, to manage National Nature Reserves (NNRs) and to develop research and scientific services. Also it could designate Sites of Special Scientific Interest (SSSIs), although these enjoyed no statutory protection. It was given powers to enter into agreements with landowners for the management of nature reserves, to buy land for this purpose (compulsorily if need be) and to make byelaws for their protection. It was free to recruit the most suitable people.

It is hardly surprising in the circumstances that the Conservancy went forward to establish a national and international reputation, whereas the Commission turned out to be a weak and ineffective body. The intimate association between landscape and nature that Dower, Hobhouse and Huxley all wanted was not realised in practice. Giving evidence to the Sandford Committee (1974), the Nature Conservancy said that the national park authorities had failed to take account of nature conservation to the extent envisaged; nor, with one or two exceptions, had the Nature Conservancy been able to fulfil its intended advisory role as it would have wished. The very existence and separate development of the two agencies, one staffed largely by natural scientists and the other by generalists, effectively delayed movement towards common ground. Yet the first chairman of the Nature Conservancy, Sir Arthur Tansley, admitted in 1953 that it was difficult, if not impossible, to separate nature from 'amenity' and confessed to his embarrassment at having to refer to the beauty of landscape or vegetation in an almost apologetic tone (Mabey 1980).

Ministers attempted to conceal the gulf that separated the 1949 Act from the Dower and Hobhouse reports by claiming that 90% of their recommendations had been accepted. But H. H. Symonds, chairman of the Friends of the Lake District and a lifelong campaigner for national parks, described the Commission more accurately as 'a wraith' or, to change the metaphor, as 'window-dressing for sub-standard goods' (Symonds 1949). Inside the Civil Service the National Parks Commission (to Symonds a non-commission) was seen as an unnecessary body the only real function of which was to provide a sop to the national parks lobby (Cherry 1975).

Certainly the scientists are right in thinking, as Max Nicholson has put it, that the Nature Conservancy could hardly have become 'the first [body] in the world to progress from rule of thumb conservation done on hunch and intuition to scientific management' (Nicholson 1980, p. 5) had it been tied to the National Parks Commission and made subservient to local government committees. But the scientific reasons for the split were probably of less importance than the political ones. The original 1941 Conference on Nature Preservation had already forewarned of the disfavour with which the local authorities viewed the intervention of a strong National Parks Commission and the prospective loss of some of the extensive planning powers they then expected to acquire. But in addition, the very popularity of the national parks' cause over the years and its emphasis on access and recreation had allowed ample time for opposition to develop among farmers, landowners and local authorities and within factions of government.

Lowe and Goyder (forthcoming) have suggested that the SPNR and NRIC avoided controversy by divorcing the case for nature reserves from that of national parks and by concentrating on the scientific aspects of nature conservation. Nature conservation was identified as a scientific matter in the hands of experts, which seemed to pose a threat to no one and was seen as an academic concern which had a bearing only on small areas of land.

By initially limiting the scope of their work to research, the provision of advice and the management of reserves, scientists were able to lay a foundation of knowledge for an attack on problems affecting the natural environment. But the emphasis placed today on the protection of the whole environment, not merely the reserves or areas of scientific interest, necessarily calls in question both the political wisdom and the scientific validity of the split between nature conservation and landscape and the limited role of the Nature Conservancy Council (NCC) – as it became in 1973. The loss of the Conservancy's research branch, hived off to form the Institute of Terrestrial Ecology (ITE) in 1973, breached the basic principle of the Conservancy – that research and practice should be combined in the same hands. But these changes have not fundamentally changed the relationship of the NCC to the Countryside Commission or to national parks. We shall return to these issues in Chapter 13.

Footpaths and access

The access provisions of Part V of the 1949 Act (which applied to the whole of England and Wales, not only to national parks) stood the principles of the Scott, Dower and Hobhouse reports on their heads. The Committee on Footpaths and Access to the Countryside (Hobhouse 1947b) firmly recommended that the public should have a legal right of access (subject to certain conditions and exceptions) to all open or uncultivated land. Part V of the Act in effect provided that the public should have *no* rights of access to open country whether in a national park or not, except by agreement or order. The reasoning behind this decision was that where access was enjoyed by custom it was better, in Silkin's words, to let sleeping dogs lie and not to risk provoking landowners into withdrawing the 'privilege' of access. This was to be provided by law, as opposed to custom, only where an access agreement had been made with the landowner or, in default of agreement, an access order had been made by a local planning authority and confirmed by the secretary of state. The county councils were required to review their areas and to advise what action was necessary to secure public access. With few exceptions, the county councils reported that little or no action was needed.

The access provisions have not been used widely outside the Peak District National Park, which has used them to provide access to the moorlands where the battles of the 1930s were fought. A survey (Gibbs & Whitby 1975) showed that in the whole of England and Wales by 1973 only 98 access areas covering 35 260 ha, or 86 625 acres, had been created, of which 80% were in national parks and 56% in the Peak. The reasons for the limited use of access agreements and orders include the strong opposition of landowners and farmers, cost and administrative inconvenience, the reluctance of national park and other land planning authorities to enter into agreements or to make orders and the extent of *de facto* access. The consequence of this limited use of the Act was probably less to deny the public access, which in most places it took anyway, than to save public money, to exacerbate conflicts with land-owners and farmers and to diminish the role of the national park authorities. For it was only in access areas that the authorities could provide wardens to help visitors, repair damage, make byelaws about behaviour, or pay compensation. The 1949 Act enabled the NPAs to duck the job of managing the open country in the interests of all its users.

One of the more successful parts of the 1949 Act, Part IV on public rights of way, broke entirely new ground by giving the public statutory rights it had never enjoyed before. Almost at a stroke it arrested the piecemeal and widespread loss of rights of way that had been taking place throughout the 1930s and 1940s and earlier – a process that could be arrested previously only by taking costly and risky legal proceedings for each individual path separately. The Act was intended first to identify and protect the public's rights of way that had been built up over centuries and then, where necessary, to adapt the system of footpaths and bridleways to the needs of modern recreation. County councils were required to survey their areas and to prepare maps which would become statutory, definitive maps of rights of way after objections had been disposed of. The county councils were given powers also to close or divert existing paths, to create new rights of way by agreement or compulsorily and to pay compensation. But when the Sandford Committee on national park policy reported 25 years later in 1974 it found that three county councils in national park areas had not even completed the definitive maps of existing rights of way.

It is, unfortunately, characteristic of the 1949 Act that the detailed drafting tended to delay or prevent the achievement of the desired result. In the case of footpaths, the delay was caused by the complexity of the procedures designed to protect private interests and by the failure of the county councils to provide the will or the resources for their implementation. County councils are far more representative of farming and landowning interests than of ramblers (Newby *et al.* 1978, see Ch. 5). Footpaths and bridleways or RUPPs

(Roads Used as Public Paths) are a highway responsibility, but the highway authorities were obsessed with roads and motor traffic and still do not take their footpath responsibilities seriously. Footpaths are, with open country, the main recreational asset of a national park, yet the NPAs had no statutory role, even for their upkeep, unless the county councils delegated footpath functions to them. The only roles of the National Parks Commission were to suggest the routes of long-distance paths to the minister for confirmation and to offer 100% grants to the local authorities for implementing the proposals on the ground. It took the local authorities 21 years to complete the Pennine Way, the route of which was approved by Hugh Dalton within two weeks of its submission to him in 1951. Even today, it is only in the Lake District and the Peak that the NPAs have the statutory power to create, divert or close rights of way.

1949—74: downhill (nearly) all the way

The low priority given to national parks in 1950 was evident immediately in the appointments to the National Parks Commission. The chairman (part-time of course) for the first four years was Sir Patrick Duff, a retired civil servant, who had no previous interest or commitment in the field. Few of the early commissioners and its tiny staff had any understanding of the national park concept or knowledge of the English landscape, let alone the catalogue of essential qualities prescribed by Dower and Hobhouse. The staff was headed by Harold Abrahams, an olympic athlete whose consuming passions were athletic journalism and broadcasting.

It was obviously necessary to ensure that every national park was planned and managed as a geographical entity and when the National Parks Bill was passing through Parliament firm pledges to this effect were given. Six of the 10 parks eventually designated turned out to lie within the territory of more than one county – until the reorganisation of 1974 which reduced the number to five. The Act provided (Section 8) that in these cases a Joint Planning Board composed of representatives from each of the counties would be set up under the 1947 Town and Country Planning Act. But the Minister, Lewis Silkin, insisted on providing an escape clause, by which the Minister would allow each county to administer its own part of a park, overseen by a powerless and resourceless Joint Advisory Committee (JAC), where 'by reason of special circumstances' it is expedient so to do for securing 'efficient administration' (Sub-Section 2). The Minister, Lewis Silkin, also promised that every national park would have its own planning officer or, as he would now be called, National Park Officer.

The county councils objected to the designation of all the parks except Northumberland and Dartmoor and objected even more strongly to the establishment of semi-autonomous joint planning boards that would have power to make development plans, levy a rate and appoint their own staff.

Hugh Dalton, as the Minister of Town and Country Planning, overruled the objections of the Labour-controlled Derbyshire County Council in the Peak where the first national park was confirmed in 1951. It was to be administered by a joint planning board with its own National Park Officer and staff. He weakened over the Lake District, conceding that the board need have neither a National Park Officer nor staff of its own and agreeing that the three constituent county councils would control its expenditure. A ceiling of £7500 a year was placed immediately on its budget.

The retreat turned into a rout in Snowdonia, the third park to be designated by the National Parks Commission. The new Minister of Housing and Local Government, Harold Macmillan, surrendered to the pressure of the Welsh county councils after receiving a noisy deputation. He found that there were 'special circumstances' that justified him in agreeing to its 'more efficient administration' by no fewer than four committees – three separate county council committees and a joint advisory committee. This multiple committee pattern was followed in the other multi-county parks in Exmoor, Brecon and the Yorkshire Dales. It breached the principle that each park should be administered as a geographical entity, except in the single county parks such as Dartmoor and Northumberland which were administered by national park committees of the county council. The long lead the Peak Board won through the independent status accorded to it in 1951 enabled it to build up a professional staff and to develop consistent policies that have been internationally recognised and, in our experience, are still in advance of most of the other NPAs.

The period from 1949 to the reorganisation of the parks in 1974 began with postwar austerity, but rapidly became the heyday of the affluent, mobile, consumer society. No limits could be seen to the growth in consumption. Successive governments were too deeply committed to the satisfaction of the new demands for water, power, materials and recreation to be reliable protectors of threatened environments. The NPAs were faced by pressures and demands far greater than even Dower had anticipated, but they lacked the resources, the powers and often the will to control them. National parks were obliged to accommodate massive new installations on a scale far exceeding anything that had happened in prewar years before designation – an oil port and refineries in Milford Haven, a nuclear power station in Snowdonia, high-tension transmission lines and television and radio masts all over the place, vast new reservoirs and quarries. Ministers claimed that government leaned over backwards to weight the scales in favour of beauty and remoteness. But Lord Strang, who succeeded Sir Patrick Duff as chairman of the National Parks Commission, summed up the experience of 12 years in 1962 by saying: 'Where a government department has had plans for erecting large installations of one kind or another in a national park, I can remember no case where it has been diverted from its purpose by anything that the Commission might say ...' (Strang 1963, p. 71).

By the end of the 1950s, government was already promising that some of the more glaring weaknesses of the 1949 Act – particularly its financial terms – would be remedied at some unspecified date. Eventually in 1965, after 10 years of ceaseless pressure, the new Labour Minister for Land and Natural Resources, Fred Willey, promised a comprehensive countryside policy. But the action when taken was to transform the National Parks Commission into a Countryside Commission, and to shift its interest from a concentration on national parks and AONBs towards recreation in the countryside as a whole. This shift reflected the acceptance of the doctrine, first articulated in the United States, that increasing incomes, mobility and education were changing the demands for leisure and would put immense pressures on recreational resources. Michael Dower, a son of John Dower, compared the impact of leisure to a 'fourth wave' sweeping over the countryside as the railway, the industrial revolution or the motorcar had done in earlier generations (Dower 1965).

The demands for leisure and the protection of the countryside were voiced simultaneously by the three prestigious 'Countryside in 1970' conferences sponsored by the Nature Conservancy between 1964 and 1970. Their starting point was the fear that current social and economic trends, massively reinforced by modern technology, had completely altered the delicate traditional structure of the countryside. Their aim was to secure a countryside policy acceptable to countryman and townsman alike. Their first step was to bring together all those whom the sponsors regarded as having legitimate interests in the countryside, i.e. the farmers, landowners, conservationists and recreationists who felt that the countryside was threatened by the uneducated and unorganised urban masses. The definition of conservation given by the Duke of Edinburgh to the 1963 conference as 'the total management of the rural areas . . . for the fair and equal benefit of all groups which have a direct interest in their use' (quoted in Lowe & Clifford 1979, p. 17) diverted attention from real conflicts of interest or controversial issues. Experience was showing that Dennison's minority report of 1942 had accurately anticipated the course of agricultural development. But the conferences paid little attention to the decline of rural services or depopulation, or to agricultural and forestry policies.

The government White Paper on Leisure in the Countryside (MLNR 1966) which laid the basis for the 1968 Act, simply argued that 'more money, more leisure and above all more cars' meant that 'the valuable national asset' allegedly created by national parks, access agreements and long-distance paths would be spoiled unless new provision was made elsewhere for countryside enjoyment. The chosen instrument was the country park.

The Countryside Act of 1968 transformed the National Parks Commission into the Countryside Commission. The Commission was able to offer 50% grants to the private and public sector for country parks and other recreational facilities, which hitherto were only grant-aided in national parks. Also it was given powers to undertake or grant-aid experimental or research projects. This gave it, for the first time, an opportunity to intervene directly on the ground in national parks and elsewhere. These new powers enabled the Commission to initiate positive 'management' projects in the uplands of the national parks, in the urban fringes which have become the main focus of its interest, and in the 'heritage coast' areas. Heritage coasts were identified in studies and reports (CC 1970) that led to the adoption of the concept as a non-statutory designation (DOE 1972).

The 1968 Act was a step forward in extending informal recreational policies to the countryside as a whole, instead of concentrating them on national parks and AONBs. But the 'comprehensive countryside policy' promised by Fred Willey turned out to be no more than a countryside recreation policy, if that. His new Ministry of Land and National Resources was extinguished even before the 1968 Bill could be presented. The Ministry of Agriculture, which was promoting the short-lived Rural Development Boards for upland areas under its 1967 Agriculture Act, was not involved in 'countryside' policy making. The very name 'countryside' was appropriated by the recreational interests. The preamble of the 1968 Bill as first presented to Parliament contained no reference to conservation. It only became a Bill 'for the conservation and enhancement of natural beauty' as it was amended in its passage through Parliament. Section 11, the 'amenity clause' that imposes a duty towards conservation on 'every Minister, government department and public body', is itself no more than a verbal genuflection. It requires them 'in the exercise of their functions relating to land under any enactment' to 'have regard to the *desirability* of conserving the natural beauty and amenity of the countryside' [our italics]. We have met nobody who thinks that Section 11 has had much practical effect beyond providing a legal basis on which conservation interests can rest their cases. But Section 11 is counterbalanced by Section 37, which makes it the duty of every Minister, the Countryside Commission, the Nature Conservancy Council and the local authorities to have 'due regard to the needs of agriculture and forestry and to the economic and social interests of rural areas' in the exercise of their functions under the Act.

Reorganisation and the Sandford report

National parks could hardly be left forever in the limbo to which the 1968 Act consigned them. As an integral part of local government, they were examined by the Royal Commission on Local Government (Redcliffe-Maud 1969). It recommended that national parks should not be entrusted to the new multi-purpose local authorities it proposed, but should be the responsibility of planning boards. These would be similar to the relatively successful Peak Board, but would take on a regional character by the addition of members from the proposed provincial authorities and additional funding from the same source. The Labour government accepted these recommendations, but within months an incoming Tory government had rejected the entire scheme for local government reorganisation, including the national park proposals. Its White Paper (DOE 1971) said that very little change was needed in the law governing planning functions in national parks, although it promised to retain the two joint planning boards and to consider, with the local authorities, whether boards should be set up in the multi-county parks.

This, from the Countryside Commission's point of view, was back to square one. Its response was to present the government with a report by Sir Jack Longland (1972) presenting 'overwhelming evidence' from 20 years experience that each park should be planned, administered and managed as a separate and single geographical unit by a board on the Peak model. But this was precisely what the County Councils' Association had been fighting against ever since the Dower report. Negotiations between the Commission and the county councils produced a compromise that was enacted in Schedule 17 of the 1972 Local Government Act. The Countryside Commission traded the abandonment of its main demand (the establishment of boards in every park) for a unified administration of every park and statutory requirements that every park authority should appoint a National Park Officer and prepare a national park 'management plan'. The two boards were retained in the Peak and the Lake District (which was now a single-county park in Cumbria). Elsewhere there was to be a committee of the county council as before in single-county parks. But, in multi-county parks there was to be a joint committee of several councils (as in Brecon) or a committee of the council with the largest part of the park, to which the council with the minor interest would send representatives (as in Exmoor, North York Moors and the Yorkshire Dales). The 2 : 1 split between elected and appointed members was retained. The district councils failed to win statutory representation, but made an informal agreement with the county councils by which the counties would appoint a small number of district councillors to the authorities. The majority on the authority was to consist in every case of county councillors. The present composition of each authority in 1980–81 is shown in Table 5.1 (p. 116).

The financial issue was settled in the Local Government (Finance) Act 1974 which provided for a National Park Supplementary Grant (NPSG) to be paid to the county councils separately from the local authority Rate Support Grant (RSG). The government, however, provided no new money. It simply deducted the NPSG from the RSG and promised that the NPSG would be equivalent to 75% of approved national park expenditure including administration. The result of these reforms, which were part of local government reorganisation, was to leave the 1949 Act concept intact but to remedy some of the worst defects that had arisen both from the Act and from its application by central government and the county councils. But this settlement was a remarkable cart-before-horse exercise.

The government settled the principles of reorganisation a few weeks *after* it had appointed a committee to review national park policy and two and a half years *before* it could have hoped to receive the committee's findings. The way in which the committee was set up says a good deal about the status of the Countryside Commission and the government's attitude towards it. In March 1971, John (now Sir John) Cripps, who had been made chairman of the Commission in 1970, informed the government that the Commission proposed to undertake a review of national parks 'with special reference to national considerations which should affect national park policies' (Cripps 1979). He received no reply, but two months later Peter Walker, the Secretary of State for the Environment, descended by helicopter on the shores of Windermere to address the National Parks Conference. He gave Mr Cripps five minutes notice of his announcement that the Department of the Environment and Countryside Commission would make a joint study of national park policies, through a committee chaired by Lord Sandford, his Under Secretary. Its terms of reference were

> to review how far the national parks have fulfilled their purpose for which they were established, to consider the implications of the changes that have occurred and may be expected in social and economic conditions and to make recommendations as regards future policies.

The Commission tried again in December 1971 to persuade the Department to take a wider look at countryside problems, suggesting the setting up of a Royal Commission on the countryside modelled on the Scott Committee of 1941–2. It specifically drew attention to the danger that not only recreational pressures but also developments in farming and forestry might be combining to destroy the 'natural beauty' of the countryside.

The Commission's suggestion was ignored, but in fact its hint that the sacred cow of agriculture might actually be contributing to the rural malaise was one of the earliest signs of a shift in conventional attitudes towards the countryside. Throughout the 1970s there was a marked trend towards a more comprehensive view of countryside problems and a search for compromise between the conflicting interests. This was combined with a new 'management' approach, which sought to achieve the aims of public authorities on private land or public land held for special purposes, through agreements to manage the land in ways that would satisfy both the needs of the owner and those of conservation and recreation.

The Sandford Committee was only partly attuned to this trend. Its report (Sandford 1974) took a strong consensus and management approach. It relied largely in its recommendations on toughening up development control and getting results through co-operation and agreement with landowners, farmers and other interested parties by voluntary agreements rather than the acquisition of land or use of controls. It recommended that the NPAs should have power to acquire 'open country', compulsorily if need be, for the purpose of preserving or enhancing its natural beauty and to control afforestation of 'bare land'. But the majority declined to recommend compulsory powers to acquire any other land for the purposes of conservation, or to bring forestry operations generally under control. Agreement was seen as the best means of reconciling farming practices with national park purposes and legislation was recommended to make 'management agreements' binding on landowners' successors in title. The extension of the Landscape General Development Order to bring the siting and design of farm buildings throughout national parks under some form of control was also recommended.

The Sandford Committee, as we have seen, was set up to avoid a wider, more comprehensive study. Although its terms of reference required it to study social and economic conditions, it did so only superficially and it made no significant recommendations regarding them. It recommended, however, that the 1949 Act be amended to make it clear that the enjoyment of the national parks was to be 'in such manner and by such means as will leave their natural beauty unimpaired for the enjoyment of this and future generations' (Sandford 1974, p. 54). The sentiment is unexceptionable, but it implies that the main threat to national parks comes from recreational pressure and not from economic and social change. The committee was not allowed to consider the government's reorganisation of national parks or the roles of the Countryside Commission or the Nature Conservancy Council. It could only agree that staffing and administration should be reviewed after five years.

The composition of the committee guaranteed that it would not interpret its terms of reference widely. Its 10 members included the two ministers responsible for national parks in the Department of the Environment and the Welsh Office, and two civil servants from the same departments. A third civil servant was R. J. S. Hookway, the Director of the Countryside Commission, who had been one of the principal initiators of the 1968 Act's approach to countryside recreation. One member was a local government recreation officer, two were members of the Countryside Commission and one (an industrialist and landowner) was an appointed member of two NPAs and a lifelong campaigner for national parks on the Dower model. Only one member, John Cousins, a trade union official, could be said to represent an urban interest. Even more surprising for a committee concerned with the countryside, it contained nobody who could speak with authority on nature conservation, farming, rural industries or services, or local government.

The significant aspect of the Sandford report was its confirmation of the criticisms made since 1949 of the failure of the national parks to realise their objectives. The report did not use the word failure, and failure is of course a relative term. Sandford's answer to the question 'how successful have national parks been?' was to say that 'but for designation much worse would have befallen them'. It found that there had been a marked tendency to subordinate intangible and enduring benefits to short-term considerations – so much so that it wanted the presumption against development 'to amount to a prohibition to be breached only in the case of a most compelling national necessity' (Sandford 1974, p. 11). The whole emphasis of the report, albeit in carefully measured phrases, is on the shortcomings over the entire range of issues – the government's priorities, development control, highways and traffic management, recreational facilities, the management of footpaths and commons, agricultural reclamation, afforestation and quarrying, and administrative, financial and staffing arrangements.

It would be absurd to suggest that nothing was achieved between 1951 and 1971. Clearly, more had been achieved in the Peak and to a lesser extent in the Lake District, whose semi-autonomous planning boards had shown more initiative, done more positive works and spent more money than the county council committees elsewhere. But taken as a whole, the record of the parks in positive works and management before the 1974 reorganisation was pitiful. The main successes claimed for the old system by those we have interviewed were that it stopped some bad developments, but even here the successes can only be described as modest. Things would have been worse, but for development control; but development control was far more successful in stopping the small man doing a small thing than in controlling the big private or statutory developers and development control has not been markedly more successful inside most national parks than elsewhere (Blacksell & Gilg 1981).

Those who battled hard throughout these years to get small things done on the proverbial shoestring, often in the face of the indifference or obstruction of local and central government, may resent the use of the word 'failure'. But national parks were administered throughout these years on the principle that the costs of conservation and recreation were negligible. Hobhouse had estimated that expenditure would be running at £1.475 m a year (in 1947 money) after 10 years. After 20 years, in 1971–72, expenditure was running at £1.2 m a year, which was equivalent to about one-third of the Hobhouse figure in real terms. Nearly half of this total was spent in the Peak and the Lake District. The highest rates were levied in the poorest areas but only three counties levied a higher rate than one (new) penny in the pound and five were spending less than one-tenth of a penny. The government's contribution was little more than a third of the meagre total. It is hardly surprising that Sandford called for the budgets of the national park boards to be doubled in real terms within five years of reorganisation and for those of the committees to be trebled. This would have raised total expenditure to less than £4 m a year, an amount so modest that the committee 'hardly feel called upon to justify it'. The committee was in fact pushing at an open door, for already the government had committed itself to meeting the 'lion's share' of national park expenditure and actual expenditure had been rising since 1971–2 (see Ch. 5).

The government responded to Sandford in DOE Circular 4/1976. It accepted a host of minor recommendations while rejecting or failing to implement most of the more important. It was most positive about finance and in its acceptance (spelt out in a joint circular issued by the Departments of the Environment and Transport in 1977) of the view that highway authorities must consult national park authorities and make environmental quality the 'primary criterion' in planning road systems and traffic schemes. It agreed that priority should be given to conservation where there was an irreconcilable conflict with recreation, but took no steps to give the principle statutory force. It accepted that the social and economic wellbeing of national parks was 'an object of policy', but rejected the suggestion (referred to in the circular) that this should be made a statutory purpose of the national park authorities. It accepted the recommendation that the NPAs should have power to control the design, external appearance and siting of all agricultural buildings by extending the scope of the Landscape Areas Special Development Order, but has failed to do so. It refused to give the authorities powers to buy land compulsorily for purposes of conservation or to control afforestation. Nor would it agree to a quinquennial review of defence sites in national parks.

The 10 new national park authorities took office on 1 April 1974, equipped with something resembling the basic essentials for a satisfactory administration and charged with the duty of preparing national park management plans. It had taken a quarter of a century to remove the gross shortcomings that had frustrated the serious implementation of the ideas of the 1940s. During that time the minds and energies of many people were diverted away from constructive thought about the future into desperate efforts to rectify the mistakes of the past. We have said that the national park system introduced in 1949 failed, although it had some successes too. But the idea of planning and managing the landscape and natural resources of large areas of countryside in a manner consistent with their conservation and with the livelihood of its people had not been discredited. It would be nearer the truth to say that the idea had never been tested under conditions that would enable it to achieve its objectives. The question has now to be asked whether the reforms of 1974, which belatedly applied the thinking of the 1940s to the problems of the 1970s, are capable of achieving the far broader aims that the more advanced conservation thinking now sets for the 1980s and beyond.

Part 2 *The national parks*

2 *Nature, man and conservation*

Nature

The purpose of this chapter is to give readers a sufficient understanding of the resources of the national parks to enable them to follow the argument in the rest of the book. The resources of the uplands and the severe handicaps from which they suffer both arise from the combination of geological processes, weather, climate and human activities. The hills and mountains that provide the spectacular scenery, the rocks, minerals and water that men need and the habitats for plant and animal life, also provide the harsh conditions in which the hill farmer has to wrest his living from the ground. The poor acid soils, short growing season and difficult communications in remote areas have been among the most significant factors driving the native populations down the valleys and into the cities.

Weather conditions vary immensely between and within the parks according to altitude, latitude and distance from the westerly winds of the Atlantic. The combination of these factors can produce extraordinarily severe weather conditions in the higher parts of the more northern and westerly parks, where the wet, chilling winds inhibit the growth of vegetation and can rapidly reduce the body temperature of the human being (unless he is properly shod and clad) to dangerously low levels. Conditions are coldest in Snowdonia, the Lakes, Northumberland and the Yorkshire Dales, but annual rainfall is considerably lower in Northumberland and on the east-facing fells of the Dales than in the rest of these four northern parks. In the Peak District and the North York Moors altitudes are lower and summer temperatures higher compared to the other parks of the North. The North York Moors, which is the most easterly of the parks and has the lowest altitude, also enjoys the lowest rainfall of them all. In the southern and westerly parks – Dartmoor, Exmoor, Pembrokeshire Coast and Brecon Beacons – the climate is somewhat warmer, reflecting latitude and the tempering influence of the Gulf Stream. However, rainfall varies with altitude, being highest in the Brecon Beacons and Dartmoor and much lower in Exmoor and Pembrokeshire. Looking at all the parks, the areas with the warmer and drier climates and the most favourable conditions for both agriculture and holidaymaking are the North York Moors, Exmoor, the White Peak and Pembrokeshire Coast. In the two latter, most of the land is enclosed for agriculture as are extensive tracts of the North York Moors and Exmoor.

The upland qualities that attract the visitor, the second homer, the commuter and the retired, cater for an almost limitless range of recreational interests and attract the mining companies, the water and electricity authorities, the 'improving' farmer, the commercial forester, the grouse moor proprietor, the Atomic Energy Authority and the Ministry of Defence. Conflicts over land use are built into the landscape by nature itself, not least by letting loose on it the species Man, and equipping him with rather less understanding of his impact on the natural world than his boastful title *Homo sapiens* might suggest.

We ask readers to study the maps, one of England and Wales showing relief (Fig. 2.1) and two for each park (Figs 2.2-2.21) to enable them to form a picture in their minds of the main characteristics of each park. The first park map shows the landforms of mountain, hill, valley and coast, the main rivers, lines of communication, settlements and mineral deposits. The second shows the land cover of semi-natural vegetation, which is the major constituent of the landscape and combines with landform and human artefacts to create the scenery.

The different landforms of the parks reflect the properties of the underlying rocks and the changes effected over geological time by rain, wind, ice and snow. Except for the North York Moors, the Palaeozoic rocks of the uplands are older and harder than those that form the lowlands and it is to their resilience, as much as to the earth movements that raised them in the first place, that the mountains and hills of the parks owe their existence. The glaciers of the last Ice Age, that melted a mere 10 000 years ago, created the steep-sided valleys and lakes, the hanging valleys and waterfalls and the small basins or cwms in the spectacular mountains of Wales and Northern England. The landforms and natural resources of the parks also reflect the history of the Earth, an understanding of which adds to the experience of the mountains and hills, for the rocks are visible and tactile links with the Earth's beginnings unimaginable aeons ago, and a reminder of the awesome cataclysms that made them.

The domelike masses of Dartmoor and the Cheviot Hills are granite or other coarse igneous rocks, the chemical and physical structures of which make them susceptible to surface weathering and result in a smooth, undulating terrain. They provide a complete contrast to the bare rocky crags of the highest mountains in the central Lake District and Snowdonia formed

Figure 2.1 Relief and rivers of England and Wales. Crown copyright reserved.

from hard volcanic rocks; these, in turn, are different from the lower hills in both these national parks which are formed of softer shales and slates. The spectacular gorges, the flat 'pavements' and the subterranean rivers of the southern Peak, parts of the Brecon Beacons and Yorkshire Dales are characteristic of limestone country. Sandstone country gives rise to the scarped mountains of the Brecon Beacons, the Millstone Grit edges of the High Peak, as well as the rolling plateaux of the North York Moors and Exmoor.

In the Peak, geology has created two contrasting worlds to form a single national park. A glance at Figures 2.6 and 2.7 reveals the change in landform and vegetation (and therefore in farming and human society) as one steps across the junction between the Millstone Grits of the High Peak and the limestone of the aptly named White Peak. To the north lie heather moors and the cliffs or 'edges' to which the climbers flock from Manchester and South Yorkshire. Beyond them at 2000 ft lie the inhospitable moors of Kinder Scout and Bleaklow, to gain access to which men went to prison less than 50 years ago. Anyone who has walked the Pennine Way in the High Peak will be familiar with the peat hags – islands of disintegrating 'blanket' peat separated by deep channels that penetrate down to the underlying rock, forcing the walker to go 'bog-trotting' endlessly up and down their slippery slopes. South of the gritstone moors, the white walls of the small dairy farms of the White Peak criss-cross a green, almost treeless and undulating plateau broken only by the odd clump of hardwoods planted 100 years or so ago and by the enchanting limestone dales, some with rivers and some without, where semi-natural woodlands still survive precariously. Their names are as evocative as their scenery – Dovedale, Monsal Dale, the Manifold Valley, and many others.

The Pembrokeshire Coast, the smallest of the parks, is in a class by itself. Nobody has described it better than John Barrett,

> sandstones, limestones, mudstones, conglomerates, shales, grits, slates, ashes and igneous masses – greys, greens, reds, purples, tawny browns, black and ochre – acid and base – soft as sand to hard as iron – spread at all angles – faulted, folded and contorted – facing in all compass directions – and all of them exposed in the cliffs, visible and mostly accessible from the (coastal) path.... Contemporary seas have so excavated the softer materials that the coast is mightily peninsulated. The complicated intricacies of larger headlands and little promontories constantly conjure views at unexpected angles across wide bays, sandy coves or deeply indented estuaries ... the cliff-tops support such a profusion of flowers that almost any square yard would win the rock garden prize at Chelsea (Barrett 1978, p. 78).

The extraction of rocks and mineral ores for industrial purposes gives rise to the acute conflicts of interest that are discussed in Chapter 11. Limestone is quarried and processed on a massive scale in the Peak and the Yorkshire

Key

▬▬▬	national park boundary
+-+-+-	national boundary
⊔⊔⊔⊔⊔	canal
R	reservoir
A65(T)	trunk roads
══════	other 'A' roads
────────	motorway
++++++	railway
HHHHHH	narrow gauge railway
P	power station
O	oil refinery
T	antiquity/tourist attraction
NT	National Trust (house not land)

▨	Ministry of Defence training area
▲	quarrying
△	other mineral extraction
··········	long-distance/coastal footpath (named)
+	communications apparatus
▦	land over 600 ft (185 m)
▦	land over 1400 ft (430 m)
▦	land over 2000 ft (615 m)
▲	peaks (heights in feet)
•	villages and small towns
●	towns with 4000–10 000 inhabitants
⬤	towns with over 10 000 inhabitants
▨	major urban areas

Key to vegetation maps Vegetation is derived from the Second Land Utilisation Survey, Geography Department, King's College, London and reproduced by permission of the Director on material based on the Ordnance Survey map with the sanction of the Controller of Her Majesty's Stationery Office.

Major vegetation association	*Component communities* ex *LUS*		*Ornament used*
heather	heather bilberry		▨
grassland	fescue-bent (*Festuca/Agrostis*) matt-grass (*Nardus*) purple moor-grass (*Molinia*)	moor-rush (*Juncus squarrosus*) fixed dunes	▦
bog	cotton-grass (*Eriophorum*) deer-sedge (*Trichophorum*)	bog-moss (*Sphagnum*) bog-myrtle (*Myrica*)	■
bracken/gorse	bracken gorse		▦
woodland	conifers deciduous mixed	coppice scrub	▦
water	lakes reservoirs		▦
other	in-bye built-up areas	industrial land	▢

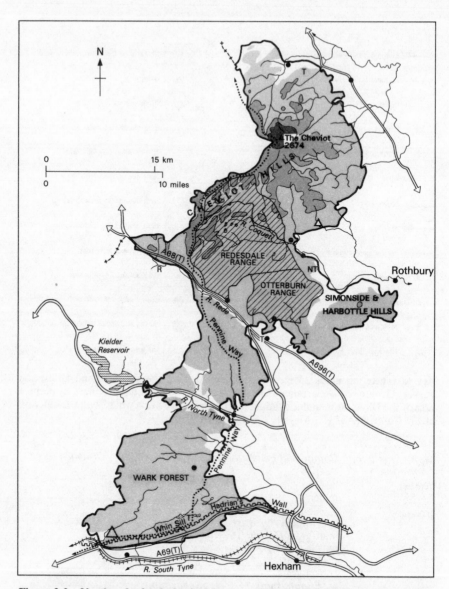

Figure 2.2 Northumberland physical features. The park is a wide strip through the three distinct tracts of country that make up inland Northumbria. Immediately north of the Tyne Gap (Fig. 2.1) is a ridge of igneous rock with north-facing escarpments (the Whin Sill) on which the Roman Wall stands. North of this is an area of undulating upland interrupted by the valleys of the North Tyne and the Rede rivers. North again is the rounded igneous boss of the Cheviot Hills (2670 ft) through which the border with Scotland runs. On the east and south of the Cheviots is a concentric belt of lower hills of fell sandstone of which the Simonside and Harbottle Hills are part. The hard igneous rocks of the Whin Sill and of the northern hills are quarried for road stone. Crown copyright reserved.

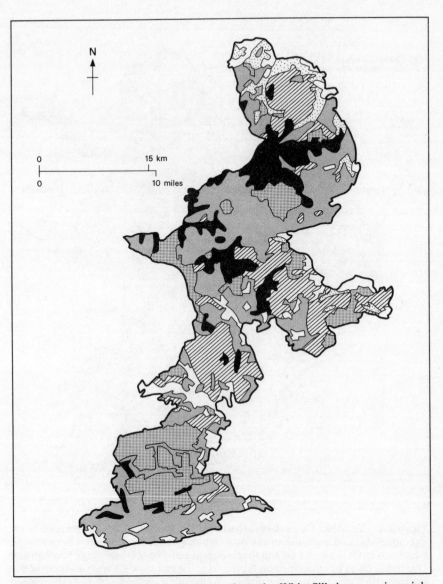

Figure 2.3 Northumberland vegetation. Along the Whin Sill the cover is mainly fescue-bent grassland with bog and marsh vegetation around the lakes at the foot of the scarps. The coniferous Wark Forest extends northwards to the North Tyne River, beyond which there is extensive heather and bilberry moorland, some of which is managed for grouse. The MOD ranges north of Redesdale are mainly purple moor-grass with bog vegetation on the peaty tops. On the southern slopes of the Cheviots the relatively good soil carries fescue-bent grassland, giving way to matt-grass and cotton-grass on the peaty topland. Further north there is heather moorland falling into bracken and gorse-sided valleys. (Surveyed by G. Sinclair, assisted by P. H. Richards, A. G. Lunn and C. J. Watson: forestry data 1975, vegetation data 1963–8.) Crown copyright reserved.

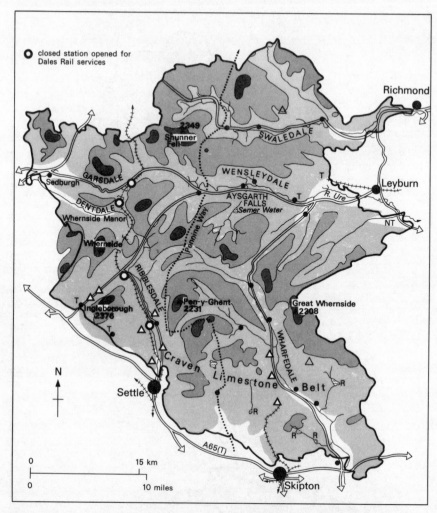

Figure 2.4 Yorkshire Dales physical features. The Park straddles the two sides of the Pennine Ridge and lies north of the Aire Gap (Fig. 2.1). Short, steep valleys descend westwards from the high fells and the three peaks of Pen-y-Ghent, Ingleborough and Whernside (2416 ft) are located on the west. On the east, straight wide dales dip gently towards the Vale of York (Swaledale, Wensleydale, Wharfedale). Their stepped profiles reflect the repeating alternation of limestones, sandstones and shales from which they are formed (the Yoredale series). In the south-west is the Craven limestone belt with its caves, pavements and crags. In the north and south-east, millstone grit predominates. Limestone quarrying is concentrated in Ribblesdale and lower Wharfedale (see Ch. 11). Crown copyright reserved.

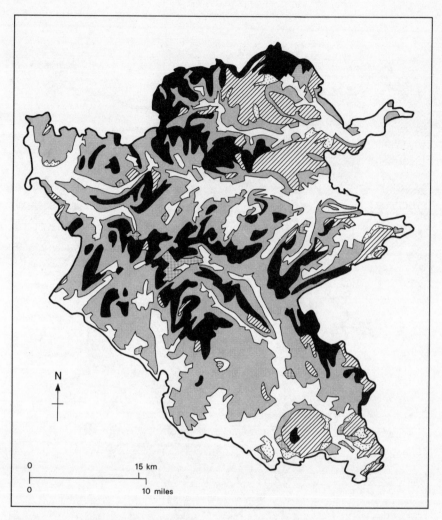

Figure 2.5 Yorkshire Dales vegetation. Permanent pasture extends well up the hillsides. Fescue-bent grassland predominates on the fells of Yoredale rocks, with mattgrass occupying much of the valley sides and lower slopes. The higher plateau tops are peat covered and in the west support extensive areas of cotton-grass. On the millstone grit of the north-east and south-east, the drier conditions favour heather moorland, often managed for grouse. Fescue-bent turf dominates in the limestone country of the south, with matt-grass where the soils are leached. (Surveyed by G. Sinclair: forestry data 1975, vegetation data 1963–8.) Crown copyright reserved.

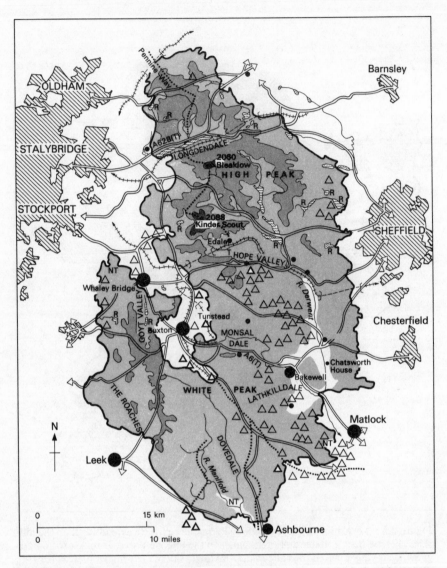

Figure 2.6 Peak District physical features. The Peak District is the southernmost part of the Pennines. Most of the park is dominated by the millstone grit moorlands of the High Peak which form a crescent on the west, north and east of the park with Kinder Scout as the highest point (2088 ft). Contained within the crescent is the lower plateau of limestone known as the White Peak which is penetrated by narrow dales – Dovedale on the southern edge of the park being the most famous. Limestone quarrying is concentrated around Buxton in an enclave excluded from the park boundary. Within the park the main quarry and cement works are in the Hope Valley on the north of the White Peak and fluorspar and other vein mineral workings are on the east. Crown copyright reserved.

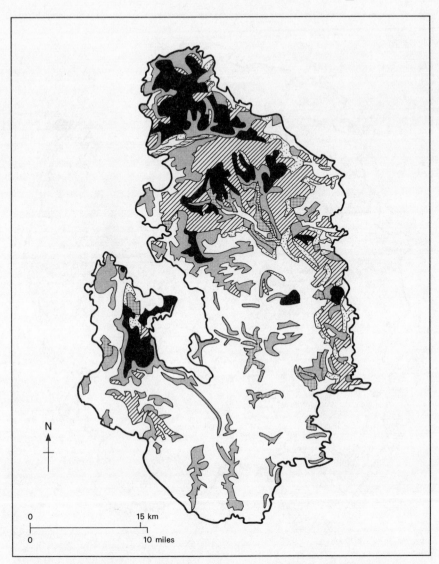

Figure 2.7 Peak District vegetation. The High Peak is typical heather moor, managed for grouse with bracken on valley sides and bilberry lining the gritstone edges. The highest peaty moorlands of Kinder Scout and Bleaklow carry cotton-grass with bilberry and crowberry and are eroded deeply and extensively. Their rolling lower slopes support large areas of matt-grassland. The White Peak is mostly farmland with a striking network of limestone walls. The steep-sided dry valleys carry fescue-bent turf, some semi-natural woodland and scrub. Elsewhere, broadleaved woodland consists mainly of beech and sycamore plantations. Conifer plantations are mainly on the gritstone valley sides. (Surveyed by G. Sinclair: forestry data 1974, vegetation data 1963–9.) Crown copyright reserved.

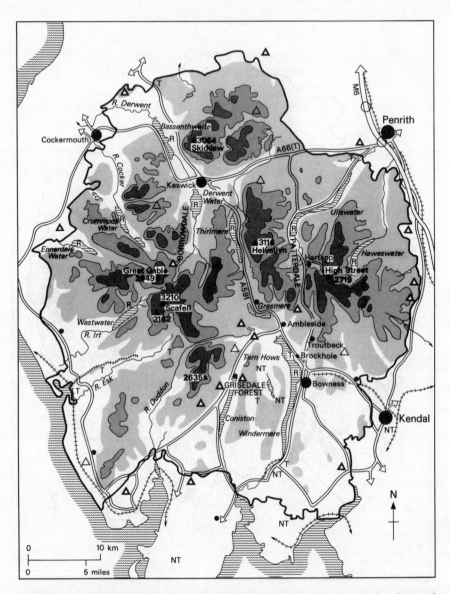

Figure 2.8 Lake District physical features. The Lake District is a complex dome of volcanic and sedimentary rocks surrounded by a broken rim of limestone. Radial drainage has been emphasised by glacial activity which froze debris off the mountain faces, scoured the valley floors with it and deposited it where the dales widened creating linear lakes. The rugged irregular mountains of the central belt are formed from volcanic rocks (Scafell Pikes, Helvellyn – both over 3000 ft). To the north, the slates that underlie Skiddaw (3054 ft) have weathered to form a smooth, rounded mountain. To the south are lower hills of under 2000 ft among which lies Windermere. The famous green slates are formed from stratified volcanic lava and are quarried still. Crown copyright reserved.

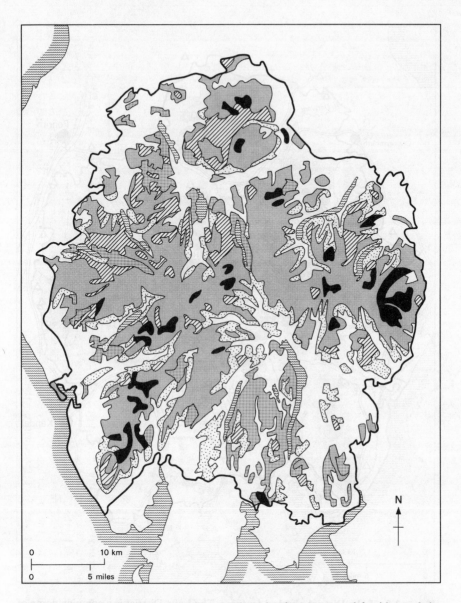

Figure 2.9 Lake District vegetation. Bracken dominates many dale sides and the lower slopes or unimproved valley floors (especially in the wetter, milder west) carry purple moor-grass. Higher up there are extensive areas of matt-grass with cotton-grass and moor-rush on peaty levels. Heather and billberry occur on crags and rocky fell sides and also in the east where heather is managed as grouse moors. There is some natural woodland in the valleys but also there are extensive conifer plantations, especially in the Grizedale area in the south. Summits above 2500 ft carry arctic-alpine heaths. (Surveyed by G. Sinclair, assisted by M. Davies Shiel: forestry data 1973, vegetation data 1962−8.) Crown copyright reserved.

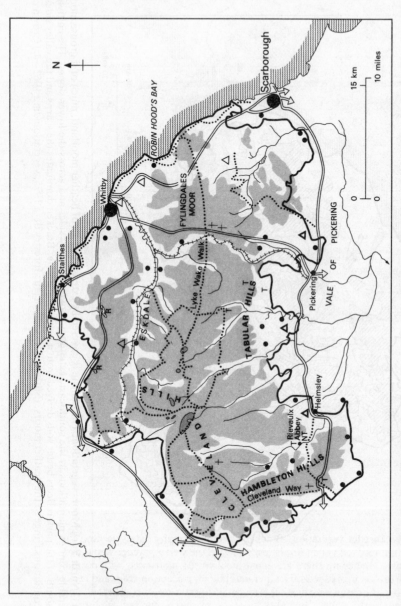

Figure 2.10 North York Moors physical features. The North York Moors lie as an isolated upland block above the surrounding country-side. In the north the moorland plateau is cut by the River Esk which flows west – east to the sea at Whitby. The highest part of the moorland is south of Eskdale and is bordered by the Cleveland Hills (1490 ft) on the north-west and by the Hambleton Hills on the west. From the moorland tops, short streams run northwards to the Esk and longer rivers have cut deep dales through the Tabular Hills as they flow southwards to the Vale of Pickering. The coastal belt is lower than the moorland with vertical cliffs of great diversity and height (Boulby, 600 ft). Potash is mined near Whitby (see Ch. 11).

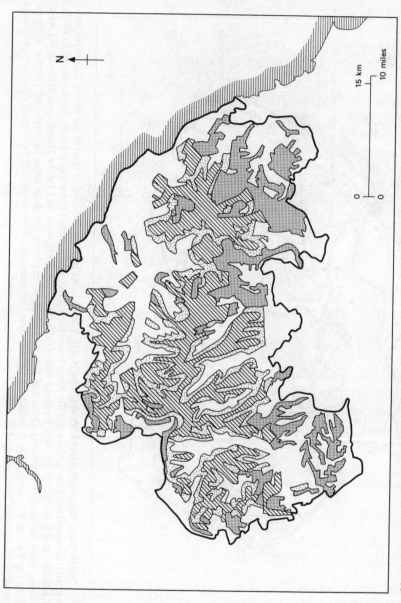

Figure 2.11 North York Moors vegetation. The plateau is covered by extensive areas of heather moorland, much of it grouse moor. There are considerable conifer plantations in the south-east, extending above the valley sides and across the lower slopes. The cultivated land across the south of the park reflects better soils derived from a belt of limestone. Bracken dominates the scarps and the valley sides to form an almost continuous fringe to the heather moors. (Surveyed by G. Sinclair: forestry data 1975, vegetation data 1963–4.) Crown copyright reserved.

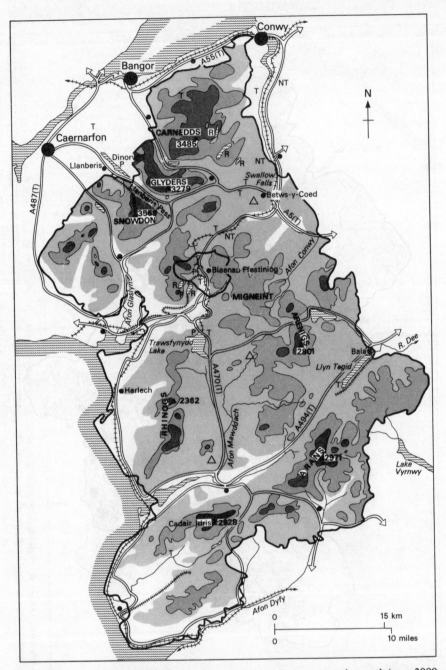

Figure 2.12 Snowdonia physical features. The Snowdon range on the north (over 3000 ft), the Arenig and Aran ranges in the east and south-east and Cadair Idris in the south-west constitute a giant arc of high mountains formed from volcanic rock. The arc encloses the lower and geologically older Rhinog range and Migneint moorland, the underlying sedimentary rocks of which appear in the form of slate on the north and south of Snowdon. Llanberis and Blaenau Ffestiniog (both outside the park) are centres of the once much larger slate industry. The low-lying land and extensive sandy beaches of the coast are interrupted by the estuaries of the Glaslyn, Mawddach and Dyfi rivers. Crown copyright reserved.

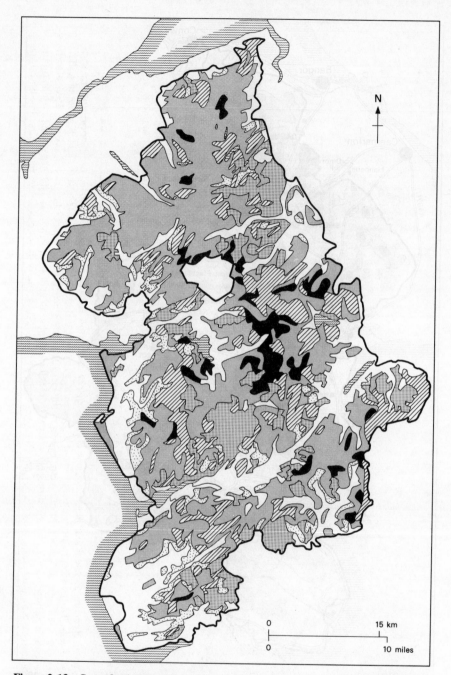

Figure 2.13 Snowdonia vegetation. Most valleys in the west and south carry bracken. Purple moor-grass is established on unimproved valley floors and lower slopes. The middle slopes are dominated by matt-grass and as drainage worsens by moor-rush, with cotton-grass and deer-sedge on the horizontal, peaty surfaces. Heather and bilberry are locally important on crags and rocky mountainsides and on a large scale in the drier east where heather moors are managed for grouse. Summits are a mixture of rock debris and arctic-alpine plants. Some western valleys have retained their oakwoods, but in the south and east of the Park there are extensive conifer plantations. (Surveyed by G. Sinclair: forestry data 1975, vegetation 1967–72.) Crown copyright reserved.

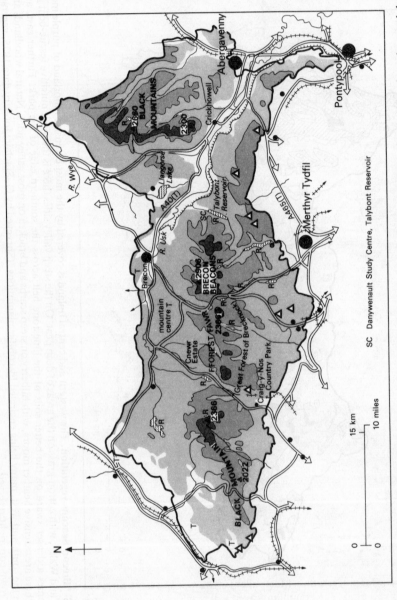

Figure 2.14 Brecon Beacons physical features. The park consists of two mountain areas separated and skirted on the north by the wide valley of the River Usk. To the west is the continuous range formed by the Brecon Beacons, Fforest Fawr and the Black Mountain. The latter must not be confused with the Black Mountains to the east of the Usk, on the western flank of which Llangorse Lake is located. North-facing scarps are a dominating summit feature of the mountains, from which slopes fall gently southwards. The limestone foothills on the south and the sandstone mountains are cut by deep, wooded gorges and by broad valleys, many of which contain reservoirs. The limestone belt is rich in caves and sinkholes and is quarried. Crown copyright reserved.

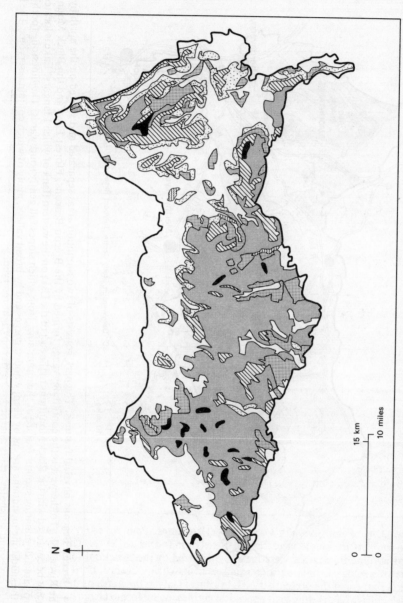

Figure 2.15 Brecon Beacons vegetation. The western and central upland is covered by the most extensive moorland of purple moor-grass in England and Wales, with cotton-grass on the areas of deep peat. On the steep valley sides there is the more nutritive fescue-bent grassland which becomes a denser sward on the better soils of the limestone belt across the southern edge of the park. Further east, as rainfall decreases, there are extensive heather moors, with bilberry on steep scarps and bracken on most valley sides. Natural woodlands are limited to valleys in the south and west, many being encircled by conifer plantations. (Surveyed by G. Sinclair: forestry data 1975, vegetation data 1970–2.) Crown copyright reserved.

N

15 km

10 miles

0

0

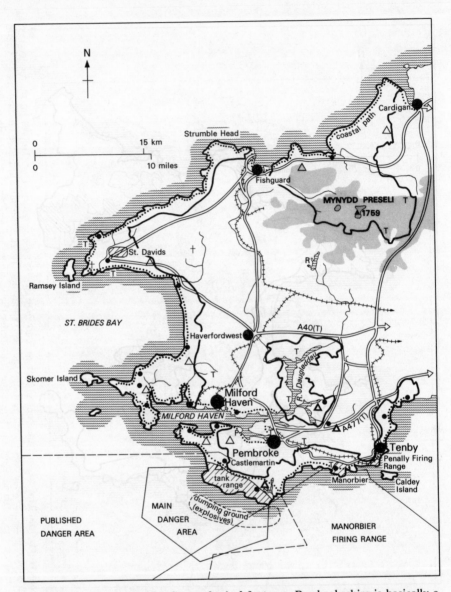

Figure 2.16 Pembrokeshire Coast physical features. Pembrokeshire is basically a wave-cut platform raised in successive stages from former sea levels. This means that its extraordinarily complex geology – as evidenced by the structural folding and the range of geological time periods exposed in its cliffs – bears little relation to the general flatness of the present-day land surface. Only in the north of the park do the Preseli Hills (1700 ft) emerge as geological entities, being formed from hard, volcanic rock. Postglacial rises in sea level have 'drowned' estuaries in the south – notably the Milford Haven, now an oil port, and its upper reaches called the Daugleddau. Crown copyright reserved.

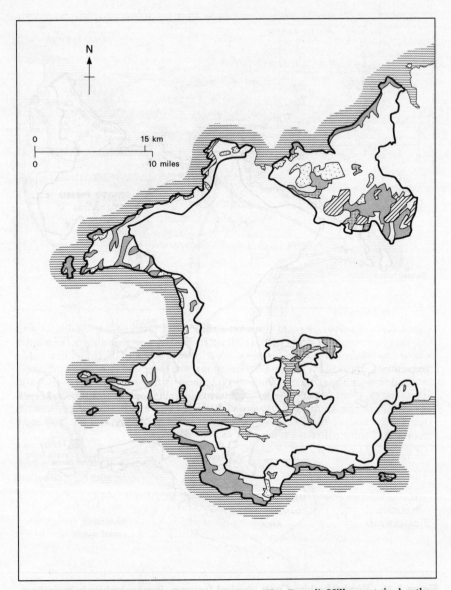

Figure 2.17 Pembrokeshire Coast vegetation. The Preseli Hills contain heather moors with purple moor-grass on the foot slopes. Along the coast, fescue-bent grassland and bracken predominate on the unenclosed headlands and there is much gorse. The fertile land used for military training at Castlemartin in the south has reverted to rough grassland and is used as winter grazing for Preseli sheep. Natural oak woodlands occur along the beaches of the Daugleddau and in some of the Preseli valleys where there are also conifer plantations. (Surveyed by G. Sinclair: forestry data 1975, vegetation data 1970–2.) Crown copyright reserved.

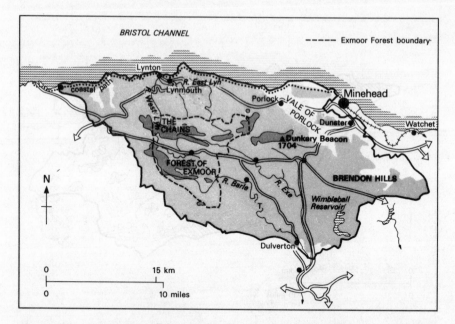

Figure 2.18 Exmoor physical features. Exmoor is a high, rolling moorland with Dunkery Beacon as its highest point (1700 ft), divided by wooded valleys. The plateau is bounded on the north by a somewhat lower coastal belt with cliffs that descend as steep convex slopes to the Bristol Channel. The rivers Barle and Exe rise on the moorland and flow southwards down long valleys to meet on the southern edge of the park. Short, swifter rivers flow north and break through to the coast in picturesque gorges. The cliff-line is broken also by the broad and fertile Vale of Porlock. The Brendon Hills to the east of the Exe are lower than the main plateau and are no longer moorland. Crown copyright reserved.

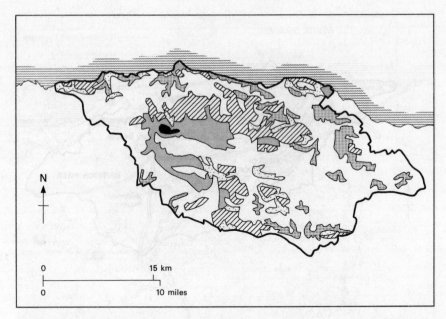

Figure 2.19 Exmoor vegetation. The central part of Exmoor is covered in purple moor-grass, capped on the desolate and boggy plateau called The Chains by what is perhaps the largest area in south-west England where deer-sedge is dominant. Surrounding the grassland is heather moorland (much fragmented by reclamation) which passes down into bracken and gorse-covered valleys, many of which retain their natural oak woodlands. Parts of the coastal ridge are still covered by heather and gorse, but the Brendon Hills on the east are largely cultivated and contain some conifer plantations (Surveyed by G. Sinclair: forestry data 1974, vegetation data 1962–4. Figure 8.1, p. 179, shows the distribution of moorland in 1980.) Crown Copyright Reserved.

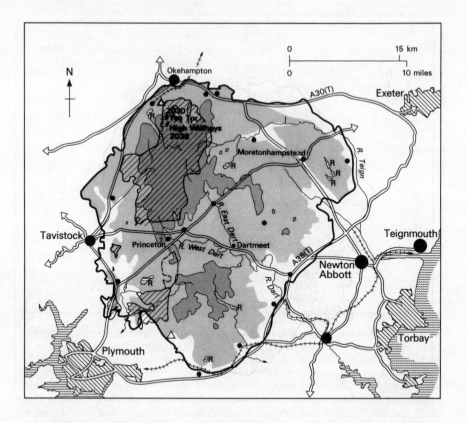

Figure 2.20 Dartmoor physical features. Dartmoor is divided into northern and southern plateaux, the former being the higher and larger (2000 ft). Each has a central area of moorland with rocky tors and steep-sided valleys on the edges. Many rivers rise in the higher northern part, the most important being the Dart and the Teign. The East and West Dart join at Dartmeet, one of the park's major 'honeypots'. Exploitation of the Park's natural resources takes the form of quarrying, mainly in the north-west, the extraction of china clay in the south-west, military training which pre-empts the northern heights and reservoirs ringing the moor in valley tops. Crown copyright reserved.

Dales and to a lesser degree in the Brecon Beacons. The granite of the Lakes and the Cheviots is used for road metal and that of Dartmoor for rail ballast. The old Welsh slate industry (now much reduced in scale) is centred on the heart of Snowdonia (although in an area excluded from the national park) and the famous green Westmorland slates are still quarried in the Lake District. A wide range of minerals resulting from igneous activity (including copper) is found in Snowdonia and in Dartmoor where china clay is worked

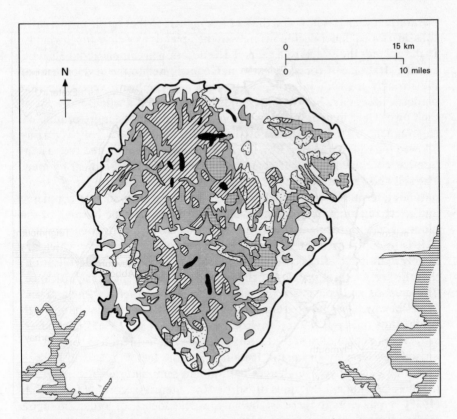

Figure 2.21 Dartmoor vegetation. The higher moorland is peat-covered supporting heather with purple moor-grass and deer-sedge on the wetter ground. Downslope purple moor-grass dominates with some sphagnum bogs, especially in the south. Better soils on the east support the more nutritive fescue-bent grassland with some heather and gorse. Many southern and eastern valleys retain natural oak woodlands and several persist at high levels. Of the four main conifer plantations, three surround reservoirs. (Surveyed by G. Sinclair: forestry data 1974, vegetation data 1963–6.) Crown copyright reserved.

extensively on an internationally significant scale. The limestone of the Peak is also rich in minerals. The lead industry has disappeared but the old workings are being mined for fluorspar, formerly a waste product but now a vital material for steelmaking. The UK's only reserves of potash are in and adjoining the North York Moors.

The natural soil and vegetation of the uplands of England and Wales have been drastically modified since the end of the last Ice Age. The climate then was warmer than it is now and the tree line higher, so that fertile brown earth soils developed under deciduous trees in the uplands as well as the lowlands. In the uplands the effects of a general deterioration in climate about 3000 BC and the clearance of forest by early man contributed to the development of the strongly leached, infertile, acidic soils and the heath vegetation that predominate today. But the moorlands have acquired a wildlife interest of their own. Once man moved down from the hilltops to the more productive environment of the lowlands, his use of the uplands for rough grazing allowed the soils to develop by natural processes in the main and the vegetation has continued to be self-generated despite some management by man. The soil and vegetation systems of the uplands are, therefore, largely semi-natural, a term that embraces low-intensity management such as coppicing and selective felling of woodlands, the grazing and periodic burning of the moors, and the grazing and mowing of some herb-rich permanent pasture.

It is in contrast to the soils and vegetation of the lowlands, which are largely man-made after centuries of cultivation, drainage and fertilisation, that the semi-natural systems of the uplands take on a special significance. The uplands and coasts are the most extensive areas left in England and Wales in which to study natural processes and to find out what happens to wildlife in a relatively natural environment. Curtis *et al.* (1976) find it necessary in their explanation of the factors affecting soil formation to concentrate on soil development in upland Britain where the factors 'can still be seen operating on relatively unaltered, natural and semi-natural soils'. And for the biologist, upland Britain is of 'surpassing interest' according to Pearsall (1965) 'because in it there is shown the dependence of organism upon environment on a large scale'. He goes on to say that 'in these marginal habitats we most often see man as a part of a biological system rather than as the lord of his surroundings'. In other words, the severe physical conditions of the uplands have limited man's scope for changing the natural environment. This is what makes the soils and vegetation of the mountains and moors of such interest to natural scientists and makes the national parks of special significance to everyone.

In the four cold parks of the North, moorland soils* predominate, particularly in Northumberland, although there are also better drained and more fertile soils on the lower land of the Lakes and Snowdonia and in the limestone areas of the Yorkshire Dales. In the climatically more favoured parks of the south-west and Pembrokeshire and in the White Peak, and also in the

---

* There are four main types of moorland soil: **peaty gleys** are water-logged mineral soils with a peaty organic surface. Wherever waterlogging has been long continued and the layers of peat have become deep, **raw peat soils** develop which are strongly acid; they may be found either in local depressions, in basins and at the foot of slopes, or on plateaus under heavy rainfall where they are known as blanket peat or blanket bog. **Peaty podsols** develop where the drainage is better and are soils in which the iron has been leached from the surface soil to form an impermeable layer – or iron-pan – that checks drainage and has to be broken through if the land is to be cultivated either for agriculture or forestry. **Skeletal soils** occur on the steeper slopes and mountain tops and are very thin and stony.

North York Moors and Brecon Beacons, the proportion of better acid brown earth soils is much higher. They predominate in Pembrokeshire and Exmoor and in the rest there is probably about as much non-peaty as moorland soil (Avery *et al.* 1975).

The peaty, acidic moorland soils have severe limitations when looked at simply as factors of agricultural production. They support grasslands of varying palatability to livestock, heathlands which merge into wetter moorlands and bogs, and woodlands or bracken on the hillsides. On MAFF's Agricultural Land Classification map of England and Wales, the uplands stand out as the areas where the two lowest grades – 4 and 5 – are concentrated. Land of these qualities is shown to be suitable only for low-output enterprises and is generally under grass or rough grazing with 'occasional fields of oats, barley or fodder crops on the grade 4 land'. The natural handicaps of the uplands are the main justification for the subsidising of both hill farming and afforestation. The hill farmer's main competitor is the commercial forester who can grow conifers on the moorland soils.

Sinclair (1979) has divided the semi-natural vegetation of the national parks into five categories (Figs 2.3, 2.5, 2.7, 2.9, 2.11, 2.13, 2.15, 2.17, 2.19 and 2.21): woodland (including planted forests which cannot be separated at the scale used in our maps); bracken and gorse; heather and bilberry moors; grasslands; and bogs. The distribution of semi-natural vegetation reveals that the widely-held image of upland scenery built up in many minds is often far removed from reality. A rough calculation based on Sinclair's work shows that semi-natural vegetation covers more than half the area in only five of the parks – Northumberland (where apart from forestry plantations there is hardly any cultivated land), Snowdonia, Yorkshire Dales, the Lakes and Dartmoor. Heather moors epitomise the uplands for many people, but they are far from being the major component of the semi-natural vegetation. Even in the North York Moors, where it is indeed possible to walk for 40 miles on heather from one side of the park to the other, the map shows the heather core to be an elongated strip poking thin fingers between the valleys, up the sides of which bracken creeps relentlessly. Every national park has heather moorland, but grassland is the dominant vegetation in the Brecon Beacons (the southern slopes of which are covered in the most extensive area of purple moor grass (*Molinia*) in England and Wales), the Lakes, Snowdonia, the Dales and Northumberland. It comes as a surprise to see that Snowdonia probably has more heather than the North York Moors, but the heather does not dominate the most visited mountain ranges. Dartmoor and Exmoor probably have no more heather, even taken together, than the North York Moors, which makes their heather moors a precious resource in South-West England. But the dominant vegetation in the former royal forest of Exmoor is purple moor-grass, unpalatable to sheep except when it is young but colourful as the purple-tinged leaves turn to tawny brown in late autumn and persist through the winter.

One key to understanding the natural life of the uplands and its changing relationship to land use and scenery is the 'upland profile' (Fig. 2.22a). By this we mean the cross-section from valley bottom to moor or fell and mountain top. The essential characteristics are everywhere the same – a transition from relatively fertile soils and diverse vegetation on the valley bottoms to poor soils and less stratified vegetation at the top. As one goes up the hillside the soil and vegetation change, providing habitats for different fauna and flora. But the line between them shifts up or down the hill in response to man's changing objectives and techniques of management, and local geological conditions and aspect produce an infinite variety in the characteristics of the profile.

The profile may begin at sea level, which it does in five of the parks, with coastlines that offer (in Pembrokeshire Coast particularly) a remarkable combination of marine, coastal and terrestrial life with spectacular scenery and extensive sandy bays. Ecologically, the wildlife of the coast is often as fragile as the mountain fauna and flora at the other end of the profile. Away from the coast, the traditional hill farm tries to exploit the full profile, as it climbs up the hill from the sheltered farmstead and inbye fields, originally cleared from woodland, on the better soils of the valley and its lower slopes, through the enclosures of rough pasture on the upper slopes (variously known as intakes, new takes or ffridd), to the rough grazing, sometimes managed for grouse, on the open moor or fell. The enormous popular appeal of the national parks lies in the changing scene and the wealth of different environments unfolded from level to level.

The range between the extremes astonishes foreign visitors and takes many English townspeople by surprise. Even in the benign climate of Exmoor with its modest altitudes and easy climbs, what Tim Burton (author of the best book on Exmoor) calls 'the high forbidding plateau' of the Chains is a world away from the teashops and putting greens of Lynmouth, only 1500 ft below and 4 miles distant. Between the valleys of the Exe and the Barle

> lies the boggy tableland which only the deer and stout-hearted walkers can cross. The lonely heights are lashed by frequent gales – even on a summer's day the wind stirs here. The rainfall is heavier than anywhere else on the moor; the land is sour, peaty, awash. There are no trees, only the coarse matted grass. Yet the desolation and the silence culminate in a sublimity that makes the Chains, for a very few, one of Exmoor's finest scenes. (Burton 1970, p. 4.)

But many of the natural features of the greatest scientific and popular interest – the caves and potholes of the limestone country, the sea-shore, lakes, dales, woodlands and rivers – are to be found at the lower or intermediate levels. So too are the towns, villages and interesting buildings. Stately homes, such as Chatsworth in the Peak, or villages like Dunster in Exmoor with its castle and intact mediaeval layout, are often the most powerful tourist attractions in the park. The easier walks and much picturesque

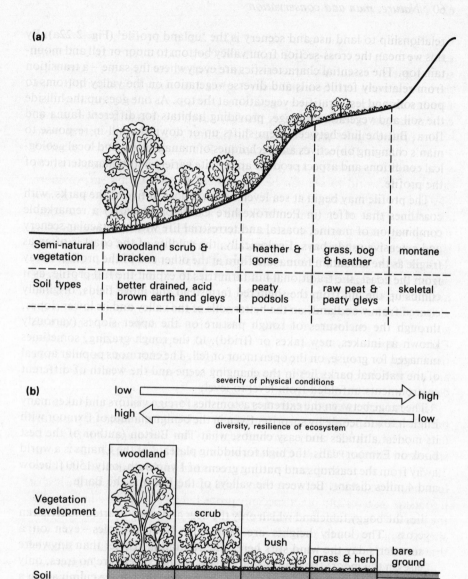

Figure 2.22 The upland profile and plant succession. (a) Upland profile, (b) plant succession, environmental conditions and ecological characteristics.

scenery, the major lines of communication and nearly all the facilities for servicing both the local people and the visitors – hotels, caravan and camp sites, hostels, restaurants, museums, information centres – are located on the lower ground. It is here that visitors come most sharply into conflict with farming as they make their way across the enclosed inbye-land, or drive their cars up narrow lanes to the valley heads to reach the fells and moors above.

The profile can be seen in a clear and dramatic form in the ascent from Porlock Vale to Porlock Common, in the Exmoor National Park, where a wide range of vegetation and land use in a seascape and landscape worth crossing the world to see can be experienced in minutes by car, or more pleasurably within a couple of hours on foot. Yet, even here one can discern disturbing signs of the reduction in the extent and diversity of the semi-natural vegetation that is, in fact, a widespread phenomenon. Deterioration is the price being paid in all the national parks for whatever benefits are derived from modern commercial agricultural and forestry techniques, neglect (often caused by an acute shortage of labour on farms and estates), mismanagement and inappropriate or excessive use. The signs are to be seen at every level of the profile. The herb-rich meadows on the lower land are going fast, as the result of spraying, ploughing and draining. Although an Exmoor experiment suggests that farmers will respond to grants for laying their beech hedges, the mechanical flail, enlarged fields and the wire fence are everywhere changing the character of hedgerows and hastening their demise.

The semi-natural woodlands that are critically important elements in the natural life and scenery of the combes and valleys of the national parks are under serious threat. Every survey made of the woodlands confirms the statement of the Nature Conservancy Council – that since 1947 some 30–50% of all ancient, semi-natural woodland in Great Britain has been lost, mainly to agriculture and commercial afforestation, and that the rest of it (outside reserves and other specially protected areas) will be eliminated by the year 2025 if the trends continue (NCC 1980b). Grazing of woodlands and shelter belts prevents natural regeneration. Former woodlands on well drained hillsides once cleared for grazing are now being overrun by bracken and gorse as sheep replace cattle and shepherding declines. Farmers are abandoning the steep, small fields on the valley sides in favour of more easily cultivated land lower down, or higher up where (in parts of Exmoor or North York Moors for example) relatively fertile soils exist on the flatter moorland tops.

On the peaty moorland soils, heather can produce a continuing supply of nutritious food for sheep, deer and grouse by means of carefully controlled burning. In the North York Moors and parts of the High Peak, Northumberland and Snowdonia, the management of heather for grouse shooting has been a major factor in its conservation. Repeated burning, however, produces a heather monoculture which favours grouse but impoverishes the moorland flora and soil (Miller & Watson 1976). Similarly, the burning of grassland and mixed vegetation communities, when skilfully carried out, can enhance their value for grazing. But when, as often happens, it is ineptly done it can destroy the desired species or even the peat itself (Phillips 1977; ITE 1979).

The most contentious conflicts of interest and changes in vegetation at the higher levels are produced by military training, reclamation of moorland for agriculture and afforestation, and excessive trampling of fragile soils and vegetation by human feet. All these problems arise from the suitability of the terrain for activities that can easily diminish the semi-natural vegetation and its associated wildlife. The first three of these activities are the direct or indirect responsibility of government departments or agencies. The difficulty of controlling these activities and resolving the conflicts is one of the themes of later chapters.

The wet and relatively mild climate of the British uplands often makes it possible to grow coniferous species more rapidly than is possible in their native habitats. Firm scientific evidence about the long-term effects of afforestation on upland soils is lacking, because there is an alarming lack of information (HL 1980). There is virtually no fundamental research, nor any central body to direct it. The Forestry Commission spends £2 750 000 (1979–80) out of total national expenditure of £4 870 000 on forestry research and concentrates on applied research biased towards the planting of quick-growing conifers. The NCC directs most of its £175 000 forest research budget towards identifying areas of importance for nature conservation (NCC 1980a). The NCC does not accept the claim of the forestry interests that coniferous afforestation replaces a uniform habitat by a more diverse one. On the contrary, the NCC takes the view that the most serious losses of plant communities and species are suffered when wet ground and upland peat bogs, many of which are undisturbed and have a largely natural character, are drained and planted. More generally, the NCC considers that although in the early years a plantation may support a diversity of wildlife, 40 to 50 years of dense coniferous monoculture excludes the moorland vegetation and supports a depauperate bird community with few mammals.

As can be seen from Figure 2.22a the upland profile reveals the changes associated with altitude, just as the plant succession diagram records the development of plant communities over time, from the simplest to the most complex that the environment can support. The profile illustrates the general relationship between the severity of physical conditions and resilience to use shown in Figure 2.22b. This diagram indicates that the more severe the environmental conditions the less diverse is the vegetation and associated wildlife, and the greater their susceptibility to damage as a result of intensive use (O'Connor 1976). Their acid soils, cold, wet wind and short growing season limit the capabilities of the uplands for self-renewal and repair.

This suggests that over a major part of the national parks the ecosystems are easily damaged, and, if they are to be conserved, should be used or managed in ways that respect their ecological characteristics. Traditional hill farming can achieve this end by using the relatively small areas of the better and more resilient bottom land for hay, silage and other fodder crops as winter keep, and using the unimproved open country as rough grazing at stocking levels dictated by the small proportion of better inbye land. If practised with a minimum of well-controlled grass or heather burning and attentive shepherding (in contrast to the present trend towards crude overburning and little or no shepherding) hill farming maintains some of the diversity of vegetation and wildlife. Sheep are selective feeders and if grazing is not carefully controlled they will overgraze young heather shoots and favourite grasses, thus allowing mat grass and other unpalatable species to take over from the bent/fescue grasses that should provide their staple diet.

Hill farming is practised under severe natural handicaps, but it is too easy to overlook the advantages of low-input farming systems. When the world comes to terms with the need to make intelligent use of one of its most plentiful resources – human labour – and to minimise the use of energy and other scarce resources, hill farming will have to be seen in a different light. John Phillips, in a report to the Exmoor National Park Committee, argued that it is unacceptable to apply costly inputs, such as fuel, phosphate and nitrogen, to upland soils where conditions preclude a maximum response. 'Agronomists from government downwards will have to start looking at native vegetation with fresh eyes, because essentially it is capable of yielding a useful annual increment on a low input/low output basis' (Phillips 1977, p. 84). Seen from this point of view, the uplands acquire value as an environment where store sheep and cattle can be reared from a reservoir of hardy breeding stocks, with economy of resources and in harmony with nature, for finishing in the lowlands. The uplands are threatened, less perhaps by the local cataclysmic changes made by vast new civil engineering works (such as reservoirs and roads) than by the insidious widespread incremental changes wrought by modern farming and forestry. A study of vegetation maps covering 1500 km^2 of Powys in Mid-Wales showed that in the six years 1971–7 'forestry and improved farming had destroyed 7% of the natural habitat ... if agricultural improvement continues at that rate only half the area covered by natural vegetation in 1971 will remain by the end of the century' (Goode 1981).

Man

The national parks have a rich history running in a continuum from man's arrival after the Ice Age, through pre-history and historical times to the present day. The evidence of man's progress and conflicting interests is to be seen everywhere – in archaeological remains, field boundaries, the lines of communication, the settlement pattern, place names, ancient buildings, forts, castles and churches. The very remoteness of the uplands has preserved much of the evidence. But the past has more than historical or archaeological interest, for it survives into the present day in language and dialect and in the habits of thought and independence of mind of the people, as well as in the landscape.

Evidence of life in the Neolithic, Bronze and Iron ages, from about 300 BC to the Roman invasion, is to be found in all the parks, although it is thin on the ground in some. In Dartmoor, as the park guide says, the antiquities are so numerous and their setting so relatively unchanged that they still give an intelligible picture of early man in relation to his environment. The Romans also left their mark on all the upland parks, mainly in the form of military forts and a linking road system. Hadrian's Wall, the central part of which is in the Northumberland National Park, is the most outstanding Roman monument in Britain. Impressive though it is as an ancient structure, the magic of the Wall lies in part in its magnificent natural setting along the Whin Sill and in the contrast that can still be felt between the friendly, fertile lands to the south and the bleak threatening moorland and marsh to the north.

But in general – and the Wall is no exception – much remains to be done, both to reveal and interpret archaeological remains and to protect them from deliberate and accidental damage. Although many ancient monuments have been officially scheduled and protected, a recent report on the conservation of Dartmoor's ancient monuments says that unscheduled sites may be of equal or greater importance and that 'only a small proportion of sites which merit scheduling have in fact been scheduled' (DNPC undated). This omission is attributed mainly to staff shortages in the DOE inspectorate of ancient monuments. The position in Exmoor probably applies to many other areas as well – 'the real value of the moor is that it has many unexcavated sites. It remains a rich and largely untapped reservoir of knowledge about early man in the south west' (Curtis & Maltby 1980).

From the early English period – the 6th to the 11th centuries – the English uplands have inherited their pattern of villages and place-names, their systems of mixed and of hill farming and the dialects of today which derive from the language of the early Anglo-Saxon, Danish and Norse invaders. Few buildings survive, but in the long, narrow S-shaped fields still surviving in parts of the Dales, North York Moors and the Peak (notably at Chelmorton) one can see the pattern of the early English strip cultivations.

During this period Wales remained a Celtic kingdom and was affected very little by the English and Scandinavian invasions. The Welsh spoke their own language, maintained their own laws and customs and, from the 6th century, developed a literature of their own. In spite of the English conquest at the end of the 13th century, much of the old way of life continued in Wales until the Tudor succession. It was Tudor policy to assimilate Wales which, as the official guide to the Snowdonia National Park says, smoothed the way for ambitious Welshmen to proceed to the English Court, but was socially disastrous – '...the leaders of the native Welsh society became gradually anglicised in speech and habit and between them and the mass of ordinary Welshmen there opened a gulf leading to two separate social classes, different in language, in religion and in politics' (Morris-Jones 1973, p. 76).

It is against this background and the subsequent attempts to eradicate Welsh as a living language that the present-day nationalist movement, opposition to second-homers from England and the fierce resistance put up in Snowdonia to a national park board has to be understood. The Snowdonia park guide itself, while admitting that tourism makes a significant contribution to the local economy, makes it clear how offensive to many Welsh people is the indifference of visitors and second-homers to the culture and language of Wales. Snowdonia is located in Wales, but primarily it is a park for the English.

While the ordinary people of Wales continued in their resistance to the English during the Middle Ages, the English in Northumberland and the Lakes were embattled with the Scots. The warlike character of the times has left its mark in the castles of the Welsh princes in Brecon Beacons and Snowdonia, in the English castles on the edge of Snowdonia and the Lakes and within the Pembrokeshire and Northumberland parks and in the pele-towers, or fortified houses, of the Lakes and Northumberland.

The royal forests were the first example in our history of the designation of extensive tracts of land for recreation, combined with severe restrictions on the local people's right to cultivate or use the land. The recreation, of course, was for the pleasure of the king and his court and the hunting preserves were protected by ferocious forest laws and forest officers. The royal forests survive today in the New Forest and in the estates of the Duchy of Cornwall in Dartmoor and the Duchy of Lancaster in the North York Moors. These apart, the royal forests were not disposed of finally until the early 19th century, but they still survive in such names as the Forest of Exmoor and the Great Forest of Brecknock.

If the economic development of the uplands was retarded by the forest law, it was accelerated by the activities of the great monastic orders. The monasteries, such as Rievaulx Abbey in the North York Moors, established farms and sheep walks and grew rich on the wool trade, thereby coming into conflict with local people and depriving them of grazing, fishing and hunting rights over large tracts of wild country. But it was the enclosures that finally settled the fate of many peasants and small farmers, whose survival depended upon the ability to graze animals or to take turf and wood for fuel from privately owned land over which they held rights of common.

Every part of the uplands was affected by the parliamentary enclosures of the 18th and 19th centuries. The results are still visible in mile upon mile of stone walls running up hill and down dale, giving their distinctive character to the fells and moors of northern England and in the earth/stone banks of the South-West. But the discerning traveller will notice that there are large areas in all the national park uplands that have not been enclosed. The enclosures were incomplete, mainly because the less fertile upland commons were less attractive to the enclosers, but also because it was not so easy, for reasons of land tenure and the independent attitudes of upland folk, to ride rough shod over the commoners. The consequence is that by far the greater part of the million and a half acres or so of remaining commons are to be found in the uplands, where they are a major resource for livestock farming, wildlife and recreation. It is now nearly 40 years since the Scott report (*op. cit.* 1942) drew attention to the urgent need to restore commons management where it had collapsed and to provide legal rights of public access, and 23 years since the Royal Commission on Common Land (Common Land 1958) recommended legislation. It is one of the scandals of the countryside that legislation now seems unlikely before the 1990s – an issue to which we shall return in Chapter 9.

Often it is forgotten that the uplands have had mixed economies in the past, the evidence of which is still to be seen in old mines, drifts, mills and quarries and the farmhouse spinning galleries of the Lake District. From the earliest times sheep-farming was often a part-time job, being combined with working on other people's land or in the mines or the home-based woollen industry. In addition to some coal, the coppiced oakwoods provided a renewable source of energy for smelting metals and a basis for trades related to both farming and industry. In the 18th century water power, now almost totally neglected despite its potential for small-scale enterprises, attracted the northern textile manufacturers into the valleys and established a widespread spinning industry in the Lake District, the Yorkshire Dales and the Peak.

When the centres of industrial activity shifted to the major coalfields and the prolonged depression in agriculture set in throughout the era of cheap labour, cheap food and free trade, the upland economy became less and less self-sufficient, more marginal and increasingly dependent on a weakened hill farming industry. At the same time, with the coming of the railways, local cultures were exposed to the influence of nascent tourism and the influx of the new rich seeking second homes or sporting estates. The scene was being set for the recreational explosion, the transformation of communications, farming, forestry and industry in the mid-20th century – changes that have exposed the uplands to a more intimate relationship with the lowlands and the cities than ever before and that pose problems of an entirely novel kind for the physical, social and cultural environment.

Looking back over history, one can see the uplands as marginal areas, continually changing in response to economic, technological, social and political trends. But in the past their remoteness and the harshness of the environment that depressed living standards also protected them from some of the worst excesses of human exploitation experienced more acutely in the lowlands where ordinary people lived closer to their rulers. The Norman conquest, concentrating power in the unholy trinity of the crown, the church and the feudal lords, reduced many free farmers to virtual slavery. But 'freemen survived, especially in the Danish area of England, in the border counties, and in other pastoral hilly regions where the peasants had hacked their own holdings out of the waste' (Bonham-Carter 1971 p. 27). This tradition can be seen in the case of free tenants who had reclaimed much of Exmoor by the time of the Black Death, in the similar recolonisation of Dartmoor, in the 'drengs' or free tenants of Northumbria who held land in return for military service and at a later date in the 'statesmen' of Cumbria, tenant farmers who enjoyed rights of succession. This tradition lingers on, surviving not only in independent minds but also in a tradition of mutual help in farm work and times of trouble and in the common management of common land. It remains one of the potential assets of the uplands.

Conservation

Parliament gave the National Park Authorities the job of conserving and enhancing the 'natural beauty' of the national parks and it defined that term widely to include nature in its broadest sense. But, as we saw in the previous chapter, the Countryside Commission tends to equate 'natural beauty' with 'landscape' and does so in the advice it gives to the NPAs (DOE 1974b). But 'landscape' has two very different meanings. The Commission tends to use it to mean picturesque scenery in the romantic landscape tradition – a prospect or scene pleasing to the eye, the elements of which can be analysed as an aid to appreciation. Once the components of a pleasing landscape are identified, a landscape can be designed from scratch and a pleasant prospect created where none existed before. From this tradition, which had its beginnings in the 18th century in the writings of William Gilpin (Barbier 1963) and the work of 'Capability' Brown and other landscape designers, springs the whole modern school of landscape evaluation and attempts to pick out the most beautiful landscapes (i.e. the most picturesque scenery) of which the Countryside Commission for Scotland's report on Scotland's Scenic Heritage (CCS 1978) is a recent example.

But 'landscape', like the German word 'landschaft', can have ecological connotations as well. Pearsall (1965) says that upland 'scenery' (which he admires for its beauty) is important to the biologist as an integration of the factors that have created it – geological, climatic, vegetational, human – and that 'often his first interest will be to look keenly at the scenery for clues in the analysis of the environmental factors at work'. We prefer to speak of 'scenery' to describe the visual appearance of the countryside and 'living landscape' to express the interaction of the natural environment and the activities of man described by Pearsall. Scenery, according to this interpretation, is an important element of landscape, but beauty is not skin deep, nor is the argument merely a semantic one. For keeping up appearances is very far from being the same thing as conserving the living landscape. In practice, since the reorganisation of the national parks in 1974, 'landscape' is being given a much wider interpretation than mere scenic beauty. The Yorkshire Dales National Park Plan, for example, treats the 'condition' of landscape as the physical, biological and cultural characteristics of an area and their interactions, and its 'appearance' as the visual manifestation of these characteristics (YDNPC 1977).

The interdependence of scenery and nature and the wide overlap between areas of great scenic beauty and areas of great wildlife value have long been acknowledged. The Nature Conservancy Council has said that

the natural scenic beauty and amenity of the countryside depends to a large extent upon the maintenance of physical features with their cover of soil, vegetation and animals, these in turn being an expression of patterns of land use evolved by man over the centuries. . . . National parks, chosen as the outstanding areas of natural beauty, necessarily express this relationship with the basic ecological features to an especially marked degree.

The NCC went on to say that national parks contain 'some of the least disturbed and developed country in England and Wales and encompass a substantial part of the country's wildlife resources' (NCC 1976, p. 564).

In these words, the NCC has put its finger on the first essential characteristic of the national parks – their appearance of wildness. They are not wild, in the sense that they have never been used or exploited by man, but within them natural features and processes are dominant. Like others, we do not want the natural world preserved as a 'museum piece', but 'want the opportunity to experience it face to face with its qualities of wildness and renewal intact' (Mabey 1980, p. 40). It is precisely the relative ascendancy of the 'natural world' that characterises the uplands of these islands in general and can be experienced to an exceptional degree in the national parks of England and Wales. We call this characteristic semi-wildness, and to it we would add three others. One is that the uplands are unique repositories both of Earth and human history. Another is that they have resources and offer space that cannot be found elsewhere. The third is that although man has left his mark and has sometimes done so with a brutal disregard for natural systems and scenic beauty, his relationship with nature is, in contrast to much of the lowlands, relatively harmonious.

The rest of this book consists largely of detailed studies of the practical operation of the system set up in 1949, and modified later, for the protection and management of these resources. In practice they get very little real protection, and they are managed for a variety of purposes that may be in the sharpest conflict with the purposes of conservation. To say that 13% of the land area of the national parks has been designated as national nature reserves (NNR) or sites of special scientific interest (SSSI) may sound impressive. The NNRs, whether owned by the NCC or leased or managed by agreement with the owners, are indeed legally protected, at least for the duration of the lease or agreement. But NNRs amount to no more than 4 % of the designated area, or about 0.5 % of the land area of the national parks. In the SSSIs, which are supposed to enjoy a special degree of protection, development is controlled by local planning authorities, which must consult the NCC. But the agricultural and forestry operations most likely to affect the SSSIs are not 'development' and are, therefore, uncontrolled. Nationwide, 4 % of them are severely damaged every year (NCC 1980c) but studies of 25 counties in England and Wales suggest that around 10 % were seriously damaged in 1980 (NCC 1981). Such protection as SSSIs enjoy is afforded mainly by the goodwill of owners and users and by consultation procedures. The Wildlife and Countryside Bill introduced in December 1980 would apply a compulsory notification procedure to a very small number of top priority SSSIs, leaving the remainder to be 'protected' by voluntary arrangements – a policy whose implications for conservation will be examined in Chapter 13. The Ministry of Agriculture now warns farmers that if they do not notify the national park authority or the Nature Conservancy Council before making 'improvements' in national parks or SSSIs, they risk losing their grants (MAFF 1980a). The effectiveness of these consultation procedures will be examined later. But there can be no doubt that the key to the conservation of the national parks, including their scenic beauty, wildlife and recreational attraction, is the conservation of the totality of their natural life and resources on the broadest possible base (see Postscript, p. 284).

The system established for the planning and administration of the national parks was never designed to control the social and economic forces that are behind the process of incremental change. A landscape that is being transformed by social, economic and cultural change cannot be protected without taking social, economic and cultural (and therefore political) decisions about its resources. Merely to designate areas or promulgate orders is likely to be a futile exercise. For conservation of resources is dependent on 'marrying natural systems and social systems to maintain stability or sustain yield' (Warren & Goldsmith 1976). But such a marriage implies a reversal of present trends and drastic changes in the objectives and priorities of agricultural, forestry, mineral and other policies (see Chs 9, 10 & 11).

Conservation is taken by the authors to mean the thrifty use of non-renewable resources and the use of renewable resources without diminishing their quality or endangering their supply. Essentially, conservation is an attitude of mind that runs counter to the prevailing ideology of growth and consumerism and implies a commitment on the part of public and private owners and users of land that goes far beyond cosmetic gestures. To husband energy and materials while encouraging and enhancing natural processes must touch the pocket too, for at the most fundamental level it challenges the conventional wisdom that never-ending growth and increasing material wealth are intrinsically desirable and attainable goals.

A shift from the conservation of scenery (and some islands of nature) to the conservation of nature and natural resources opens up a range of options for management or non-management for upland areas like the national parks. What is common to them all is that although they may or may not involve radical changes in scenery over time, they are all designed to conserve or enhance (perhaps we should say enrich) the living landscape. One option, of course, is to preserve the status quo, either because it is judged to effect a harmonious balance between man and nature, or because it is desired to conserve special habitats, communities or species. But the status quo can be preserved only by positive management that interferes with the natural processes of change.

Particularly in the British Isles where man's interference has been so widespread, there is a case at suitable places and times for letting nature take its course and allowing the natural vegetation of moor and woodland to develop without interference until it reaches its climax. Non-management of heather moorland would transform the scenery as the heather grew high and woody and scrub appeared. It might impair access and appear unsightly to those who like the managed landscape. Often untidiness is equated with mismanagement in the minds of those who regard all scrub clearance as an act of virtue. But in the right place a regime of non-management could, we suggest, be consistent with sustaining the semi-wild landscapes in the parks. Moorland can be viewed also as a degraded landscape, characterised by nutrient-poor acidic soils, or even as Britain's first, man-made, ecological disaster. Dimbleby (1962) has argued that the long-term aim should be to restore the fertility of the degraded moorland soils, and this offers another management option. The Lake District National Park Plan (LDSPB 1978) expresses anxieties about the long-term possibility that even continued grazing of the fells by sheep could lead to further soil erosion and the depletion of soil resources. The NCC's doubts about the long-term effects of continuously taking crops of conifers off moorland soils were voiced many years earlier by Pearsall. He suggested that long-term forestry policy should be directed towards the restoration of the natural fertility of moorland soils, by a combination of fertilisation and the gradual introduction of deciduous hardwood species that would enrich rather than deplete the soil (Pearsall 1965). Such a policy is ruled out today by the financial encouragement given to quick returns from coniferous afforestation.

Yet another possibility is suggested by Nan Fairbrother's idea of creating a 'man-made wild' (*op. cit.* 1970, p. 225). In some of the less exposed parts of the parks there may be scope for increasing the diversity (and hence the resilience) of the vegetation to create a landscape designed to take recreational pressure. It would be new 'scenery' but also a usable semi-wild landscape, designed with a full understanding of the ecosystem where eventually natural processes would be allowed to operate. A long-established example of man-made landscape of this kind is to be found at Tarn Hows, said to be the most popular beauty spot in the Lake District. The Tarn itself, a small lake of only 13 ha in a 20-ha site, was created by a dam in 1865. The plantations on the lake shore and the island, which are a major feature, date from the same time and are coniferous – Scots pine, larch and fir. It is a living demonstration of the fact that man, if tourist figures are anything to go by, can sometimes do as well as nature.

Even to suggest the exploration of some of these options could stir up controversy. But they are no more than part of a range of possibilities, each of which could have a role to play in the strategy of conservation. The fact that the uplands of Britain have the special characteristics that we associate with semi-wildness, and therefore need appropriate conservation measures, does not mean that they are more important than other parts of the country. It means that they are different and should be conserved for their specific qualities.

The first aims of conservationists must be a reduction in the demands that society makes on nature and natural resources, and a change in the attitudes of mind that lie behind them. Approaching conservation in this way raises many other questions that will form the themes of later chapters, including fundamental questions about protective designations and the division of responsibility for conservation between the Countryside Commission and the Nature Conservancy Council. The qualities that distinguish the national parks of England and Wales (which were our starting point) are shared to a large degree by other upland areas, some of them equally extensive if less spectacular. Whether the semi-wild 'cultural landscapes' of England and Wales should continue to be called 'national parks' is an issue to which we shall return in Chapter 12.

3 *Enjoyment*

Town, country and the national parks

The preservation and enhancement of natural beauty – the first statutory purpose of the national parks legislation of 1949 – was not an end in itself but a means to an end. The countryside was to be protected so that the public could enjoy it, and it was the popular appeal of opening up the countryside that carried the legislation through Parliament. The 1949 Act accurately reflected the mood of post-war Britain. The sacrifices made by ordinary people in 10 years of war and austerity were to be rewarded by opening up the countryside for the enjoyment of the town. In one sense there was nothing new in this. From Roman times the wealthy citizens had resorted to the countryside. From Wordsworth's day the industrialists of Lancashire had been settling in the Lake District to enjoy peace and beauty. Now the ordinary people were to have their turn and use the countryside as their playground as their masters had done before them.

Raymond Williams has identified the ideology of the upper class 'countryman' that developed on the basis of industrialisation and imperialism as a 'mode of play . . . field sports, fishing and above all horses; often a marginal interest in conservation and "old country ways"' (Williams 1973, p. 282). Hardy's *The hand of Ethelberta* captures the same idea in the wry incomprehension of the hostler, who has spent 50 years 'saddling horses that others might ride 'em' without making a penny, as he watches the 'men of money' working off their surplus energy 'doing work for play': 'aye, the toppermost class nowadays have left off the use of wheels for the good of their constitutions, so they traipse and walk for many years up foreign hills, where you can see nothing but snow and fog, till there's no more left to walk up'.

As long as this kind of recreation was the prerogative of a small, if steadily growing, rich and leisured minority, and only the toppermost class had wheels at their disposal, it was not regarded as a problem by landowners or rural authorities. But, as we saw in Chapter 1, the demand by working people to have access to open country and the resistance of the landowners has a long history. The 1949 Act struck a political compromise, but none of those concerned foresaw the full extent of the changes that were to take place between 1945 and the mid-1970s. Real disposable income per head doubled, energy costs fell in real terms, the number of private cars increased eightfold and nearly half the manual workers were entitled by 1978 to at least three weeks holiday – another third being entitled to four weeks or more (Tables

1.9, 1.10, 1.16, CC 1979c). As these benefits moved down the social scale, so did the working class take increasingly to countryside recreation. The National Survey of Countryside Recreation, undertaken by the Countryside Commission, has shown that in 1977 half the trips to the countryside were made by skilled manual workers, foremen and supervisors, who represented 33% of all households in Great Britain (Table 1.5, CC 1979c). The number of trips made by the semi-skilled and unskilled is already substantial, although far fewer in number than those made by employers, managers and white-collar workers.

There are strong echoes, even now, of the Wordsworthian view that the working masses are incapable of appreciating natural beauty, although nobody is so rash as to spell it out today as crudely as the poet did in 1844. But Fitton (1979) has shown that some 'defenders' of the countryside see it being threatened with 'invasion' by ignorant people, brought there by higher wages, shorter working hours and motor cars. He numbers the National Trust and the 1973 House of Lords Select Committee on Sport and Leisure among those who have suggested that the majority of the population are not seeking 'true countryside' but should be content with country parks or improved facilities in the city or the urban fringes. We take the opposite view, first expressed by Olmsted over 100 years ago (Roper 1973), that although the driving force for the conservation and enjoyment of nature has largely been generated by urban intellectuals who knew the countryside, the ignorance about the natural world of ordinary townspeople is the result of the historical class and functional separation of town and country, and will respond to closer contact with nature given time and opportunity.

It is often suggested that the mass demand for countryside recreation comes from the new motorists, the white-collar workers and men from the production line, who simply want to relax by their cars, with a nice view in front of them, the radio and their dogs for company and a *News of the World* on their laps. The scene at innumerable car parks by riversides or viewpoints on hot summer Sundays would seem to confirm this cynical view. A survey in the Lake District in 1975 showed that more than half the visitors did not move 'very far' from their cars, but simply wanted somewhere to relax, picnic or take a short stroll to a viewpoint (LDSPB 1978). In Dartmoor, just under a third of the visitors stayed within 100 yards of their cars and 13% drove around without stopping (DNPC 1977). This reluctance to get out of the car and explore the countryside is, to our mind, understandable. Visitors include many elderly and disabled people, mothers with very small children and men and women whose daily work gives them all the exercise they want. Add the pleasures of idleness, sunbathing, picnicking and paddling and unfamiliarity with the countryside, and one can understand why so much countryside recreation is passive.

Equally, there can be little doubt that some proportion of these passive visitors would be happy if similar facilities could be provided nearer to their homes. A Peak Survey in 1971 and 1972 suggests that about 38% of visitors would use such facilities as country parks, instead of going to the Peak, if they were conveniently located (PPJPB 1974). This points to a gap in the spectrum of recreational provision. Often country parks are not available because rural authorities give a very low priority to the satisfaction of the recreational needs of the towns. But it is entirely wrong to think of country parks as facilities for a special class of people for whom the unique qualities of the national parks have no appeal. Those who visit the Craig-y-Nos country park in the Brecon Beacons one day, may be out on the mountain the next. The family that first gets to know the Lake District on a trip to Windermere may be fell walking next year. The original destination, the tourist honeypot, becomes the base from which the whole range of experiences offered by the national park can be explored. People cannot be pigeonholed, once and for all, as active or passive, car-bound or liberated. They develop and change.

Let us look at the figures more closely. The Lake District survey showed that the most popular activity was walking (55%) with 28% going more than a mile, 11% more than 4 miles and 10% fell-walking. Even in Dartmoor, which has less appeal for the long-distance walker, about a quarter of all visitors walked over a mile, of whom more than half walked between 2 and 5 miles. Such data as can be extracted from national park plans suggest that in all the national parks about one person in five goes for a walk of 2 miles or more. This confirms the findings of the 1977 General Household Survey and the Countryside Commission's Recreation Survey of the same year (CC 1979c), that at least 21% of those interviewed had been on a walk in the countryside of 2 miles or more in the previous four weeks. The result of a 1975 questionnaire to visitors to information centres in Exmoor suggests 'a keen predeliction for exploring the wildness' and walking and less interest in the more traditional 'tripper' activities such as visiting well-known tourist spots (ENPC 1977b). What stands out from these surveys is not so much the high proportion of passive visitors, but the remarkably large and apparently increasing numbers of those who do make an effort to experience the natural world direct.

These 'middle distance walkers', to use a convenient phrase to describe those who fall between the two extremes of athleticism and passivity, need more access, a more extensive footpath system and appropriate transport. Neither their existence as a group nor their specific needs have been recognised sufficiently. They are responding to the call of Norman Nicholson, the Lakeland poet:

to see the Lakes clearly . . . we must penetrate the living landscape behind the view. We must get out of our cars, feel the rock under our feet, breathe the Cumbrian air, and learn to know something, at least, of the complex organic life of grass, herb and tree, something of the changing pattern of the weather, water and rock, and something of the way man has helped to shape the landscape in the past and is shaping it today' (Nicholson 1975, p. 6).

But the case for encouraging more people to get out of their cars and experience the living landscape is not based on the paternalistic idea that it is good for the soul to experience nature in the raw, like cold baths before breakfast. It rests on other considerations. Olmsted emphasised above all the total contrast between the rhythms of nature and of the modern industrial world and the need for man to disengage from all the forces that impel his daily routine (Sax 1976). Only by detaching himself from all the pressing, short-term considerations that dominate contemporary society, and by understanding nature in a deeper and broader perspective, can urban man make sound decisions about the natural world on which he is totally dependent for survival. As townspeople regain familiarity with the countryside they will wish to extend their active enjoyment of it and should have opportunities to do so.

The Countryside Commission's survey demolishes the notion fostered by the media that the British are above all compulsive watchers of competitive sports. People now make trips to the countryside three times more often than they watch any sport and eight times more often than they take part in one. As a leisure activity, countryside trips are second in popularity only to gardening, which itself reflects the desire to work with nature. They are twice as popular as visiting the seaside and these preferences extend across the social spectrum. Unskilled workers undoubtedly spend their leisure time in ways that differ markedly from those of the middle or professional classes. But no less than 69% of the unskilled workers expressed a preference for countryside recreation over town recreation compared to 90% of the professionals (Fitton 1979). However, whereas 69% of the professionals had made a trip to the countryside in the month before the interview, only 31% of the unskilled workers had done so.

Davidson and Wibberley (1977) and others have shown that opportunities for countryside recreation are circumscribed sharply by income and social class. What holds the unskilled worker back is low pay, inaccessibility of the countryside from the inner city, chronic unemployment (or conversely, weekend work or overtime), and lack of a car or the means to run it for leisure trips, as well as unfamiliarity with the countryside. The Countryside Commission's survey suggests that were the suppressed needs of the lower income groups to be met, the demand for countryside recreation would double. In present economic circumstances it seems likely that the working and lower middle classes will in fact get less access to the countryside, not more. This trend can and should be reversed. Arthur Gemmell, an appointed member of the Yorkshire Dales National Park Committee, has drawn this conclusion from nearly half a century of active participation in the field, in the urban fringe between the West Riding conurbation and the Dales: 'there can be no greater social benefit at less cost and less harm to the environment and the local community than to help an under-privileged family to go by public transport from an industrial town and walk the Dales' footpaths or fells' (Gemmell 1978). We hope to persuade the reader that the national parks, although overcrowded at times and places, have under-used space to provide part of the additional recreational capacity that will be required.

National and regional roles

The national parks were to be available to everybody, in John Dower's eyes, 'to people – and especially young people – of every class and kind'. Hobhouse looked to the national parks to provide 'open-air recreation to the advantage of the whole nation'. But the founding fathers tended to see national parks in isolation, rather than as part of a spectrum of recreational resources extending from the city playground at one end to the national parks at the other. Nor could they have anticipated the immense changes in social attitudes and habits produced by the greater affluence and mobility of the 1960s and 1970s, or the immense changes wrought in recreational possibilities by new technology. Entirely new mass sports, such as hang-gliding and pot-holing, have been invented and the scope for many long-established sports as different as rock-climbing and sailing has been vastly extended. In all probability the numbers now enjoying the national parks exceed anything that Dower or Hobhouse imagined. But the post-war explosion in motorised recreation has not, in fact, succeeded in making the national parks or the rest of the countryside available to 'the whole nation'.

In designating national parks, the National Parks Commission was required, by Section 5 of the 1949 Act, to have regard both to their potential for open-air recreation and 'to their position in relation to centres of population'. But the priority given to agricultural improvement and the objections raised by landowners and farmers persuaded the National Parks Commission to abandon any idea of designating the South Downs, and the designation of the Broads has been continually frustrated. The fields and downs of the lowlands became part of the 'factory floor' of the farming industry, where the townsman who wants to stretch his legs or have a picnic is technically the equivalent of a weed or a pest. The geographical distribution of open country in the hills and mountains of the north and west, when combined with the intensification of agriculture in the lowlands, has had the effect of depriving Londoners in particular of easy access to open country. The construction of the motorway and improved trunk road system had, by the 1970s, brought the national parks within two or three hours drive of every large city and conurbation in England and Wales, except in the south-east (Fig. 3.1). Because it is difficult and costly to get out of London, Londoners make little more than half as many countryside trips as do residents in the south and west. For most practical purposes the national parks are outside the range of a day trip from London (although the Peak and Brecon Beacons are both within three hours drive). Most Londoners and residents in the south-east will get to the parks only on holiday or a long weekend. But country recreation is also related to income and car ownership. The fact that

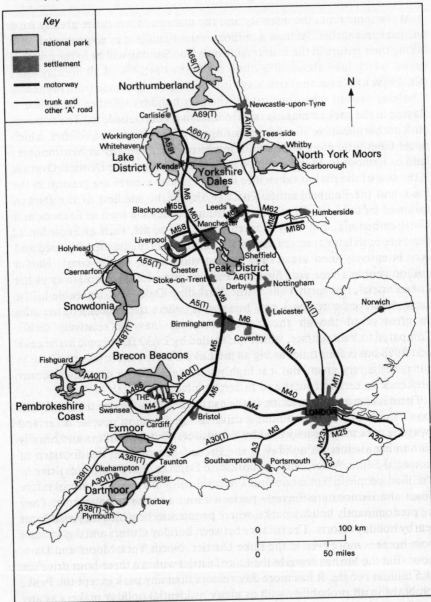

Figure 3.1 National parks, national road networks and towns. Crown copyright reserved.

residents in the economically depressed north-west make markedly fewer countryside trips than the people of the more prosperous south, despite the open country on their doorsteps, suggests that those with the greatest need are least able to enjoy it. The use of the national parks is skewed, both geographically and socially, to the disadvantage of London, the south-east and the inner city areas.

At the same time, the intensity and the manner of use differ greatly from one park to another. At least a million of the 10 million or so people who are taking their leisure in the countryside on a fine Sunday will be in the national parks, which take about 10% of all day visits but 14% of all holiday visits (CC 1979c). (We use the term 'day visit' to mean a visit made from home and a holiday visit to mean one made when on holiday, whether the visitor is staying in the park or making trips to it from a base outside it.) The national park authorities have all made guesstimates of the number of visitors, which range from little more than a million visitor days annually in Northumberland or Exmoor to 15 to 20 million in the Peak or the Lake District. Overall, if the size of the park is taken into account, the pressures are greatest in the Peak and the Pembrokeshire Coast (which is the smallest of the Parks), followed by the Lake District and Dartmoor; they are least in Exmoor and Northumberland. But even in intensively used parks, such as Snowdonia, there are both large tracts of mountain or hill country that are little used and very intensively used areas such as Snowdon itself, or the coast. Half a million people a year visit Swallow Falls in Snowdonia, Tarn Hows in the Lake District, Aysgarth Falls in the Yorkshire Dales and Dovedale in the Peak. However, every park has 'honeypots' where the intensity of use may be great, even though the overall numbers may be relatively small. Compared to Yellowstone, which was visited by 2 630 000 people in the peak year 1978 but is four times as big as the Lake District, the intensity of use in our parks is very great. But it is highly seasonal, peaking on a few summer weekends on certain routes and in certain places.

There is also a wide variation in the use of the parks for day trips and holidays. The Peak, within an hour's drive for 16.5 million people, is far and away the park most heavily used by day visitors. But day visitors also heavily outnumber visitors on holiday in the Brecon Beacons (on the doorstep of industrial South Wales) and the Yorkshire Dales (within 90 minutes drive of 8 million people in Yorkshire and Lancashire). Snowdonia, Pembrokeshire Coast and Exmoor are the only parks without a major regional role. They are predominantly holiday parks, where people stay or which they visit from nearby holiday resorts. The balance between holiday visitors and day visitors from home is more even in the Lake District, North York Moors and Dartmoor. But the M6 has brought the Lake District within a three-hour drive for 14.5 million people. It has more day visitors than any park except the Peak, combined in all probability with as many residential holiday makers as any other park. North York Moors is the traditional 'lung' for industrial Teesside and part of the park actually lies within the district of Cleveland. Dartmoor not only serves the local needs of Plymouth and Exeter and the seaside resort of Torbay (whose coach operators specialise in trips to Dartmoor with a view of the prison and cream teas at Dartmeet), but lies athwart the tourist routes to Cornwall. Northumberland really consists of two parks. The Roman Wall, its only major 'honeypot', is an outstanding tourist attraction which draws a quarter of its visitors from south-east England and a fifth from overseas. In contrast, the Cheviots are the least used part of any park and take day trips on a modest scale, mainly from the conurbations of the Tyne and Wear.

There is a common tendency to denigrate the day visitor, to whom often the opprobrious adjective of 'tripper', with its connotations of tin cans, orange peel and noise, is often applied. This often extends to a more general dislike of any visitors who have little money to spend. The tourist 'industry' and the local authorities perceive the visitor as a source of income, but the visitor perceives his trip as a source of enjoyment that can be marred by expenditure beyond his means. In reality, both the day trip and the holiday satisfy important needs, although there are contrasting views about the relative quality of the different experiences they offer. Olmsted took the view that natural places had to be experienced 'at length and at leisure' (Sax 1976). One survey (Yapp 1969) has shown that the holidaymaker is five times more likely than the day visitor to study nature, picnic away from the car or go for a walk of more than a mile; twice as likely to go for a short walk; and more likely to laze by the lakeside. On the other hand, for people living in big cities there is enormous value in having areas of wildness and beauty relatively nearby where, as the editor of the Peak park guide says, they are most needed and most appreciated: 'living so near at hand they do not need to stay for weeks at a time, as they might in North Wales or the Lake District. They come for the inside of a day, taking nature in sips' (Monkhouse 1975, p. 1). Far more opportunities are needed for people in the great conurbations, particularly in London, to make short day trips to open and accessible countryside. If national parks are 'for people of every class and kind', there is a need not only for cheap transport and easy access from towns within day-trip distance, but also for cheap holiday accommodation for those who are beyond the day-trip range – in fact, for social recreation policies.

Accommodation

A study group set up by the Trades Union Congress and the English Tourist Board in 1974 identified a huge gap in our social services, which do not regard holidays as a social need. Those who are most in need of the benefits a holiday can bring – the economically disadvantaged and one-parent families, the elderly and the handicapped – are least able to take one (ETB 1976). Although local authorities can subsidise holidays for the elderly and disabled, they only spent £50 on average per 1000 of the population in 1975 on doing so. There is no special provision for family holidays. By way of contrast, half the French budget for tourist development is allocated to 'social tourism', and substantial funds are concentrated on providing family holidays through public and private organisations. Dower and Hobhouse both saw the provision of cheap accommodation as one of the keys to making the national parks accessible to everybody and the 1949 National Parks Act

(Section 12) does empower the NPAs to provide accommodation, meals or refreshment. But it does so in a grudging spirit, by insisting that they may do so only where the existing facilities are inadequate or unsatisfactory. (Oddly enough, Section 23 of the 1968 Countryside Act gives the Forestry Commission unrestricted powers to provide accommodation and other facilities, including shops, and to make such charges for them as they think fit.) Satisfying the needs of the economically, socially or physically deprived is seen still to be the job of charitable organisations or voluntary bodies such as the Youth Hostels Association (YHA).

This goes some way to explain the failure of the NPAs to provide or to subsidise much in the way of simple, small-scale places to stay, or to ensure high standards in the cheaper, privately owned accommodation. Private enterprise provides nearly all the holiday accommodation in or adjoining the parks and the majority of visitors cater for themselves, in caravans, tents, rented cottages, chalets and second homes. Leaving aside hostels and out-door centres, the self-serviced sector accounts for 85% of the accommodation in Snowdonia, 70% in the Lake District and over 60% in Pembrokeshire Coast – the three parks that between them contain about three-quarters of all the holiday bedspaces in the parks.

The main exceptions to private provision are the hostels run by the Youth Hostels Association, the outdoor centres belonging to local authorities and other bodies, and the sites for touring caravanners and campers managed by the Caravan and Camping Clubs, the National Trust, public bodies such as the park authorities themselves and the Forestry Commission. That there is a demand for cheap places to stay is shown by the fact that the numbers using youth hostels in the parks have been increasing, although as a proportion of total bedspaces they remain small. In the Lake District, which has the largest number of hostels (22), there has been a 6% annual increase in use since the late 1960s, but they contain only about 3% of total bedspaces. In the Peak, where hostels account for just over 11% of the holiday accommodation, there was a 30% increase in use between 1973 and 1976 and a new hostel was opened in 1977 (making 13 in all). Several of the park plans point to the need for more hostels and light-weight camping sites, particularly in relation to walking routes, and a number of park authorities have provided financial assistance to the YHA.

Static caravans provide one of the cheapest ways of holidaying in the national parks. But about half the parks' total of 16 000–17 000 pitches for static caravans are located in the Snowdonia and Pembrokeshire Parks, each of which has over 4000, sited mainly on the coast. The Lake District also has about 4000 pitches and the bulk of the remainder are in the Yorkshire Dales or on the coast in the North York Moors. Thus the main function of the static caravans in the parks is to provide seaside and lakeside holidays. Concentrated as they are in three parks, they cannot be said to be satisfying the general need for cheap accommodation. Furthermore, the sites are unsubsidised business enterprises and commercial viability dictates large concentrations to keep down overheads and the rentals charged to visitors. Long experience of low-cost housing, whether subsidised by tax relief on mortgages or direct subsidies to tenants, should have taught us by now that it is impossible to provide reasonable standards of accommodation for low-income families *and* high standards of environment without public support of some kind. The result of a purely commercial approach to low-cost holiday accommodation, if it is provided at all, is often a low standard of environment within the site and a blot on the landscape when seen from outside. High standards of development control merely force the development to move up market. There is no way in which the sprawling sites that disfigure the Snowdonia and Pembrokeshire coasts or the Limefitt camp and caravan site at Troutbeck in the Lakes could now be removed or redesigned except by paying large sums in compensation. It is small wonder that all the NPAs frown on further developments of this kind, although they are now more sympathetic to small numbers of caravans or chalets carefully sited on farms. But the motivation behind this growing tolerance is a desire to help the farmer and has little to do with the provision of cheap accommodation.

The touring caravan provides a relatively cheap and attractive holiday for the family that can afford to buy the caravan in the first place. We ourselves could not have afforded the family holidays we enjoyed in this country and abroad in the 1950s and early 1960s had we not bought a caravan in 1950 for £300, a sum that bought the freedom of the countryside and was repaid many times over by the savings it made possible. But from the standpoint of the NPAs, the huge upsurge in the number of touring caravans (which increased by 120% between 1969 and 1976) faced them with what many regard as their most serious problem. The static caravan is under the planning control of the NPA and the licensing control of the district council. But the gaping loopholes in the law for touring sites has created big problems that the authorities are unable to control. The principal enactments are the Caravan Sites and Control of Development Act 1960 and the Town and Country Planning Act 1971.

At least three major loopholes in the law have been identified. The most serious is the 28-day rule, by which any area of more than five acres can be used for up to 28 days in any one year by up to three caravans at a time or by any number of tents without the need for planning consent. The law is unenforceable without continuous monitoring, and because there is no limit to the number of tents, sites with hundreds of them can spring up overnight. The second major loophole is the exemption from development control of the activities of the Caravan Club and other camping and caravanning organisations exempted by the secretary of state. This exempts sites of any size directly managed by them, sites up to five caravans certificated but not managed by them, and caravan rallies of any size for up to five days. Although the exempted organisations normally consult the planning authorities, the exemption of rallies is abused grossly where the same site is used almost continuously without planning permission by hundreds of caravans.

Grasmere and Ullswater in the Lake District are two of the most notorious examples. The third loophole is the difficulty of checking on the numbers using licensed sites for which planning permission has been given.

We found complete unanimity among those we interviewed on the need for effective powers to close these loopholes. The secretary of state could withdraw exemptions, but has not done so. NPAs could, if they wished, apply to the secretary of state for Article 4 Directions under the General Development Order 1977, which bring uses of land that are not defined as 'development' within the scope of development control. They can be used to bring all camping and caravanning under planning control, as the City of Swansea has done in the Gower peninsula. But Article 4 Directions involve paying compensation. The tendency in the plans is to attempt to control illegal pitches, to stop overnighting on laybys and car parks, to provide caravan advisory services (as the Lakes Board has done), and to connive at breaches in the law. There is, for example, a general move to license fields with minimal facilities for use at the holiday peaks.

In November 1980 the government announced its intention to introduce caravan and camping legislation some time in the present (1979–84) Parliament, which will go some way to meet the complaints of the local authorities (DOE 1980b). The sites of the exempted organisations would come under development control. The exempted organisations would be required to consult the planning authorities about uncertificated sites and, within 'sensitive' parts of the national park designated by the secretary of state, to consult about their rally programmes. Tents would be subject to the same numerical limits as caravans – a rule that if strictly enforced could reduce the number of pitches in the Lake District from 7000 to 2000 – with an exception for up to 10 tents for backpackers camping in the wild. In general, the government's policy is to continue to rely on the good behaviour of the exempted organisations and to spread the peak load as the only alternative to the 'unacceptable' idea of excluding caravans from heavily used areas if they have not reserved a pitch. The proposals seem, on the whole, to be acceptable to the NPAs, although most of them have regretted the decision that exempted organisations will have to consult the NPAs about rallies in 'sensitive areas' only and not throughout the park. The strength of the caravan lobby in Parliament can be detected in the government's reluctance to control a minority which can inflict enormous inconvenience on the majority.

There is considerable scope for the provision of more cheap holiday and bed and breakfast accommodation on farms. Farm holidays are popular and, as they are a supplementary form of income, they do not have to carry the same overheads as purely commercial enterprises. But farm accommodation is a small proportion of the total. In Pembrokeshire Coast, where 15% of the farms offered farmhouse accommodation in 1975, they probably provided only about 2% of the bedspaces. In Exmoor about 5% of the holiday bedspaces were on farms in 1976. The main reasons given by farmers for not accommodating visitors according to the Peak Structure Plan (PPJPB 1980) are lack of time and room, particularly in the case of small farmers. It is true that some farmers and some farmers' wives do not want to take in visitors, although others we have met not only profit from it but enjoy it. The main reason is that Britain fails to provide the assistance that many European farmers get for this purpose. Our Ministry of Agriculture decided not to make use of Article 10 of the EEC Less Favoured Area Directive (EEC 1975), which provides capital grants for tourist and craft developments on hill farms, on the ground that this is the job of the Tourist Boards. But the Tourist Boards can pay grants only in assisted areas, and they are not seriously interested in small farm projects. The Peak Board is the only NPA to subsidise farm holiday accommodation. By contrast, when we visited the chairman of the farmers' organisation in the Vercors Regional Park in France, we found that he (and several of his neighbours) had received 80% grants for the conversion of redundant buildings into holiday accommodation. This enabled him to run a 15-cow dairy unit that would have been closed down long ago in Britain as 'non-viable'.

Money spent by the visitor on bed and breakfast accommodation or farm house holidays generates considerably more local income than the same amount of money spent in hotels and guesthouses (WTB 1974), many of which are not locally owned and depend neither on local labour nor supplies. Visitors like farm holidays, which bring them into contact with friendly local people, and help them to understand farming and its problems. Farmers like them because it brings in money and improves visitors' behaviour. Farmers in Langdale in the Lake District complained to us that when the National Trust banned caravans on their tenants' farms and concentrated visitors in a single site, they were deprived of an important source of income and the visitors became less considerate. Perhaps the most agreeable part of our book was the welcome we received in farms and cottages, in pubs and small hotels. Small scale tourist accommodation, if it takes the form of sensitive building conversions or a few well designed, sited and oriented cabins – which can be as cheap as luxury caravans and far superior in appearance, comfort and durability – can be accommodated in the landscape. The effects would be benign, both for the local community and the visitors, in contrast to the cataclysmic destruction inflicted by mass tourism that swamps local life and culture.

Interfering busybodies or ministering angels?

There is a school of thought, which sounds off very loudly from time to time in the local press, which holds that national park authorities are interfering busybodies and largely irrelevant to the public's enjoyment of the parks. But if one looks closely at the different kinds of recreational activities, it is not difficult to identify the essential recreational role of the national park authority. It is to control the excesses, regulate the conflicts and remedy the deficiencies that arise from the reliance on private enterprise and voluntary effort, and to intervene positively to enlarge the opportunities for individual and group enjoyment.

The conventional distinction between active and informal recreation obscures some important differences between the two, not the least of which is that between activities that yield a profit to the private entrepreneur and those that do not. Active recreation embraces, at one extreme, the long-distance fell-walkers, climbers, cavers and other countryside athletes or enthusiasts who come to enjoy the natural features of the park in their various ways. They are well served by the voluntary organisations to which many of them belong. They cause relatively few problems and these are, in any case, localised. They need little in the way of facilities beyond transport, car parking, somewhere to stay, access to the resource and rescue services if things go wrong. They do not attract large crowds. It is to the public authorities that these individuals or organisations must turn if essential facilities are lacking or deficient, or beyond the resources of the voluntary bodies, because there is no money to be made out of them. Private enterprise, for example, would not provide the moderately priced courses in caving and pot-holing available at the Whernside Manor Cave and Fell Centre run by the Yorkshire Dales NPC; nor would it cater for the relatively low-cost provision at field-study centres such as those run by local education authorities and voluntary bodies, through which thousands of young people have been able to learn about and enjoy the national parks.

At the other extreme, active recreation embraces pursuits involving the use of costly equipment – such as sailing, canoeing, gliding, hang-gliding, riding, pony-trekking, power-boating and water-skiing – or in which competition plays a big part or is the object of the exercise – such as car-rallies, scrambles, trail-riding and endurance walks or runs against the clock. Participation usually involves either joining private clubs, if you have the means, or hiring equipment from commercially run enterprises. Some people own the necessary equipment individually, in which case they may need special facilities to use it and, if there is no profit in such provision, it falls to the public authorities to fill the gap. For example, public launching places are provided on Windermere for the use of people with privately owned boats. These activities can be in competition with each other for the use of a limited resource such as water and can conflict with the more passive recreational activities. The motorised sports are noisy and often destructive of the terrain. Others, such as pony-trekking, are peaceful in themselves but if intensively pursued (as in the Brecon Beacons) can erode footpaths seriously, destroy vegetation and be a nuisance to others. Hang-gliding and gliding are also quiet in themselves but attract crowds and may need large car parks and base installations. Competitive events or sponsored walks, such as the Lyke Wake Walk across the North York Moors or the Three Peaks walk in the Yorkshire Dales, can be destructive of soil and vegetation.

The role of the NPAs should be to control these activities in time and space and to uphold standards of use and behaviour that will respect both the environment itself and the needs of different users. In principle, the NPAs all give the highest priority to the peaceful use of the parks for quiet, informal recreation. In practice, they all face the problem that they have few powers to control active sports however destructive of the environment or of its peaceful enjoyment they may be. Private owners are free to permit the use of their land for noisy sports. Motor rallies on public roads are the responsibility of the Royal Automobile Club. There are powers to make byelaws for lakes and rivers and some use has been made of them to bring power boating and water-skiing under a degree of control in the Lake District. But, as the proposed plan for Windermere (WSC 1980) shows, the agreement of several public authorities and private bodies is required to realise any kind of management plan for water, despite the existence of a byelaw-making power. On the coast, the problems of recreational management and wildlife conservation are even more complex. In the Pembrokeshire Coast Park

> the peculiarities of ownership, problems of nomenclature, archaic legislation, overlapping rivalries and aspirations of various government departments, differing claims of ownership and jurisdiction, make attempts at comprehensive planning or managing a disconcerting experience

according to the National Park Officer (Wheeler 1980). Most of the problems remain unsolved. It is a tribute to the good sense of those concerned that despite the authorities' lack of powers the national parks are still immensely enjoyable places. But voluntary arrangements have been unable to resolve many acute conflicts of interest, as the classic case of Llangorse Lake in the Brecons (which is discussed in Ch. 7) vividly illustrates.

The term 'informal recreation' also obscures some significant distinctions, the most important of which is that between the more or less vehicle-tied, passive visitors who experience the national park from their motor cars (or coaches) and people who get out and explore the 'living landscape behind the view', in particular the middle-distance walkers. It is not surprising that the NPAs, faced as they were with the rapid post-war growth in the number of car-borne visitors, should have concentrated their very limited resources on the three Ps and the two Is – parking, picnicking, public conveniences, information and interpretation. Nearly 80% of the money available in the national parks after paying for administration and planning, goes on information and recreation (see Table 5.6, p. 129). The lion's share of this expenditure is on services and facilities designed primarily to benefit the least active visitors, although the more active benefit from it too. Some of the investment, particularly in the interpretive services, is intended to extend the horizons of the passive visitor unfamiliar with the countryside or the area. But a recent study of visitor centres, such as the Lake District Centre at

Brockhole, suggests that they have the greatest influence on those who are interested in the subject already and the least influence on those visiting them for the first time (DART 1978b).

The tourist industry will provide whatever goods and services the public will pay for, whether or not these are necessary for the quiet enjoyment of the parks, and without too much regard to any jarring or harmful effects they may have on the natural environment or the beauty that attracted the visitors in the first place. But the tourist industry contributes little or nothing to the maintenance or enhancement of the resource and it looks to the public authorities to solve the problems that its activities generate. There is money to be made out of the sale of boots and anoraks, but not out of the walk itself. Unless the public authorities promote a comprehensive network of rights of way, nobody else is in a position to do so.

The path and access systems, which are a primary recreational resource, actually deteriorated over wide areas before 1974 through a mixture of increasing use and neglect, and despite waymarking and the opening up of some new areas by the Forestry Commission, the National Trust and some park authorities. The expansion in the number of walkers was not matched by a corresponding increase in resources until the Countryside Commission sponsored the first Upland Management Experiment (UMEX) in Snowdonia and the Lake District in 1969. Virtually nothing was done to create a footpath network to meet walkers' needs or to create a bridleway network for riders. John Barrett, the Pembrokeshire naturalist, has related how the two district councils took 17 years to negotiate the Pembroke Coast long-distance path with landowners and having done so, allocated half a man to look after its 168 miles (Barrett 1978). It was not until 1980 that the Countryside Commission appointed a project officer with a staff of 10 to maintain and improve the path and to study the problems of management.

Since 1974 there has been a considerable improvement, the degree of which varies from park to park in the management of footpaths and access systems, but it would be entirely wrong to suppose that they are now satisfactory. There are, as we saw in Chapter 1, fundamental defects in the law governing rights of way and access that have been amply documented for years and seem to be no nearer solution. There is a continuous loss of rights of way for both walkers and riders. In 1978, 43 orders creating new rights of way were made in England and Wales, but in the same year 303 path closure orders were made, extinguishing the public's rights over some 150 miles (RA 1980). Even preliminary work on legislation to give the public a legal right of access to common land has been stopped for at least two years (HC 1980). The official view in central and local government is shockingly complacent and was well illustrated by the Countryside Review Committee's paper on leisure in the countryside (CRC 1977), which argued that the present system of '*de facto* access', in which the public's presence is tolerated by landowners, covers most needs. But the truth is that definitive rights of way are scarce in many parts of the hill country. In the Yorkshire Dales, for example, the only well-known fells the summits of which can be reached by definitive rights of way are Ingleborough and Shunner Fell. The definitive path maps are severely defective because they were compiled by parish councils, with the result that footpaths and bridleways stop at parish boundaries, or are omitted altogether. Many walkers are reluctant to risk trespassing by leaving a definitive path. Notices may tell the walker that a permissive path, on which he walks at the landowner's pleasure, has been provided, or they may warn him not to trespass off the right of way. But they never tell him that *de facto* access to open land is permitted. Ordnance survey maps are of very limited use as guides to a walker's or rider's right of way, or to the practicality of a particular route for horses or pedestrians.

As for the CRC's view that local authorities are 'best placed to decide the need for public access', an expert offered this comment to the Department of the Environment:

> their record in this field is appalling; they consistently fail to understand the aspirations of those who seek actively to enjoy the hills and the field paths on foot and, with few exceptions, they have neglected for years their statutory duties of maintenance. The access area provisions of the 1949 Act have only scratched the surface of the problem (Gemmell 1978).

The Government's intention (in the Wildlife and Countryside Bill introduced in November 1980) to give county councils the final say in the determination of rights of way, which now rests with the Secretary of State for the Environment, was criticised in *The Times* on the ground that councils on which landowning interests may be strongly represented 'may often seem not to be an impartial adjudicator'. It is indicative of the councils' bias against footpaths that of the 250 appeals against council decisions that go to the Minister each year almost half are upheld (*The Times* 29 November 1980). The government's proposal was so outrageous that it was defeated in the House of Lords on 16 March 1981.

On balance, the development of water resources and afforestation has probably diminished the recreational opportunities of the national parks by excluding the public from large areas and closing access routes, but also it has created some new facilities that the public is using in increasing numbers. Now both the Forestry Commission and the water authorities are required to make positive provision for recreation. But it will take a long time to undo nearly a century of water management based on the old-fashioned view that the cleanliness of water depended on the total exclusion of humanity – farmers, walkers, sailors and even fishermen – from the vast catchment areas the authorities impounded. Two of the Forestry Commission's seven 'forest parks' are in or adjoin the national parks of England and Wales. One, Kielder in Northumberland, is a vast blanket of sitka spruce and must rank as one of the least interesting landscapes in the United Kingdom. The other, in Snowdonia, includes some spectacularly beautiful woods and forests around Betws y Coed. The Commission has made imaginative use in some areas of the land it has not blanketed with conifers and of lakes and streams and other natural features to provide forest drives, picnic sites, nature trails, campsites and chalet settlements. By 1976, the Commission was providing nearly two-thirds of all the nature trails and picnic sites in Snowdonia. But then the Forestry Commission owns 43 times as much land in Snowdonia as does the NPA (see Table 7.1 p. 158). The figures reflect credit on the Commission, but they also reveal the haphazard way in which the provision of recreational opportunities is determined by the policy of the landowner rather than by the needs of the public.

One reason for the rural authorities' reluctance to extend access is the blighting impact of recreation and tourism on the environment. A major concern is the serious erosion of popular walks and climbs and the damage to wildlife and habitats. The people who feel the pressures most – or are the most vociferous about them – are the farmers and landowners. The farmers to whom we spoke talked of the harassment of sheep by visitors' dogs, the hazards of lambing time which coincides with Easter holidays and the lack of discipline amongst youngsters on school parties and attending field-study centres; and they voiced complaints about people who picnic in hayfields, leave gates open, block gateways with their cars and damage fences and walls. They told apocryphal stories (that are repeated up and down the country as if they were first-hand evidence) to illustrate the visitors' alleged belief that everything in a national park belongs to the nation.

In all this there is a kernel of truth and it is undeniable that visitors damage both the countryside itself and the interests of some of its inhabitants. But these stories are often best taken with a pinch of salt. One review has found that 'the actual evidence offered that recreation is often detrimental to farming amounts to a small number of studies, much quoted, of incursion and vandalism mostly based on very unsophisticated research' (Fitton 1979, p. 75). Nor is research in this area entirely free from bias. A university-based survey of farm vandalism sponsored by *Farmers' Weekly* started with a questionnaire which asks 85 questions based on the explicit assumption that farmers suffer 'social and financial injustices' caused by visitors and other urban pressures, but not one seeking more positive reactions or inquiring how farmers have benefited from tourism or rising land prices (Coleman & Feaver 1980). We do not underestimate the very real pressures on some farmers, or the damage caused to the terrain and to wildlife by countryside recreation. Irreversible damage may result in some locations if recreational use continues at the present level or increases still further. More must be done through education, the warden services and other means to encourage visitors' understanding and consideration. But vandalism is by no means confined to the urban visitor. National park wardens in the Lake District told the authors that a group indulging in the dangerous pastime of 'stone rolling' on the fells were young farmers. One does not have to look very far to see the squalid refuse, old cars, bedsteads and farm machinery, the plastic bags and other local litter scattered over the countryside or accumulating around the farms.

If farmers in national parks want relief from the nuisance that some visitors cause, it is in the main to public enterprise and public funds that they must and in fact do look to put more resources into positive management. But it should not be imagined that more management calls for a greatly enlarged bureaucracy. Large numbers of both town and country people are willing to spend their own time doing voluntary conservation work or serving as part-time wardens or in other ways. The Peak Board has so many volunteers that it employs two full-time staff to organise them. An experiment in guided walks revealed the existence of a large reservoir of skilled and knowledgeable people who were prepared to share their love and knowledge of the countryside with others for little or no reward (CC 1980c). The NPAs could, we believe, mobilise more volunteers and part-time workers than they do; and by so doing they would be helping not only the visitors but also the local community.

Cars and people

No development has had a greater impact on the national parks, positively or negatively, than the motor vehicle. It has been the lifeblood of modern countryside recreation, just as the roads have been its circulation system. The motor car has been the magic carpet transporting the urban family with its recreation gear to the mountains, lakes and beaches. It is not surprising that the national park and highway authorities have been pre-occupied with coping with the problems presented by the growth in traffic, or that traffic and highway policies have generated some of the most bitter conflicts since the Second World War. Geoffrey Beard, in his account of a century of conservation in the Lake District (Berry & Beard 1980) devotes a third of his space to the conflict between traffic and environment. But we take the view that, although acute problems remain unsolved and there are still some damaging road projects in the pipeline (such as the improvement of the A470(T) in Snowdonia and the A39 Okehampton bypass in Dartmoor), we are unlikely to see many more confrontations of the old kind in the national parks between the highway engineers and groups of residents or conservationists. The days when the Ministry of Transport would bulldoze the A66 through the Lake District to connect West Cumbria with the national motorway system, or was planning to build a new Manchester–Sheffield motorway through the Peak (a project abandoned in 1980), are probably numbered. It is now government policy to avoid national parks in developing new trunk routes (DOE 1976b) and to make environmental quality the primary criterion in the planning of road systems, road alterations and traffic management in national parks (DOE 1977).

There are three reasons for the shift in policy. The first is the gradual recognition, dating back to the report on Traffic in Towns (Buchanan *et al*. 1963), that there are limits to the capacity of environments to tolerate traffic. The second is the stagnation in the British economy (accelerating as we write into a rapid decline) which has cut down the resources that were available in the 1960s and 1970s for highway construction or improvement. The third is the recognition that the world's reserves of hydrocarbon fuels are finite, are largely located in politically difficult or unstable areas, and will probably become prohibitively expensive for mass private transport by the beginning of the 21st century if not earlier. There are those who believe that some tech-nological fix (oil from coal, the hydrogen engine or the electric car propelled by nuclear-generated power) will enable mass private motoring to continue into the indefinite future. We have concluded from the evidence available to us that on the contrary, if the urban population of the British Isles is to have adequate access to the countryside for recreation in the 21st century, it will need recreational transport systems that make more efficient use of scarce and costly resources than the private car, however fuelled, can ever do.

During the next 20 to 25 years, if the world has the luck to enjoy peace and a degree of political stability, the level of private car ownership is likely to remain high and may even grow for a time. The problem will continue to be to minimise the damage to the physical and social environments caused by the numbers of vehicles, the conflicts between through traffic, local traffic and holiday traffic on main routes and in settlements, the growing size of commercial vehicles using minor roads, the litter of parked cars and caravans and the ever-increasing penetration of the wilder areas by vehicles. But the capital resources available for modifying the road system will be small and it will be necessary, in this phase, to initiate a decisive shift towards traffic management and public transport policies appropriate to the 21st century. Twenty years are not a long time to develop appropriate modes of transport and infrastructure.

In practice, although major new roads are now unlikely, resources are going into various measures designed to improve traffic circulation, the environment and the enjoyment of the parks for the visitors who do not want to move far from their cars. These include the banning of heavy lorries from taking a short cut through the heart of the Lake District on the A591(T) and the designation of scenic routes in the Peak. But they also include piecemeal road widening and the improvement of sight-lines at the expense of verges, banks, hedges, walls and trees. The facilities for the car-tied visitors are being located on or near the main roads to discourage penetration of the wilder places. However, there is a danger that the network could degenerate into the tarmac corridor characteristic of some American national parks where the price paid for conserving the wilderness is the confinement of the motorist to an essentially urban experience of the landscape. The average visitor to Yellowstone National Park has access to 1% of the park area and spends 1.1 days on the tarmac corridor. He 'does' the sites in between taking his lunch at a fast-food counter and hooking his trailer into the comforts of modern civilisation. He learns about nature in the main from interpretive panels, audiovisual presentations and camp fire talks. Far from escaping from the city, he brings it with him.

In our national parks the fine web of roads that links the farms and settlements and enables the motorist to penetrate some of the remotest areas makes it infinitely more difficult to confine the motorist to a tarmac corridor. The existence of this network is both a blessing and a curse, bringing a walk in the wild within the reach of every motorist but simultaneously threatening the destruction of the very qualities the visitor is seeking. The landforms, vegetation and intimate scale of our national parks have been remarkably successful in preserving what is often no more than a miraculous illusion of the wild. But access roads for farming, afforestation, grouse shooting, water undertakings and military training (none of which requires planning consent and most of which are paid for largely by Government) are everywhere increasing the level of vehicular penetration. The use of cross-country vehicles is increasing and motor bikes have been seen at the summits of most of the Dartmoor Tors. The motorist now can penetrate almost to Cranmere Pool, for walkers a hard day's slog to one of the loneliest spots in Dartmoor, since the Ministry of Defence tarred the military road and opened it to the public when firing on the ranges is not taking place.

But the national parks can also demonstrate alternative transport systems which exploit the advantages of the fine road network to make the wilder country accessible, without allowing the motor car to penetrate to the furthest corners or to dominate the landscape. Imaginative and romantically named recreational bus and rail services are to be found in nearly every park. The outstanding success story is Dales Rail, an experiment initially funded by the Countryside Commission (CC 1979b), which re-opened some remote stations on the Leeds–Carlisle main line to passengers. It provided rail and bus links for walkers between the West Riding conurbation and the Yorkshire Dales and Lake District National Parks and enabled the Dales people once more to make shopping or other trips to the cities by rail. Attempts to restrict the penetration of the motor vehicle, to which several national parks plans pay lip service, have been much less successful. Nearly 10 years have passed since the Peak Board first closed the Goyt Valley to cars at peak holiday times and provided mini-buses for those who could or would not walk. This experiment was immensely popular, but the Goyt Valley is in an exceptional situation as it only gives access to a reservoir. Attempts to introduce similar schemes in valleys giving access to farms or villages (as in Malhamdale in the Yorkshire Dales and Watendlath in the Lake District) have foundered on the rock of local opposition.

Probably the energy crisis will have to become more acute before NPAs or local communities are prepared to face up to these problems. It is ironic that cuts in public expenditure now jeopardise the future of public transport services that do exist. Their scale is insignificant, when contrasted to the tens of millions of people who travel by private car, and their scope is limited by the requirement that national park transport services must not be designed primarily to serve local people. The significance of these services, and of the pedestrianisation of the Goyt Valley, lies in the fact that they offer, in embryo, a working prototype for a transport policy that would both conserve energy and enhance the public's enjoyment. The question is whether either central government or the NPAs have the imagination and the political will to develop these prototypes into working systems. If they lack the will or the powers to curtail the use and penetration of the motor vehicle, or to initiate the provision of alternative systems, we may have to wait a long time before the rising price and shrinking supplies of fossil fuel relieve congestion and force the change upon us.

Elitism and democracy

We shall be returning in Chapter 12 to the place of the existing national parks within a countryside recreation policy. But before passing on to other themes, we should rebut the view that national parks as conceived by Dower and the national parks lobby reflected an essentially middle-class, elitist approach to recreation. Marion Shoard (1978) regarded Dower and the entire prewar national parks movement as a middle-class minority, whose 'cult' of the wilderness led them to indulge in solitary activities such as climbing and walking on the moors and mountains of the North and West. This led, she has argued, to the geographical maldistribution of national parks and to the failure to make all but a few of the extensive woods and parklands of lowland England available for public recreation. As a result the national parks have taken the lion's share of the very limited government moneys spent on countryside recreation. She is right, we believe, about the inadequacy and maldistribution of recreational resources and money, and she has argued a convincing case in *The theft of the countryside* (Shoard 1980) for a major expansion of the opportunities for countryside recreation in the lowlands. But to regard hill walking and access to semi-wild landscape as a middle-class fad can itself be interpreted as an elitist point of view and one that flies in the face of the findings of the surveys we have summarised. The hills and fells, to which working people have taken as readily in the past 50 years as the professional classes did in Victorian and Edwardian times, are an important element in the national spectrum of recreational provision. In addition, as Marion Shoard has demonstrated, there should be far more public access to the woods, parkland, downland and other semi-wild landscape of the lowlands. Whether such areas can meet the criteria appropriate to a 'national park' is another matter, which will also be discussed in Chapter 12.

Nor is it elitist to argue that a high level of management may be necessary to ensure that intensively used areas in the semi-wild retain their natural beauty. The popular places immediately accessible from the main road network should not be so planned and provided with public and tourist facilities that it becomes impossible to experience their natural qualities. They are after all the only places inactive visitors are likely to see. But there is a case for some constraint and for controlling or limiting access in the most heavily used areas. We share Christopher Hall's strongly held view that the countryside can be over-signposted, over-interpreted and over-managed, and his dislike of the pseudo-scientific language of interpreters and managers (Hall 1978). But our eyebrows shot up when we read his criticism of the National Trust's management of Tarn Hows, the most popular beauty spot in the Lake District. For he asserted, surely with his tongue in his cheek, not only that 'freedom is what the countryside is about' but that this freedom 'includes freedom to walk places bare and to overcrowd the most popular viewpoints, if that is what people want'. But there is no evidence that that is what people do want. Christopher Hall, we know, does not in fact share the view of those elitists, to be found in every national park, who refer disparagingly to 'those people' who allegedly do not mind overcrowded and degraded surroundings.

It is another thing to argue, as Price (1979b) does, that if gregarious people like places of spectacular beauty, benefits are maximised by catering for as many people in them as possible, while leaving the less spectacular landscapes for those who place the highest value on solitude. The price to be paid, if large numbers are to be catered for at the popular places, should be a degree of management and constraint, not the degradation of the resource by the superficial attractions of souvenir shops, ice-cream vans and other devices for parting the visitor from his money. In towns and settlements the visitor should find most of the things he needs, but he should be able to experience the natural world (as Olmsted advised at Niagara Falls a century ago) with the minimum of intrusive management, carefully planned essential facilities and a complete absence of commercial exploitation. Olmsted's answer to those who said that the commercialisation of Niagara Falls was giving the public what it wanted, was to say that commerce offered the public no choice but to take what it offered. 'The fact that they accept the arrangements is no evidence of their approval' (Sax 1976). The fact that people will buy an ice cream or a Coke wherever an enterprising operator spots a big enough crowd to make a profitable pitch, does not mean that the majority of visitors prefer it that way, or that vans should be allowed to intrude wherever the operator finds it profitable to go.

In a democratic society, management does not consist of doing whatever a show of hands or a count of feet suggests. Those who have been entrusted with the management of a precious resource, and the promotion of its enjoyment by the public, should be properly accountable for their decisions. But the test to be applied is whether they have succeeded in their aims of conserving the resource and enabling people to enjoy its special qualities. Skilful management, embodying a degree of constraint or guidance (as at Tarn Hows) can increase the capacity of the resource to absorb visitors and enhance their enjoyment (Brotherton *et al.* 1977). But where (as at Tarn Hows) there is a limit to the car parking that can be provided, there is nothing undemocratic or elitist in imposing a limit or in excluding excessive numbers of vehicles or even people. There are limits to everything. The peace of the Königsee, the Alpine lake in the heart of the Berchtesgaden National Park in Bavaria, is in marked contrast to the noise and conflict to be found in Llangorse Lake, Semer Water in the Yorksire Dales or Windermere in the Lake District. All private boating is prohibited, and access is provided entirely by silent, electric publicly-owned launches, because there is no other way in which such an immensely popular lake could retain its natural qualities. If one is looking for elitism one is likely to find it in the decisions of landowners (public and private) or commercial operators who are accountable to no one but whose property or other rights enable them to say where the public may or may not go, or what the public may or may not do and buy. Or one may find it in the 'tyranny of small decisions' by which, in the absence of management, a multitude of unco-ordinated individual decisions frustrate the desires of majorities and minorities alike. The real issue, to which we return in Part 3, is whether the national park authorities have the powers, the money, the will and the concern to manage the landscapes entrusted to their care, and whether they are sufficiently accountable to the users.

4　*The upland paradox*

The success or failure of policies designed to preserve or enhance 'cultural landscapes' that are inhabited and exploited by man, must be determined very largely by social and economic trends for which national park authorities have little or no responsibility. The duty imposed on them (as on all public authorities) by the 1968 Countryside Act, to have regard to the social and economic interests of rural areas, has misled some people into crediting them with far wider social and economic powers or responsibilities than they possess. For their duty is only to have regard to social and economic interests when exercising their development control, conservation and recreational functions. Economic trends are determined or influenced by the decisions of those who own or control land and other resources, and by central government's policies, incentives and resource allocations. We have attempted in this chapter to draw some general conclusions about economic trends and their impact on the national parks. In doing so we have been very conscious of the immense diversity of the parks and of the fact that, as their boundaries were drawn for aesthetic reasons, they do not correspond to political, administrative or statistical areas. Nevertheless, using the best data there are (incuding the 1971 census returns, county structure plans and national park plans) and the information obtained by interviews and personal observation, some broad conclusions can be reached about social and economic change.

The national parks are by and large the more economically handicapped parts of the least prosperous regions of England and Wales – the industrial north, Wales and the predominantly agricultural south-west. The structure plans of the counties in which national parks are situated (the 'park counties') show that, compared to England and Wales as a whole, these counties have lower incomes, a higher rate of unemployment, a higher proportion of seasonal, lower-paid and women's jobs, greater reliance on the primary industries of agriculture, forestry and mineral extraction, more self-employed and fewer economically active people of working age. Whereas the population of all rural districts increased by 29% between 1951 and 1971 (and their small towns by 22%), the total population of the park counties grew little, if at all – in Gwynedd it fell. The only exceptions were Somerset, an industrial growth area, and Devon with its expanding tourist industry – both of which also attracted a large number of elderly or retired people.

It is in fact the flow of people into the park counties from the outside that has caused their populations to grow, or to be held relatively stable. The natural increase of population through an excess of births over deaths has been declining in nearly all of them, in line with national trends, and in some deaths now exceed births. Moreover, the natural trend towards an ageing population has been exacerbated by the pattern of migration. The younger people of the working and child-bearing age groups have been forced to leave by lack of jobs or have been attracted by the opportunities of city life. They have been outnumbered by the inward flow of people of retirement and pre-retirement age, attracted by the remoteness, peace and beauty of the park counties.

The problems of declining jobs and services tend to be more acute in the uplands and the national parks than in the rest of the relatively depressed counties of which they are part. The parks rely even more heavily than do their counties on the primary industries, in which employment has been falling sharply. They have benefited little from the measures taken within the depressed regions to promote economic growth by such means as assisted area grants and loans, or providing infrastructure at key growth centres. These measures have been concentrated on the larger enterprises and on settlements in the lowland areas where communications and the availability of labour can attract large-scale industry. Furthermore, these measures have aggravated the social and economic problems of the remoter uplands by drawing people away from them.

The small amount of help the national parks received in the past from assisted area programmes for tourism and job creation has been heavily cut by the government's decision in 1980 to reduce the extent of development and special development areas and concentrate the money on a few heavily depressed industrial areas (Fig. 4.1). Whatever the justification of such a decision, its effect on national parks could be serious. Until 1977 all the Welsh parks, the Lake District, Northumberland and parts of the North York Moors, Yorkshire Dales and Exmoor were in development areas, and were eligible for some measure of assistance for new or expanding industries, including tourism. Since 1980 Pembrokeshire Coast (apart from Tenby) is the only national park that lies wholly within a development area, although small parts of Snowdonia, Brecon Beacons, the Lake District, North York Moors and Dartmoor enjoy this status. This withdrawal of development area status has cut off labour supplied under Manpower Services Commission programmes, and has made nonsense of the management of each park as an entity. The areas in which grants to assist farmers to provide farm holidays are available, for example, bear no relation to the need of the farmer or the holidaymaker. For example, the Brecon Beacons may employ unemployed people from the Welsh industrial valleys on conservation programmes in the southern segments of the park that lie within the county of Mid-Glamorgan, but may not employ them in the far greater central segment that lies in Powys.

For many years, Wibberley has described the uplands as consisting of 'interlocking vicious circles of natural, economic and social difficulties

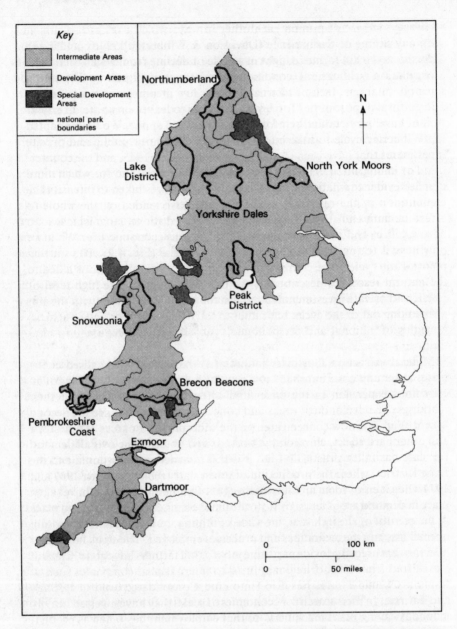

Figure 4.1 Assisted Areas as defined by the Department of Industry 1980. Financial incentives are offered for development in the assisted areas, which are divided into three categories. Since 1980 the extent of the development and special development areas in which the main incentives are concentrated has been drastically reduced and that of the intermediate areas increased. This has curtailed the assistance available in several national parks, Pembrokeshire Coast (with the exception of Tenby) being the only one now wholly situated in a development area. Source: Department of the Environment 1979. Crown copyright reserved.

which act and interact upon each other in ways which are hard to change with any degree of permanence (Davidson & Wibberley 1977, pp. 132–3). This shows the hill farmer caught in a cycle of decline from which there is no escape, as harsh natural conditions, limited agricultural opportunities, uncertain markets, lack of alternative jobs, low incomes and limited social and cultural opportunities force young people to leave, cause the deterioration of rural services and reinforce the downward spiral. We have adapted the Wibberley cycle to take into account the enormous public and private investments that have been made in the uplands since 1945, and the counter-trend of immigration. The conclusion we have reached, and for which more detailed evidence will be provided, is that the measures taken to intensify the exploitation of the resources of the uplands have tended on the whole to effect the same end as the cycle of decline described above – that is, to lead to depopulation and the deterioration of social and economic life. What we now have is the cycle of intensification and decline (Fig. 4.2). The starting point of the cycle is the combination of severe physical limitations allied to the natural resources described in the previous chapter. The high level of public and private investment has not, on the whole, been made with the aim of breaking out of the cycle, but rather to satisfy urban needs and to achieve a medley of national and personal goals associated with resource exploitation.

Mineral extraction illustrates the way in which highly capitalised enterprises lower unit costs but shed jobs, or increase their number by means of an enormous expansion in the scale (and often the destructiveness) of their workings. The demand for rocks and minerals has changed since the Second World War. It is now concentrated on the widespread resources of limestone and other hard rocks, china clay, fluorspar and potash. The overall demand for slate has fallen drastically, but it is still quarried in Snowdonia and the Lake District, where the production of green slate trebled between 1967 and 1974 when it enjoyed an architectural vogue. But the changes that have taken place in demand are of less significance than the changes that have taken place in the control of the industry, the scale of mining, quarrying and processing operations, and the techniques and processes employed. The small mines and quarries that used to provide part-time jobs for hill farmers have gone. Control has shifted from local or regional firms to international companies such as Imperial Chemical Industries, Rio Tinto Zinc, Consolidated Goldfields, Shell and Tarmac. In their search for economies of scale, they have invested heavily in labour-saving plant machinery, so that employment has fallen as production has increased. In the Peak Park, for example, the number of limestone quarries fell from 23 to 12 between 1953 and 1974, while production increased from around 1.4 to 5.4 million tons per annum over roughly the same period. The Peak Board has estimated that the output of aggregates from the national park increased nearly twice as fast as the national output between 1953 and 1974. But the number of jobs in stone mining and quarrying in and around the Peak fell by a fifth between 1961 and 1971 (PPJPB 1974).

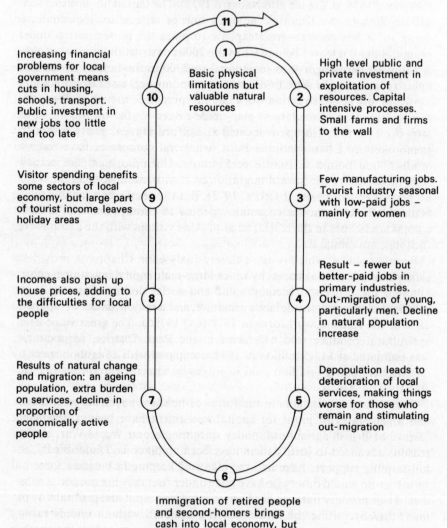

Central government gives inadequate support to rural development on the one hand, and on the other continues with grants and support to primary industries in a form that accelerates job decline

11

1 Basic physical limitations but valuable natural resources

10 Increasing financial problems for local government means cuts in housing, schools, transport. Public investment in new jobs too little and too late

2 High level public and private investment in exploitation of resources. Capital intensive processes. Small farms and firms to the wall

9 Visitor spending benefits some sectors of local economy, but large part of tourist income leaves holiday areas

3 Few manufacturing jobs. Tourist industry seasonal with low-paid jobs – mainly for women

8 Incomes also push up house prices, adding to the difficulties for local people

4 Result – fewer but better-paid jobs in primary industries. Out-migration of young, particularly men. Decline in natural population increase

7 Results of natural change and migration: an ageing population, extra burden on services, decline in proportion of economically active people

5 Depopulation leads to deterioration of local services, making things worse for those who remain and stimulating out-migration

6 Immigration of retired people and second-homers brings cash into local economy, but does not reverse the downward spiral

Figure 4.2 Cycle of intensification and decline.

The effects of major construction schemes are another aspect of resource exploitation. Studies in Gwynedd, for example, suggest 'that the long term effect has been to help prevent the growth of employment in more stable industries, as a result of the impact on local wage levels and labour supply' (Gwynedd 1976, p. 26; see also Nabarro 1973). The CEGB has invested some £500 million in the Dinorwic pumped storage scheme in Snowdonia. In doing so, it has gone to great expense to place the power station underground, but all it leaves behind when the 2000 construction jobs have folded is about 90 permanent jobs (compared to 2700 in the heyday of the slate industry, acording to the CEGB), a local economy depressed by the counter-attraction of the construction work, an interpretive centre for visitors and a tourist attraction in the largest man-made cavern in the world. One of the largest oil ports in Europe is located at Milford Haven, partly within the Pembrokeshire Coast National Park, where oil companies have received multi-million pound assistance area grants. Unemployment has actually been increased by the inward migration of construction workers for whom no permanent jobs exist (PCNPC 1977). But the resources available to the National Park Authority to employ people to protect one of the finest coastal landscapes in the world, or to provide visitors with the best possible facilities, are minimal.

Farming policy, which is more closely analysed in Chapter 9, provides a classic example of the process by which large-scale capital investment contributes to the process of demographic and social decline. Farming is the principal land use in the uplands generally, and a major industry employing 18% of the resident workforce in 1971 (CC 1979d). The gross value of all agricultural produce sold off farms in the Peak District, for example, was estimated at £11.5 million in 1972, compared with £8 million spent by day trippers and £4 million paid in wages by mineral enterprises (PPJPB 1974).

Subsidies to hill farmers in the forms of headage payments on livestock and higher rates of grant for capital investment have been a permanent feature of British agricultural policy since the Second World War, but the reasons advanced to justify them have been ambiguous. Undoubtedly, the hill-farming supports have had the effect of keeping in business some hill farmers who would otherwise have gone under. But they are not social subsidies. Their primary purpose has been to increase output and profitability per man, thereby raising the farmer's living standard without unduly raising prices to the consumer. The aim throughout has been to reduce the number of hill farms, farmers and farm workers, by creating fewer but larger and more productive units. As the hill support system was continued virtually unchanged when the UK entered the EEC, the payments are now made within the Common Agricultural Policy (CAP) through the EEC directives on the less favoured areas (shown on Fig. 4.3) and on farm modernisation (EEC 1975, 1972a). But there is a sharp contradiction between the basically agricultural aims of UK agricultural policy and the explicitly social and even

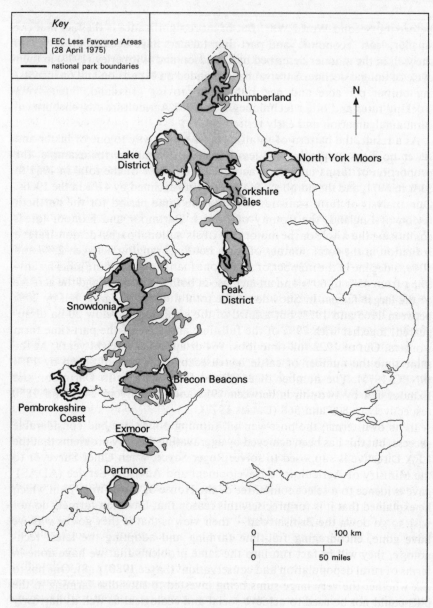

Figure 4.3 Less Favoured Areas. Crown copyright reserved.

conservation aims of the EEC directives, which we discuss more fully in Chapter 9.

Hill farming has changed out of all recognition since 1945. Better roads, mains electricity, piped water and drainage, the mobility conferred by the car and the larger incomes generated by larger, more productive, subsidised units have given the remaining hill farmers living standards unattainable before the Second World War. But of more significance is the fact that the smaller, least 'economic' and part-time farmers have been going slowly to the wall in the manner described by Davidson and Wibberley (1977) in their cycle of upland decline. Survival has depended on expansion and on increasing output per acre and per man by improving grassland, intensifying stocking rates and other techniques. The 1967 Agriculture Act encouraged farm amalgamation and early retirement.

As a result, the pattern of small farms is giving way to one of larger and fewer holdings employing far less labour. In Cumbria, for example, the proportion of farms under 100 acres fell from 74% of the total in 1951 to 53% in 1971, and the number of farm workers declined by 47% in the 1960s. Our analysis of farm statistics covering the same period for the northern region of England, the County of Powys, Dartmoor and Exmoor (areas comprising the whole or the major part of six national parks) demonstrates a reduction in the total number of farm holdings ranging between 23% and 50%, a decline in the number of small (one man) and part-time units by anything from 45% to 60% and an increase in both the number and the acreage of the larger farms. In Snowdonia the total number of farms fell by 20% between 1965 and 1973, but a third of the small farms below 20 ha disappeared, together with 79% of the full-time and 70% of the part-time farm workers. Out of 1222 full-time jobs, 964 disappeared in eight years. At the same time the number of cattle increased by 37% and of sheep by 13% (SNPC 1975). The number of employed farm workers in Dartmoor and Exmoor fell by two-thirds between 1952 and 1972, from 2411 and 1850 respectively to 809 and 568 (Davies 1977).

In its own terms, the post-war hill-farming policy has had considerable success, but this has been achieved by aggravating the very problems that the LFA Directive is supposed to solve. Roger Sayce, when Chief Surveyor to the Ministry of Agriculture's Development and Advisory Service (ADAS), gave evidence to a select committee of the House of Lords in 1979 in which he explained that it is for precisely this reason that Bavarian farmers do not wish to go down the British road – 'their view is that if they go the way we have gone, encouraging full-time farming and adopting the latest technology, they will in fact run into the same problems that we have done in terms of rural depopulation and conservation' (Sayce 1980, p. 8). One has to ask whether the very large sums being invested to subsidise farming in the hills could not be used to achieve social and ecological as well as narrowly agricultural objectives. It has been estimated that almost three-quarters of the farmers and farm holdings of the LFAs of England and Wales are in the national parks (Leonard 1979). As the estimated cost of livestock headage payments under the LFA directive in England and Wales for 1981 is £54.3 million (MAFF 1980c), it may be inferred that MAFF's support for hill farming in national parks may be around £40 million a year excluding capital grants. The combined total of National Park Supplementary Grant and Countryside Commission grants to national parks in 1980–1 was estimated at £5.2 million (ACC 1980d), of which only a small fraction is available to encourage farmers or foresters to employ labour or to conserve nature or landscape.

What we have established so far is that large-scale investment and technological change directed at purely economic or financial objectives have been the cause of dramatic, even catastrophic, losses in jobs. This situation usually provokes one of two responses. The first is to argue, as one National Park Officer did when he met the authors, that the fewer people there are in the hills the fewer the problems he would have to face. In short, the process is not only inevitable but, from the point of view of conservation and recreation, desirable. Nan Fairbrother (1970) implied as much with characteristic vigour when she questioned the view that the continuing depopulation of the uplands is 'a continuing tragedy', and argued that 'all poverty is a prison, but poverty in the uplands is a prison in a wilderness'. But there are many people (as our interviews with farmers and others confirmed) who want to live in the uplands, who are prepared to meet and even to savour the challenges they offer, and can lead what they believe to be a good life if the resources are sensibly used and equitably distributed. The nation needs the resources of the uplands and the people to manage them. Hill farming is integral to the traditional upland landscape and an essential part of the British livestock industry and, as we saw in the last chapter, has the advantage of a low-input system the merits of which will become more apparent as energy costs rise.

The second response is to suggest alternative ways of creating new jobs, for which the best prospects are seen in forestry and tourism. The Centre for Agricultural Strategy (CAS) has given academic backing to a campaign launched in the late 1970s, clearly with the broad support of private forestry interests and of the Forestry Commission, to persuade government to double the forest area in the next 50 years, by planting anything up to 2 million ha of mainly coniferous species in the uplands (CAS 1980). Most of the planted area would be in Scotland, but the plantations in England and Wales would be substantial. One of the main arguments used to support this campaign is that afforestation would create more jobs. The reasons for our scepticism towards this claim are developed in Chapter 10. All we wish to say at this point is that forestry is on the same technological treadmill as farming or quarrying. Forestry and forest products have to expand continuously even to keep pace with the loss of jobs through mechanisation. In employment terms, it is another case of having to run hard to stay in the same place.

Tourism, the other widely canvassed source of jobs, is in the business of making money out of satisfying the demand (which may have to be artificially stimulated if the business is to succeed) for recreation. Tourism is important to the economies of all the parks and it is probably the major industry of the Pembrokeshire Coast, but accurate information is hard to come by. Insufficient is known about the 'multiplier effect' by which the income from tourism is passed on to others in the area, or about the reverse process by which a large part of the tourist income leaves the tourist areas to pay for food and petrol, souvenirs produced by externally based enterprises and the wages of seasonal employees from outside the area. Visitors certainly help to keep marginal village shops and services going, but they also push up prices and stimulate the change from convenience to specialist shops. The jobs are seasonal, mainly for women, low paid and even servile. It has been reported that more than half the people working in the hotel industry earn less than the Supplementary Benefit level (CIS 1980). With the trend towards self-catering holidays, jobs are not expected to increase in number even if the visitors do.

Welcome as the extra income undoubtedly is to local people – and it makes the difference between survival and defeat on many hill farms – tourism cannot be the answer to the employment problems of the national parks. If it is seen as the answer, the objectives of policy are likely to be the attracting of richer tourists and the provision of the facilities they demand. The season could be extended but there is no realistic prospect of a winter sports season. In moderation tourism may be benign; in excess it can have cataclysmic or corrupting effects on the physical, social and cultural environments. Whatever else tourism may do, it will not halt the emigration of young people, particularly young men, who will stay only if there is a prospect of reasonably paid employment the whole year round.

The cycle of intensification leads, in fact, to the upland paradox – that the measures taken to exploit the resources of the uplands have on the whole had the reverse of the desired effect, if the desired effect is to conserve the human and natural resources of the uplands. The more capital is invested, the more rapid becomes the cycle of decline. Some of those who remain enjoy higher standards of life, but others are relentlessly squeezed. There are no longer enough people on the land to suport the necessary services or to maintain the landscape that attracts the visitor.

The results can be seen in the changing population structure. Age pyramids for each national park, based in 1971 census data (Fig 4.4) show a top-heavy age structure indicative of decline. The parks have a lower proportion of children and adults below the age of 45 and a higher proportion of women between 45 and 60 and of men between 50 and 65, than the average for rural districts in England and Wales. Exmoor and Dartmoor, followed by North York Moors, have the most top-heavy pyramids. The immigration of commuters, second-homers and the retired masks the emigration of the young, whose departure in turn masks the true level of unemployment and the lack of job opportunities. The growth in towns and large villages masks the decline in the remoter upland valleys, some of which can no longer reproduce their population. In common with most rural areas, the picture in the parks is one of decline in shopping and transport services, the closure of schools and the failure to meet local housing needs. External pressures on the housing market combined with inflation have taken house prices beyond the reach of local people, particularly the young. In the Lake District, housing rather than lack of job opportunities is now regarded as the main social problem.

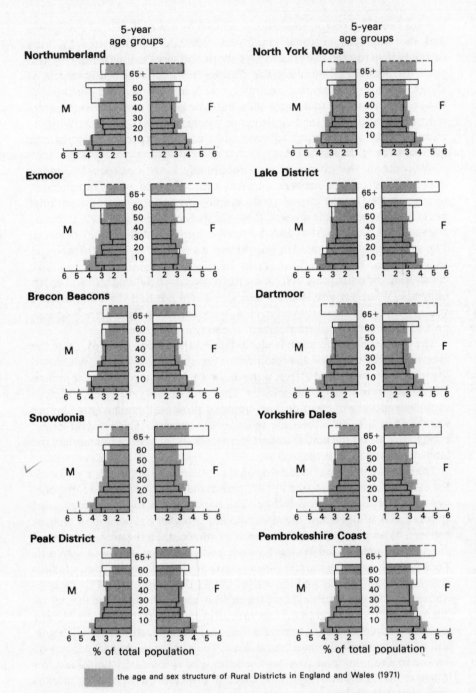

Figure 4.4 Age and sex structure by national parks, 1971. All those over 65 years are shown in a single 65+ group to emphasise the proportion of elderly people in the national parks.

The effect on local life and culture should not be ignored, nor should 'local culture' be dismissed as a romantic desire to perpetuate quaint old customs or accents that amuse the visiting townsman. Nobody who is familiar with the work of Arthur Raistrick (in, for example, *The Pennine Dales* (1978) and the official guides to the Yorkshire Dales and North York Moors National Parks), could entertain for one moment the notion that nothing would be lost if the indigenous population were to be submerged completely or displaced by incomers. This is not to deny that local people's attitudes are unchanging or that an inflow of newcomers of working age would invigorate many declining communities, as has happened repeatedly in history. But, although the uplands are repositories of local customs, traditions, crafts, skills and dialect, local culture is discussed in English policy documents, if at all, in terms of its value as a tourist attraction. Well-dressing, town criers in the 18th century costumes and Morris dancing on the green may amuse visitors, but once local culture is valued in these terms it is being deprived of its true purpose – which is to transmit human experience.

In Wales the inward migration of English-speaking people with higher incomes and the overwhelming impact of English-language television are seen by Welsh speakers as threatening a deathblow to a language and culture that have proved astonishingly resilient under centuries of English domination. The areas of greatest population decline are also those, such as Gwynedd, in which the proportion of Welsh speakers is the highest. Snowdonia is in the Welsh-speaking heartland, but in the eastern side of the Brecon Beacons anglicisation is far advanced and in the southern part of Pembrokeshire Coast ('little England beyond Wales') it has long been complete. Snowdonia is the only national park committee in Wales where the proceedings are in Welsh (with an English translation for non-Welsh-speaking members), all documents are printed in both languages and a knowledge of Welsh is essential for most officers. It is here that the cultural changes being wrought by tourism and by second- or retirement-homers are felt most deeply and the national park is perceived by some as a factor that undermines the Welsh position. This feeling is not confined to members of Plaid Cymru, the nationalist party. The Meirionnydd structure plan refers to the 'diluting and disruptive effect' of the purchase of second and retirement homes by English-speaking people who can outbid local residents.

It would be wrong to give the impression that nothing has been done at national or local levels to counteract the effects of the cycle we have described. But in setting up national parks as playgrounds for the nation, governments and parliaments treated them initially as a free resource, calling for negligible investment or maintenance. They saw no need for special policies to sustain a social and economic structure that would conserve the resources that nature and man had provided, because it was assumed, as we saw in Chapter 1, that traditional farming would do so. The water, electricity, quarrying and other interests were not expected to put much, if anything, back into the areas that they were exploiting. The successful efforts of the

Shetland County Council to insist on major investment in social and economic infrastructure and strong measures of environmental protection, as the price of its consent to North Sea oil development, is in marked contrast to the relative failure of the upland authorities in England and Wales to extract similar benefits from the exploitation of their resources.

The measures taken by the Development Commission, the Council for Small Industries in Rural Areas (CoSIRA) and the Development Board for Rural Wales have been aimed in a useful direction, at the encouragement of small scale local industries or crafts in the countryside. The Development Commission has concentrated its investment in special areas (see Fig. 4.5) but its influence on the national parks and other upland areas has been minimal, and matches neither the scale nor the character of their problems. Too little has been done and too late. The Development Commission programme to provide 1500 new jobs a year over rural England cannot provide more than a handful in the remoter uplands.

The measures taken by the government in 1979–80 to reduce local authority services and expenditure, and to oblige local authorities to sell their council houses or cut down their direct labour departments, have not only aggravated all the problems we have described, but have been bitterly resented by many of the government's most loyal supporters. The reports from Somerset in 1980 that 20–30 schools may be closed in the next four years, and reports that Exmoor may lose what little was left of its public transport services almost immediately, are typical. *The Countryman* has reported that 'the natives are getting restless' in the shire counties, as sacrosanct market forces and government policy kill off rural petrol stations, post offices, schools and shops (Aldous 1980). Speaking at a conference called to discuss the rural crisis in November 1980, Michael Heseltine, the Secretary of State for the Environment, defended the government's decision to withdraw grants for village halls, which are now the responsibility of largely urban local authorities (Heseltine 1980). In practical terms he had little to offer, beyond the offer of £250 000 in prize money for a competition to be run by Rural Voice to encourage 'innovative village schemes'. It remains to be seen, given the government's apparent conviction that state intervention is an evil to be avoided at almost any cost, whether the rural electorate can be persuaded so cheaply to tolerate the impact of reductions in government expenditure and the continuation of conflicting sectoral policies.

Davidson and Wibberley (1977) have tried to distinguish between the 'external' pressures on the countryside associated with changes in urban society (such as the demand for building land and recreation) and 'internal' pressures arising from within the rural economy (such as technical changes in agriculture, commercial afforestation and mining). It is clear from our necessarily brief and over-simplified survey that this distinction is mistaken. The critical decisions about the countryside, such as those about farming, forestry, mining or rural policy, are made in the city. Raymond Williams (1973) seems to us to get far closer to the truth when he identifies the division

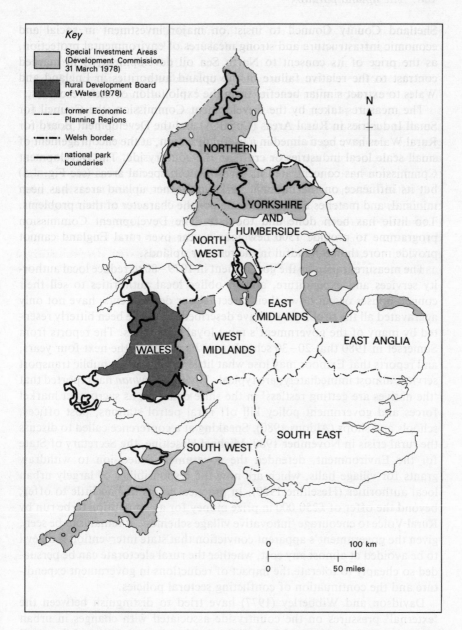

Figure 4.5 Special Investment Areas, Development Commission 1978, and area of the Development Board for Rural Wales. Crown copyright reserved.

and opposition of city and country, in their modern forms, as the critical culmination of the specialisation and division of labour.

According to this view, the role of the country is to specialise in the production of a very limited range of goods and services and to hook itself into the production and marketing systems of the city. It gets rid of local self-sufficiency and marginally profitable enterprises. The city provides the specialist outlets and the capital (public and private) for the new technologies, thereby lowering unit costs, displacing labour, increasing productivity and profitability and promoting capital growth. The major benefits accrue to the large investors and the basic decisions are taken by those who control the political, financial and industrial institutions. At the local level there may be immense differences in outlook and practice between and among agri-businessmen, traditional landowners and family farmers, and acute differences with central government or big business. But local decisions, public or private, are taken within the general framework determined by market trends and city-based decisions.

Conclusion to Part 2

At this point we ask the reader to pause and to look back over the ground we have covered before moving on in the next part of the book to the working of the National Park Authorities at the local level. In appraising their efforts it must be borne in mind continuously that they took over an inherently weak system, made even weaker by 25 years of low political and financial priority. Moreover, it has become clearer since the reorganisation of 1974 that the national parks do not present simple problems with easy solutions, but extremely complex ones that may prove very difficult to resolve. The failure to identify these problems clearly enough, or to diagnose their causes, during the legislative periods of 1967–8 and 1972–4 and more recently 1980–81, has not made it easier to take appropriate action in the 1980s.

In Chapters 2 and 3 we described the physical characteristics of the national parks and the extent to which they are being changed by human intervention and enjoyed by the public. In so doing we have reached a preliminary conclusion. Despite the establishment of a reformed administration in 1974, success in achieving the twin purposes of conserving and enhancing natural beauty (in its full statutory meaning embracing fauna and flora) and promoting the enjoyment of the public still eludes the national park system. The splitting apart of the functions of conserving nature and conserving natural beauty has led both the NPAs and the Countryside Commission to concentrate their efforts on the protection of the 'landscape', interpreted by the Commission to mean 'scenery'. We understand 'landscape' to be a living system produced by natural and human forces, of which scenery is the visual expression. We do not undervalue scenic beauty, which is probably the most powerful force attracting people to the national parks and gives the most powerful emotional impulse to the movement to protect them. But we believe that, in spite of management by man, the essential characteristic of the national parks is the relative ascendancy of the natural world and natural processes. The emphasis on appearance has been a handicap both to understanding and to action. It has encouraged the idea that problems deeply rooted in the exploitation of the resources of the national parks for economic purposes can be dealt with by protective designations of limited areas, while ignoring the social and economic trends or policies that are literally changing the face of nature. We suggest that incremental changes induced by man's activities are threatening the living landscapes of the national parks and can only be brought under control if conservation of natural and human resources on the broadest possible base becomes an integral element of social and economic policy.

The evidence about the recreational use of the national parks has been misinterpreted to create a widespread impression that the great majority of townspeople do not appreciate the 'real' countryside and are happy to remain by their cars along the tarmac corridor. On the contrary, the open country of the national parks is a major element in the spectrum of recreational resources of the highest value for many people. The commonsense view that recreational use must not be allowed to destroy the resource has been transformed subtly into a rather negative attitude towards recreation. Little effort is made to satisfy the needs for recreation in open country of those who are socially or geographically disadvantaged. The NPAs are most concerned with two groups of visitors – the very active but not very numerous long-distance walkers, climbers and cavers, and the inactive, very numerous, more or less car-bound visitors. But in between there is a very large and growing middle-band of people who, as the recreation surveys show, do get away from their cars, do walk and are able to enjoy the natural world of the parks by exerting themselves to a modest extent. Contrary to the prevailing view that the urban hordes are already destroying the beauty and wildness of the areas they came to experience, we believe that there is still scope in all the national parks for more walkers to enjoy the remote areas without inflicting unacceptable damage on them. But this implies reducing their accessibility to motor cars, more positive management to restrict the penetration of the remoter areas by cars and to ration access to them by physical effort.

Although the government decided in 1976 that the satisfaction of social and economic needs in national parks was 'an object of policy', it is clear from our analysis of the cycle of intensification and decline that this object is not being achieved. The substitution of capital for labour in agriculture, forestry and mineral working has sustained or increased the incomes of the more fortunate, while accelerating the outward flow of the young and the active and the rundown of rural services. Tourism cannot reverse the trend as long as it offers low-paid seasonal jobs, although it is an indispensable source of supplementary income. The NPAs have no responsibility for satisfying social and economic needs, except as a spin-off from conservation and recreation policies, but social and economic trends are working against the achievement of conservation and recreation aims. The social and economic context in turn is determined largely by the policies and attitudes of central government, which we shall examine in Part 4.

Part 3   *The system at work*

Introduction

Having surveyed the history of the national parks, their characteristics and problems in Parts 1 and 2, we now examine the working of the national park system as it was reorganised in 1974. Chapter 5 is concerned with administration – the merits of the two different kinds of national park authority (planning boards and county council committees), the characteristics of the elected and appointed members and the resources of money and manpower of which they dispose. Chapter 6 examines the policies expressed in the structure and national park plans and development control. Chapter 7 deals with the implementation of policies and looks at the effectiveness and the limitations in practice of various techniques for national park management. Finally in this section, Chapter 8 is an extended case study of moorland reclamation in Exmoor, which illustrates in some detail how the system actually works.

When considering how the system functions, it is necessary to bear in mind the limited range of powers available to NPAs. The two national park boards are structure plan authorities and exercise, with minor exceptions, the planning and countryside (essentially recreation) functions of both district and county councils. The national park committees exercise as of right the development control and countryside functions conferred on them by Schedule 17 of the 1972 Local Government Act, within the policy framework of the county structure plans. County councils may also delegate to them (and usually do) such functions as the preparation of local plans, the conservation of areas of historic or architectural interest, the making of tree preservation orders, advertisement control, footpath maintenance and the conclusion of management agreements under Section 52 of the 1971 Town and Country Planning Act. The 1980–1 Wildlife and Countryside Bill, removes legal doubt about the powers of local authorities (including national park boards or committees) to conclude management agreements. The 1972 Local Government Act required every NPA to publish a national park management plan within three years of reorganisation in 1974, and to review it thereafter at intervals of not less than five years.

Certain special powers are available in national parks. But they are so limited that generally speaking it is true to say that NPAs have the same planning and recreation powers as local planning authorities elsewhere. They have compulsory powers to buy land for access or to make access orders, but not to buy land for the purpose of conserving its natural beauty. The Landscape Areas Special Development Order 1950 (LASDO) enables NPAs to control the design and materials of farm buildings in certain parts of the Lake District, the Peak and Snowdonia; Section 13 of the 1949 National Parks and Access to the Countryside Act empowers them to improve waterways for recreation; Section 13 of the 1968 Countryside Act enables them to make byelaws regulating boating on lakes; and Section 14 of the 1968 Countryside Act empowers the minister to make orders requiring landowners or land users in national parks to give six months notice (to be extended by the 1980 Wildlife and Countryside Bill to 12 months) of their intention to convert land that has been moor or heath for 20 years to agricultural use.

The NPAs have no highway, or traffic management powers, although consultation between the national park and the highway authorities is now encouraged by DOE Circular 125/1977. The 1949 Act purports to confer a sweeping power on the NPAs to 'take all such action as appears to them expedient for the preservation and enhancement of natural beauty' but in practice this means very little. The differences between national parks and other areas lie in the interpretation of policies, the higher levels of government grant aid for national park purposes and the exclusion of district councils from the exercise of development control within national parks. A new distinction was introduced by the Local Government, Planning and Land Act 1980 and by the general relaxation in development controls under the 1981 amendment of the General Development Order 1977. The national parks were excepted from the relaxation, thereby creating a new source of resentment. For example, a householder outside the national park can build a small addition to his home without having to seek planning permission from the district council. But his neighbour inside the park who wishes to do the same thing has to make a planning application and pay a fee for it to the national park authority.

5 *National park administration*

Boards or committees?

Few issues have generated more heat in national park circles over the past 30 years than the conflict between the county councils on the one hand and the amenity and national park lobby on the other over the administration of the national parks. The county councils, as we saw in Chapter 1, succeeded in frustrating the clear intention of the National Parks Act 1949 that multi-county parks should be administered by joint planning boards. The 1972 agreement between the County Councils' Association and the Countryside Commission, by which the Commission dropped its demand for boards in all 10 parks in return for national park management plans, a National Park Officer and a unified administration in every park, was intended to end the controversy. But the issue is still a live one. Cumbria County Council has voted twice (in 1976 and 1978) for the replacement of the Lakes Board by a county council committee. The national park committees of the Yorkshire Dales (in 1975) and of Pembrokeshire Coast (in 1980) have voted for the replacement of committees by planning boards.

The difference between boards and committees lies in their relationship to the county councils, not in their composition. In both cases the Secretary of State appoints one-third of the members and the county councils appoint two-thirds*. The county councils, by agreement with the district councils, appoint a small number of district council nominees, but the Wildlife and Countryside Bill gives each district council one member, subject to a maximum of one-seventh. The composition of the National Park Authorities in 1980–1 is shown in Table 5.1.

The boards are autonomous local planning authorities. They settle their own budgets and levy a rate by precepting on the constituent county councils. They employ their own staff and determine both the size of their staff establishment and the salary grades of their employees. They are free to use or not to use the services of county council officials, to hire their own staffs or to engage specialist consultants. They can buy land or conclude management agreements on their own authority. They combine the plan-making and

---

* Schedule 17 of the Local Government Act 1972 gives the Secretary of State greater flexibility than he uses in practice. He must appoint no less than one-third of the members, but may appoint more subject to the requirement that county councillors must form a majority of each committee – although not of each board. Also he may substitute, with the consent of the Countryside Commission, a minimum proportion of one-quarter in particular cases.

Table 5.1 Composition of National Park authorities 1980–1. Three of the multi-county committees are committees of the county council responsible for the greater part of the national park area. Somerset County Council administers Exmoor, the North Yorkshire County Council administers Yorkshire Dales and North York Moors. The Brecon Beacons are administered by a joint committee of the four counties, but attached to Powys for purposes of staffing and finance.

Park	County Council	County	District	Appointed	Total
Boards					
Peak	Cheshire	2			
	Derbyshire	8			
	Greater Manchester	2			
	Staffordshire	2			
	South Yorkshire	2			
	West Yorkshire	2	18	4	11	33
Lake District	Cumbria	16	2	9	27
Single county committees					
Dartmoor	Devon	12	2	7	21
Northumberland	Northumberland	15	3	9	27
Pembroke Coast	Dyfed	10	2	6	18
Snowdonia	Gwynedd	14	4	9	27
Multi-county committees					
Brecon Beacons	Dyfed	2			
	Gwent	2			
	Mid-Glamorgan	2			
	Powys	8	14	4	9	27
Exmoor	Devon	4			
	Somerset	8	12	2	7	21
North York Moors	Cleveland	2			
	North Yorks	12	14	4	9	27
Yorkshire Dales	Cumbria	1			
	North Yorks	12	13	3	8	24
totals		138	30	84	252

the development control functions of both county and district councils and prepare both structure plans* and local plans. They are responsible for the conservation of historic buildings and areas. They make their own standing orders about procedure and administration.

The extent to which a board uses its autonomy depends in practice on local political factors. The Peak Board has six constituent county councils, the largest of which (Derbyshire) has less than a quarter of the Board's membership and is in no position to control it. The Lake District Board lies wholly within the county of Cumbria, but Cumbria cannot force the Board to toe its

---

* The Peak Board publishes its own structure plan; the Lake District structure plan is incorporated in the Cumbria Structure Plan.

line in matters of policy, finance or staffing unless it can muster a political majority on the Board. In practice, this has not proved to be very easy. When the Tory Party won control of Cumbria County Council in 1977, it was able to use its majority to replace two of the four district council representatives on the Board by county councillors, thereby increasing the size of the county council majority. But even threats that county councillors might be deprived of committee chairmanships failed to win a majority on the Board for the Ennerdale reservoir scheme, to which virtually every organisation in the Lake District except the county council was opposed.

Some county councillors and officers argue that because the work of a board is not 'subject to scrutiny by county councillors', boards are less 'democratically accountable' than county council committees. In fact, the elected members of boards are accountable to their electorate in exactly the same way as members of committees. Only a minority either of boards or committees is directly accountable to the resident population of the parks and none of them is accountable to the visitors for whose benefit the parks were established. The real objection behind the argument about 'democratic accountability' is quite different. The autonomous status of the board enables its members and officers to be freed both from the grip of the party political caucus that controls the county council through its policy and resources committee and from the all-pervading influence of the county council chief executive and his management 'team' of senior officers. The question at issue is not democratic accountability or efficiency but political and bureaucratic power.

The autonomy of the boards does not extend beyond the limits of their statutory planning, amenity and recreation functions. For example, the Peak has initiated traffic studies in consultation with the highway authorities, which was itself a step forward. But neither boards nor park committees have highway or traffic powers, any more than they have powers to deal with the social and economic problems of their areas, such as jobs, housing, public transport, or the support of tourism or farming. For example, the Lake District Board had to rely on Cumbria County Council to implement its policy of banning heavy through traffic from West Cumberland from using the A591 through the heart of the Lake District. The County Council blew hot and cold for several years before making the necessary Order.

The national park committees are committees of a county council* (see Table 5.1) and are subject to its political and financial control. Their decisions on development control and on countryside matters, under powers delegated to them by statute, cannot be challenged by the county council, and they alone appoint the National Park Officer. But the county council decides the size of the national park budget and the amount of the annual bid made by the national park for its share of the National Park Supplementary Grant (NPSG). The National Park Officer and his staff are officers of the

* The Brecon Beacons National Park Committee, as a joint committee of four county councils, enjoys a higher degree of administrative autonomy than other committees, although it lacks the autonomy of a board in such matters as finance, staffing and structure plans.

county council, which decides the total staff establishment, its distribution and the salary gradings for each post; whether capital can be provided for unforeseen purchases; whether capital spending should be frozen in times of retrenchment; and whether recruitment to established posts should be allowed, or new posts created.

The national park committees are also tightly integrated into the county council administration, on which they are dependent for legal, financial, administrative and technical staff for many of their key services. County Council officers write the agendas and the minutes. It can be advantageous for a national park department to make use of architects, landscape architects, engineers, solicitors and other professionals on the county council staff, but the national park has to take its place in the queue for their services, is charged for them at rates fixed by the county council and is not allowed to go shopping elsewhere if it is dissatisfied with the speed, quality or the cost of the service it gets.

The autonomy of national park committees in development control does not extend to 'county matters', which are defined in the 1972 Local Government Act as applications that are not in accordance with the 'fundamental provisions' of the county development or structure plans, or straddle national park boundaries. Some county councils allow the national park committees to determine all but the most important county matters. Others call in the most trivial applications if the County Planning Officer thinks that they transgress the policies of the development plan, or the County Surveyor thinks that they do not satisfy his detailed highway design requirements. The secretary of state's right to call in important applications, or to settle them on appeal, means that usually the most controversial proposals are taken out of the hands of the NPAs.

Since 1974, several county councils have allowed national park committees to oppose them at public inquiries. Devon allowed the Dartmoor NPC to object to the A30 Okehampton bypass and the North Yorkshire County Council allowed the North York Moors NPC to oppose a potash mining application. Both county councils supported the proposals. But this autonomy is a privilege not a right and it places the county council legal staff in the position of having to present evidence and arguments on both sides of the dispute, for the county solicitor provides the national park committee with its legal service.

National park committees are also subject to the standing orders of the county council to which the committee is attached. Standing orders regulate the procedures of the council and its committees in fine detail. They enable the county council to discipline awkward elected (but not appointed) members by removing them from committees*. Members of other councils,

---

* The majority on the county council can remove a county councillor from a park committee at any time, but it cannot remove him from a board. The Labour majority on Derbyshire County Council attempted to remove one of their colleagues, Peter Jackson, from the Peak Board in 1975 but Jackson won a ruling from the High Court that he could not be removed before the end of his three-year term.

or members appointed by the secretary of state, are ineligible under standing orders for the chairmanship of the national park committee. In some parks they are also ineligible for the vice-chairmanship, or even for the chairmanship of sub-committees. In Dyfed, the Pembroke Coast National Park Committee may only be represented by county councillors on outside bodies. In certain counties the permission of the county council is required for the establishment of new standing sub-committees of the national park committee, capital expenditure above a certain figure, whether budgeted or not and the acquisition of land.

The minutes of the Yorkshire Dales National Park Committee for 1974–5 document the control exercised by the North Yorkshire County Council. The Personnel Sub-Committee of the County Council reduced the National Park Officer's salary. The county council refused to permit the expenditure of some £35 000 on the purchase of Whernside Manor (for which funds were in fact available) as a caving centre, or to appoint a footpath officer despite the fact that a 75% grant had been obtained for this purpose. The national park committee, with the support of its politically independent elected chairman, twice voted by a majority that the committee should be replaced by a planning board. The seven appointed members sent a deputation to the secretary of state to complain about the council's interference. He listened politely but would not commit himself. The Yorkshire Dales got its caving centre and its footpath a year later and the 'revolution' petered out in the face of the obduracy of the County Council, whose chairman firmly told the committee that the 1972 agreement between the County Councils' Association and the Countryside Commission meant that 'the eight national parks not already run by boards should be controlled by county councils through national park committees' (Fletcher 1975).

Opinions differ as to whether Schedule 17 of the 1972 Local Government Act gives the county councils the right to the control they exercise. The Countryside Commission has argued that the committees are legally entitled to use their resources as they see fit (Hookway 1975b). But the above statement by the chairman of the North Yorkshire County Council reflected the reality of power. Nevertheless, the row in the Dales was one of the factors that led the Association of County Councils to commission a study of national parks by Clem Hurley, formerly chief executive of Northumberland County Council, in anticipation of the government review expected in 1981. His report (Hurley 1979) catalogues 'what may appear at first reading a formidable list of rules, regulations and restrictions laid down by standing orders', but he concluded that the county councils interfered very little and he found little wrong with the system. Hurley spent very little time with the two national park boards and made no attempt to evaluate their advantages or disadvantages by comparison with committees. This did not stop him from commenting adversely on the boards' salary levels and some other aspects of their administration. The entire report is permeated, as might have been expected, by the conventional view that the national park 'department' should be regulated in the same way as other departments of the county council, on the ground that county councils are responsible to their ratepayers and cannot abdicate all financial control over national park expenditure. The ratepayers' contribution, as we shall see, is in fact about 12%, for which the county councils get effective control.

The minutes of the Pembrokeshire Coast National Park Committee for 18 March 1980 illustrate the degree of control exercised by the county council that led the committee to vote (in its response to Hurley) for its replacement by a board. The committee was debating a report in which the chairman of the sub-committee concerned, Guy Hains, complained about decisions on staffing by the Personnel Sub-Committee of the county council. He was never consulted when the short listing or appointment of staff was made, or given an opportunity to discuss or comment on the salary gradings that had caused acute staff dissatisfaction, a very high staff turnover and led to NALGO blacklisting posts in the department. The minute reveals the impossible position in which the National Park Officer found himself, torn between his duty to the committee that appointed him and his obligation as a county council chief officer to carry out county council policy.

> The National Park Officer . . . stated that as the National Park Department was part of Dyfed County Council the Sub-Committee had to adhere strictly to the policy of the county council. The appointments which Mr Hains referred to had all been undertaken within the guidelines set down by the County Council and therefore he had no alternative when making appointments at officer level but to appoint staff at the first incremental point of the grade . . . He did appreciate that chairmen of sub-committees were not consulted. This, however, was the policy of the county council and he had to adhere to this. (PCNPC 1980)

We do not suggest that petty interference of the kind revealed in this minute is typical of all county councils. The reorganisation of 1974 has raised the standard of administration and extended the professional skills and competence of the new authorities. But also we have seen nothing to invalidate the conclusion of the Longland report, referred to in Chapter 1, which argued that the boards have a much better track record than the committees. In our view boards benefit from being compact, local organisations freed from the tentacles of the larger bureaucracy. The Association of County Councils, however, has argued on the basis of the Hurley report that national park administration should continue on the same general lines as at present within the financial and political control of the county councils (ACC 1980a). While grudgingly admitting that for historical and practical reasons the boards are here to stay, the ACC rejects them as models for national park administration on the ground that they 'lack some of the advantages flowing from the closer integration which can be achieved by national park committees'. The ACC concedes that standing orders should not be allowed to hinder national park committees in discharging their statutory duties. It recommends 'extensive financial freedom' for the committees – but 'within the overall financial control exercised by the county council', which it regards as the only bodies capable of co-ordinating land uses in the parks and the rest of the countryside. The county councils will not readily loosen the political grip on which they have insisted for the past 35 years.

Membership characteristics

The unstated assumption of the Hobhouse report (1947a), which recommended that the National Parks Commission should appoint half the local committees and the chairman, was that the appointees would act as a solid block in support of national conservation policies. The same theory underlies the observation of the Countryside Review Committee (CRC 1979) that central government is liable to be resented because of 'undue interference' in the national parks through the appointed members.

In reality, the appointees rarely form a solid block and are more representative of special interests than of the government. Although the Countryside Commission is consulted about the appointments and puts up names to ministers, many of its nominations are rejected and other persons appointed. The appointees have no lines of communication either to the Commission or to the Department of the Environment or the Welsh Office. They are selected, according to a typical letter of appointment,

> for their personal qualities and experience and not as representatives of any particular organisation or group. The Secretary of State is primarily concerned that they should be able to bring to the Committee's (or Board's) deliberations the wider national viewpoint, whilst at the same time having regard to the interests of all who are concerned with the park.

Despite ministers' insistence that appointees do not represent particular interests, the tendency is to ensure that every NPA has one member drawn from such groups as the CPRE, the Ramblers' Association, naturalist groups, the NFU, CLA and so on. It is not surprising that appointed members are seen (and even see themselves) as representatives of those interests. On the occasions that they have temporarily formed a solid block (as in the Yorkshire Dales in 1975), they were in no sense acting as representatives of the Countryside Commission or the government.

The evidence from our membership survey and from interviews suggests that elected members who are seriously concerned either about conservation or about social and economic problems regard the appointed members as essential makeweights to counter the philistinism, indifference and parochialism of many councillors. A sub-committee of the Association of County Councils recorded its unanimous view of 'the valuable contribution' made

by appointed members, and proposed no changes in the existing arrangements (ACC 1980b). In some counties, few councillors volunteer to serve on
the national park committee, regarding it as of minor importance, but
troublesome and unpopular. One appointed member described to us 'the
desperate unconcern' of some of his elected colleagues who (in his view) only
joined the committee to make up the numbers and only turn up at meetings
to collect their attendance allowances. District councillors in particular are
widely held to be concerned mainly in pushing through planning applications
for their constituents, although there are district councillors of whom this
could not be said. We heard almost as many criticisms of appointed
members from their appointed colleagues as from the elected members.
Appointed members expressed to us their astonishment at some appointments and their unease over the lack of expert knowledge and weak commitment of some of their fellow appointees.

However, such generalisations tell one very little about the make-up of the
NPAs, the range of members' interests or skills or their representative
character. Therefore, we have constructed a 'profile' of the members of
NPAs, in the year 1978–9, from members' answers to the questionnaire
referred to in the Introduction on page xii (Table 5.2). The response rate of
72% gives us confidence that the profile is accurate for the parks as a whole
and for both elected and appointed members.

The characteristic elected member is a male Conservative of the socio-
economic groups A and B, aged about 58, most likely to be retired (the
largest single 'occupation') or to be engaged in farming or landownership,
and unlikely to have academic qualifications. The characteristic appointed
member is a male of socio-economic groups A and B, aged about 52, more
likely than an elected member to hold Labour, Liberal or other minority
political views (although Conservatives form the largest single group),
holding an academic or professional qualification, very unlikely to be retired
and most likely to be working in an academic job or in farming. The
membership as a whole is highly unrepresentative of the urban users of the
national parks. The proportion of manual workers is 3% (all elected)* and
of trade unionists 17% (14% of the elected, 21% of the appointed members)
most of them being members of white-collar unions. The overall proportion
of women is very low (12.5%).

The appointed members, as one would expect, have a strong commitment
through membership (69%) to amenity and conservation bodies such as the
CPRE or County Naturalist Trusts. The commitment of elected members to
amenity/conservation bodies, although much lower (25%), is probably
considerably higher than one would expect from county or district councillors in rural areas. The involvement of members in recreational bodies is at a

* Percentages are related to the total number of members returning the questionnaire (183)
or, where appropriate, to the numbers of elected members (118) or appointed members (65)
returning the questionnaire. Similarly, numbers (eg. five elected members) are the number
returning the questionnaire.

Table 5.2 Response to questionnaire.

Park authority	Elected members			Appointed members			Total		
	No. on NPC	No. of responses	Percentage	No. on NPC	No. of responses	Percentage	No. on NPC	No. of responses	Percentage
Lake District	18	17	94	9	6	67	27	23	85
Northumberland	18	14	78	9	9	100	27	23	85
Pembrokeshire Coast	12	9	75	6	6	100	18	15	83
Yorkshire Dales	16	13	81	8	6	75	24	19	79
Peak District	22	17	77	11	9	82	33	26	79
Exmoor	14	9	64	7	6	86	21	15	71
North York Moors	18	13	72	9	6	67	27	19	70
Brecon Beacons	18	11	61	9	6	67	27	17	63
Snowdonia	18	10	56	9	6	67	27	16	59
Dartmoor	14	5	36	7	5	71	21	10	48
totals	168	118	70	84	65	77	252	183	73

far lower level – 29% of the appointed 10% of the elected members belong to such bodies as the Ramblers' or the Youth Hostels Associations.

We asked members to say whether they had any professional or academic qualifications relevant in some way to national park functions. (Relevant qualifications included natural science, geography/geology, architecture/surveying/planning, estate management, recreation, degree or Higher National Diploma in agriculture.) Only five elected members (4.2%) have relevant qualifications compared to 29 appointees (44.6%). Elected members are more likely to be involved in professional or trade associations such as the NFU or CLA (36%) than in amenity, wildlife or recreation bodies. Appointed members, while nearly as active in professional or trade associations (27%) are also far more active in the other fields. On the other hand, a high proportion of farmers (42%) and a very high proportion of landowners (89%) are members of amenity/conservation bodies.

By far the largest interest group consists of farmers and landowners (Table 5.3). Farmers and landowners constituted 37% of the elected respondents and 25% of the appointees. Their influence is clearly stronger in some parks than in others. If farmers and landowners are treated as a single group, half are owner-occupiers, several of whom also rent land. Only 10% are tenants who own no land. A substantial proportion of farmers have other jobs, usually in a professional or commercial field. A significant fact is that 42 of the 52 farmer respondents employed full-time hired labour outside the family. It may be remarkable that as many as ten family farmers who employed no labour found the time to take part in local government or national park affairs. But there is not a single farm worker or member of the National Union of Agricultural and Allied Workers on a National Park Authority, and the family farms which form the majority are seriously under-represented by comparison with other farmers. The influence of farmers on the NPAs is out of all proportion to their numbers in the rural community – under 3.5% of the working population in national parks in

Table 5.3   Farmers and landowners.

Park authority	No. of replies to questionnaire	No. of farmers and landowners	Percentage
Brecon Beacons	17	9	53
Pembrokeshire Coast	15	7	47
Exmoor	15	6	40
Northumberland	23	9	39
Lake District	23	8	35
North York Moors	19	6	32
Dartmoor	10	3	30
Snowdonia	16	4	25
Yorkshire Dales	19	4	21
Peak	26	4	15
all parks	183	60	33

1971. In 1978–9 no less than six of the ten NPA chairmen were farmers or landowners.

Farmers and landowners do not, of course, form a homogeneous group and individual farmers or landowners are to be found in diametrically opposed camps on both farming and conservation issues. But within any group certain characteristics tend to be dominant. A committee in which farmers and landowners are the single largest group is unlikely to be an impartial arbiter where landowning and farming 'rights' are in question. Some members were unwilling to answer the question 'how did you normally vote in general elections between 1964 and 1974?', but 82% of those who replied did so as shown in Table 5.4. Whereas 63% of the elected members vote Conservative and 37% for other parties, among the appointed members the percentages are reversed – 63% vote for the other parties and 37% for the Conservative Party, which nevertheless retains an overall majority with 54% of the national park membership. It is true that most issues in NPAs are decided on a free vote without any caucus decisions by the ruling group at county hall, but the ruling group influences national park policies both through its members' participation and by its control of the key county council committees where the party line is applied to finance, policy and staffing. (Powys County Council does not operate on party lines.)

The complaint is frequently voiced in national parks that those who live and work in them are represented inadequately on the authorities. Analysis of the full membership of NPAs in 1978–9 shows that of the 41 district councils lying wholly or partly within the parks, 31 are represented on the authorities by one or more members. Of the 149 county council electoral areas lying wholly or partly within the parks, 66 are represented on the NPAs by their county councillors. However, county councillors representing substantial national park areas have no right to membership of the authority and sometimes are excluded. North Yorkshire County Council's Tory party group decided in 1977 to exclude the Liberal member for Settle (the Yorkshire

Table 5.4 Party Political support on National Park Authorities 1964–74.

	Elected members		Appointed members		All members replying to political support question	
	Numbers	%	Numbers	%	Numbers voting	%
Conservative	61	63	19	37	80	54
Labour	21	22	12	22	33	22
Liberal	7	7	13	25	20	13
Plaid Cymru	5	5	1	2	6	4
other	1	1	0	0	1	1
unsure/floating	2	2	7	14	9	6
total replies to political support question	97	100	52	100	149	100

Dales National Park Committee's only woman member) on political grounds, and the Somerset County Council excluded the member for Exford from the Exmoor National Park Committee on personal grounds. Both were re-admitted after an interval. These figures and facts explain why some electors feel that they are not represented, but they also exaggerate the degree of 'under-representation'. Many of the unrepresented areas are small, even tiny, fragments of land or very sparsely inhabited. In six of the parks every district council has at least one representative on the NPA. Normally all of Exmoor's eight county council electoral divisions are represented, as are all but two in the Yorkshire Dales. Of the elected members of NPAs, 35% live in the Parks, as do 29% of the appointees.

We conclude that the NPAs contain a reasonable proportion of members who are familiar with the area they are administering and sufficient to enable most electors to make their views known to an accessible representative. But we reject entirely the view that NPAs, or even their elected component, should consist largely of local residents. The real question is *which* interests are represented? As we have seen, the people whose interests are most seriously under-represented are the lower-income groups and workers within the parks, women and millions of users who live in the cities and conurbations. The 1949 Act envisaged (Section 99) that the cities or adjoining rural areas might contribute financially to the national parks – a provision that has never been used – but made no arrangements for their direct representation. The Royal Commission on Local Government (Redcliffe-Maud 1969) recommended that the regional authorities it proposed should be represented on and contribute to the NPAs. In France, cities are represented on the governing bodies both of the national parks and of the regional parks and contribute to them financially. Extending membership to the cities and conurbations could provide a useful source of funds and represent the townsman's interest in both conservation and recreation. The desire for better local representation could be met by a re-allocation of the county and district council seats, or by directly electing a small proportion of the authorities' membership.

The membership profile shows that the effect of removal of the appointed members, as suggested by the Countryside Review Committee (CRC 1979), would be to reduce the number of women, to increase the average age, to increase the proportion of retired members, to reduce the number of members with interests and qualifications relevant to national park purposes, to reduce the proportion of members with Labour, Liberal and independent political outlook and to increase the dominant influence of the Conservative landed and farming interests. It would tend to diminish the proportion of members committed to or professionally involved in conservation issues. It would diminish still further the already meagre representation of urban interests and of working-class interests whether urban or rural. This is not to say that the present arrangements are the best way of securing the representation in national park and other countryside agencies of major national, urban or even rural interests. But we see great merits in attempting to combine representative local democracy, in which councillors would ideally be drawn from all groups of society rather than from the retired and better-off, with appointees to represent other national and regional interests.

Money and manpower

As we saw in Chapter 1, the Local Government (Finance) Act 1974 gave the national parks an exceptional financial status by replacing specific percentage grants for individual projects by the National Parks Supplementary Grant (NPSG). This extended grant aid for the first time to the administration and management of the parks, and it is also intended to cover both capital projects and running costs. It is a block grant calculated at about 75% of the budgeted 'approved net expenditure' (i.e. after deducting receipts from income-producing activities). It is paid in advance on the strict understanding that the local authorities will provide the remaining 25% (Howell 1974). (The 90% grant paid in Exmoor for moorland conservation as a 'special case' is explained in Chapter 8.) Those who are unfamiliar with the baffling complexities of local government finance could be forgiven for thinking that this means, in simple terms, that the ratepayer has to find 25% of the cost of running national parks. We calculate that the ratepayer's contribution is about 12%, in return for which the county councils secure control of the national park committees and a majority of members on the boards. There are several reasons for this discrepancy. The local authorities tend to spend less than they have budgeted for and have used the unspent balances to build up reserves in some national parks. The public make a substantial contribution in payments for car parks, caravan sites, information and other services, which are disregarded in calculating the 75% grant. The government itself pays about half the rate-borne contribution through the Rate Support Grant to local authorities. The NPAs' income is broken down as shown in Table 5.5.

The NPSG is paid direct to local authorities by the Department of the Environment or the Welsh Office, but under Section 86 of the 1949 Act the Countryside Commission grant-aids information and publicity services separately. It also makes specific grants for other projects, but not on a substantial scale. The information grant is paid in arrear, traditionally at 75%, but the Commission cut back its grant by 15% in June 1979 for the year 1979–80, to the acute embarrassment of authorities who were committed to a higher level of expenditure for a season that was already under way. Separate funding compels the authorities to devote a larger proportion of their resources to information services than they might wish to do if free to choose their own priorities. The merger of the grants has been discussed for many years, but is said to have been blocked by a Treasury

Table 5.5 Who pays for the national parks? Sources of national parks' finance 1979–80 (from National Park Statistics, *County Council Gazette* November 1980, vol. 73, no. 8; Finance, General and Rating Statistics 1979–80).

	£('000s)	%
From the public		
payments for services [a]	1500	17
From the taxpayer		
National Park Supplementary Grant [b]	4634	53
Countryside Commission Grants [c]	767	9
Rate Support Grant, resources element [d]	750	9
From the ratepayer		
rates levied on ratepayers	1080	12
total income	8731	100

[a] Services include camp and caravan sites, car parks, information etc.
[b] NPSG is estimated at 75% of 'net grant-related expenditure', i.e. gross income less income from services. In 1979–80 it was 75.48% of actual net expenditure.
[c] Countryside Commission grants are 75% of net information expenditure and 100% of expenditure on long-distance paths.
[d] The county councils levy a rate on the Government as a notional ratepayer to provide the 'resources element' of the Rate Support Grant. In 1979–80 the 'resources element' contributed 41% of the share of national park expenditure borne by the rates.

quibble over having to find an extra £100 000 in the transitional year because of the change in the basis of accountancy (Ridley 1979).

The Sandford Committee (1974) recommended that net expenditure should be raised over four or five years from £1.2 million a year in 1971–2 to nearly £4 million in 1978 or 1979 at constant prices. This made no allowance for land acquisition. The Association of County Councils' Treasurer has estimated (ACC 1980c) that in real terms expenditure increased 2.6 times between 1971–2 and 1979–80 when spending seems to have reached a peak. Tables 5.6 and 5.7 show how the pattern of expenditure has changed between 1973–4 (the last year before local government reorganisation) and 1979–80 using the allocation of functions adopted by the Association of County Councils.

The breakdown of expenditure between the individual parks and functions in 1979–80 is shown in Table 5.7. The allocation of expenditure between functions made by the Association of County Councils is arbitrary and, in the view of several National Park officers, it seriously understates the expenditure on positive management and the conservation of landscape. One officer went so far as to say to the authors that in his view his entire budget contributes towards 'conservation' in one form or another, through management, administration, development control, wardening, tree planting, the educational effect of the information services and so on. There is substance in this argument and allowance must be made for it. But it also reflects a reluctance to admit that despite the rapid growth in conservation

Table 5.6 Changes in national park expenditure by function, 1973−4 and 1979−80. Inflation calculated from the price increases accepted by Government as relevant to local government expenditure in the annual updating of the Rate Support Grant, taking November 1973 as 100 and November 1979 as 233; 1 : 1 means no change in real expenditure, 2 : 1 means doubling and so on. (From National Park Statistics, November 1974 and 1980, re-arranged to show the total expenditure before deducting income and to include capital expenditure in the totals for the various functions. The 1973−4 figures have been adjusted to bring them, as far as possible, into line with the classification adopted from 1974−5 onwards.)

	1973−4 £('000s)	%	1979−80 £('000s)	%	Ratio of 1979−80 expenditure to 1973−4 expenditure in real terms
administration and planning	842	44	3196	36.6	1.63 : 1
recreation	490	26	2744	31.5	2.4 : 1
information, publicity, national park centres	430	22	1608	18.4	1.61 : 1
conservation and estate management	57	3	680	7.8	5.12 : 1
land acquisition	−	−	235	2.7	−
debt charges	42	2	28	0.3	0.28 : 1
miscellaneous	55	3	240	2.6	1.87 : 1
gross expenditure	1916	100	8731	100	1.96 : 1

and estate work, which have increased by 511% in real terms in six years, they still get less than 8% of the expenditure. Administration and planning, although taking a smaller proportion than before, still get the largest share and recreation and information together account for half the total expenditure. The proportion of national park budgets spent on the ground is still very small (Table 5.8)

One reason for the low level of expenditure on estate management is that although more than 25% of the land in national parks is owned by public or semi-public agencies, only 1.16% is owned by NPAs, three of which own less than 200 ha apiece (Table 7.1, p. 158). The low level of landownership is partly due to the fact that the system is particularly ill adapted to providing capital for buying land, the purchase of which often cannot be foreseen when the estimates are prepared. The approved budgets are supposed to cover capital expenditure, but in reality they provide little or no capital for land purchase. All but two of the NPAs accumulated reserves through underspending in the early years after 1974, but these reserves are being eaten into already to offset cuts in central government grant. Significantly, the two boards (the Peak and Lake District) have by far the largest reserves, Dartmoor and Brecon Beacons have none. The replacement of the National Land Fund in 1980 by a National Heritage Memorial Fund with a capital of

Table 5.7   National park expenditure 1979–80 (from National Park Statistics, *County Council*

	Brecon Beacons £('000s)	%	Dartmoor £('000s)	%	Exmoor £('000s)	%	Lake District £('000s)	%	Northumber-land £('000s)	%
management, administration and planning[a]	183	35.4	292	47.2	223[b]	51.0	522[b]	34.9	133	40.8
recreation[a,d]	264[c]	51.0	169	27.3	105	24.0	415	27.8	79	24.2
information[a] and publicity	48	9.3	67	10.8	52	11.9	341	22.8	71	21.8
conservation[e] and estate maintenance	18	3.5	74	12.0	46	10.5	124	8.3	28	8.6
land acquisition	–	–	3	0.5	–	–	–	–	–	–
debt charges	–	–	7	1.1	3	0.7	–	–	–	–
miscellaneous[a]	4	0.8	7	1.1	8	1.8	93	6.2	15	4.6
total expenditure	517	100	619	100	437	100	1495	100	326	100
park's total as percentage of all parks	5.9		7.1		5.0		17.1		3.7	

[a] Includes capital expenditure; [b] includes part cost of offices; [c] includes canal rehabilitation; [d] includes car parks, picnic areas, caravan and camp sites, accommodation, catering facilities, access agreements and distance routes. Acquisition of land for access (£228 000) is included in land acquisition; [e] includes management agreements; [f] includes £247 000 capital expenditure. Very minor discrepancies caused by rounding off.

£12.4 million for 1980–1, and an annual grant from the Treasury of a sum – expected to be of the order of £3 million for 1981–2 – cannot make more than a very occasional contribution to land purchase, as the fund is primarily intended to buy works of art and stately homes.

One of the intentions behind the introduction of the NPSG was to enable the low-spending authorities to catch up with the levels established by the two boards. While some NPAs, notably Dartmoor and North York Moors, have increased their shares greatly, the Peak remains the biggest spender and actually has increased its share. The two boards, which were responsible for 46% of expenditure in 1973–4, were still spending 43% of the total in 1979–80. But the share of Snowdonia, the needs of which are possibly as great, remained at 10.4% over the same period. One reason for the partial failure of the new system to redistribute resources lies in the reluctance of local authorities to bid for a larger share of the NPSG, as this would call for matching expenditure from the rates. In fact, as we have seen, the contribution made by ratepayers is small and the proportion borne by national park residents very small indeed, as the county councils' share of expenditure is borne by the ratepayers of all the counties within which any part of a national park is situated. Whereas the landowners and farmers, who play a large part in national park management, pay no rates on farm land or farm buildings, no matter how profitable, the ratepayers of Plymouth, Sheffield,

Gazette, November 1980, vol. 73, no. 8).

North York Moors £('000s)	%	Peak £('000s)	%	Pembroke-shire Coast £('000s)	%	Snowdonia £('000s)	%	Yorkshire Dales £('000s)	%	Totals £('000s)	%
252	37.1	717	31.7	283[b]	36.3	299[b]	33.0	292[b]	41.0	3196	36.6
225	33.1	669	29.6	340[f]	43.6	203	22.4	275	38.6	2744	31.5
133	19.6	448	19.8	85	10.9	267	29.4	96	13.5	1608	18.4
50	7.4	195	8.6	22	2.8	102	11.2	21	2.9	680	7.8
–	–	196	8.7	36	4.6	–	–	–	–	235	2.7
–	–	–	–	10	1.3	1	0.1	7	1.0	28	0.3
19	2.8	35	1.5	3	0.4	35	3.9	21	2.9	240	2.8
679	100	2260	100	779	100	907	100	712	100	8731	100
	7.7		25.9		8.9		10.4		8.2		

Manchester, Derby, Carlisle, Bangor, Taunton, Pembroke and many other towns and cities outside the parks contribute a share. However, although the burden on the ratepayer is small everywhere in absolute terms, it weighs far more heavily on the poorer rural counties than on wealthier counties or conurbations. The disparity in resources between the Peak, whose constituent counties could raise £15.5 million in 1979–80 by a 1p rate, and Gwynedd which could raise only £383 000, is enormous. It must influence councillors' attitudes towards national park expenditure and explains why the Redcliffe-Maud report (1969) recommended that contributions should be paid by regional authorities. The authors calculate that in 1978–9 the Gwynedd householder with a house having a rateable value of £175 paid 69p a year towards Snowdonia, whereas the householder with a house of the same rateable value in Devon paid 19p towards the two national parks of Dartmoor and Exmoor and a similar ratepayer in Manchester paid 1p towards the Peak.

Additional finance has made it possible to expand the national park staffs. Before 1974, except in the Peak, the only full-time national park staff were a handful of wardens. By 1980 all the parks had a cadre of professional and managerial staff. In 1949 it was thought that a National Park Officer should be a land-use planner, but in 1980 only four of the ten were chartered planners and the others included a naturalist, a forester, a land manager and

Table 5.8 Expenditure on land acquisition and management and access agreements in national parks 1979–80 (from National Park Statistics *County Council Gazette* November 1980 vol. 73, no. 8).

	£	% of NP expenditure
acquisition for public access	228 000[a]	2.6
woodland acquisition	7 000	0.1
access agreements/orders	37 000	0.4
management agreements	32 000	0.4
totals	304 000	3.5

[a] Includes £185 000 in the Peak District, for the purchase of the Roaches (see Chapter 7).

a soil scientist. The shift away from conventional planning and visitor services towards land management and conservation is also shown in the still very small but growing number of naturalists, ecologists, farmers and foresters on the staff. Tables 5.9 and 5.10 show the full-time staff establishment in each park and the breakdown between the various functions. The figures in these two tables have to be interpreted with some caution, as there is no common system of departmental organisation or job classification and often it is impossible to draw hard and fast lines between park management and planning. Many wardens or rangers are providing upland management services; they also play a part in information and interpretation. Seasonal and part-time staff and volunteers play an important part in the visitor services. In 1980, for example, the Lakes Board employed 75 seasonal information staff, 42 weekend wardens, 5 seasonal rangers and 23 people on car parking, litter collection and similar services. Dartmoor, by contrast, employed 20 full-time seasonal staff (11 information assistants, 5 rangers and 4 student researchers) and 1 part-time car-park attendant. Some authorities, notably Snowdonia, have relied heavily on Manpower Services Commission job creation schemes for the unemployed to provide additional manpower, mainly unskilled but including a few professionals. But MSC programmes tend to be here today and gone tomorrow. In 1980 Snowdonia's MSC personnel were cut back from 70 to 14 and Exmoor lost half its ground force because it was unable to satisfy MSC requirements. The MSC schemes are difficult to administer, there is a continuous turnover in personnel and they cannot provide a career for those who turn out to have a liking and an aptitude for the job. Having made these allowances, it is reasonable to conclude from Tables 5.9 and 5.10 that a relatively large managerial, planning and administrative staff in the national parks is responsible for a relatively small force of workers engaged on positive management and conservation in the field.

National park officers are local government chief officers, whose salaries are related to the population of the county, which may bear little or no relation to the demands of the national park or to the responsibilities of the

Table 5.9 National park staff 1980 (full-time staff, excluding part-time, seasonal and temporarily 'frozen posts' and labour provided by the Manpower Commission). F = female, M = male.

	Brecon Beacons		Dartmoor		Exmoor		Lake District		Northumberland		North York Moors		Peak District		Pembrokeshire Coast		Snowdonia		Yorkshire Dales		Total	
	M	F	M	F	M	F	M	F	M	F	M	F	M	F	M	F	M	F	M	F	M	F
numbers	26	10	32	13	28	8	74	26	24	3	35	14	87	43	47	8	74	20	40	14	467	159
totals	36		45		36		100		27		49		130		55		94		54		626	

Table 5.10 National park staff functions 1980 (data from National Park Officers).

	Park management administration		Planning (land use and park plans)		Information and interpretation centres		Visitor centres		Wardens (rangers)		Project and estate management (professional)		Project and estate management (manual)		Total	
	M	F	M	F	M	F	M	F	M	F	M	F	M	F	M	F
numbers	64	80	94	18	35	20	42	28	76	3	59	10	97	0	467	159
totals	144		112		55		70		79		69		97		626	

National Park Officer. Variations at the top affect salary levels lower down. They are aggravated when county council establishment committees refuse to give to the national park staff gradings comparable to those of other people doing similar jobs in the same area. In 1979 salary scales and grades showed, for example, that the planning staff of the Pembrokeshire Coast National Park, who were supposed to be achieving a higher standard of development control than the district councils, are being paid less than their opposite numbers on the district councils' staffs and far less than staff with similar responsibilities in some other national parks. The ecologist on the Pembrokeshire Coast staff was on the same salary scale as the display assistant in the information section of another park. The higher level of professionally qualified staff in the Peak District is clearly related to the fact that salary levels are higher there than they are elsewhere.

In several parks the wardens (or rangers) felt that the high level of enthusiasm they bring to the job, and the enormous demand for open-air jobs, enables the county councils to exploit them by paying low salaries. There is substance in this complaint. Wardens are often maids of all work and labourers too, and dirtying one's hands carries a severe wage penalty in local government. Wardens are 'established', but manual workers are not. Staff charts shown to us named or identified every member of the office staff and the wardens, but never gave the names of labourers or manual workers. They, too, are key workers, but their wages are determined by the level of agricultural workers' wages and are therefore low enough to qualify recipients with children for the poverty benefit called Family Income Supplement. We noted that, in 1978–9, Devon County Council paid the chargehand who led the Dartmoor 'estate gang' 28p a week less than the minimum salary at that time for a 21-year-old local government typist.

It would be agreeable to conclude on an optimistic note. But the NPAs have been required by the 1980 White Paper on Public Expenditure to reduce expenditure progressively in line with other local government environment expenditure by 5% in real terms. As the government only allowed 7.5% for inflation the cut seems likely to prove even more severe in reality. It also seems possible that the contribution hitherto made by government through the Rate Support Grant to the county councils' 25% share will be reduced by the effect of the changes in RSG made by the Local Government, Planning and Land Act 1980.

A new and potentially serious obstruction has been introduced into the procedures for buying land and other capital expenditures. From April 1981 all capital expenditure (including expenditure on vehicles or plant) in excess of £5000 must be covered by 'a central government payments allocation' (PFA 1981). What this means is that even if a national park committee has the money in hand and is within its approved budget it must compete for a share of an allocation made by central government to the local authority for 'environmental services'. The two boards are given their own capital allocations, but the committees have to fight for an allocation (to buy a Land

Rover or to acquire land) in competition with refuse collection, cemeteries, libraries, museums, smallholdings and a host of other local services. Devon and Somerset County Councils learned to their astonishment in 1981 that, in order to buy land at Larkbarrow in Exmoor for £235 000 with a 90% grant from the DOE, they were required to spend £235 000 less on 'other environmental services'. Exmoor National Park Committee even advised the county councils not to proceed with the purchase on these terms and the government made Exmoor a 'special allocation'. Nothing could be better calculated to increase the unpopularity of the national parks than to force them to obtain capital allocations by denying them to other services to which local residents may understandably attach greater importance.

How the new arrangements will work out remains to be seen. But even before these changes were made Lord Ridley, in his valedictory address as chairman of the ACC National Parks Committee, when national park expenditure was nearing what proved to be its peak, said: 'this miserable sum ... hardly qualifies us to use the word "national" when we talk about national parks' (Ridley 1979).

6 *Plans and policies*

Two kinds of plan

It is our purpose in this and the two succeeding chapters to look at the reality of planning and management in the national parks and to do so without involving the reader unnecessarily in the technical complexities or esoteric rituals of planning legislation, statutory orders and circulars. It is the existence of the national park plan that gives the planning system of the national parks a special significance, for it introduced the concept of 'management' into the vocabulary of 'planning'. However, it is not possible to draw a very clear line between 'planning', for which the structure and local plans are the venicle, and 'management', for which national park plans are the prototype. The Department of the Environment's Circular 65/74 (DOE 1974b) offers the explanation that ' "planning" provides a basis for policies and decisions affecting the physical, social and economic environment'. 'Management', on the other hand, means the organisation and provision of services and facilities related to national park purposes 'and the use and management of land and resources to serve these purposes'. But the circular goes on to say that there is a good deal of overlap between planning and management and that each type of plan will influence the other. In short, the distinction is blurred and one has to hunt through both structure and national park plans to identify the policy on any issue. The essential differences would seem to be that planning is more concerned with control, and management with doing; that the structure plan is formal and inflexible and requires the approval of the secretary of state, whereas the national park plan, although submitted to the Countryside Commission for comment, is informal and flexible; and that planning policy, except in the two board parks, lies in the hands of county councils or their planning committees on which there are no appointees of the secretary of state.

In looking first at structure plans, our intention is not to review the entire system (a pastime much enjoyed by the planning profession) but to explain its barest outline and shortcomings for the benefit of those not already familiar with it. The purposes of the structure plans are *first*, to set out the main planning policies and the main strategy for the development and use of land and the provision of essential facilities and services, including transport; *second*, to interpret national and regional planning policies; *third*, to provide the framework and statutory basis for the control of development and for the preparation of local plans.

Forecasts of future population and jobs provide the basis for the ritual of setting up and evaluating alternative 'planning strategies', each one optimising on a particular set of aims. The 'preferred' strategy usually draws something from each of the alternatives in an effort to do the impossible and satisfy all objectives. It is apt to fog or evade those issues or conflicts of interest that cannot be tackled through development control or other forms of positive action within the council's powers and (since 1980) rapidly shrinking resources. The strategy is developed in more detailed local plans for particular districts or subjects (such as caravans) prepared by county councils, district councils or the NPAs. The industrial strategy in rural areas may be developed in non-statutory action plans prepared by local authorities for small-scale industrial development within the Development Commission's Special Investment Areas (Fig. 4.5).

Structure plans contain two kinds of policy statement. The first kind state where and under what conditions development will be allowed, on what scale and of what kind. These statements find expression in proposals to concentrate development in 'key' settlements and to prevent sporadic building in the countryside. They become policy commitments when approved by the Secretary of State and, at least when compared with the second kind, are reasonably clear. They can be implemented negatively through development control, by refusing applications that do not conform to the policy, and to some extent positively through programmes to provide roads, housing, industrial estates, schools and other facilities. Where the authorities have powers but their resources or the will to use them are limited, policies are often heavily qualified by the phrase 'within the limits set by resources'.

The second kind of statement expresses aspirations or intentions that the council has little or no power to implement. Here the structure plan is attempting to play a co-ordinating role, by expressing broad economic and social aims which should influence the decisions of public or private agencies or individuals. Policy statements of this kind, however strongly put, are often ambiguous and even misleading for, as the Association of County Councils complains, the objectives of public and statutory bodies often conflict directly with one another (ACC 1980a). As a basis for decision-making, both kinds of statement leave officers and members a fairly free hand to reach conclusions on the basis of local knowledge and expediency and it is difficult to know what, if any, effect policy statements have had. It has been observed that 'the (structure plan) policies are not framed in such a way as to make any judgement about their practical effectiveness possible. The greatest care is taken to leave every policy open-ended' (Pharaoh & Anderson 1980, p. 117). There are advantages in keeping options open, particularly in times of acute economic instability. But a recent study by a professor of planning who has had long experience as a county planning officer concluded that structure planning had 'only limited influence over major decisions; little relevance to corporate management and implementation programmes; a precarious relationship with local planning and ... a poor public image' (Smart 1980).

We should not be misled by the seductive language of countryside planning into exaggerating the scope of national park management plans. They have been described by the Countryside Review Committee (CRC)* as plans 'for the co-ordinated management of large areas of land' (CRC 1976), or as 'in simple words, getting things done to reduce the conflicts' (Hookway 1977). Their merits are said to include providing 'a far better focus for our agricultural, forestry, water, tourist and conservation authorities than the structure plans can hope to do' (Hookway 1978). But they are concerned with recreation and landscape, not with the management of the total resources of an area or resolving major conflicts over land use. The Countryside Commission's guidance notes on the preparation of national park plans spell this out: 'In every case the fundamental aims from which these policies will be derived will be the two statutory ones of conservation and enhancement of the landscape, and the provision of opportunities for the public to enjoy the park'. While the NPA must show that it has had due regard to the needs of agriculture, forestry and the economic and social interests of the area, 'these broader planning aims will be explained in full in the development plan' (i.e. structure plan), 'and included in the park plan *only in so far as they condition the pursuit of the conservation and recreation aims* and the extent to which they can be achieved'. (DOE Circular 65/74; our italics). Aspects to be covered in detail are listed under 'recreation', 'landscape', 'conservation', 'transport and traffic' and 'other aspects', the last including not only the basic national park warden and other services, but also 'nature conservation' which (characteristically) is treated separately from 'landscape'.

The national park plans are an immense step forward when compared with the void that preceded them. They have escaped from the clutches of the local government officers, civil servants and ministers who scrutinise every dot and comma of the structure plans to ensure their conformity with established dogma or government policy. The need to produce a plan obliged every authority to present (for the first time outside the Peak) a comprehensive picture of the problems, conflicts and opportunities in the park as a whole, an analysis of its physical, financial and human resources, and a phased programme of implementation over five years with its associated costs. National park plans have a greater sense of immediacy than structure plans, which look up to 15 years ahead, and they are intended to be altogether more action oriented.

The process of preparing, revising and implementing the plan has brought the NPAs into a continual dialogue with a wide range of national and local interest groups and with individual members of the public. But the plans also

* The CRC was a committee of civil and public servants, including representatives of MAFF, the Countryside Commission, the NCC and the Forestry Commission, set up within the Department of the Environment in 1974 to review the countryside and pressures on it.

reflect the authorities' sense of weakness and their reluctance in many cases to question or resist government policy, particularly for agriculture, forestry and defence. They reveal the authorities' unwillingness to use even the powers they do have and a determination to produce plans and policies that will be acceptable to all. For this reason the national park plans, like the structure plans, are inclined to fudge issues that provoke conflicts of interest and to imply that with sufficient goodwill conflict can be wished almost out of existence.

A revealing analysis of national park policies is made in the Pembrokeshire Coast National Park Plan which divides them into three categories. 'Active policies' are those which can be initiated by the NPA, if it has the resources and the will to do so, but are limited to practical functions such as the provision of information, interpretative and warden services, car parks, toilets, tree planting and similar matters. The second category consists of 'passive policies' where the NPA has powers but is largely dependent either on other people taking the initiative (for example, by submitting a planning application or applying for a tree-planting grant) or giving their consent (for example, to an access or management agreement). Finally, there are 'general recommendations' where the NPA can do no more than give encouragement or advice (as in farming, forestry and highways) or organise pressure to secure the powers or resources it lacks.

The plans show that the strongest pressures on landscape and wildlife (apart from recreational pressures) come from the policies, grants, subsidies, tax reliefs and development projects of the government departments, notably the Ministries of Defence, Transport and Agriculture, the public agencies such as the Forestry Commission and the water and electricity authorities, and private developers, notably the mining and quarrying companies, backed by the Department of Industry. But for the most part these pressures fall into the area where the NPAs depend on decisions by others or can do no more than offer 'general recommendations'. However, the main thrust of the plans lies in the formulation and implementation of 'active policies' which cover important but essentially tactical matters and do not impinge on the underlying threats to the landscape and life of the parks. There is, therefore, an inverse relationship between the scale of the problems and the capacity of the NPAs to cope with them, as will be seen very clearly from the studies of central government influence in Part 4.

Conservation policies

In their approach to the conservation of nature and natural resources, both structure plans and national park plans reflect the transitional period in which they were written. We are moving over a period of years or even decades from the days when natural resources were squandered without thought for the future to the time when their conservation is the condition of our wellbeing and probably of our survival. When Lewis Silkin, as Minister of Town and Country Planning in 1949, laid down the Silkin test by which new mineral workings in national parks should be developed only in case of compelling national necessity, and even then under strict conditions, he was concerned about amenity and not about the need for society to reduce its demand for resources. He merely wanted to be satisfied that the minerals could not be obtained from somewhere else. Even today, although several of the plans express concern about the demand for minerals and water and lay down conditions rather similar to the Silkin test for their exploitation, the overriding concerns are amenity and recreation. Both afforestation and agriculture now require large inputs of energy and their products (such as paper and packaging) may be wastefully consumed. But the plans discuss neither of them in terms of conserving scarce supplies of energy or other resources, apart from the emphasis on protecting good agricultural land from development.

Nevertheless, a significant change is taking place at least at the level of plan-making and broad brush descriptions. For example, there is a conflict (which is discussed in some detail in Ch. 11) over the use of chemical-grade limestone, which is being quarried on a large scale for use as aggregate in road and other construction. The Peak Board and the Yorkshire Dales Committee object to the waste of a finite resource of great value to industry on purposes for which lower-grade rocks could be used, but they have been frustrated by government in their efforts to secure control over the end use of the product. The North York Moors National Park Plan expresses concern over the proposed rate of potash extraction. All the park plans now take ecology seriously. Several NPAs have ecologists on their staffs, or get ecological advice from the Nature Conservancy Council or the Institute of Terrestrial Ecology. Without exception the plans recognise that conservation goes beyond the protection of scenic beauty and of specially designated nature reserves or SSSIs but extends, in the words of the Lake District's Plan, to the conservation and enhancement of 'the ecological resources of the park as a whole'. Several identify large areas of nature conservation interest, the Devon Structure Plan going so far as to identify the whole of Dartmoor and the Devon portion of the Exmoor National Park as 'nature conservation zones'. But, having started almost from scratch in nature conservation, the plans focus mainly on the need to collect information and to monitor change and the authorities rely heavily on the county trusts for nature conservation to keep them informed. A similar attitude informs their approach to archaeology.

The Peak Structure Plan, as we have seen, is the only one prepared exclusively for a national park. This explains why the Peak Structure and National Park Plans, when taken together, go further than any others (although Dartmoor comes close) in attempting to imbue their policies with a spirit of conservation and to rest them on an ecological base. The natural qualities of the park are seen as the essential qualities to be conserved: 'Many parts of the park are in a near natural condition where man's influence is barely notice-able. Even in the remainder of the park the character reflects a close relation-ship between man and nature. Although man's influence is strong he can still be seen almost as part of nature' (PPJPB 1980, p. 23). To provide a context for land use, land management, conservation and recreation policies, the park (outside the main settlements) is divided into a natural and a rural zone. Broadly speaking, the natural zone is open country where vegetation is almost entirely self-sown with only minor modifications by man. It covers the gritstone moors, shale/grit semi-natural woodlands, limestone dales such as Dovedale and the limestone moors and rough grazings. The rural zone consists predominantly of enclosed farmland and plantation wood-lands and includes farmsteads, isolated dwellings and hamlets. The interface between the two, where enclosed land can revert to rough grazing or rough grazing can be enclosed for agriculture or afforested, is regarded as a shifting frontier of potential change for which special policies will be needed.

In the natural zone the intention is to keep its existing character and quali-ties substantially unchanged. In the rural zone, however, the ecological approach weakens. Nature conservation is not given any priority except in those bits and pieces not required by the farmer for food production and in a few specially protected sites and areas. When the Board's plans proceed from broad analysis to detailed policy, they reveal unconsciously the embar-rassment of the draftsmen when required to produce policies that will muffle serious conflicts of interest. The Board's report of survey (PPJPB 1974) was sharply critical of the narrow focus of the Ministry of Agriculture's policies on making farming profitable and its disregard of the wider role of farmers in the rural community and landscape. Yet, despite all the evidence to the contrary (of which the Board reveals itself to be well aware), the Structure Plan relies on farming and forestry as the major agencies of conservation. Its policy, in consequence, is a masterpiece of so-whattery: 'the policy frame-work . . . will balance all interests, yet enable farming and forestry interests to develop so that they remain profitable enterprises whilst respecting the character of the park and continuing to be the main means of conserving that character' (PPJPB 1980, p. 37). The policy for protecting the few remaining herb-rich meadows might be discussing something as speculative as putting a man on Mars, so tentative is its approach: 'the *possibility* of carrying out *studies* aimed at *identifying* the important areas of herb-rich meadows will be *examined*' (PPJPB 1978a, p. 49, our italics). The Peak Board's attempts to relate specific policies to its ecological framework have been discouraged by the Secretary of State, who has deleted all reference to the natural and rural zones from the policy statements of the structure plan on the ground that they make insufficient allowance for changing circumstances.

The Lakes Board, which firmly attributes landscape deterioration to the decline in the farming population and the vulnerability of the small hill farm, is equally hard put to devise any conservationist farm policies. It is the only NPA to draw attention to the fragmentation and destruction of farms resulting from the sale of holdings in lots, a process encouraged by estate agents to realise a higher price for the parts than could be got by selling the farm as a going concern. But it can offer no hope of doing anything about the land market, beyond discussing the problem with MAFF and the farming interests and hinting that it might in some cases buy viable farms to keep them in being. It is because NPAs face powerful forces beyond their control that all the plans pin their hopes on greater involvement in the major decisions by the farmers and landowners who apply for agricultural or afforestation grants. For this reason all the NPAs have welcomed the Minister of Agriculture's decision requiring farmers to notify the NPA or the Nature Conservancy Council before applying for grant for capital projects in national parks or SSSIs. The arrangements for consultation about afforestation projects, over which the NPAs have no control, leave so much to be desired that the NPAs in the Lake District, Brecon Beacons, Snowdonia, Northumberland and the Peak, as well as the Association of County Councils, have called consistently for afforestation to be brought under planning control. Their reasons for doing so will become apparent in Chapter 10.

Oddly enough, more effort seems to have gone into identifying areas of importance for nature conservation on a broad scale than into the assessment of scenic quality. Only half the authorities identify landscapes that require special protection. The best known of these is probably Exmoor's 'critical amenity area' of moorland, now superseded by new maps recommended by the Porchester report (1977) which forms the subject of our study in Chapter 8. The Lake District Plan has identified 11 broadleaved woodland conservation zones, where the planting of conifers even as a nurse crop is to be resisted. The Brecon Beacons Plan has identified 'landscapes vulnerable to change', either because they are not subject to common rights or because there is a strong presumption inherited from earlier policies that afforestation would be acceptable. All the plans fasten on the need to remedy the wholesale neglect of small woodlands and the loss of hardwood trees. Eight of the NPAs are acquiring broadleaved woodlands, or are prepared to do so, and all are prepared to enter into management agreements for this purpose. The reason for this emphasis on trees is not only the seriousness of the loss of semi-natural woodland but also the opportunity for undertaking practical work of benefit to landscape and wildlife, with grant aid from the Forestry Commission or the Countryside Commission and, above all, without any risk of serious conflict with landowners or farmers.

The abiding fear of the NPAs, which is reflected in all the plans and was expressed openly by chairmen and other members when interviewed, is that any use of compulsory powers, or the merest hint of it, will forfeit the co-operation of farmers and landowners. When it comes to implementation, therefore, the plans rely almost entirely on securing agreement with public agencies and negotiating voluntary management agreements with landowners and farmers. Only in rare cases and only in some parks is the acquisition of land regarded as a serious possibility. It is not very surprising that authorities which are strongly influenced, and in some cases dominated, by farmers and landowners should regard their goodwill and co-operation as the key to implementation. However, the question at issue is not whether co-operation is desirable (for clearly it is) but whether total reliance on persuasion and goodwill does not give those who have property rights in land the power to determine policy. Unless the authorities have the ultimate power to control major land use decisions they are not in a position to 'manage' the countryside. Fears that legislation involving compulsion will be introduced to control the reclamation of moorland or afforestation have been a major influence on the behaviour of farmers, landowners and the Forestry Commission. There is plenty of historical evidence to show that some obstinate donkeys will not be persuaded to move by carrots alone. Sticks are necessary, particularly if the donkey is inclined to insist on an excessive quantity of carrots. In other words, the NPAs need reserve powers to make appropriate orders or to acquire land compulsorily for conservation purposes and the will to use them if necessary.

An independent study of the national park plans led to the following conclusion:

> The long-term shifts in emphasis advocated by Sandford, and supported by the government and the NPAs, must await more prosperous times. Almost nothing will be spent on major landscape conservation; items such as buying land, large-scale management agreements, compensation for expensive conservation work, and subsidies for planting and managing broadleaved woodlands are all way beyond present budgets, even were powers and willing spirits to coincide . . . Proposals for major (landscape) changes, if they prove beyond negotiation are undoubtedly beyond the control of the national park authorities (Dennier 1978, pp. 180–81).

Our study of the conservation policies of the structure and national park plans raises in our minds the question whether the NPAs are not attempting the impossible. They rely almost entirely on persuasion, negotiation, influence, public relations, encouragement and hope to protect some of the finest landscapes in England and Wales against a formidable battery of threats and pressures which are largely financed by public funds and promoted by public agencies.

Recreation policies

National parks are an important element in the spectrum of recreational provision that stretches from the city playgrounds to the mountain tops. Designation does not mean that national parks are more important than other recreational areas. It means that they are different, and that recreation appropriate to their unique characteristics should have high priority within the designated area in terms both of land use and finance. National parks should find an appropriate place in the recreational 'strategies', as they are called, of the regional councils for sport and recreation set up in 1976 (DOE 1976a) and in the more localised recreational strategies of the county council structure plans. But national parks play only a minor role in either.

The 1975 white paper on Sport and Recreation treated the local authorities as 'the primary providers' of recreation, but it was oriented strongly towards the provision of facilities and took an extremely cautious, even negative, attitude towards active countryside recreation. It referred, not to the need to expand opportunities for access to open country, but to the need 'to uphold the tradition of public access to the countryside and coast' – in short, to uphold the status quo by which the public has very limited legal rights of access and is dependent on the toleration of landowners and farmers. It argued that the modification of footpath networks by agreement with farmers and landowners could only be achieved 'if it is clear from the start that the objective is neither to pare down the existing network *nor to enlarge it*, but to adapt it in ways which, taken together, are clearly beneficial to farmer, rambler and rider' (DOE 1975, p. 15, our italics). This policy is applied to national parks by DOE circular 4/76, and reinforced by allocating insufficient resources for a more positive policy. The national park plans tend to concentrate on maintaining or improving selected high priority paths.

In other words, the white paper selected what the Countryside Review Committee, in its paper Leisure and the Countryside published two years later, called 'the low cost approach'. By implication it rejected the alternative possibility, also discussed by the CRC, 'to stimulate demand as a deliberate act of policy, both expanding opportunities and assisting a wider cross-section of the public to "discover" recreation in the countryside' (CRC 1977, p. 5). It is not surprising, given that kind of a lead from a Labour government at the centre, that the structure plans of the shire counties reflect an even more negative approach towards active countryside recreation. As one might expect, the structure plans of county councils in the least prosperous regions are primarily concerned with economic development and do not attempt to articulate the unsatisfied needs of people in the adjoining cities or distant conurbations. They concentrate not on the expansion of recreational opportunities, but on maximising the economic benefits of tourism and protecting local life and the environment from its adverse effects.

Recreation strategies are expressed largely in terms of encouraging tourists (i.e. overnight visitors) because they spend more than day visitors, and indicating where tourist accommodation and facilities should be located. National parks tend to be seen as sensitive areas, from which recreational pressures should be deflected into more robust locations, such as forests, reservoirs, restored wasteland and country parks. For city dwellers without cars, new facilities are suggested on the edges of cities adjoining existing public transport routes, making use wherever possible of derelict land. The budgets for such provision were small or non-existent even two years ago. However, the Chairman of the North Yorkshire County Council, one of those with a nil budget for this purpose, directed the authors' attention to the eventual use of some worked-out gravel pits. The recreation policies of the shire counties are not designed to encourage townspeople of all classes to experience nature in the countryside.

The national park plans, although far more positive than the county structure plans in their approach to recreation, also reflect the preoccupations of local authorities and politicians with tourism (as a business and a problem) rather than with recreation. This can be seen, for example, in the emphasis put by the plans and by NPA members on the need to shift the tourist trade and visitor accommodation 'up market', so that more income is generated by the same number of people. The strongest influences at the time of their preparation (1974–7) were the knowledge that there was a huge backlog of neglect and the fear that the rising tide of car-borne visitors still had a long way to go before it reached a peak. At that time the Director of the Countryside Commission, R. J. S. Hookway, was confidently predicting that recreation pressures would treble in the next 20 years 'right across the board' (Hookway 1975a). The fear has receded, but it has left a strong imprint on recreational policies, which tend to be defensive, reacting to the immediate problems caused by the car, and are not fired with enthusiasm for creating new recreational opportunities.

The recreational 'strategy' that emerges from the plans has three arms. The first is to focus on management schemes for honeypot areas and the provision of car parks, toilets, picnic sites and interpretive and warden services for the mass of car-borne visitors. New opportunities for the enjoyment of visitors are to be within easy reach of the main settlements and roads, or located in such places as new forests or forested reservoir catchments where cars and people can be hidden from view. The second arm is to protect the more remote and fragile areas by not spreading the load of recreational pressure throughout the park. The third arm is the integration of recreational management with the county councils' policies for highways, traffic management (including parking) and public transport. The main concept here is a road hierarchy that distinguishes between the busiest routes for heavy and recreational traffic and scenic routes and roads giving access to recreational areas. But the hierarchies remain largely on paper and the public or shared transport services that provide a theoretical alternative to the private car play a much bigger part in publicity than they do on the ground. This is not for lack of enthusiasm (for NPAs have been outstanding in their efforts to pioneer public bus and rail transport) but is due to lack of means and powers and the public's overwhelming commitment to the private car. Therefore, while the plans reflect interest in experimental ideas, such as park-and-ride, their approach to innovation is cautious. They rely, as they must, on the transport operators and the county councils not so much to improve public transport as to prevent or delay its further deterioration.

The Dartmoor Plan is the most explicit in formulating a recreation strategy with an order of priorities. First comes the management of the heavily used sites; second the reduction of vehicle use in the remote high moorland which is categorised as an 'area with a low capacity for car-borne recreation'; third is the reorganisation of the road, bridleway and footpath systems to relieve congestion and to improve access. The negotiation of management or access agreements comes last because they are expected to take time. The Peak Plan is the only one to base its strategy on the relationship between different types of recreational activity and the ecological characteristics of the 'natural' and 'rural' zones it defines. No facilities are to be provided in the natural zone, but a spectrum of activities is proposed for the rural zone, ranging from small-scale facilities on the edge of the natural zone to motorised land and water sports under strict control in the least sensitive parts of the rural zone.

In general, although there are great differences in detail, the plans tend to focus on the two extremes, catering for the least energetic, car-tied visitors in the busy areas and the more athletic, energetic long-distance walkers, cavers, climbers and others in the quiet areas. The large and growing middle group we identified in Chapter 3, the middle-distance walkers, tend to fall between these two stools. The plans point to the need to improve the footpath systems (although resources are insufficient to clear the backlog of maintenance) but the specific problem of enabling substantially *more* people to have access to wild country, without increasing penetration by the motor car or damaging fragile environments, is inadequately recognised. The plans also betray the difficulties inherent in translating the intentions behind the highway and traffic policies into reality.

The plans rely heavily on the advice given by the Secretary of State in DOE Circular 4/76 that 'the recreational use of the national parks should be related to the particular qualities and capacities of the different types of area'. But the plans give the word 'capacity' a bewildering range of meanings including 'environmental', 'ecological', 'landscape', 'carrying', 'maximum', 'optimum' and 'capacity for cars'. Moreover, the NPAs experience great difficulty in reconciling two apparently contradictory policies that run through all the plans. One is that the recreational use of any area should be limited to its 'capacity', by which is meant the highest level of use consistent with sustaining the quality of the natural environment. The other is that in the remoter or more fragile areas (such as the western dales of the Lake District) recreational activity should be kept at a low level 'irrespective of the capacity of a particular lake or area of woodland to accommodate large numbers of people' (LDSPB 1978). For example, the Peak Structure Plan states that it is 'desirable' to keep the activity in some areas *below* their capacities so as to offer the visitor the opportunity to experience some dales in peace without great crowds and the inevitable restraints of management.

In his modifications to the plan, the secretary of state rejected this point of view. He said in effect that capacity and the desirable level of recreational use are one and the same thing. So they are, but he failed to make it clear that the capacity of any one place is not a fixed quantity but a variable that can be controlled within wide limits by management. Where to fix the limit is largely a subjective matter as opinions differ on what is tolerable, but above all it is a policy or a political decision, not a technical one. Where it is impossible to divert visitors away from popular beauty spots or viewpoints, such as Dovedale or Snowdon, the only practical solution may well be to increase the capacity of the site to absorb visitors by minimising the damage they can do and preventing the degradation of their experience. But in other limestone dales and on other mountains the policy may be to keep the capacity low.

As we saw in Chapter 3, there is both a limit to what management can do and a price to be paid if visitors are to find beauty spots more or less in their natural state at the times it suits them best to go there – that is, at holidays and weekends. There is the cost of physical works and visitor services, which has often been evaded in the past; there are bound to be restrictions on where visitors can park or walk; and they cannot expect to have the place to themselves. In Dovedale, for example, people will have to walk a little distance from their cars when the management plan becomes fully effective, and they will also have to keep to the path and to one side of the river. They will be discouraged from exploring the dale sides and will view the natural beauty of the far bank from a distance (PPJPB 1978a). But there is ample evidence that people are ready to pay this price.

On the other hand, the view that the quieter and remoter areas cannot absorb more visitors without a fatal loss of character, implicit in decisions not to 'spread the load', does not always stand up on examination. There are some quiet and remote areas of which this is true and the case for retaining a very low level of use so as to protect fragile environments and habitats from excessive human interference makes sense. We would endorse the view, put most clearly in the Lake District Plan, that visitors should be able to choose from a range of experiences, from the crowded beauty spots to the wilder areas where nature can be experienced with few signs of human influence. But there is much good walking country in nearly all the national parks where, with a very modest input of management, more walkers could be accommodated without doing any harm to farmers' interests or causing any lasting damage or detriment to the distinctive natural character. The Snowdonia Plan is explicit in giving lack of resources as the reason for concentrating management on Snowdon, the Glyders and Cadair Idris and for not encouraging people to walk on the Arans and other little-used hill and mountain areas that constitute the greater part of the open country in the national park.

The Arans – a superb range of hills in the south of Snowdonia – offer safe and delightful ridge walks of a mountainous character in an environment that from the standpoint of nature conservation is less fragile than that of Cadair Idris or Snowdon. But if one asks why more people do not walk there, one of the answers one gets is that the farmers do not concede *de facto* access, but expect walkers to keep to the very few public rights of way. The lack of management to sort out the problems that visitors create only strengthens the farmers' intransigence. Nor is Snowdonia unique, as many landowners are cool towards increasing recreational use of their land. The Peak Board is franker than most authorities in acknowledging that the attitude of landowners is one of the factors limiting access. It has found no evidence that existing access arrangements have diminished the value of the grouse moors and its policy is to negotiate more such agreements if it can. 'However, there is a reluctance by owners to allow public access to the most valuable grouse moors such as the heather moorlands, *few of which are currently subject to access agreements*' (PPJPB 1978a, p. 65; our italics).

Lack of resources and the fragility of the ecosystem can, therefore, be no more than a pretext for a policy the roots of which lie in the reluctance of the NPA to face up to the difficulties created by some farmers and landowners. Arthur Gemmell, a member of the Yorkshire Dales National Park Committee, has cited various cases where rights of way had been obstructed by farmers or landowners (in one case for more than five years) without any effective action by the Park Committee. He summed up the problem of improving or extending the footpath network by saying 'it seems nothing can be done without the agreement of the landowners and occupiers who can successfully defy the park authority' (Gemmell 1980). This explains why the government's intention, stated in the Wildlife and Countryside Bill 1980–1 to entrust local authorities with the final say in issues concerning rights of way is regarded by the Ramblers' Association as a betrayal of the public's interest, and was defeated in the House of Lords.

Opening up the Arans and similar areas would call for a whole package of measures. The upland management service would have to be introduced, on a modest scale, legal rights of access extended to commons and to private land and rights of way extended to form a comprehensive network related to car parks and bus services. The need to start and finish a walk from the same car park severely circumscribes walkers' opportunities. The absence of public transport in the Arans, for example, rules out the most exciting linear walks for all but the most athletic. The public needs comprehensive bus and rail timetables, of the kind pioneered in the Peak, and maps similar to Stile Publications' admirable walkers' maps for the Yorkshire Dales, designed by Arthur Gemmell, which tell the walkers everything they need to know for their comfort, safety and enjoyment.

One of the main omissions from the national park plans is a strategy or a plan for walkers, riders and cyclists. Nowhere has the full potential of a national park for these activities been assessed and developed into a costed plan and programme. The elements of such a plan are to be found in every park. The economic recession and the rising cost of energy give the park authorities an opportunity to give a higher priority to the needs of walkers, riders, cyclists and the users of shared or public transport. They could re-allocate such resources as they have and, when this country has a government less obsessed with reducing the number of people employed in public service, could bid for more resources to provide the transport, management and information services required. We do not want the fells to be way-marked with colour-coded signs, or to take the adventure out of finding one's way. Nor do we want visitors to trample the hay, knock down the walls or disturb the stock. But the evidence is that people who walk regularly are not causing the problems – and farmers know this. As one farmer told the Exmoor National Park Committee, and as other farmers have told the authors, the 'ramblers' are welcome because they understand the country-side.

The basic problem is that active, informal recreation has never been given the financial or the legislative back-up that it requires, either in central or local government. Enactment of the private members' Bills presented by the late Arthur Blenkinsop MP and by David Clark MP in 1979 and 1980, to secure legal rights of access to 'open country' as defined in the 1949 National Parks and Access to the Countryside Act and to commons, with appropriate safeguards, should be part of a long-term programme for walkers, cyclists and riders. Improved access, restraints on the private car, the promotion of shared forms of transport and the provision of inexpensive accommodation would have a double pay-off. If combined with social policies to benefit those who are disadvantaged socially and geographically it would encourage the active enjoyment of 'the living landscape behind the view', particularly for those who have no ready access to cars. And it would build up an alternative, more economical access system in preparation for the 21st century.

Development control

The conservation of the built environment is accepted by every NPA as a major element in its conservation strategy. It tries to achieve its aims by establishing conservation areas, making grants (on a very modest scale) to conserve buildings of architectural and historic interest and, above all, by the control of development. Unfortunately, although development control takes a large slice of the time and energies of the members and staff of NPAs, central and local government have not bothered to evaluate the claims made for it. The result is a dearth of hard information. The most recent study of development control in the countryside concluded that 'the welter of words over the past five years . . . has served to expose the lack of factual information about what is happening' (Blacksell & Gilg 1981). The crude statistics about the number of planning applications and the proportions of refusals and appeals can be misleading. They say nothing about the quality of the decisions or of the buildings that are permitted or refused. Nobody knows how many would-be applicants are deterred by the NPAs' reputation, to quote the words of a parish councillor in the Lake District, for 'turning everything down'. In fact the rate of refusals in the Lake District is very close to the average of 21% for all national parks and there is no solid evidence to show that NPAs are very much 'stricter' than other planning authorities (Table 6.1).

Table 6.2 shows that the disparity between the authorities in the number of decisions is immense. The Northumberland National Park has so few applications (around 50 a year) that development control is handled for it by the Planning Department of the County Council. At the other extreme in the Lake and Peak District it is normal to have 900 decisions or more in a year.

The relatively small scale of development in national parks can be judged by comparing the total of 6247 decisions in 1978–9 with the total of 579 160 by other planning authorities in England and Wales for the same period. National parks cover 9% of the land area of England and Wales but gave rise to only about 1% of the applications. Table 6.1 suggests that after local government reorganisation in 1974, the new NPAs took a tougher line initially (by rejecting 31% of all applications in 1974–5, or 50% more than in 1972–3), but within two years had reverted to the former level.

It was the almost unanimous view of those we interviewed that the main success of the NPAs has been to restrict urban development in the open countryside and that the national park designation has been a material factor in this success. Development control does not, of course, protect the countryside against agricultural, forestry or other practices that require no planning approval. Whether in fact NPAs have been more successful than other rural planning authorities in restricting the urbanisation of the countryside is a difficult question to answer. The Sandford report (1974) was very critical of the laxity of development control in some national parks before reorganisation. In several parks, chairmen and other members regard the problem of buying out earlier planning permissions for quarries and caravan sites as insoluble. Our impression that the planning system has confined the spread of urban areas and concentrated new development in the countryside within existing settlements is confirmed by Blacksell and Gilg. But they also say that it has failed to reverse the general decline in the dispersed village pattern that used to typify rural Britain and has had only a limited success in mounting a cosmetic operation to preserve local building styles and materials. 'Both the design and materials of rural housing are now little different from that in urban areas, even in protected landscapes such as national parks' (Blacksell & Gilg, *op. cit*).

Blacksell and Gilg's evidence also suggests that development control is not very successful in steering homes or jobs to the areas selected for growth in the structure plan. Between 1963 and 1974, 34% of the new housing development in the Dartmoor National Park was located in non-key areas and only 22% in the three key centres. The balance was in open country, the high proportion being accounted for by the very heavy demand from people

Table 6.1 Planning decisions in national parks 1972–80 (from National Park Statistics, *County Council Gazette*).

	1972–3[a]	1973–4[a]	1974–5	1975–6	1976–7	1977–8	1978–9	1979–80
(1) decisions	9362	8888	5854	6058	6324	5606	6247	6224
(2) refusals	2014	2310	1815	1544	1371	1286	1371	1316
(3) (2) as % of (1)	22	26	31	25	22	23	22	21

[a] Decisions for 1972–3 and 1973–4 preceded reorganisation.

Table 6.2 Planning decisions by national parks 1979–80 (from National Park Statistics, *County Council Gazette*, November 1980).

National park	1 Decisions	2 Approvals	3 Refusals	4 3 as % of 1	5 Appealed	6 Appeal dismissed or withdrawn	7 6 as % of 5
Brecon Beacons	635	519	116	18	27	22	81
Dartmoor	593	454	139	23	36	24	67
Exmoor	293	256	37	13	5	5	100
Lake District	1164	827	337	29	93	78	84
Northumberland	68	65	3	4	0	0	–
North York Moors	721	572	149	21	30	25	83
Peak District	909	747	162	18	24	19	79
Pembrokeshire Coast	646	488	158	24	21	17	81
Snowdonia	669	547	122	18	21	12	57
Yorkshire Dales	526	433	93	18	13	9	69
totals	6224	4908	1316	21	270	211	78

working in Exeter and Torbay and the needs of agriculture in an area where farms are scattered and dwellings in short supply. But the evidence also shows Dartmoor to be one of the two areas in Devon where the refusal rate for development in open country is substantially higher than elsewhere. Development control can succeed in preventing sporadic housebuilding near towns and cities but not in promoting growth in selected centres if the prevailing commercial trends and policies for schools, water supply, sewerage, post offices, transport and health services are pushing in the opposite direction. The key settlement concept, moreover, is now being challenged on the ground that it is socially retrograde and economically wasteful. It requires major investment in the key areas, imposes large costs on those who are forced to go there and fails to use the facilities in the existing settlements. The lower the rate of growth, the stronger these arguments are said to be (Gilder 1980).

The efforts of the Peak and the Lakes Boards to make new housing available to local people illustrate the difficulties inherent in trying to achieve social goals through planning policy and development control. In response to protests that local people could not get homes, the Peak Board's Structure Plan published in 1976 contained a series of policy statements limiting new housing to local needs. Peter Shore, the Labour secretary of state, proposed to delete them all from the plan and Michael Heseltine, the Tory secretary of state, did so. He struck out the social criteria for housing policy but retained the aesthetic ones. Both insisted that under present planning law, planning applications must be decided by the merits of the proposed use, not by reference to the user. From 1965 the Lakes Board had tried to halt depopulation by allowing more houses to be built in the towns and larger villages. The policy had some success in crude statistical terms, in the sense that between 1961 and 1971 the decline in population was halted. But by 1975 second homes accounted for more than 30% of the housing stock in some of the remoter parishes (LDSPB 1978). Although about 5000 new houses were built in the Lake District between 1962 and 1976 (2000 of them for letting by district councils), thereby increasing the housing stock by nearly 50%, the total population remained static and the depopulation of the remoter areas continued (LDSPB 1978).

The failure of this policy led the Board to give priority from 1977 onwards to building for local needs. This was to be achieved primarily by requiring developers to sign agreements under Section 52 of the Town and Country Planning Act 1971, restricting the ownership or occupation of new houses to people who live or work in the national park. But until a case has been tested on appeal, it is uncertain whether the board is legally entitled to insist on the condition. Local estate agents argue that the policy concentrates demand on existing houses and building plots, thereby inflating their prices still further. The most claimed for it by the National Park Officer is that it has slowed down the trend towards rural depopulation and second-home ownership, without bringing home ownership any closer for the lower-paid Lakelander (Clouston 1980).

Since then, rural authorities have been confronted by the government's 1980 Housing Act requiring them to sell council houses, which offer local people the only chance of obtaining a house at a moderate rent. Despite protests from NPAs and Tory-controlled shire county and district councils, the Act makes only one concession to the rural areas. Section 19 offers district councils two ways of restricting the resale of council houses in national parks, AONBs and such 'rural areas' as may be designated by the secretary of state. Resales may be confined for 21 years to people who have lived or worked for three years in the 'region' (as defined by the secretary of state) in which the house is situated. Or the council may retain a right to buy the house back at market value should the owner decide to sell it within 10 years. Neither option does more than defer the moment when the house passes out of local control. In the face of such policies, the moratoria and cutbacks in council and housing association programmes and the sharp rises in council house rents, the issue of who should occupy a few high-priced new *private* houses pales into insignificance.

Moreover, the concept of 'local need' raises other problems that are equally difficult. It is national policy to allow building in the open country only if an agricultural, forestry or other local need can be established. The NPAs are now looking with more favour on the farmer who wants to supplement his income by converting a barn to holiday accommodation or by providing some caravans or chalets, but they have great difficulty in deciding whether a farmer has a 'need' to supplement his income. They are reluctant to investigate means themselves and MAFF's approach to the determination of agricultural need is not of much help, for MAFF interprets 'need' in technical, not social terms. Normally it will not certify an agricultural need unless it regards a farm as a full-time viable holding. Although ADAS officers individually often try to help, the system operates against the small farmer whose greatest need may be to earn some non-farm income, probably from visitors. Another difficult question is whether, should social 'need' be established, a planning authority should approve on social grounds development that it would reject on planning grounds. Planning authorities are very reluctant to refuse permission for development for which MAFF has established an agricultural 'need' (meaning that it is required by modern farm practice). 'Once a genuine agricultural need has been established a planning authority is almost powerless to oppose the development because it will be over-ruled on appeal by the Secretary of State' (Blacksell & Gilg 1981, p. 129). However, to permit holiday accommodation for which the farm has an economic need can alienate public opinion if permanent homes are being refused on the ground that they put a strain on services. In the Lake District the view now seems to prevail that in the last analysis the survival of the farmer is more important than a blemish on the Lakeland scene. But it is not an easy line to hold, for (as one committee chairman put it) some farmers are 'pretty fly' at spotting a loophole in the relaxations in their favour and then driving a flock of sheep through it – thereby forcing the planning authority to deny the relaxation to others. The truth is that development control is a clumsy and inefficient way of achieving social goals in the absence of positive social policies and programmes.

Conclusive evidence that development control has been totally unable to keep alive the use of traditional building styles, forms and materials even in national parks is also provided by Blacksell and Gilg. Their survey shows that in Exmoor, whereas 79% of pre-1945 buildings had slate roofs, 80% of post-1945 buildings were tiled. In Dartmoor 86% of all pre-1945 houses were of two or more storeys, but 79% of all those built since 1945 were bungalows. Rendering has taken the place of stone almost everywhere. The visual evidence in all the parks confirms the findings of the Exmoor and Dartmoor surveys. Development control has been reasonably successful in conserving buildings and groups of buildings from earlier times and much of the familiar street scenes in the centres of towns and villages. Some care has been taken in siting buildings in the countryside, or screening them with new planting. But not even the Peak and the Lake District Boards, despite their attempts to achieve higher design standards and to require the use of stone in certain cases, have been able to avoid the suburbanising effects of building 'off-the-peg' bungalows within the ruling standards of road widths, privacy distances, turning circles, hammerhead reversing areas, visibility splays, parking provision, lay-bys, lamp standards and access for dustmen or fire engines and all the other technical requirements that make it impossible to retain the feeling of intimacy and cohesion that distinguishes earlier development.

The answer is not, of course, to try to compel 1980 man to build in the styles and materials of another period for 1980 purposes at 1980 costs. Nor is there necessarily anything wrong with a tiled, rendered, single-storey house, even of a standard design, if it can take advantage of the site and sit easily in the landscape. The tragedy is that so many of the new buildings deny their occupants the internal and external benefits of good design, and damage or even destroy the harmonious relationship between man and nature that the earlier buildings ensured by the use of local materials, traditional construction and an unconscious sense of place.

Planning authorities should stop trying to compel developers to imitate the superficial characteristics of the vernacular, but should try to inculcate (as some do) some of the basic lessons that the vernacular has to teach about siting, design, craftsmanship and landscape. The appearance of a building is not a cosmetic, like powder and paint, to be changed at the whim of a committee that has heard the designer's case only through the summary of an official. The appearance is one aspect of a total design that springs from the resolution of the conflicting requirements of the user, the site, the structure and the bank or the building society. Committees need a better understanding of design in terms of basic criteria, that are susceptible to more objective judgement than appearances – whether a building is in scale and sympathy with its surroundings, how it relates to the access system and to public and private spaces around it, whether it provides an efficient shelter and filter between the internal climate and the elements outside, and how well the spaces have been arranged to meet the needs of users and others who may be affected. The façade of a building is not just a pattern of door and window openings in a wall, to be re-arranged to suit the fancy of the committee or the officers, but expresses a reconciliation between internal arrangements and external factors. Where buildings satisfy a range of such criteria the area of dispute over appearances can be diminished greatly (Smith 1976).

The authors listened to the Dartmoor National Park Committee engaging in a debate over the colour of the roof of a new addition to a road haulage depot in Moretonhampstead. A large business operating on a national scale had been allowed to grow by stages on an abandoned railway station. It could only be approached through the park along picturesque B roads that are totally unsuitable in width and alignment for heavy vehicles. Clearly, the Committee had had to make difficult decisions. Moretonhampstead is a key centre, but had failed to attract new jobs. How could the committee refuse to allow a successful enterprise to grow? It could in theory revoke the planning consent and buy the business out, but where would the money come from and what would the local people say if the national park committee sent the business and its jobs elsewhere? If the business were to stay, should the roads be widened, as the county surveyor proposed, which would be contrary both to government policy and to the national park plan? Expediency usually wins in such cases. The business grows, the roads are not widened, jobs are bought at the cost of the environment and the public's enjoyment of it, while the national park committee debates the colour of the roof. It strains at the gnat but swallows the camel.

7 *Getting things done*

Introduction

The purpose of this chapter is to give a realistic picture of what can and cannot be done (or can be done only in very exceptional circumstances) to implement national park plans and policies. Because there has been so much rhetoric in recent years about the successes of countryside management, the chapter is focused on the mismatches between promise and performance, while recognising the successes that have been achieved. It deals very briefly with the basic warden and information services and then with the three main techniques by which the NPAs hope to achieve their aims – the management of publicly owned land, practical, problem-solving management projects and management agreements.

A key role in implementing every management project or agreement and in sustaining the visitor services is played by the wardens, or as the Countryside Commission and some authorities now prefer to call them 'rangers'. The adoption of the American term 'ranger' with its suggestion of the wide open spaces reflects the tendency of the wardens to specialise in visitor management and interpretation of the countryside. The parks are in fact divided between those who see their rangers as part of the visitor service and those who see wardens playing a multiple role including close liaison with the farming community and physical labour on land and management projects. It is significant that the Countryside Commission's advisory booklet on countryside rangers (CC 1979a) places the management of the natural resources of the site, including the protection of wildlife, ninth on the list of 16 duties normally undertaken by rangers. The first eight are concerned with informing and advising the visitor (the no. 1 job), public relations, managing interpretive facilities, supervising the visitor for his own safety and the good of the countryside and ensuring good relations with neighbouring landowners and farmers by, among other things, 'preventing trespass'.

In practice many wardens and rangers are torn by conflicting loyalties and handicapped by confusion about their role. Their functions are defined somewhat vaguely by Section 92(2) of the 1949 Act as being to secure compliance with byelaws, to advise and assist the public and to perform 'such other duties . . . as the authorities may determine'. But there are no byelaws except over the very limited areas owned by the NPAs or subject to access or management agreements. The government conceded powers in the Wildlife and Countryside Bill to enable wardens 'to advise and assist the public' on *de facto* access land (HL, 13 February 1981) and to operate on footpaths and bridleways on the understanding that no additional wardens would be employed (HL, 16 February 1981). Wardens have no powers (as rangers do in the US, for example) to enforce byelaws. They operate over wide areas by tacit agreement, and rely with considerable success on persuasion, and on bluff that is easily called. A Snowdonia study suggests that if wardens concentrate on helping the visitor, they may fail to win the farmers' confidence (Fitton 1978). If, on the other hand, they lean over backwards (as some do) to be the farmers' friend, they run the risk of doing too little for the visitors. They are supposed to be the eyes and ears of the NPA, but in our experience communications between the wardens and the national park office can be limited, and communications with the members almost non-existent. Wardens tend to combine a high level of personal commitment with a strong sense that the park would be better managed if those in authority listened more to their representatives in the field.

The stress now being put on the wardens' interpretive role reflects a shift since reorganisation away from the provision of large, sophisticated visitor or field study centres, of which Brockhole on Lake Windermere and the Brecon Beacons Mountain Centre are the most spectacular examples, towards simpler, more direct and cost-effective ways of helping visitors to extend their knowledge and experience. Modest information centres, interpretive panels at points of interest, self-guided trails, guided walks, farm open days and a steadily expanding range of printed material have raised the standard of service. Without warden and information services of a high standard to win the understanding and co-operation of both residents and farmers, no management projects or agreements are likely to get very far.

The management of public land

A high proportion of the land in national parks is owned by public or semi-public bodies, but very little of it is owned by the NPAs or managed primarily for national park purposes.

Table 7.1 shows that although 26.9% of the land is in some form of public or semi-public ownership, only 1.16% of the area is owned by the NPAs. The area managed by them through agreements is as yet barely measurable, although at the time the statistics were published a few more agreements were in preparation. If the area owned by the Nature Conservancy Council is added, the area publicly owned and managed specifically for the purposes of conservation and recreation is only 1.38%.

There are two practical reasons why NPAs should take a positive attitude to land acquisition. The first is that they are now claiming the role of land managers for their entire area. Their plans are supposed to co-ordinate the land management strategies of all the public and private landowners and this must lead to some involvement in detailed implementation. But an authority

Table 7.1 Public and semi-public landownership in national parks 1980 (from National Park Statistics, *County Council Gazette*, November 1980, vol. 73, no. 8; Table iv.2, *Digest of recreation statistics*, Countryside Commission 1979; information from National Park Officers).

	Brecon Beacons	Dartmoor	Exmoor	Lake District	Northumberland	North York Moors	Peak District	Pembrokeshire Coast	Snowdonia	Yorkshire Dales	Total	Percentage of total NP area in public or semi-public ownership by body
total area of national park (ha)	134 420	94 535	68 636	224 300	103 119	143 200	140 400	58 350	217 100	176 113	1 360 173	100
National Park Authority	563	1984	1623	8336	132	865	1281	193	775	84	15 836	1.16
other local authority (1979)	20	409	142	c.2000	–	190	NA	155	19	–	2935	0.22
National Trust	4733[a]	1882	6605	50 500	756	1200	14 200	1741	19 218	1721	102 556	7.54
Central Electricity Generating Board	–	–	–	–	–	–	–	–	2496	–	2496	0.18
Forestry Commission	11 122[b]	1807	1340	12 734	22 379	23 690	2600	720	33 850	424	110 666	8.13
Nature Conservancy Council (1979)	779	302	–	303	36	–	139	313	1140	11	3023	0.22

											totals	%
Water Authority	8624	4710	332	15 560	1202	271	–	19 940	1955	221	52 815	3.88
Ministry of Defence	1006[c]	3987[d]	–	461[c]	22 700	768	2710	1200	300	716	33 848[d]	2.4
Department of Environment	332	–	–	–	–	–	–	–	–	–	356	0.03
Welsh Office	–	–	356[f]	–	–	–	–	–	–	–	356	0.03
Duchy of Cornwall	–	–	–	–	–	–	–	–	5263[g]	–	5263	0.39
Duchy of Lancaster	–	–	27 952[h]	–	–	5032	–	–	–	–	27 952	2.06
other	798[i]	–	2422[j]	–	–	–	–	5032	–	–	5032	0.37
											3220	0.24
totals	27 645	43 033	12 820	89 894	47 205	32 016	5832	39 360	65 016	3177	365 998	26.91
% total NP area in public and semi-public ownership by park	20.57	45.52	18.68	40.07	45.78	22.36	9.99	28.03	29.96	1.80	26.91	–

[a] Including 283 ha leased from Ministry of Defence.
[b] Including land leased from Welsh Water Authority.
[c] Including 283 ha owned by National Trust and 64 ha managed by Nature Conservancy Council.
[d] Excludes 10 000 ha owned by Duchy of Cornwall and used under licence by MOD.
[e] Land and foreshore: clearance and firing rights over a further 484 ha, mostly foreshore.
[f] Land at Larkbarrow acquired in 1979–80 for transfer to Exmoor National Park Committee with 90% grant in 1981–2.
[g] Vaynol Estate, sales to tenants under negotiation.
[h] Excluded from national park and Countryside Commission statistics, but shown in Sandford report (1974) and unchanged since then. Includes 10 000 ha leased to MOD.
[i] 57 ha British Waterways Board, 741 ha National Coal Board.
[j] Includes Crown Estate Land.

that owns no land is an amateur in the land management business and its staff lack credibility as expert advisers, co-ordinators or negotiators. Yet only five parks (Dartmoor, Exmoor, North York Moors, the Peak and the Lake District) are even modestly in the business of land management with an estate of 775 ha or more apiece. None of the authorities manages nature reserves and by a strange legislative quirk the two boards do not even have the power to do so. The second reason is that public acquisition is often the only way to solve complex management problems created by a combination of conflicting land uses, divided land tenure and the presence of landowners or users who are unable or unwilling to co-operate with each other or with the public authorities. But landownership is an acutely sensitive and a highly emotive subject. The figures in Table 7.1 reflect the view, most strongly put to the authors by members of the Yorkshire Dales National Park Committee and clearly shared in some other parks, that the public acquisition of land, even by a freely negotiated voluntary agreement, is an evil to be avoided at almost any cost and therefore should play little or no part in the implementation of national park policies.

Table 7.1 brings out both the enormous differences in the pattern of public landownership from one park to another and the huge potential for implementing public policies on publicly owned land were it possible to alter the management objectives of the different agencies and departments and to co-ordinate their policies and programmes. In the Lake District around 40% of the land is now in some form of public or semi-public ownership, and in Dartmoor and Northumberland the proportion is about 45%. The Duchy of Cornwall, the Ministry of Defence and the Forestry Commission own most of the hill country in Dartmoor. The Forestry Commission owns more than a fifth of the Northumberland National Park and nearly as big a proportion of the North York Moors. The Ministry of Defence owns another fifth of Northumberland National Park and one of the most sensitive stretches of the Pembrokeshire Coast. The Central Electricity Generating Board and the Forestry Commission hold key areas in Snowdonia.

The Forestry Commission, which increased its holdings in national parks by 8608 ha in 1979–80, is the largest landowner with 8.13%. But it is being overtaken by the National Trust (now 7.54%) which received 13 000 ha of land in 1979 on the Derwent Fells and Scafell in the Lake District, that had been accepted by the Treasury in lieu of death duties from the estate of Lord Egremont (NT 1979). The Trust is by far the largest landowner in the Lake District, where it owns or manages under protective covenants about a fifth of the land. It is also a substantial owner of land in Exmoor and it has significant holdings in every park except the North York Moors. It owns over 6 times as much land as the NPAs and can legitimately claim to have done far more to conserve the landscape.

The National Trust is a hybrid, semi-public, semi-private body. It is a private corporation, supported by its 800 000 members, private donors and the general public with subscriptions, gifts and legacies which they would not give to the state or to a local authority. It manages its estates as if it were a traditional, paternalistic private landowner of the old school. It is free to pursue its own policies in conformity with its mandate and often does so, in the experience of many of those we have consulted, without too much regard to involving the NPAs or anyone else in its decisions. But it is a public body because it owes its special status to an Act of Parliament of 1907, which defines its functions as to preserve 'land and buildings of beauty and historic interest for the benefit of the nation'. The Act gives it the unique power of declaring its property inalienable, so that it cannot be sold, given away or expropriated even by government without the express approval of Parliament. It can give more permanent protection to land and buildings than can a public authority.

In exercising this power, the Trust is not accountable to anyone except its members. Its constitution ensures that it is a self-perpetuating oligarchy over which neither its membership nor its tenantry can exercise much control (Lowe *et al*. 1979). But its public purposes are almost identical with those of the national parks and make it a major element in the 'public estate' although it is not, in fact, accountable to the public. The Trust is an ingenious political device that secures the conservation of scenic beauty without disturbing the landed interest, which in turn supports the Trust and exercises great influence within it.

The large concentrations of public and semi-public land, coupled to the influence of the Ministry of Agriculture, the Forestry Commission and the Department of Industry, explain why, as long ago as 1967, R. J. S. Hookway (later the Director of the Countryside Commission) called for legislation to require each public landholding body 'to make available for public inspection its management plan or policy for each distinctive area' (Hookway 1967). Neither central nor local government took the challenge seriously. The idea that public authorities should publish their land management plans was watered down to the idea that they should, in the words of the Sandford report (1974) 'review the extent to which their holdings could make a positive contribution to the achievement of national park purposes'. In September 1977, Dennis Howell, the Minister of State, asked government departments and agencies holding land in national parks and the National Trust to implement Sandford's recommendation by undertaking 'a comprehensive review in consultation with the NPA' and to consult the NPA at an early stage on any new substantial management action or physical developments (CC 1979e). His request that land should be managed to protect wildlife, safeguard natural beauty and facilitate recreation was made 'without prejudice to the body's primary statutory function'.

There is no evidence that any of the public bodies paid much attention to this modest request. None of the replies has been published, but they are believed to have expressed the complacent view that the authorities were already doing all they could to manage their land sympathetically and to consult NPAs at an early stage. The NPAs are, as a rule, consulted on specific issues, but our studies suggest that the agencies normally take a policy decision first and begin consultations thereafter. The Countryside Commission found Howell's letter encouraging, but the response disappointing. In its comments on the national park plans two years later it urged the NPAs themselves to initiate the discussions, so that agreed statements of policy could be included in the revised plans due in 1982–3 (CC 1980d). Hookway's hopes that government bodies might publish their land management plans seem to have faded. The problem remains, in the words of one National Park Officer, that even where the top management in bodies like the Forestry Commission appear to be helpful, the 'primary function of timber or water production takes priority at the lower levels of management: nothing less than making support of national park aims a statutory responsibility on a par with the existing statutory duties will ever have much effect'. The policies of the Forestry Commission and the Ministry of Defence are examined in Chapters 10 and 11.

Practical projects

All the national park plans describe a range of what Hookway (1978) has called 'practical, problem solving, action-oriented projects over limited areas of countryside'. Some are being prepared as local plans, others as management schemes and others are less advanced. They may involve wide-ranging consultation with local people, private interests and other public agencies. Often they call for a combination of all the techniques and skills at the disposal of the county and district councils and the park authorities – land acquisition, management and access agreements, development control, tree planting, litter collection, work on the ground to protect or restore heavily used areas, traffic management and bus or rail services. Wardens, information services, ecologists, foresters and ground staff all have their parts to play. The characteristics of management projects can be illustrated by describing the Snowdon Management Scheme and the Upland Management Experiment.

Snowdon (Wyddfa in Welsh) is the highest mountain in England and Wales. It is also one of the main British centres for mountaineering. The mountain railway provides a spectacular railway journey but culminates in squalid surroundings at the summit. All six of the paths leading to the summit are badly eroded. Walkers pass continually in large numbers over the major national nature reserves (NNRs) on the mountain plateau. Conditions on the road encircling the mountain are chaotic at peak times. The Welsh county councils which sought to prevent the establishment of a unified national park board in 1952 had provided by 1974 a total ground staff of two part-time men for the whole national park, of which the Snowdon massif is but a small part and by no means the only area that is subject to intensive recreational use.

The Snowdon Management Scheme (SNPC 1979), introduced with the collaboration of the Countryside Commission, the Welsh Development Agency and Gwynedd County Council, has a five-year programme from 1979 to 1984 to tackle a multiplicity of problems in a combined operation. The scheme begins, as all area management projects must, with traffic management. It aims to reduce congestion by providing car parks at the base of the mountain, linked to Pen-y-Pass and other access points by the successful Snowdon Sherpa bus service. The summit will be enhanced by laying out new paths from the railway station to the cairn, landscaping and (if the railway company co-operates) improving the station building and its facilities.

An immense amount of work is needed to restore the six main footpaths, and to develop techniques that will discourage walkers from passing through the sensitive NNRs en route to the summit. The information services have a big part to play in persuading inexperienced walkers to control their dogs and their litter, and not to walk inadequately shod or clad on the mountain. The scheme will employ 40 people when fully developed. For 1980–1 it had already a staff of 31, including four wardens and 23 ground staff. The whole project is the responsibility of a senior project officer. The cost is estimated at £600 000 over five years. The cost of a 'face lift' and improvements to the dilapidated and unsightly summit building was estimated at £316 000 in 1980. Providing mains water, electricity, telephone and a septic tank would bring the total to £1 million. The NPA decided to offer the private railway company £7500 (SNPC 1981) to improve the lavatories. It is a measure of the exceptional nature of the Snowdon scheme that in 1980 nearly a quarter of the permanent ground staffs of all ten national parks are employed on it. Even so, it seems improbable that the arrears of work can be overtaken in five years. No resources are in sight for similar projects badly needed in other parts of Snowdonia and elsewhere. The Manpower Services Commission (MSC) has refused to continue the scheme that has done similar work on Cadair Idris for several years – despite the fact that the MSC has the money to pay for it and jobs are needed urgently by road maintenance men made redundant by the local authorities.

A very curious aspect of the Snowdon situation is that the Welsh Office, which acquired a large part of the mountain when it bought 5243 ha (13 000 acres), for what now looks like the bargain price of £40 000, from the Vaynol Estate in 1967, has spent the past 13 years trying to sell it off to the tenant farmers, subject to access agreements, retaining only a small area at the summit and some land for car parks for the NPA (WO 1967, 1971, 1979). By July 1980, 6 out of 22 agreements had been negotiated although not legally completed. In the meantime, the Estate has been allowed to fall into a shocking state of dereliction that is all too visible from the railway. The Welsh Office, having got the key to management in its hands, threw it away.

The first Upland Management Experiment (UMEX 1) was launched jointly by the Countryside Commission with the Ministry of Agriculture (but not the national park board) in the Lake District in 1969 and in Snowdonia in 1970. The objective was 'to test a method of reconciling the interests of farmers and visitors in the uplands by offering financial encouragement to farmers to carry out small schemes which improve the appearance of the landscape and enhance the recreational opportunities of the area', and to assess what effect this had on farmers' attitudes towards landscape and recreation (CC 1976, p. 1).

The key to the success of UMEX proved to be the appointment of a project officer, who was given a wide discretion to take practical steps to solve the problems he had identified and to spend modest sums of money without reference to a committee. For the first time in the history of the national parks, an officer appeared on the scene offering jobs and money and handing over the cash to the farmers even before the job was done. The Ministry of Agriculture lost interest in UMEX when James Prior killed the Ministry's Rural Development Boards in 1970. But the first stage was sufficiently successful to be extended by the Countryside Commission and the NPAs into a wider area for a second stage (UMEX 2) with a full-time officer independent of MAFF.

After the second stage, the Upland Management Service (UMAS) was incorporated into the national park administration in the Lake District in 1976. It employs two full-time officers with a budget (1980–1) of £115 000. It has taken over responsibility for the network of footpaths and other rights of way from the local highway authority and therefore much of its work is repair and maintenance jobs that are done in other parks by wardens and ground staff. In Snowdonia, the service has a less clear identity. The Welsh-speaking Agricultural Liaison Officer has to spend so much time advising on farmers' planning applications and improvement schemes, negotiating access agreements on the Vaynol Estate and organising farm trails that he has little time left for upland management. Government-imposed economies froze the appointment of an assistant officer in 1980. The agricultural liaison budget for 1980–1 is £8000, a trifling sum, although some 'upland management' work is carried out by wardens and ground staff and charged to different headings in the budget.

The success of upland management (particularly in the Lake District) has been considerable in terms of minor works such as erecting stiles, bridges and gates, repairing walls and fences and repairing or diverting paths. It has provided some much needed part-time jobs and has, for example, enabled three men who would otherwise have left to remain in Patterdale. It has changed the attitudes of many farmers from resentment towards a remote bureaucracy into something approaching enthusiasm for a service that knows them, helps them and employs some of them. Every Lakeland farmer the authors met spoke highly of UMAS and some of this popularity has even rubbed off onto the board itself.

The concept of the area project run by a project officer has been extended on a modest scale to other national parks, to heritage coasts, to a few AONBs and to some areas on the fringe of large cities or conurbations. In all of them it has proved to be a successful technique for getting minor recreational works done and easing the friction between farmers and visitors. UMEX and UMAS have every right to claim that they have been successful on their own terms. But it is also necessary to recognise the limits of these schemes which have been spelt out clearly by the Countryside Commission itself in its reports on the Lake District and Snowdonia experiments (CC 1974, 1976 and 1979f). 'It was evident during the course of Stage 1 that it would . . . only scratch the surface of the real social and economic problems faced by the farming community . . . with less and less indigenous help to keep the fabric of the area intact there was every chance of the dereliction accelerating' (CC 1976, p. 4).

The Commission's report on Snowdonia (CC 1979f) demonstrates that the friction between farmers and visitors can be attributed in part to the total failure of the NPA, in earlier years, to make even the most elementary provision for visitors to park their cars or to make their way on to the hills in the absence of the traditional footpath system found in the Lake District. The Snowdonia farmers faced far more difficult conditions and had to cope with far more day trippers from coastal resorts than the Lakeland farmers but got less help from the NPA. The fundamental problem in Snowdonia, as we saw in Chapter 4, was found to be the sheer lack of labour on the farms as a result of a drop of 79% in the number of full-time farm workers, of 70% in the number of part-time workers and 20% in the number of farms in the eight years from 1965 to 1973 (SNPC 1975).

The irrelevance of upland management to the solution of deep-seated economic and social problems, revealed by UMEX 1, led the Commission and the Lakes Board to commission a study of the Hartsop Valley. The report presented a vivid picture of an ageing, declining community living on the margin of survival, whose farmers had neither the time, the labour, the economic incentives nor the capital to maintain landscape features that brought no financial benefit to them (Feist *et al*. 1976). The report rejected the theory that management agreements could solve these problems and looked rather to a small-scale tourist development and a permanent upland management service to provide some additional support. But its main conclusion was that neither the Lakes Board nor the local authorities could solve the problems: 'it is imperative that the government should provide financial and legislative backing for measures aimed at attacking rural housing shortages, assisting hill farmers and maintaining a national asset' (p. 113). Much the same conclusion about the limits of 'countryside management' was reached in a report on farmers' responses to experiments in 'countryside management', sponsored by the Countryside Commission in the urban fringe. Farmers tolerated the experiment, even welcomed it, as long as it did not impinge on their economic interests. The report concluded that, as regards the broader problems of land-use conflict, '. . . the potential of countryside management has hardly begun to be explored' (Newby 1979b).

The House of Lords Select Committee on European Communities has asserted that in the upland management experiments in the Lake District and Snowdonia 'hill farming and recreation were reshaped so as to accommodate and improve both' (HL 1979). It was precisely because upland management could not even attempt to reconcile countryside policies or reshape hill farming that the Lakes Board urged major changes in agricultural policy and initiated a third experiment – UMEX 3 – which attempts to integrate tourist development and landscape and nature conservation on 25 farms with Ministry of Agriculture grant-aided farm development plans. But the authors sensed a lack of enthusiasm and confidence concerning UMEX 3 on the part of officers of MAFF, the NFU and even the board. The reasons are not hard to find. It will be several years before UMEX 3 will yield results. Neither MAFF nor the board seem to accept full responsibility for managing it and it is up against fundamental problems created by central government policies and economic trends.

Management agreements

'Management agreement' is a much-abused term. NPAs have used it to include: informal maps agreed with the timber-producing interests to define areas where there are presumptions for or against afforestation; unwritten arrangements by which landowners provide picnic sites; *de facto* access to land without any agreement; permissions granted for the use of footpaths; and bargains struck with farmers by which the authorities maintain footpaths, repair walls, build stiles and provide a warden service. The Countryside Commission defined a management agreement in 1973 as 'a formal written agreement between a public authority and an owner of an interest in land (the term 'owner' may here include lessees and occupiers) who thereby undertakes to manage the land in a specified manner in order to satisfy a particular public need, usually in return for some form of consideration' (Feist 1978, p. 1).

In attempting to assess the contribution that management agreements can make in resolving conflicts, three inherent limitations were spelt out in a report to the Countryside Commission (ibid.). First, management agreements cannot remedy deficiencies in the system, such as conflicting policies in central government, lack of co-ordinating or notification machinery or lack of money. Second, certain problems admit of no solution without legislation or the exercise of legal powers. Third, management agreements cannot tackle the causes of adverse situations, such as the underlying structural problems of agriculture in marginal areas. Feist saw the main value of management agreements in holding situations or initiating experiments: 'Without adequate back-up powers, management agreements do not offer much in the way of long-term security for the public interest or public investment.' (p. 29).

In situations where there is no serious conflict of interest, mutual respect and goodwill often create a climate in which it is possible to achieve results, albeit on a small scale. The multitude of informal agreements made under the Upland Management Service in the Lake District, or by similar means elsewhere, show that large dividends of goodwill and co-operation can be earned by small investments of money and manpower on minor works. Informal, year-by-year conservation agreements in Exmoor (of which there were two in 1980) fall into the same category. The management agreement at Upton Castle in Pembrokeshire Coast National Park illustrates the case where the owner of a stately home who cannot afford to keep up the grounds is relieved of the cost of doing so, in return for opening them to the public. At Deeper Marsh on the River Dart, Dartmoor National Park Committee has agreed a management plan with the landowner, the commoners and the SW Regional Water Authority to improve parking, protect grazing areas and restore the river banks to the mutual benefit of all concerned.

All the NPAs can show examples of formal or informal agreements for tree planting or the leasing or purchase of land for this purpose. The Peak Board has a long lead here and has acquired a considerable area for planting. The Brecon Beacons have shown what an enterprising authority can do in a short time. By using Forestry Commission small woodland grants for schemes between 1/2 and 10 ha and getting free labour from the Manpower Commission to supplement its staff resources, it was able by 1979 to enter into 17 management agreements covering 50 ha and carried out over 140 smaller schemes ranging from 1 or 2 to 200 trees. By 1979–80, it was planting 16 ha a year. The cost to public funds in 1979–80 was £26 000. Owners, on average, had to meet only 20% of the cost. 'Management' worked because there were no serious conflicts of interest, the NPA offered favourable terms and the schemes made only small demands on the pockets or the energies of the farmers or owners. The limitations of this particular enterprise are obvious. The 'best guess' that the National Park Officer can make is that the rate of planting is about one-third that required to halt the progressive loss of woodland. But the contributions from public funds are falling and one must question whether private owners will follow the lead so ably given by the NPA once the cuts in public funds and Manpower Services Commission projects made in 1979–81 take effect.

The most extensive management agreement in any national park is the result of the Treasury's agreement to exempt 6235 ha (15 400 acres) of moorland on the Nawton Tower Estate in the North York Moors National Park from Capital Transfer Tax (CTT) (NYMNPC 1978). Since the 1976 Finance Act, land of outstanding scenic, historic and scientific interest can be exempted from CTT provided that the character of the land is protected and public access secured. The Estate secured the exemption by entering into a management agreement with the NPA by which the Estate will be managed for sheep, grouse and informal recreation. An agreement that might have cost £30 000 a year indexed linked against inflation on the terms negotiated in Exmoor (see Chapter 8) costs the NPA nothing. The true cost is hidden, being met by the Treasury forgoing large sums in CTT once in every generation.

In fact, very few management agreements in the Countryside Commission's meaning of the term have been concluded in situations where there have been basic conflicts of interest. The cases referred to in later chapters, such as Stowey Allotment, Glenthorne and Haddon Hill in Exmoor and the Cnewr Estate in Brecon Beacons, not only confirm all Feist's reservations about management agreements but demonstrate some other difficulties. The most serious, apart from their cost, is the impossibility in most cases of persuading landowners and farmers to sign away for all time their right to improve or develop land. So far as we know, no management agreements exist that permanently protect a resource, because owners insist on break clauses at frequent intervals (usually three years) when the agreement can be terminated by either side and the terms of compensation renegotiated. The adoption of 20-year agreements without breaks in the Exmoor compensation guidelines (see p. 247) goes some way to meet this objection. Another difficulty is that the negotiation of agreements consumes a lot of time and professional manpower. Four years after the publication of a report recommending management agreements at Monsal Dale, a honeypot in the Peak (Wager 1976), the board had not been able even to begin to negotiate the 20 or so leases, contracts and agreements required.

But the most formidable difficulty is cost. Where the owner is an 'unwilling seller' he has to be 'persuaded' by paying him 'over the odds'. As things are, the money is simply not available to conclude agreements on any large scale. The Nature Conservancy Council said so explicitly in its annual report for 1978–9 and so did the Countryside Commission in its evidence to the House of Lords Committee on EEC rural policies in 1979. The Nature Conservancy Council points out that 74% of the 130 000 ha (320 000 acres) of National Nature Reserves in the UK are managed under nature reserve agreements or leased from the owners on terms negotiated in the 1950s or 1960s (NCC 1980a). Agreements and leases affecting 44 of the 164 NNRs expire in the 1980s. To renegotiate them the NCC may well have to pay in a single year as much as would have bought the land 20 or 30 years ago.

The contrast between the success of short-term, informal, small-scale understandings and the failure to conclude a single major long-term management agreement led Hookway who was their original advocate (Hookway 1967), to change his mind. He told the Town and Country Planning Summer School in 1977 that experience had demonstrated 'that it is better to have informal short-term agreements that achieve something, than to go for long-term formal bonds, with positive and negative covenants and all the other legal refinements, *which no one seems to want . . .*' (Hookway 1977, our italics). Management agreements, he said, should be 'short-term contracts subject to continuous review'. But if management agreements are informal, short-term, small-scale arrangements, what is left of Hookway's view (1967) that they provide 'the most promising technique to bridge conflicting public and private interests in an area of land'? The answer seems to be not much.

There would seem to be only two ways of resolving basic conflicts of interest once the considerable possibilities of offering sweeteners and re-adjusting financial and fiscal incentives have been exhausted. One is to make statutory orders regulating the use of the land, for which precedents exist in Tree Preservation Orders (TPOs) and Access Orders. TPOs are entirely negative and do not ensure lasting management. The power to make access orders has been useful in persuading owners to conclude voluntary access agreements. The other way is to acquire the land. It is significant that the number of access agreements has been falling in recent years because authorities have preferred to buy land to secure access (Gibbs & Whitby 1975). Two recent cases at The Roaches in the Peak (Roaches 1977–80) and Larkbarrow in Exmoor (see Chapter 8) illustrate both the need to acquire land and the difficulty of doing so.

The Roaches are a gritstone outcrop in an extensive area of heather moorland providing popular climbs as well as attractive scenery and habitats for Britain's only wild wallabies. On the break-up of the Swythamley Estate, The Roaches were put up for auction in 1977 as part of a lot of 460 ha (1134 acres) of moorland and were bought by two agricultural entrepreneurs for £60 000. The Peak Board tried to buy at the auction but the District Valuer imposed a limit of £45 000 on its bid. The buyers stocked the moorland with 2000 sheep and spent £30 000 (half of it provided by MAFF grant) on constructing a stockproof fence several miles long around the perimeter. Climbing was prohibited and signs were erected warning that trespassers would be prosecuted. The Board tried to negotiate an access agreement, but the owners would offer access to only 81 ha (200 acres) at a non-negotiable price. In this case the Board had two trump cards. It was one of only two NPAs with reserves big enough to finance a purchase on this scale and, although it stated publicly that it did not intend to use its power of compulsory purchase to secure access, the knowledge that it might do so in the last resort was probably the decisive factor in persuading the owners to sell about 405 ha (1000 acres) to the Board for £185 000 in December, 1979. The Board is preparing a management plan to re-establish the moorland ecology and provide for public access (NPN 1980a). The owners' speculation in national park land paid off handsomely.

In 1979 the Fortescue Estate informally told the Exmoor National Park Committee that it was contemplating agricultural improvements at Larkbarrow in the very heart of the former Royal Forest of Exmoor. When the Committee initiated discussions on a management agreement it was informed that the Estate was already negotiating the sale of the land. It was pointless to offer a management agreement to an owner who was contemplating a sale and equally pointless to negotiate one with a buyer who would have to be compensated over and above the purchase price. The Estate was willing to sell 357 ha (880 acres) for £235 000, but the NPA did not have the money to buy. Tom King, the Minister of State for Local Government and an Exmoor MP, arranged for the government to buy the land under Section 14 of the National Parks Act 1949. The land has been leased back to the Estate and the freehold will be transferred in 1981–2 to the National Park Committee, which will have to find only 10% of the price. The terms of the lease ensure both the conservation of the landscape and public access. The deal is an excellent one if it is considered reasonable to pay £235 000 for 880 acres of rough grazing, thereby compensating the owners for the loss of the agricultural grants they would probably have received had they reclaimed the moorland. This solution was only possible because the owners were willing sellers and the government was willing, for reasons discussed in the next chapter, not only to put up the capital but to treat Exmoor as 'a special case' by providing a 90% grant.

The case of Llangorse Lake in the Brecon Beacons provides a fitting conclusion to the discussion of 'getting things done'. It illustrates in an extreme form the difficulty of implementing planning policy, of enforcing planning decisions under the present law and of initiating management policies in the face of non-cooperation. Llangorse is the largest natural lake in South Wales, set in a natural amphitheatre of great beauty formed by the western end of the Black Mountains. It is small (only 0.75 square miles) and very shallow, being rarely more than six feet deep. It is of exceptional wild-life interest, noted for the variety and rarity of its bird, fish and plant life and for microscopic fauna and flora. The sediments on the lake bottom contain fossil remains from which a detailed record has been made of the 7000 years of ecological history in which it has evolved an intricate balance of animal and plant life. It was designated as an SSSI by the Nature Conservancy in 1954 (a piece of information omitted from the national park plan) and recognised as a Grade 1 site in 1977. It is 'unique in Wales and notable among all British Lakes' (Cundale 1979). But it is also said to be dying, apparently for much the same reasons as the Norfolk Broads – eutrophication from agricultural fertiliser run off and domestic sewage plus excessive and conflicting recreational usage. Yet the Nature Conservancy Council has neither undertaken the research required to establish the cause of its decline nor taken action to establish a National Nature Reserve and the NPA has been unable to control recreational use.

The valley in which Llangorse lies has become the biggest pony-trekking area in Wales, with 23 centres. Because the Welsh Water Authority restricts the recreational use of its numerous reservoirs, Llangorse Lake is the only water in South Wales open to the public for water-skiing and power boating as well as for fishing, sailing (the club having 146 dinghies), canoeing (by 12 centres) and pleasure boating (four commercial operators). Efforts made since 1954 by the NCC and the NPA to establish the lake as a statutory nature reserve by agreement with the Lord of the Manor, who owns the lake bed, have come to nothing. The Brecon County Council attempted to make byelaws to bring power boating and water-skiing under control in 1971, because over-intensive use was believed to be causing disturbance, noise, danger and damage to the ecology of the lake. The byelaws were resisted by the recreation and commercial interests and rejected by the minister, who preferred to rely on voluntary rules framed by a Lake Users' Committee. The Countryside Commission, the Sports Council and Brecon County Council combined to commission a Recreation Survey (DART 1973) because they were concerned at the damage being done to the lake, the spread of caravans (then numbering about 200) and the public use (or abuse) of the common which provides the only access to the lake – on a busy day for more than 1000 cars. The survey established the facts about recreation, but led to no action. The community councils of Llangorse and Llangynidir repeatedly complained of breaches of planning laws, traffic congestion and disturbance. The local people, though some profited from the visitors, felt they were being overwhelmed.

The attractions of Llangorse led two adventure holiday companies controlled by a Midlands businessman, P. G. Lawrence (PGL Voyages Ltd and PGL Young Adventure Ltd), to develop Llangorse and a nearby hill farm as adventure centres for children, primarily for water sports and pony-trekking. From the start in 1962, PGL's principle was to open a site first, or extend it, advertise its holidays, take bookings and apply for planning permission later. Its response to planning refusals or enforcement notices or even the rejection of its appeals by the minister was to extend its operations. The facts were established at public inquiries held in 1973 and 1976 into 12 appeals by the PGL companies against enforcement notices or refusals (WO 1973, 1976). Although PGL had planning permission in 1976 for a total of only 200 holidaymakers and staff, it took bookings for 600 guests and had 770 people on the sites. It had permission to use 5.5 acres, but was using 15.5. Its associated pony-trekking centre had trebled in size in three years and was the largest in Europe, with 200 ponies churning up the tracks and causing traffic jams of up to half an hour. But for PGL this was only the beginning. It was planning for 2000 bedspaces by 1980. The NPA informed the Inspector at the inquiry that Mr Lawrence

> disregards planning law and it is questionable whether he will abide by any permissions granted. He is able to disregard the rules because his business is not capital intensive ... The law related to enforcement, particularly the ability to stop the unauthorised use of land or buildings pending the determination of planning applications and appeals, is inadequate (WO 1976, paras 129, 136).

The minister upheld the NPA on all essentials in these appeals, but little changed. A further six-day inquiry was held in 1978 following 24 more appeals by the two companies against planning decisions and enforcement notices. With minor exceptions, the minister again upheld the NPA, in particular insisting on the closing down of two holiday centres and refusing permission for another (NPN 1979/80). The NPA hopes that these decisions will at last bring the commercial exploitation of the area under some control. In the meantime, there have been some improvements also in the management of the common and a new sewage plant to reduce eutrophication will soon be in operation. A representative Llangorse Working Group has been studying various ameliorative proposals at infrequent intervals since 1975. But Llangorse has still a very long way to go before it even has a comprehensive management plan on paper. It could have had one many years ago had the NPA been willing and able to acquire all the interests in the land and the lake. The NPA is said to be making some progress quietly through negotiation on regularising and tidying up two recreation sites adjoining the common, but the main issue of management of the lake remains unsolved as the owner is reluctant to change anything. The Nature Conservancy Council (but not the NPA) could acquire land compulsorily for purposes other than access, but it has not attempted to do so.

Llangorse Lake is dying . . . However, this natural progression has been greatly speeded up by human factors. Changes that may normally take several millennia have occurred within a few decades at Llangorse and other similar lakes . . . It may be difficult in present conditions to reverse the process or even conserve the present stocks of wildlife. It is perhaps sad to reflect that we do not even know what some of these stocks are. Sadder still that conservation measures are baulked by conflicts of interest rather than by technical problems (Cundale 1979).

8   *Conflict in Exmoor*

The background

The controversy over the reclamation of moorland in Exmoor, which culminated in the Porchester Inquiry of 1977, has raged with varying degrees of intensity for nearly 20 years. It has acquired a symbolic significance out of all proportion to the importance of Exmoor on the national scene, in terms either of its agricultural output or its recreational use. It has done so because it raises issues of principle and policy. All parties to the conflict have seen Exmoor as creating, or threatening, precedents that could be applied in other parts of the country where the interests of landowners or farmers are in conflict with those of others. The specific circumstances are local. The implications are of national significance.

It was inevitable, given the conditions in Exmoor, that it would become the scene of a conflict between those to whom the national park purposes were primary and those to whom the moorland was an agricultural resource, a source of livelihood, of profit or of capital gain. Many farmers argue that there is nothing more beautiful than a green field and it is undeniable that the beauty of Exmoor lies in the interlacing of the patchwork of fields in the valleys with the woodlands in the combes and the moorland on the hilltops. But the moor provides a totally different experience from enclosed pasture – the feel of the ground under foot, the scents, the wildlife and above all the sense of wildness and space. Had it not been for the moorland, Exmoor would not have been designated a national park in 1954. With Dartmoor, the moorland of which is more than twice as extensive, Exmoor forms one of the only two large areas of more or less wild, open country in southern England. It is a precious but fragile resource. In 1954 the moorland was about a third of the Park's area. Today it is about a quarter, so cut up into fragments that even the smallest further encroachment of reclaimed pasture may destroy the sense of limitless space that is already largely a visual illusion. The Nature Conservancy Council has argued systematically since 1977 that there should be no further significant reduction or fragmentation of the remaining areas of moorland if viable wildlife populations are to be maintained (NCC 1980e).

The mild climate, the lowish altitudes, the flattish tops of the moorland plateau, some relatively good soils and the lowest rainfall of the western national parks provide favourable conditions for reclamation – so favourable that when hill farming subsidies were introduced in 1949 strong pressure had to be exerted by the NFU to persuade MAFF to include the Exmoor upland within the hill line. Nor is there anything new in the reclamation of Exmoor. The Midlands industrialist, John Knight, who bought 15 000 acres (6000 ha) of the royal forest in 1815, established new farms and changed some soils on Exmoor from waterlogged peats, silts, clays and an iron pan into well-drained soils in little more than a century (Curtis & Maltby 1980). The conflict arose in the 1960s because modern technology gave a new impetus to reclamation at the time when the rapidly shrinking remnants of the moor had been recognised as a wildlife, scenic and recreational resource of national significance. The introduction of the tractor, liable to overturn, and new techniques for direct drilling instead of ploughing have led to the reversion of the steeper slopes to bracken, gorse and scrub and encouraged the cultivation of the flatter tops. But the tops constitute the moorland plateau that is the heart of the national park – Exmoor's major open space. Behind the tractor stands the Ministry of Agriculture, encouraging reclamation and new technology through its advisory service and offering both grants of 50% or more for reclamation or other improvements and headage payments on additional stock that can be carried on the improved land. MAFF's advisory service, capital grants and the headage payments for hill livestock in less favoured areas under EEC Directives are discussed in more detail in Chapter 9.

1962–8: the first round

The struggle between 'farming' and 'amenity' interests, to use over-simplified jargon words, began in 1962 when it was proposed to reclaim 220 acres of heather moorland at Countisbury on the coastal ridge where the moor stands 1000 ft above the Bristol Channel. The three national park committees (from 1954 to 1974 Exmoor was administered by two National Park Committees of the Devon and Somerset County Councils with a Joint Advisory Committee (JAC)) rapidly discovered that they were without financial resources and completely powerless to deal with the situation*. There was no notification system. The Devon Committee asked the Devon County Council to buy the Countisbury moorland compulsorily, but the council refused to do so. The JAC asked the Minister for Housing and Local Government to make an order (known as an Article 4 Direction) to bring fencing over 12 520 acres of moorland under planning control, but he too refused. Ministers were invited to visit Exmoor, but were 'too busy' to do so until 1968.

* The factual information about the proceedings of the Exmoor National Park Committees from 1962 onwards is derived from their minutes, from the file of evidence to the 1977 Inquiry by Lord Porchester which is available at the Department of the Environment, from his report (Porchester 1977), from the Hansard reports of the Countryside Bill 1968, from committee papers available to one of the authors as a member of the Committee, from contemporaneous notes and from transcripts of tape recordings made by the National Park Officer of certain committee meetings.

In an attempt to establish the facts about reclamation, the Exmoor Society commissioned a scientific study of land use and vegetation from Geoffrey Sinclair, who had surveyed the area already for the Second Land Utilisation Survey of Great Britain. His map and his report, *Can Exmoor survive* (Sinclair & Bonham Carter 1966), showed that the moorland had shrunk from 58 745 acres in 1957—8 to 49 655 acres in 1966, mainly because of agricultural reclamation.

But the National Farmers' Union and the Country Landowners' Association published a statement (NFU & CLA 1966) which accused the Exmoor Society of grossly exaggerating the problem. They estimated the loss of moorland to agriculture at 'less than 100 acres a year'. However, a minute of the JAC (February 1967) records that officials of MAFF and the Devon and Somerset County Councils accepted Sinclair's figures as being accurate to within plus or minus 3%. In 1969, on the basis of Sinclair's survey, officers of the national park committees prepared a map of the areas of moorland 'critical to amenity', as defined by a wide range of criteria. The 'critical amenity area' extended to 43 657 acres (17 675 ha). The NFU and CLA refused to recognise the map as a definition of areas in which there was any presumption against reclamation and held up its publication until 1974. By then reclamation and revisions of the map had reduced its area to about 40 000 acres. It was not until Porchester reported in 1977, that the NFU and CLA had to recognise that Sinclair's figures had been vindicated. But the argument was not really about figures. The real conflict was over the rights of property and the rights of farmers to exercise an unfettered control over agricultural operations in a national park. The NFU and CLA asserted that 'where conflicts of interest do arise, agriculture should be accorded first place in the order of priorities'. It was the right and the duty of farmers 'to expand their enterprises and to improve their productive capacity to a maximum' (NFU & CLA 1966).

The first phase ended with the passage of the Countryside Act 1968. When the government published the Bill omitting the powers that the JAC had asked for, the JAC resolved that unless powers to control ploughing and fencing were provided, the government should repeal the provisions of the 1949 National Park Act requiring the NPAs to preserve and enhance the natural beauty of the parks. But the NFU and CLA lobbied successfully to persuade the government to ignore the requests from the Exmoor National Park Committees and the Devon and Somerset County Councils for powers and resources to control the moorland. At the last moment, when the Bill was in the Lords, the government introduced two new clauses without consulting either the park committees or the National Parks Commission. As a result, Section 14 empowered the Secretary of State for Housing and Local Government (later for the Environment) to make Orders applicable to specific areas requiring farmers to give six months' notice of their intention to convert moor or heath to agricultural land. Section 18 made it possible for agreements to be concluded for access to open country that would prevent its conversion to agricultural land.

Lord Kennet, the Minister responsible, held out the prospect that Section 14 would encourage farmers to negotiate agreements. When asked what would happen at the end of the six months if it had not proved possible to negotiate an agreement, he argued that the county councils could make compulsory purchase orders or access orders. As the law then stood – and still does, despite the recommendation of the Sandford Committee (1974) – compulsory purchase orders can in fact only be made to secure access, not to conserve or enhance natural beauty. But Lord Kennet gave the game away when he resisted an amendment moved by Lord Foot to make it unequivocally clear that CPOs would in fact be available if negotiations failed. Lord Kennet objected that 'to make the conservation of the appearance of a given piece of land the explicit purpose of a compulsory purchase operation would be a big change in principle. *This would not be accepted by the other side of the deal, by the landowning and farming interests*, without a good deal of bad blood and sourness' (HL 1968, our italics). Back-up powers had been vetoed by the farming and landowning interests. But Lord Kennet had the grace to tell the House of Lords in 1981 (commenting on the loss of moorland in Exmoor and the North Yorks Moors): 'here we are 13 years later and I think the figures we have heard today are pretty conclusive. It has not worked. I think now it was an error of judgement on our part' (HL 1981).

1968–74: the lull before the storm

The new Act seemed to herald the introduction of a statutory notification system for the whole of the critical area through 'blanket' Orders under Section 14. But to avoid compulsory notification, the NFU and CLA proposed a 'gentleman's agreement' under which they would advise their members to notify the park committees of their intention to reclaim moorland. A revised critical amenity area map would indicate the area within which the voluntary notification system was to apply. The Ministry of Agriculture agreed to advise farmers that they should notify the committees voluntarily. But the agreement did not bind members of the NFU or CLA, still less non-members, and no funds were provided to smooth the path to agreement.

The JAC struck a bargain on these terms. No blanket Section 14 Orders were ever made, although intense ill feeling was aroused in 1972–4 when the minister, at the request of the Somerset Committee, made orders against two farmers, one of whom was co-operating with the NPA in negotiating an agreement while the other was concerned with land that was not within the agreed critical amenity area. The voluntary notification system worked reasonably well in the sense that the great majority of farmers honoured it by notifying their intentions. But as a device to control reclamation it was a complete failure. Nineteen proposals were notified between 1969 and 1973, but notification did not lead to a single agreement on the lines Lord Kennet had anticipated, nor was compulsory purchase ever considered. The most that can be claimed for the voluntary system in these years was that some farmers were persuaded to modify the boundaries of the reclaimed areas to make them more sympathetic to the contours. The controversy died down in the early 1970s because the poor economic situation in hill farming brought reclamation to a full stop. In 1973 MAFF paid out no grants for reclamation and in 1974 it only grant-aided the reclamation of 36 acres.

At this time MAFF was required (as were all government departments and public bodies) by Section 11 of the 1968 Act to 'have regard to the desirability of conserving the natural beauty and amenity of the countryside' in the exercise of its functions. But MAFF interpreted this obligation in the most formal way. It treated all applications as confidential and argued that it was statutorily obliged (despite Section 11) to pay grant for all proposals that satisfied agricultural criteria. It gave the farmer the best advice it could in *his* interest and, although it advised the farmer to discuss his proposals with the national park committee, it declined to do so itself. An officer of MAFF who explained its *modus operandi* to the committee in 1975 said that, as far as he knew, MAFF had never advised a farmer against reclamation on grounds of amenity or conservation. For its part, MAFF was not contradicted when it told Lord Porchester that it had never been asked by the NPA to withhold grant on Section 11 grounds. Nobody, in short, tried seriously to control reclamation.

1974–7: war breaks out

On the surface, a more hopeful period began with the reorganisation of 1974, when a single committee of the Somerset County Council, equipped with new resources in money and staff, assumed responsibility for the whole park. But, whereas before 1968 the NPAs and county councils had been pressing for more powers, the new committee was strongly imbued with the philosophy that it wanted no more powers and, as Lord Porchester was later to point out, would be unlikely to use them if it had them. Both the chairman and the vice-chairman were prominent landowners and the first National Park Officer was a retired major-general who farmed on the edge of the national park.

The committee's first job was to prepare the national park plan. Before doing so it commissioned the report on moorland management (to which we referred in Chapter 2) from John Phillips, an expert on heather management recommended by the Institute of Terrestrial Ecology. Phillips urged the desirability in the long run of retaining low-input low-output farming systems, as opposed to the intensive systems associated with reclamation, and strongly urged the committee to identify those areas of high quality moorland which should not be enclosed or reclaimed under any circumstances. He concluded 'unless strong and constructive steps are taken along these lines Exmoor as it is today will go on being eroded, until one day people will wake up to the fact that it has disappeared except as a name on the map' (Phillips 1977, p. 89). These conclusions were obviously valuable ammunition in the hands of those members who wanted the national park plan to conserve the moorland. But they were most unwelcome to the National Park Officer and to the vice-chairman of the committee who was also chairman of the national park plan steering group. Not only were all the discussions of the draft national park plan held in private, but the Phillips report was withheld from members until the discussions had been concluded – allegedly on the ground that members might have been 'confused if they received it out of context' (Wilson 1976).

The national park plan's policies for agriculture, finally adopted in 1977, gave the first priority to maintaining and strengthening liaison with farming and landowning interests (ENPC 1977a). The plan expressed its support for conservation in terms of 'encouraging' the conservation and enhancement of 'traditional features of the agricultural landscape, on the basis of full financial compensation should any constraints be set upon the profitable practice of agriculture'. It relied on voluntary management agreements and, as a secondary course, on land acquisition to protect the critical amenity area.

The suppression of the Phillips report and attempts to censure a member of the committee for publishing its 'confidential' conclusions attracted local and national publicity and stirred both local and national amenity groups, the Exmoor Society and the CPRE, into action. It helped to precipitate a crisis because it coincided with two major proposals in 1976 to reclaim moorland in two of the most sensitive critical amenity areas. The first was made by Ben Halliday, the vice-chairman and an appointed member of the committee until he resigned in 1977, and the owner of the Glenthorne Estate. Glenthorne (Fig. 8.1) lies on the coastal ridge between the Oare valley and the Bristol Channel, sloping precipitately for 1000 ft from the last remaining strip of heather moorland to the sea. The authors have always taken the view that Glenthorne, a very difficult estate to manage profitably, is precisely the kind of spectacular landscape that should be owned and managed by the NPA or the National Trust for the primary purposes of conserving the landscape and facilitating its enjoyment by the public. In fact much of the estate had been given or sold to the National Trust in earlier years. But Halliday was unwilling to part with any more land and wished to make the estate profitable by taking advantage of the 50% grants provided for reclamation by the Farming and Horticulture Development Scheme (now Agriculture and Horticulture Development Scheme). He proposed a comprehensive management agreement to embrace farming, woodlands, nature conservation and public access. He insisted on reclaiming moorland, but said that his initial proposal to reclaim the entire 250 acres (101 ha) of heather moorland on Yenworthy and North Commons (Fig. 8.1) – which were only commons in name, common rights no longer existed – was negotiable.

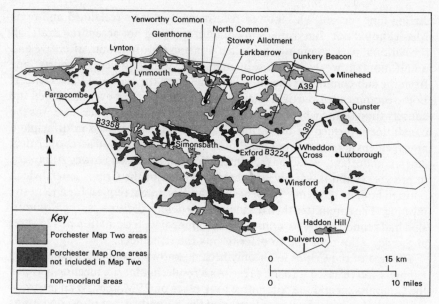

Figure 8.1 Exmoor moorland 1980. Map 1 shows the total area, and map 2 the area within which there is the strongest possible presumption against reclamation.

In the summer of 1976, 375 acres (152 ha) of moorland at Stowey Allotment to the south of Glenthorne came on the market. The NPA immediately saw its significance and agreed to bid for it at auction, for it adjoins moorland aready owned by the committee and reaches from the Oare Valley to within a mile of the centre of Exmoor's heartland. But the County Valuer, despite the protest of one of the farmers on the committee who said that the figure was much too low, put a limit of £26 000 on the bid. The land went for £35 000 to one of Halliday's neighbours, a young farmer in the Oare Valley, who immediately gave six months notice to the committee of his intention to reclaim 300 acres – all that was technically reclaimable. Had the committee been allowed to seize this first chance to prevent reclamation all the later troubles would have been avoided.

The notice ran out on 13 March 1977, but by mid-February neither the NPA nor the special Glenthorne sub-committee to which Stowey Allotment had been referred had discussed the matter. This dilatoriness was one of the factors that led John Cripps, the chairman of the Countryside Commission, to write to the chairman of the Exmoor National Park Committee on 18 February expressing the Commission's concern and its view that it was 'essential' to have a joint meeting on the sites, to discuss both the Glenthorne and Stowey Allotment proposals (Cripps 1977). He urged the committee to postpone final decisions on them until the visit had taken place. The Glenthorne sub-committee, four of whose five members (including its chairman) were farmers or landowners, had its only serious discussion about Stowey Allotment on the morning of 1 March. The chairman had drafted a report stating nine reasons why Stowey Allotment should be reclaimed and none why it should not. But as the sub-committee would not accept the draft, all the national park committee got when it met in the afternoon, after five and a half months 'work' by the sub-committee, were two verbal reports, one from the sub-committee chairman and one from the National Park Officer. Both recommended partial reclamation and neither had even discussed the conservation of the whole of Stowey Allotment with the owner. Nor was the committee informed of the Cripps letter before it approved in principle a management agreement for Glenthorne by which at least 130 acres of critical amenity moorland would be reclaimed. When it discussed Stowey Allotment in private session it was given a garbled version of the Cripps letter, which omitted both its reference to Glenthorne and its urgent request for a joint site meeting. The committee then decided not to defer a decision, as the Commission had requested, but to consent to the immediate reclamation of 125 acres at Stowey Allotment and to offer to buy the remainder.

The text of the Cripps letter only became known to members because the Commission released it to the press. As a result, a joint site meeting between the Commission and the committee took place on 25 March. At an informal meeting between the commissioners and the committee that afternoon it was reported that the owner had rejected the committee's offer to buy two-thirds of the land but had offered a management agreement for the whole or any part of it. The commissioners again asked the committee to defer a decision until 5 April, to give the Commission a chance to consider the matter. But the moment the commissioners were out of the room the committee held another private meeting. The County Valuer then advised the committee to reject the only terms he had been offered for a management agreement as 'financial suicide'. The terms were £9000 a year, indexed against inflation, for an agreement not to reclaim the moorland. Either party would be free to terminate the agreement at regular break points and further compensation would be payable should the committee ever exercise its right to terminate the agreement. The committee not only rejected the terms but decided by a majority to raise no objections to the reclamation of the entire 375 acres. A second chance to conserve the moorland had been lost.

The committee was given a third chance on 5 April when John Cripps and Reg Hookway, the Director of the Countryside Commission, came personally to the committee to make an offer to which the Commission had agreed on 1 April. This was to make an 87½% grant towards a management agreement for one year only at £9000 a year provided that no reclamation took place. The aim was to buy time because Lord Porchester's study was already being set up and its report could be expected by the end of the year. The committee rejected the offer by 11 to 6, the majority arguing that the issue had been closed by its decision of 25 March. The last chance of conserving Stowey Allotment was thrown away.

In May 1977 the Countryside Commission submitted a lengthy report on the committee's mishandling of these matters to the Secretary of State for the Environment under Section 6 (3) (b) of the 1949 Act, the first time that its power to 'report' an authority had been used (CC 1977a). But already the adverse nationwide publicity had persuaded the political leadership of Somerset County Council that it had to take its national park committee in hand. In March, without informing the committee, Mrs Phillips, the chairman of the Council's Policy and Resources Committee, had led a small deputation to Dennis Howell, the Minister of State at the DOE, to ask the Secretary of State to intervene. This led in April to the appointment of Lord Porchester jointly by the Secretary of State for the Environment and the Minister of Agriculture to study 'land use in Exmoor'. The rows had forced the two departments not only to act but to co-operate for the first time.

1977: the Porchester Inquiry

The choice of Lord Porchester to study the Exmoor problem turned out to be a happy one. The fact that he was himself a landowner and a former chairman of the County Councils' Association added greatly to the force of his conclusions. His skilful handling of the public sessions took the heat out of the situation and obliged all parties to the argument to expose their prepared positions to a polite but penetrating examination. The only real surprise in the evidence was a resolution by the North Devon District Council, carried by a substantial majority, 'that the most effective form of control is public ownership, and this would appear to be the only long term solution to the issue' (NDDC 1977). First of all Porchester established the facts and compelled the NFU in particular to recognise the figures that had been staring them in the face since 1965. Relying on recent studies by MAFF he found that 64% of the hill land within the critical amenity area was physically improvable. After excluding land in public or National Trust ownership or subject to common rights he arrived at a figure of 12 800 acres (5182 ha) theoretically at risk. Using aerial surveys dating from 1947, Porchester found that the area of moorland, which in 1947 was just under 59 000 acres, had been reduced to 47 000 acres (19 000 ha) in 1976. Of this 12 000 acre loss, 9500 acres had gone to agricultural conversion, an average of 317 acres (128 ha) a year. The annual rate of loss was higher before 1964 than after that date. These findings substantially vindicated Sinclair's figures.

Porchester saw the moorland as a major component in the mixture of elements that give Exmoor its special quality of 'mottled charm', which in turn depended on the maintenance of a reasonably stable balance of its components. But the moorland was fragile and serious inroads had been made into it by a series of operations by individual farmers, each of which (he said) was defensible on agricultural grounds. The solution he recommended was to bring the process under control; to tell MAFF to take conservation seriously; to define those moorland areas of exceptional value that should be made as safe from reclamation for all time as the uncertainties of both human and natural affairs may allow; to stop reclamation grants in those areas and to pay farmers both for the resulting loss of capital value and for managing the moorland in ways not essential to farming practice.

He recommended a 'virtually rigid regime of conservation' for the heartland of Exmoor (which included Stowey Allotment) because it was already so narrow that 'erosion of the fringes could insidiously over time do much to damage the rare environment of remoteness'. Other areas of exceptional value, including the coastal heaths of which Yenworthy and North Commons on the Glenthorne Estate were among the most valuable remnants, should be 'protected with a similar rigour'. Outside these areas, on the flanks of the moorland, some improvement was possible without harm to the characteristic scenery. But even these areas, he warned, were not expendable.

This analysis led Lord Porchester to recommend the preparation of two maps to replace the critical amenity area map. Map 1 would identify the total area of heath and moorland, including both the areas that should be rigidly protected and the flanks where a 'flexible approach' was possible. Map 2 would define 'those particular tracts of land whose traditional appearance the NPA would want to see conserved, so far as possible for all time', and within which there would be the 'strongest possible presumption against agricultural conversion'. This emphasis on conserving the appearance of the landscape left the door open for later disagreements on the value to be attached, in drawing Map 2, to wildlife values and ecological principles. Porchester noted the Nature Conservancy Council's view that the diversity of plants and animals depended on conserving the largest blocks of semi-natural vegetation. But the 'exceptional values' he wished to conserve appeared to be largely, if not exclusively, scenic.

Perhaps the most valuable contribution made by Porchester at the national rather than the Exmoor level was to be found in his criticism of the Ministry of Agriculture's handling of conservation. He found that MAFF's ADAS advisers worked out reclamation schemes with the farmer without consulting the NPA, so that by the time the farmer consulted the NPA he was already committed to the scheme. Porchester endorsed the view of the Sandford report, which MAFF had ignored, that the environmental implications should be taken into account in the development of the plans rather than be presented to the farmer as an obstruction at a later stage. While accepting the need to keep a farmer's personal and financial details confidential, he saw no justification for MAFF's habit of treating the entire application as confidential. He advised that MAFF should submit an appraisal of each proposal to the NPA and send its officers to discuss proposals with the committee.

His most important recommendation was that 'the Ministry should recognise and support the policy of conservation . . . and feel obliged to withhold grant for the reclamation of *any* moorland shown on Map 2.' First, the ADAS advisers should explore with the farmer all the other options open to him that might avoid the need for reclamation. As for the loss of meat production, he found that on the national scale this would be minimal. Even if all reclamation were stopped in the critical amenity area, the potential production lost would be no more than 708 tonnes a year of mutton and lamb (0.003% of UK production) and 610 tonnes of beef (0.0005% of UK production).

Porchester did not reject management agreements totally, but he expressed the most serious reservations about them unless some major changes were made. He said that their track record was against them – none had been concluded at that time. He thought it unrealistic to expect a mutually acceptable agreement to be concluded so long as MAFF was offering reclamation grants, there were no back-up powers to deal with the farmer who was determined to proceed and no statutory ground rules for determining compensation. Nor, in the absence of a statutory compensation code, could there be an appeal to the Lands Tribunal to settle differences.

Porchester fastened on the fact that representatives of the farming and landowning interests in their evidence to him had accepted the principle of restricting certain farming activities on the moorland, if the price paid was sufficient. This was not the view put in evidence by all the farmers and landowners. But taking the NFU and the CLA at their word, he recommended giving statutory force to the notification system and giving NPAs the power to make Moorland Conservation Orders (MCOs) binding in perpetuity, for which a lump sum would be paid in compensation. The MCO, as Porchester saw it, was to have the characteristics of a management agreement. It would ban prescribed agricultural operations, such as ploughing or reseeding, but it would also provide for public access and the control of any operations or practices likely to affect the vegetation or the character of the moorland to any degree. Because radical change can be brought about in the vegetation by many different management techniques without ploughing, the MCO might also contain restrictions on fencing or the use of fertilisers or chemicals and it might specify maximum stocking rates. In addition, Porchester recommended that farmers could enter into conservation agreements, by which they would be paid annual sums for any management operations required to conserve the character of the moor but not justified by agricultural practice.

The NFU had insisted that 'fair compensation' must take the form of an annual sum equivalent to the loss of potential profit from reclamation, to be renegotiated periodically to take account of inflation. Already this had produced the startling figure of £30 per reclaimable acre quoted for Stowey Allotment and was the basis adopted both in the Glenthorne and the Haddon Hill management agreements concluded in 1977 and 1979 for £20 and £15 an acre respectively. But Porchester objected that this basis would not protect the moorland 'for ever'. Nor would it be 'fair' to the paying authority, which would come to the negotiating table armed with nothing but its powers of persuasion and the offer of an agreement or purchase. On the contrary, he saw annual renegotiable payments as 'opening up the possibility of worsening relations between the national park authority and the farmer in the almost predictable eventuality of dispute. There being no machinery for resolving such disputes, collapse of negotiations – and discontinuance of the agreement – may well result' (Porchester 1977, p. 64).

For these reasons he advised that the ground rules for compensation must be statutory and that compensation for the permanent loss of the right to reclaim should be a once-and-for-all capital payment equal to the depreciation in the capital value of the asset. This has been the statutory basis for compensation for nearly a century and a half and no government is likely to change it. But it remains an anathema to the NFU and the CLA. Lord Porchester estimated that over a period of years once-and-for-all payments in compensation for MCOs would cost between £750 000 and £1 million at 1977 prices. It can be calculated that were compensation to be paid for the entire 12 800 acres that Porchester found to be at risk at the rate claimed for Stowey Allotment, the cost would be £384 000 *a year* at 1977 prices, increasing periodically in line with inflation. From the point of view of the landowner or farmer this would turn the 'waste' of Exmoor into an excellent investment. From the point of view of the taxpayer it could be seen as a bottomless pit.

1977–80: un uneasy peace

The Porchester report received an almost rapturous, and deceptively unanimous, reception when it was published in December 1977. On 6 December the national park committee endorsed its recommendations, with reservations about compensation, by 19 votes to 0 with one abstention and found itself in complete agreement after many years of conflict with the amenity bodies. The reason for this remarkable *volte-face* is not hard to find. The Department of the Environment had already indicated that it was embarking on speedy consultations with a view to early legislation. The Chief Executive of Somerset County Council advised the committee that if it did not accept the main recommendation to introduce Moorland Conservation Orders, either the government would reorganise the committee as an autonomous board or it would take these matters out of the hands of the committee altogether and entrust them to the Countryside Commission. Many elected members were persuaded (albeit temporarily) that some compulsory powers were unavoidable and were delighted that Porchester had turned down the Countryside Commission's advice to extend compulsory purchase powers. However, the committee's split personality was revealed by its decision at the same meeting to approve by 11 to 5 the Glenthorne management agreement, which provided for the reclamation of 100 acres of moorland on the coastal ridge at East Yenworthy Common that Porchester had identified as part of an area to be rigorously protected. The majority attempted to defend this decision on the ground that it had been agreed that Glenthorne would not be governed by the Porchester recommendations, but the record proves that this was not so.

The outcome of the Porchester report was settled by the election in May 1979 of a Conservative government that was closely identified with the farming and landowning interests and opposed in principle to restrictions on the rights of property owners. The Labour government's Countryside Bill, introduced in December 1978, had been amended in committee to emphasise the primary role of management agreements in conserving moorland. But it also gave the minister the power to make orders applicable to specified national parks, within which the NPA could make Moorland Conservation Orders, for which compensation would be a once-and-for-all payment equal to the difference between the value of the land before and after the MCO had been made. Grants for moorland conservation at the rate of 90% were promised. The Bill was unsuccessfully opposed by the Conservatives on second reading and had completed its committee stage when the Callaghan government fell in April 1979. The Bill fell with it.

The Conservative victory destroyed the credibility of the earlier warning given by Somerset's Chief Executive, that failure to accept MCOs might result in government intervention. The new Minister for Local Government was Tom King, the Conservative MP for Bridgwater whose constituency included part of Exmoor. Porchester's solution was split in two. The preparation of Map 1 to identify all moor and heath and of Map 2 to identify those areas that were to be protected, as far as possible, for all time went ahead. The other part, legislation to introduce MCOs and to provide once-for-all compensation for the right to reclaim moorland (with conservation agreements where necessary) was abandoned in favour of a completely voluntary system.

Map 1 (ENPC 1981b) was completed in 1979. It found the total area of moor and heath to be 48 300 acres (19 500 ha) or 28% of the area of the national park, of which 4700 acres (1900 ha) were intermediate or fragmented areas where semi-natural vegetation was less dominant. Map 2 was more contentious, although the area of agreement far exceeded the area of contention. As finally agreed at the end of 1980 (ENPC 1981b), it included 39 610 acres (16 036 ha) or about 82% of the total area of moor and heath shown on Map 1 (Fig. 8.1). Once again the wide overlap between areas of scenic beauty and nature conservation interest was evident. Although Map 2 was based entirely on scenic criteria, the NCC and the voluntary conservation bodies accepted over 90% of it as being of exceptional value for nature conservation. But the NCC's request that 1400 ha should be added to the map revealed a fundamental conflict of attitudes. The committee and its officers insisted that Map 2 was directed in Porchester's terms at conserving 'the traditional appearance' of Exmoor. The NCC regarded moorland and woodland as a single ecosystem and wished to protect the integrity of all the remaining blocks where semi-natural vegetation was dominant. The committee rejected the NCC's offer to argue its case before it and rejected most of the NCC's recommendations to extend the area of the map on ecological grounds. It agreed to ask the NCC to prepare a separate map of areas of nature conservation value, but the fundamental inconsistencies remain. One part of the semi-natural vegetation – the moorland – enjoys a special status and its conservation is financed by 90% grant, whereas other parts – the woodlands, coast and riverine systems – are not.

The policies adopted for Maps 1 and 2 reflected the more positive attitude taken by the committee after Porchester had reported. The appointment in 1978 of Dr L. H. Curtis, a soil scientist with long experience of Exmoor, as the National Park Officer and the assumption of the chairmanship of the committee by the chairman of Somerset County Council were both indicative of a shift in attitude. The policies adopted in 1980 for Map 2 contrast sharply with the flabby statements incorporated in 1977 in the national park plan. They comprised 'the strongest possible presumption in favour of the conservation of natural flora, fauna and landscape . . . the strongest possible presumption in favour of traditional rough grazing compatible with conservation' and 'support, financial and otherwise, for management schemes that conserve natural flora, fauna and landscape features' (ENPC 1980). Proposals to reclaim moor and heath on Map 1 but not on Map 2 were to be considered on their merits, but the exclusion of areas from Map 2 'does not mean that they are expendable' (ENPC 1980b).

However, Porchester intended that the Maps should provide the basis for withholding MAFF improvement grants and for the making of Moorland Conservation Orders, which the new Government had firmly rejected in principle. It took the NPA some months to adjust to the new situation. Its initial reaction to the consultation paper, in which the government announced its intention to include no compulsory power in the proposed Wildlife and Countryside Bill (DOE 1979a), was to continue to press for the inclusion of MCOs and to express profound scepticism about the government's assurances. The government asserted the 'national interest' in conserving the heath and moorland of national parks and declared that a significant change in the overall character of Exmoor would be unacceptable. But it was happy to accept what it called the 'small-scale losses' that Porchester had found to be insidiously damaging Exmoor and to take the risks inherent in a voluntary system. As soon as it became clear that the farmers and landowners were not prepared to go along with MCOs and that the government would not budge from its reliance on the voluntary approach, the NPA's resistance weakened.

The NFU objected to MCOs from the start. Within days of the publication of Porchester's report, an Exmoor farmer (soon to be appointed to the NPA as the NFU nominee) described the report's recommendations as a proposal 'to tie our hands behind our backs while delivering the knock-out blow' (Pugsley 1977). Two months later the national Annual General Meeting of the NFU adopted a hostile resolution. It was moved by another prominent Exmoor farmer, an appointed member who had voted for accepting the report on the park committee but now described it as 'a recipe for confrontation of the highest order' (Edwards 1978). Finally, a meeting of NFU members in Exmoor in November 1979 voted unanimously to support the government's voluntary approach. On the next day the committee, while recording in its minutes 'the brute fact' that the government's proposals left it powerless to prevent the destruction of areas of natural beauty, agreed not to press 'at this juncture' for the inclusion in the Bill of powers to enable it to make MCOs. But the fact that two farmers had reclaimed 66 acres of moorland without the committee's consent – in one case without notification – in the previous year had persuaded even farmer members that some reserve power had become essential. The committee resolved unanimously on 5 February 1980 to urge the government strongly to include a reserve power, to be activated by the minister, enabling either the minister or the park committee to make MCOs. The government rejected even this modest request. An all-party amendment to this effect to the Wildlife and Countryside Bill, supported by Lord Ridley for the Association of County Councils, was resisted by the government and defeated in the House of Lords on 16 March 1981 by 97 votes to 91. The government's refusal to provide compulsory back-up powers had no basis in evidence or logic. But logic had nothing to do with a decision that was clearly political, motivated by ideology and deference to the NFU and CLA. The Bill in fact sheds a great deal of light on the Tory government's approach to conservation, but we defer that wider issue to Chapter 13 and its Postscript.

Management agreement guidelines

The immediate question is whether the voluntary system can work. The Porchester report had led to the introduction of a systematic, businesslike and ultimately public procedure for dealing with reclamation proposals under the 'gentleman's agreement'. Porchester dealt a death blow to MAFF's traditional stance that the confidentiality of grant applications precluded publicity for reclamation proposals and any discussion of them between MAFF and the committee. From 1978, the committee received formal assessments of reclamation proposals from MAFF, the NCC, the Countryside Commission and the National Park Officer. The NFU encouraged its members to notify all proposals voluntarily and agreed to the extension of notification from the critical amenity area to the more extensive area of Map 1. It extended the voluntary period of notice from 6 months to 12, when the Minister had made it clear that the Wildlife and Countryside Bill would amend Section 14 of the Countryside Act 1968 to give him a reserve power to impose a compulsory 12-months notification period.

Table 8.1 shows that 30.6% of the area covered by Map 2 – the area within which there is the strongest possible presumption against reclamation – was protected by public or semi-public ownership at the end of 1980, 1.2% by

Table 8.1 Moorland conservation in Exmoor, 31 December 1980. (From Countryside Commission press notice, 7 July 1980, giving figures agreed by NFU, CLA, Nature Conservancy Council and Exmoor National Park Committee for period 1977–9: Exmoor National Park Committee statement to authors on Maps 1 and 2, March 1981.)

Conservation within the top priority area		Area in hectares (acres)		% of total priority area
moor and heath where there is the strongest possible presumption against reclamation (Porchester Map 2)			16036 (39610)	100
conservation in perpetuity by ownership				
Owned by NPA, (i) prior to Porchester report (1977)		914 (2256)		
(ii) acquired since 1977, Haddon Hill (1979)	64 (159)			
Larkbarrow (1980)[a]	356 (880)			
total		420 (1039)		
(iii) total owned by NPA			1334 (3295)	8.3
owned by National Trust			3569 (8815)	22.3
total conserved by ownership			4903 (12110)	30.6
conserved temporarily by formal and informal management agreements				
formal agreements (i) Glenthorne (1978)	61 (150)			
(ii) Haddon HIll (1979)	91 (225)			
(iii) total		152 (375)		0.9
informal arrangements[b]		195 (483)		1.2
total conserved by formal and informal agreements			347 (858)	2.1
grand total conserved within Porchester Map 2			5250 (12968)	32.7

[a] Purchase by Department of Environment on behalf of NPA, title to be transferred to NPA in 1981–2.
[b] Informal arrangements for 1 year with agreed programmes for controlled liming and slagging at 31 December 1979. Figures for 1980 not available.

management agreements and 0.9% by informal arrangements. The detailed figures provided by the Exmoor National Park Committee for its decisions on proposals formally notified to it by farmers between the setting up of the Porchester inquiry and the end of 1979 are open to different interpretations, and they exclude some areas that were the subject of informal consultations that led to purchase (e.g. Larkbarrow) or to informal arrangements. But the change in the trend is reflected in the notification over this period of farmers' intention to 'improve' 621 ha (1536 acres), of which the NPA was able to conserve 228 ha (564 acres) by one means or another; 27 ha (66 acres) were reclaimed without the consent of the NPA, and it raised no objection to the 'improvement' by various techniques of 235 ha (580 acres). A number of proposals were withdrawn or were undecided. Apart from the 40 ha (100 acres) reclaimed under the Glenthorne management agreement and 74 acres (30 ha) at Bye Common in the Exe valley, the rest of the area to which no objection was raised by the NPA consisted of small parcels of moorland of marginal importance for scenic beauty. The NCC, however, objected to the improvement of some of these areas on ecological grounds.

The figures demonstrate both the upsurge in reclamation in 1977–9 and the greater degree of success achieved by the NPA in conserving the moorland or in persuading farmers to modify their intentions. But 'conservation' is a relative term. Ownership assures conservation in perpetuity, but the protection afforded by the management agreements only lasts until the break-points at three-year intervals, at which either side can terminate the agreements. Both the informal arrangements concluded up to the end of 1979 were only for one year, and the Glenthorne agreement was a package deal which traded off environmental gains and losses against each other. Throughout this period doubts over compensation persisted. The farmers and landowners continued to insist that if the voluntary system was to work, they had to be assured of two things: that compensation would take the form of annual payments related to loss of profit, and that the money to pay for it would be forthcoming.

The confirmation by the incoming Tory ministers of the 90% grant for moorland conservation in Exmoor, which was treated as a 'special case', and the payment of £45 000 in grant for 1980–1 to initiate a moorland compensation fund, seem to have persuaded the farmers that there was money on the table. The purchase by the secretary of state of Larkbarrow was another sign of the government's political commitment. The secretary of state stepped in because the NPA did not have the money to buy the land. Had Larkbarrow been sold at a price reflecting its potential for reclamation, and had the new owner reclaimed it, the government's voluntary approach would have been totally discredited.

The future of Map 2 and of the voluntary approach adopted by the Government depended on the outcome of negotiations opened in November 1979 between the NPA (representing both Somerset and Devon County Councils), the CLA and the NFU at national level on financial guidelines for management agreements. The DOE, MAFF and the Countryside Commission participated as observers, but made no commitments. Both the CLA and the NFU raised objections in principle to the publication of Map 2 (Halliday 1980), but seemed to be prepared to drop their objections of principle if they were offered enough money. The NPA decided, in response to this pressure, that it would not publish Map 2 until the financial negotiations had been concluded. Agreement was finally reached in April 1981.

The guidelines (ENPC 1981a) are an ingenious attempt to overcome some of the difficulties that have inhibited management agreements, particularly the haggling over compensation and the renegotiation every three years. The guidelines offer the farmer a choice between an agreement binding in perpetuity, for which a lump sum is paid, and an agreement lasting for 20 years. In the latter case he may choose between a lump sum in compensation for the restrictions on reclamation and annual compensation for the loss of future profits, indexed against the profitability of sheep farming in Exmoor. The key to the guidelines is the offer to any farmer of a standard compensation sum, calculated by the Agricultural Economics Department of Exeter University, and updated every year to provide the index of profitability. It is based on the profitability of 34 Exmoor sheep farms 'per adjusted forage hectare'. The index shows that the standard sum would have been £73.87 a hectare (£29.90 an acre) in 1977–8, £51.54 a hectare (£20.86 an acre) in 1978–9 and £20.65 a hectare (£8.36 an acre) in 1979–80 – a drop of more than two-thirds in three years. The standard sum is offered where the land does not exceed 74 acres (30 ha), can be improved at reasonable cost and requires no drainage works or additional labour except of a minor nature. It assumes that MAFF improvement grants and subsidies would have been paid, although MAFF was reluctant throughout the negotiations to commit itself to saying in advance whether grant would be payable in particular cases. There is a range of variants on the standard, to reflect the degree of restraint imposed by the management agreement on farming activities, so there is some scope for negotiation. There is also provision for financial differences to be referred to arbitration. The farmer who claims that his profit is higher than the standard compensation sum has to produce certified accounts, and to accept the outcome even if the negotiated payment turns out to be less than the standard sum.

How farmers and landowners will respond to the guidelines for compensation remains to be seen. The offer of a known sum for the first year, indexed against the profitability of sheep farming in future years, makes the deal an attractive one for farmers. It must also encourage some farmers to notify their intention to reclaim moorland, even if their real purpose is to claim compensation. The substantial increase in headage payments in 1980, followed by the introduction of the EEC sheepmeat regime which raised the guaranteed price, has encouraged some hill farmers to believe that the index will rise above the low figure for 1979–80. Our guess is that if the NFU, which wants the guidelines to succeed, can hold the greedier or more wilful farmers in line the terms are attractive enough to conserve Exmoor for a time. But for how long and at what price? The farmer of below average efficiency is guaranteed a profit for 20 years in excess of what he would have made had he taken the risk of reclaiming the moorland. The more efficient farmers can expect to receive higher sums. Should even half the land that Porchester estimated to be at risk become subject to agreements at the standard rate the annual cost at £20 per acre per year at 1980 prices would be £128 000 a year. The bill could be much higher. But some farmers will opt for a capital sum equal to the loss in land value, and this might well run to £400 an acre, or £40 000 for 100 acres. Although the government has promised 90% grant, the upper limit of £45 000 is to be cut in future years in the same proportion as other local government expenditure. The NPA has no capital resources to make land purchases on the Larkbarrow scale. The National Heritage Memorial Fund, to which the secretary of state expects the NPAs to look for help, has (as we saw in Ch. 5) an initial capital of £12.4 million and an income of perhaps £3 million to finance all the nation's purchases of 'heritage', whether works of art, buildings or land, and will have little or nothing to spare for moorland.

The first big question mark, then, is whether government will continue to put its money where its mouth is. Our guess is that, sooner or later, Exmoor will cease to be such a 'special case' that government will continue to push up the moorland conservation grant to match the expenditure. For one thing, the Exmoor moorland is not a special case at all, in the sense that its landscape is specially deserving of government funds that are not available to protect other parts of the national countryside heritage. The woodlands of Exmoor itself are equally valuable and so are the landscapes and wildlife of many other national parks, AONBs, heritage coasts, SSSIs and undesignated areas. The North York Moors are as vulnerable as those of Exmoor, although afforestation has been a bigger threat there than agricultural improvements. Nor should it be assumed that county councils, even with a 90% grant, will continue to pay up on the agreed scale. The purchase of Larkbarrow, at the very moment when the Conservative government was embarking on its first round of cuts in essential local services, caused local resentment. The influential MP for Taunton, Edward du Cann, voiced his criticism. An Exmoor People's Association was formed at a crowded meeting in Exford in November 1980 to complain about 'waste' in the national park and to demand the replacement of government appointees on the committee by representatives of district and parish councils. Locally elected members will be sorely tempted, if nothing else is changed, to cut back expenditure on such 'frills' as conservation in national parks while allowing MAFF's large and often destructive subsidies on agriculture to pass unchallenged.

The second question is, what happens if the money or the will to pay it runs out? The answer seems to be that if the NPA cannot offer a management agreement based on the guidelines, MAFF may offer grants for reclamation. It is difficult to put any other interpretation on the refusal of MAFF, despite pressure to do so, to commit itself not to pay reclamation grants on Map 2 land (as Porchester firmly recommended) or even to accept as conclusive the NPA's overwhelming presumption against reclamation. Both in a letter to the NPA (Harland 1980) and in the guidelines, MAFF spelt out the fact that it reserved the right to pay grant for reclamation within Maps 1 or 2, even where the farmer had not followed the notification procedure or where the NPA had offered a management agreement on the terms of the guidelines to conserve the moorland. It would go no further than to say that the farmer risked losing grant if he failed to follow the notification procedure and that it would deal with each case on its merits. This raises another question. Why should landowners or farmers be compensated, whether by capital sums or annual payments, for not receiving government grants and subsidies if the national interest lies in the conservation rather than the 'improvement' of the 'national heritage'? Why, too, should landowners and farmers be compensated without regard to their means or their needs, at a time when public expenditure on essential services is being reduced and the real value of social security benefits even of those on the poverty line are being cut?

This points to the absurdity of the entire conflict between farming and conservation. MAFF encourages reclamation with unlimited funds directed exclusively at agricultural ends, which include higher production, higher profits and a reduction in the farm labour force. The Department of the Environment and the NPAs, with only a fraction of the resources, can stop or deflect the process only by matching MAFF's bounty pound for pound. Such is the scale of MAFF's support that in Exmoor it will often be cheaper to the public purse to pay the standard compensation sum than to subsidise the farmer to reclaim and farm the moorland. The root of the problem can be seen to lie in the failure of MAFF to direct its abundant resources, as the EEC Less Favoured Areas Directives intend, to the support of agricultural practices consistent with conservation and to the support of the rural population and its economy.

However, the main danger in the Exmoor guidelines lies not in the probability that they will collapse under the weight of the financial burden, but that they set a standard for compensation that will raise the price of conservation everywhere else to prohibitive levels. Repeated assertions that Exmoor is a 'special case' will cut no ice. Landowners and farmers elsewhere, who are asked to negotiate management agreements, are bound to turn for a model to Exmoor where their political power and property rights have secured guidelines more or less on their terms. The broad principles of compensation for loss of grants and subsidies, based on annual payments related to loss of profit and indexed against the profitability of farming, are capable of universal application. The guidelines may be local, in the sense that they are tailored in detail to Exmoor conditions, but they were negotiated at national level by the CLA and the NFU under the eyes of the DOE,

MAFF and the Countryside Commission. Lord Iddesleigh, who signed the guidelines agreement for the CLA, said it was a 'blue print for the future of similar areas throughout Britain' and the NFU signatory described it as a 'model for similar agreements elsewhere' (WSFP, 10 April 1981). But if the price of conservation throughout Britain is based on full compensation for loss of future profits, indexed against the profitability of farming in perpetuity, it will be raised to prohibitive levels and no government will be likely to meet 90% of the cost.

The government's view that Exmoor is a 'special case' was challenged, during the committee stage of the Wildlife and Countryside Bill in the House of Commons, by the publication of a survey by the Moorland Change Project at Birmingham University. A team led by Dr Martin Parry concluded that 'Exmoor, far from being a special case was in fact typical of the plateau uplands' (Parry *et al.* 1981). The survey showed that 37 200 acres (15 060 ha) of moorland were reclaimed for afforestation or agriculture in the past 30 years in the Brecon Beacons, Dartmoor, North York Moors and the northern part of Snowdonia national parks – most of it 'primary' moorland untouched by the plough for at least 1000 years and the nearest thing we have to a 'natural' landscape. The government's response was to insert in the Bill a clause requiring every national park authority to publish a map, similar to Porchester's Map 2, showing the area of moor or heath that the authority thinks it 'particularly important to conserve'. Other modifications made to the Bill are discussed in the Postscript (p. 284).

The Porchester inquiry would never have taken place had a minority of appointed members of the Exmoor National Park Committee, whose numbers shrank at times to one and rose at times to five, not shattered the cosy consensus within the committee. The challenge within the committee could have been frustrated easily had the local conservation movement and the press not taken it up vigorously, both locally and nationally. The Porchester report compelled all parties to reassess their position, and its influence went far beyond Exmoor. It might have produced a lasting solution had its recommendations been implemented simultaneously with a radical redirection of agricultural policies. But the NFU and CLA perceived its recommendations as a threat to the dominant political and property interests in the countryside. The Conservative electoral victory in 1979 strengthened these interests, and ensured the emasculation of the recommendations. But this does not mean that the previous state of affairs has been restored. Nothing in Exmoor will be the same again. The case for conservation has been conceded, and the argument henceforth must proceed on the basis of recognising it. The management agreement guidelines are not the end of the story but the beginning of a new chapter. Central government holds the key, in this as in other countryside matters. The impact of government policies on the national parks is, therefore, the theme of the next part of this book.

Part 4 *The impact of government*

9   Lives and livestock

Hill farming policies

In Chapter 4 we argued that the success of post-war hill farming policies in creating fewer, larger, more technologically advanced units was a major factor in pushing upland communities to the verge of collapse. Our study of Exmoor has demonstrated that whatever the conflicts of interest at the local level a decisive role is played by central government both in creating them in the first place and in resolving them. No government department has a bigger influence on land management decisions than MAFF and its Welsh counterpart the Agricultural Department of the Welsh Office (popularly known as WOAD). We ask Welsh readers to forgive us when we refer generally to MAFF to mean both the agricultural ministries, but their policies are identical. As the agricultural ministers retain ultimate responsibility for forestry, they are therefore the major determinant of land management decisions in the national parks, because farming and forestry are the principal uses over 96% of their land surface (Anderson 1980). In this chapter we take a closer look at hill farming policy and its impact on the national parks, before turning to forestry in the next chapter.

The key to MAFF's success has been the ability of the Agricultural Development and Advisory Service (ADAS) to win the confidence of individual farmers by advising them, in the farmers' best interests, how to apply the results of technological research and development with the help of the available grants, subsidies and tax concessions. Until the UK joined the EEC in 1973, the farm prices fixed by government at the annual price review were not intended to keep pace with rising costs. Price reviews between 1960 and 1970 covered two-thirds of the increase in costs (Beresford 1975), thereby compelling the farmer to expand production with a reduced labour force, or to get out. This encouraged capital investment and higher productivity. The rewards for those who could run fastest up the down escalator, assisted by generous capital grants for improvements to land or buildings and for farm amalgamation, could be enormous.

But hill farming was always the odd man out. The hill farmer can benefit very little from guaranteed prices for fat stock or crops, because he is, by definition, farming in an area where neither fat stock nor crops can be produced in any quantities. He relies for his income mainly on the price he gets for store lambs and calves sold for fattening to lowland buyers at the autumn markets. The store market, however, is a gamble in which the small farmer particularly is at the mercy of the dealer who knows that he cannot afford either to take his stock home or to feed them if he does.

Sir Emrys Jones, formerly the Director General of ADAS, put his finger on the uncertainty of store markets as the main cause of the hill farmer's lack of confidence (Jones 1972). A guaranteed price for sheep continued to operate in the UK until the EEC 'sheepmeat' regime was introduced late in 1980. But it did nothing to iron out the violent fluctuations of the store market. Nor does the sheepmeat regime, despite the higher prices it guarantees for the finished product, seem likely to remove the basic cause of the uncertainty except for those farmers who can finish their animals. Until the hammer falls in the auction ring the hill farmer, and more particularly the small hill farmer, has little idea what his income for the year will be. A succession of bad years culls the farmers who lack the capital to survive as surely as it culls the weaker animals.

The dilemma has always been seen by MAFF as an agricultural one, unrelated to other aspects of upland life and economy, and its answer has always been exclusively agricultural. Since the Second World War it has compensated farmers within the 'hill line', defined under the 1946 Hill Farming Act, for natural handicaps from which they suffer by paying a flat rate headage payment for livestock. (The 'hill line' is not a fixed contour and was determined by various criteria indicative of handicap, of which altitude was one. In parts of Scotland the 'hill line' comes down to sea level.) But its overall aim has been to increase the scale and efficiency of the farm so that it can yield an adequate income from agriculture alone and have sufficient reserves to tide the farmer over the fluctuations of the market. The advisory role of ADAS is crucial, particularly when the farmer is considering how to increase his income. ADAS feeds through to the hill farming community the results of research on animal health and nutrition, grass and livestock management and chemical and mechanical engineering. But also it disseminates the philosophy of growth and expansion – and its counterpart, the philosophy of the retirement or elimination of the weaker. The view that the application of scientific knowledge to livestock production goes hand in hand with ever-growing, more highly capitalised farms is now built into the ethos of the research institutes, the agricultural colleges from which the next generation of farmers is emerging, the farmers' organisations and the farmers themselves despite the resentment that many of them express about a trend that is driving numbers of them to extinction.

The policies of MAFF were given powerful encouragement by other social and economic trends and by the pull exerted by the prospects of more rewarding jobs in the cities. The consequence in terms of rural depopulation and the precipitous decline in the number of farms, farmers and farm workers in the national parks and other upland areas was spelt out in Chapter 4. It was precisely to counter the depopulation encouraged by earlier EEC policies on restructuring farms into larger units that the EEC Directive 75/268 on farming in the less favoured hill and mountain areas was introduced in 1975.

Its aims, as we saw, were to sustain a minimum population, conserve the countryside, promote rural crafts and provide for leisure needs. This Directive provides for the payment of hill livestock compensatory allowances (LCAs), the old headage payments under a new name. It also allows higher rates of grant for capital development to be paid in the less favoured areas, under Directive 72/159 on farm modernisation, to farmers who prepare six-year plans under the Agriculture and Horticulture Development Scheme (AHDS). Under a third EEC Directive (72/161) a socio-economic service is provided for the disadvantaged sectors of the farming industry, of which clearly hill farming is one and small or part-time farms another (EEC 1972b).

Livestock compensatory allowances are estimated to cost £100 million for the UK in 1981, of which £54.3 million are for England and Wales (FW 6 December 1980). It is instructive to examine how MAFF applies the EEC Directives in distributing these large sums. The LCAs are paid at a uniform rate throughout the less favoured areas, regardless of the differences in the degree of handicap between, for example, the relatively good climate and soils of Exmoor or the harsh climate and barren soils of Snowdonia or much of the Scottish highlands. The same rate of subsidy is paid to the farmer struggling to make ends meet on a small farm, the social need of which is high, as to a rancher with thousands of head of sheep or cattle whose social need for a subsidy may be nil. The subsidies are not related to social need or, for that matter, to agricultural efficiency. Subject to a maximum stocking rate per hectare, the LCAs are paid whether the ewe lives or dies and whether the farmer achieves a high lambing percentage or a low one. The effect is to encourage the hill farmer with capital to increase the size of his enterprise and, as we saw in Exmoor, to enhance the productivity of his land with the help of grants. Because the UK pays every hill farmer at the same rate, MAFF finds it too costly to pay LCAs at the maximum rate permitted by the EEC, which in December 1980 was 97 European Currency Units or £60 per livestock unit of one cow or 0.15 sheep, although it does apply the same EEC maximum per hectare. When the government increased LCAs for 1981 by nearly 75% compared to 1979 it nevertheless kept the LCAs for cows below the permitted maximum and that for sheep well below it. (The rates for 1981 are hill cows £42.50 or £54.87 with the suckler cow premium (EEC maximum £60), ewes of a hardy breed £6.25, other ewes £4.25 (EEC maximum £9), maximum rate per hectare £60 (FW 6 December 1980).) The Minister of Agriculture, Peter Walker, justified the increases by saying that although some areas had higher incomes in 1980 than in 1979, others had lower incomes. But the application of a flat rate rewards the more favoured areas and the larger producers, while denying to the smaller producers and the least favoured areas the maximum benefit allowed by the EEC.

Although no government in the EEC seems to have found satisfactory answers to the problems of depopulation in the hills and mountains, some governments apply Directive 75/268 with far more flexibility and discrimination than does the UK. We learned when visiting France and Western Germany in 1979 that in both countries there is an upper limit to the size of herd for which headage payments may be made. In France the maximum payment then was for 40 livestock units (i.e. 40 cows or 240 sheep) or a total of F8000 (about £900 in 1979). This goes far to explain French ill-feeling about British competition in the lamb market. A French mission which reported on Scottish hill farming in 1978 expressed amazement at the fact that the UK places no ceiling on the payment of LCAs. 'We were astonished to see very rich "farmers"' [their quotation marks] 'receive enormous sums by way of these subsidies; £17 000 a year for a farm of 4000 ha, with 2000 head of cattle and 4000 sheep. This same "farmer" also owned, in addition, 5 other farms of the same importance, which were also entitled to "compensatory allowances"' (Guimet & Martin 1978). Both in France and Bavaria the less favoured areas are graded according to the degree of handicap, the top level of subsidy being paid in the Alpine zone and none being paid in the most favoured of the least favoured areas. Recognising that the EEC Directive on farm modernisation provides insufficient help for the very small and part-time farmers who form the great majority of the farming population, the Bavarian Government has also introduced a number of supplementary programmes available to any farmer regardless of the size of his farm (Arlington 1981).

Directive 72/159 on the modernisation of farms is designed to help a middle group of farmers to achieve a target income, which was set initially at a level comparable to the average industrial wage. The target was lowered in 1980 to 90% of that wage, but MAFF defines 'comparable income' as 'the average earnings of full-time workers in occupations other than agriculture' (MAFF 1980a). The AHDS grants under this Directive are paid at a higher rate in the uplands, ranging up to 50% for land improvements such as ploughing and reseeding, or 70% for drainage. The farmer has to find the balance and commit himself to a six-year development plan agreed with ADAS. To qualify for the AHDS benefits, which may include a cash 'guidance premium', the farmer must have an initial income below the comparable income. Also he must have enough land, capital and personal ability to be able to achieve the target income from agriculture alone. Once the target is achieved, the farmer may double his income from non-agricultural sources without disqualifying himself. ADAS grants have been subject to a maximum of £136 000 per business since 1980, but the farmer whose unit is too small to enable him to achieve the target is ineligible. The Directive allows member countries to reduce the target income by 30% in less favoured areas, but the UK has not taken advantage of this provision which is designed specifically to help the small or part-time hill farmer.

Farmers who do not qualify for AHDS or who do not wish to commit themselves to a six-year plan can be grant-aided at lower rates under the Agriculture and Horticulture Grants Scheme (AHGS), which is not funded by the EEC. But all capital grant schemes incorporate inherent biases against those small or part-time farmers who are least able to raise their share of the capital required. European countries have a large repertoire of measures, of varying effectiveness, for assisting small farmers (including young farmers) to obtain land, borrow money more cheaply, run co-operatives and get relief labour for holidays or sickness, that have no counterpart in the UK. We are almost alone in placing no limits or controls on the sale of farmland or the size of farm units.

How seriously MAFF has taken the provision of socio-economic advice to disadvantaged farmers can be judged from the ADAS policy review (MAFF 1979a). It does not even discuss the role of the small or the part-time farmer. It anticipates that 'farm businesses on the borderline will tend to lose ground and to present social problems'. It concedes, too, that there may be growing interest in the contribution of the less viable farms to the maintenance of rural communities. But it is ADAS policy to concentrate advice on the viable farms, because advice to the disadvantaged sector (which contributes only 8% of production) yields a low economic return. In 1979 ADAS allocated nine full-time advisers to its socio-economic service out of a total of 4770 professional and technical staff. A massive research base is provided for technological advice, but none of the £120 million spent on research in 1978–9 by ADAS and the Agricultural Research Council was applied to socio-economic problems or to labour-intensive farming systems. An expert from the Centre for Agricultural Strategy has said that 'the needs of small farmers in terms of research and development have been very poorly served' (Spedding 1981). Individual ADAS advisers often lean over backwards to squeeze the marginal farmer through the gates designed to exclude him from AHDS, but they are powerless to remedy the inbuilt obstacles of the system they operate. The ADAS review announced that socio-economic advice was to get no extra funds and no priority over the primary purpose of giving advice on applied technology. A disillusioned ADAS regional socio-economic adviser described the report to the authors as 'a bucket of cold water on our socio-economic role'. A high proportion of the small and part-time farmers seem to get their advice mainly from the representatives of the chemical companies.

Living with the consequences

Hill farmers, as one might expect, have come to regard the headage payments as their saviour because they provide some cash income in bad years or good. In 1977 subsidies contributed some 16% to 18% of the gross 'output' by value of the hill farms (as compared to 2% for all farms in England and Wales) and from 20% to 100% of their net income (Sayce 1978). A Lake District study (Capstick 1972) has shown that subsidies provided the entire incomes of the smaller hill farmers in the 1960s. But we have sensed, both from interviews with farmers and from other sources, a growing realisation, most strongly expressed in the Lake District, that the headage payments have helped to conceal a wide range of social and environmental problems caused or aggravated by the acute shortage of labour on the farms.

In every park small farmers have confirmed, often in the most graphic terms, the general findings of a study of manpower in Welsh hill farms in 1973 (Gasson 1979). This showed that Welsh farmers appeared to be working inordinately long hours and habits of co-operation were being undermined by shortage of labour. Even the largest farmers seem to be chronically undermanned for all but routine tasks, but the family farm is acutely pinched for labour at both ends of the family development cycle. The young farmer and his wife, on their own with young children, and the elderly farmer, who can no longer make the effort of which he was capable when younger, are exceptionally stressed. A Lake District dairy farmer with four young children called his life 'a mad scramble'. It was not so much that his living standard was low. His wife burst in to say 'I have a good living but a bad life. You work every daylight hour and there's still jobs to be done, but there's not enough money in it to take on another man. You work yourself silly until 10 o'clock at night until you can't work another hour, but you see the Water Board man going home, finished, at four in the afternoon'.

The drive for expansion in output with a smaller labour force can change the entire agricultural and social pattern. In Snowdonia, farmers said that it was now common practice for hill farms to be acquired as summer grazing by lowland farmers, who sell off or abandon the farmhouse and run the land from as far away as Anglesey or the Lleyn Peninsula. This marries complementary assets, but results in the gradual extinction of the local farming population. Occasional visits by Land Rover, facilitated if tracks are bulldozed up the hillsides for afforestation, take the place of shepherding. A Lake District national park warden of farming stock remarked 'the more stock they carry the less they care'. This criticism was reflected in the remark of a very money-conscious young farmer, an incomer to the Lake District who had just bought a large farm on the fells. His simple philosophy was 'the more stock, the more profit', and he had no objection to visitors walking over his land provided he got 'a few thousand' for the privilege. He had no intention of maintaining any of the internal walls on his farm. We met many farmers who do care, and one in particular in the Lake District who said wrily that the harsh winter of 1978–9 had taught him that one man could not lamb even 300 ewes. The chairman of the Snowdonia National Park Committee, a vet and a farmer, told the National Park Conference in 1980 of his worries over the misuse of hill farming subsidies by a minority of farmers. This type of farmer did not put enough back into the land or spend enough on labour and was inadequately supervised by MAFF. He knew of cases where the subsidy was banked, or spent on cars. It enabled 'the rapacious farmer to take over more land, and thus to hasten the area of dereliction' (Tudor 1980). Another member of a national park committee, himself a successful sheep farmer, put it this way 'I know farmers who are putting sheep out and looking at them every week or three weeks instead of once a day. One farmer with 2500 acres near here had eight shepherds, and now he has one to manage 2000 ewes or more. For good shepherding he would need four or five'. A Northumberland sheep farmer said that hill farming was being run by 'a skeleton labour force'. Many jobs now done by machine were done less efficiently 'hedging for example – instead of laying it, you slash the top off with a flail, it's neither a stock nor a wind barrier, it's open at the bottom and it hasn't the wildlife. Nobody bothers about hedges in this county'. His own farm (rented from the Ministry of Defence) would, he said, make four viable farms if money were spent to train more shepherds and re-open the schools. As a man involved in training he knew of 'a huge queue of youngsters waiting in the wings to get into agriculture' who had no hope of getting a farm at a reasonable rent or price.

The consequences of rural depopulation for the landscape of the Lake District were spelt out long ago by Margaret Capstick who found that in many parishes the number of children was well below the level required for the self-renewal of the population. 'If units become large, and labour is scarce, there will not be time for farmers to maintain structures which demand so much laborious attention. The labour figures . . . show by what a narrow margin some of the hill parishes have, hitherto, managed to maintain their attractions. Seven men in Grasmere, eight in Troutbeck valley, four-teen in the whole length of Mallerstang, form a very small labour force to maintain, as a by-product of their farm work, the physical appearance of those valleys. In the Lakes and much of North Westmorland, the environment has hitherto escaped by the "skin of its teeth"' (Capstick 1972, pp. 58–9). The consequences can be seen everywhere in the neglect and removal of walls and hedges, the degeneration of small woodlands, the neglect and consequent overgrazing or undergrazing of commons and the spread of intrusive species such as gorse, rushes, rhododendron and bracken as labour is reduced and stock management adjusted accordingly.

It was not until the late 1970s that MAFF was forced by a series of damaging reports and well-publicised confrontations to reconsider its approach and to some degree to modify its public stance. The 1977 Porchester study of Exmoor (*op. cit.*), which invited MAFF to approach the grant-aiding of moorland reclamation in an entirely different spirit, was in respectable company. The Countryside Commission's study of 'New Agricultural Landscapes' (Westmacott & Worthington 1976) accepted almost without question the trend in agricultural technology, but demonstrated its devastating effect on tree cover and other landscape features that had lost their function. The Nature Conservancy Council's report on Nature Conservation and Agriculture (NCC 1977) said that 'all changes due to modernisation are harmful to wildlife except for a few species that are able to adapt to the new simplified habitats'.

The National Farmers' Union and the Country Landowners' Association responded to these criticisms by publishing a joint statement, 'Caring for the

Countryside' (NFU & CLA 1977), in which they re-asserted their claim to be the 'custodians of the countryside' and accepted in general terms their responsibility for conserving scenery and wildlife – provided that government and the conservation movement would provide advice, practical assistance and money.

The Ministry of Agriculture's own Advisory Council for Agriculture and Horticulture recommended in the Strutt report on Agriculture and the Countryside (Strutt 1978) that MAFF must take a wider view of countryside affairs. Strutt wanted it to acquire a 'rural affairs capability', to take over the Nature Conservancy Council from the Department of the Environment and to equip ADAS officers with the skills required to enable them to advise farmers on landscape and nature conservation. The interdepartmental Countryside Review Committee (which included a representative of MAFF) agreed that virtually all the changes produced by new agricultural technology had been 'unfavourable to wildlife and landscape' (CRC 1978). It implied, in cautious phrases, that MAFF's 'overwhelming emphasis' on increasing agricultural efficiency was creating conflicts in the uplands with other uses of land. It even hinted that ADAS could not be trusted to be the main source of advice on non-agricultural matters in the uplands until MAFF's methods for 'promoting the well-being of hill farmers' had been reconsidered. But, as one might expect from a committee of civil and public servants determined not to tread on each other's toes, it could see no real conflict of interest between farming and conservation and looked to consensus and co-ordination to provide the answers.

The significance of these reports lies in the philosophy that underlines them all. None of them challenges directly either the aims or the direction of basic agricultural policy, although CRC comes nearest to doing so when it implies that it is the inflexibility of national agricultural policies that has prevented agreement on objectives for the uplands. The consensus view, which treats 'hill farmers' or 'the agricultural industry' as a single interest, runs away both from the very real conflicts of interest within the farming community and from the social and economic problems that present agricultural trends are creating. It ignores or underplays the basic structural problems and the long-term threats that current social and economic trends pose both to the landscape and to the majority of the hill farming community.

The Labour government's response in *Farming and the nation* (MAFF 1979b) was, on the one hand, to recognise that there are 'special cases' (as in Exmoor) where food production must take second place and improvement grants may have to be withheld, and on the other to accept in principle the wider role for ADAS. The Countryside Commission has been encouraging and financing a variety of projects designed to harmonise agriculture and recreation or conservation. But the ADAS policy review, while recognising that increasingly farmers would seek advice on environmental problems, insisted that environmental concern must not absorb resources to the detriment of the primary, technological responsibilities of the service. The incoming Conservative government in 1979 confirmed its acceptance in principle of ADAS's role in conservation, but deferred its implementation to better times. Neither government matched its fair words with men or money. The new procedure for processing grant applications under the Agricultural and Horticultural Development Scheme and Capital Grant Schemes is designed, in fact, to save 400 staff posts in ADAS by eliminating the need for farmers to get any advice from ADAS (except in the national parks and SSSIs) before proceeding with capital improvements. The Nature Conservancy Council believes that this will accelerate the destruction of wildlife habitats throughout the country (NCC 1980c). It is beginning to look as if conservation is to be concentrated on the 'sensitive areas' and that even there (judging by Exmoor) the nation will have to pay the farmer or landowner for it.

The neglect of the commons

The failure of the government to make a serious or effective response to the problems of the uplands can be seen in the neglect of the commons, which constitute one of the major resources of the uplands for livestock farming, for recreation and for wildlife. Common land is not public land (unless owned by a public body). It is privately owned land over which, by custom, individual commoners (not the general public) enjoy such rights as grazing livestock or taking turf or firewood. The area of common land in England and Wales was estimated by the Royal Commission on Common Land in 1958 at about 1.5 million acres (510 000 ha) (Common land 1958). The true figure is probably higher. Of this, the greater part is in the uplands. Commons form no less than 41% of the total area of the Dartmoor National Park and 35% of the Brecon Beacons; there are extensive commons in the Lake District and North York Moors and considerable areas elsewhere. There has been a widespread, although not universal, breakdown in the traditional systems of management by which associations of commoners acting by unanimous decisions regulated such matters as stocking rates. Both the rule of unanimity and the collapse of management have prevented such changes as reclamation or afforestation, but they have also resulted in widespread non-management, overgrazing, undergrazing and under-utilisation of the resource.

The public has no legal rights and the public authorities have, as a rule, no powers to provide warden services or manage recreational use. In practice the public walk over many commons, but the Commons, Open Spaces and Footpaths Preservation Society estimates that they have a legal right to do so only over about 25% of the area of common land. They have a legal right to walk over 'urban commons' (commons situated in the area of a former Borough or Urban District Council), which form about a fifth of the total common land, over National Trust commons and some other commons over which legal rights have been conceded by the lords of the manor, or acquired by local authorities. By an accident of history, many of the Lake District commons are 'urban commons', including the central fells, an accident of history that goes far to explain the relative absence of conflict over access in the Lakes.

The concern expressed by the Scott committee (1942) and the acute difficulties experienced by the War Agricultural Committees in securing the effective management of commons whose owners could not be traced, led in turn to the Royal Commission of 1958 and to the Commons Registration Act of 1965. Once registration had been completed, legislation to set up schemes of management and to secure public rights of access (subject to appropriate regulation) was to follow. But the process of investigating claims and reaching final decisions on registration was far from complete in 1980. The process seems likely to last another decade, largely because the government has failed to appoint enough commissioners to determine the claims. In the meantime, registration has made it easier for farmers and others to buy out commoners, with the result (as it was reported at a conference on common land at University College London in December 1980) that common rights are now being extinguished every year. One case, Bye Common, has occurred within the critical amenity moorland area in Exmoor. The area of non-management or mismanagement expands. In 1978 an interdepartmental working party on common land recommended legislation to secure the public's right of access and to establish schemes of management (DOE 1978a).

Because no legislation was in sight, the Devon County Council promoted a private Dartmoor Commons Bill in 1979, on behalf of the Dartmoor National Park Committee, to deal with the virtual non-management either for livestock or recreation of nearly the entire area of Dartmoor commons. This had led to undergrazing and overgrazing, scarring of the more popular spots by people and vehicles, damaging heather-burning and the invasion of the moor by bracken, gorse and matt-grass. The Bill was passed by the House of Lords, but defeated in the Commons on 23 April 1980 on second reading. MPs objected strongly to the proposed Commoners Council, to be set up to manage the commons with 2 members of the national park committee and 16 graziers out of 23 or 26 members. By surrendering control on such a scale to the graziers the park committee sealed the fate of the Bill. The Secretary of State for the Environment then announced that no more work would be done on commons legislation for at least the next two years – i.e. until the 40th anniversary of the Scott report that recommended action.

The human resource

The official response to the growing concern over conservation has been ambivalent and the response to the evidence of social and economic problems has been negative. The Countryside Commission, in evidence to the Strutt committee (1978), argued that long-term depopulation could make all but the most extensive system of farming impossible and lead to important changes in the landscape. 'The resource' it added 'is more than the land; it includes those who work it and those who share with them a community life' (CC 1977c). The Strutt committee's response was to say that the steady rise in the number of bigger farms at the expense of the small had 'obvious implications for farming methods and the viability of rural communities'. The committee then dropped the subject, implying that this was somebody else's problem.

This point of view was spelt out by Dr Keith Dexter, the Director General of ADAS, in the 1978 Bledisloe lecture. He affirmed MAFF's intention to accelerate the technological revolution. But he looked to 'administrators' and to 'society' at large to meet what he called the 'enormous social costs' imposed by the new technologies. He anticipated that the family farm (which he defined as a farm with several workers controlled by one family) would grow in turnover, acreage and profit; and that in this process today's medium-sized farm would become tomorrow's marginal farm and today's marginal farm would become tomorrow's part-time farm. We prefer the more common definition that the 'family farm' is one where the farmer and his family provide the main or only source of labour. Most national park farms are family farms in this sense. But this is precisely what Dr Dexter calls a 'marginal farm', for which the only future he can see is that its occupier gets out – a process that he would assist by offering redundancy payments 'to those farmers whose production is no longer required' (Dexter 1978).

The plain truth is that small and part-time farmers 'are hardly considered in policy formulation . . . the majority of small farms are not eligible for the AHDS – the very scheme that is meant to enable small farms to become commercially viable' (Tranter 1981). The small or the part-time farm has no place in MAFF's scheme of things. But this does not prevent MAFF from claiming, with specific reference to national parks, that 'it is (hill) farming and the other employment generated by farming, which keeps rural communities in being and ensures that basic services are there for the many people who enjoy visiting these scenic areas' (MAFF 1979b). Farming and ancillary employment do indeed provide a bigger proportion of jobs in national parks than they do in rural areas as a whole. The Countryside Commission's analysis (CC 1979d) of the 1971 census figures (which record many more jobs in farming than now exist) reveals that 16 880 of the 95 790 jobs (or 18%) held by residents in national parks were in agriculture. The percentage ranged from 13% in the Lake District to 35% in Northumberland, and exceeded 20% in three other parks – Exmoor, North York Moors and the Yorkshire Dales. But the number of jobs is shrinking (and with it the number of ancillary jobs generated by farming) as the amount of capital that has to be invested to provide them is increasing.

The rising volume of protests coming from among the smaller farmers themselves, who formed a Smallfarmers Association in 1979, is beginning to receive some support from experts in agriculture. Bob Lord, Head of the Economics Department of the East of Scotland College of Agriculture, has complained that the concentration of grassland research on complicated and expensive silage and feeding systems has left the smaller man 'out in the cold' (Lord 1979). Sir Goronwy Daniels, Principal of Aberystwyth College of Agriculture, has criticised the high energy costs of modern farming techniques, particularly for meat production, and argued that the slogan of 'back to the land' will carry more conviction in the 1980s and 1990s when labour is in surplus than it did in the 1920s and 1930s (Daniels 1979). Professor Gerald Wibberley, of Wye College, believes that, if handled in the right way, part-time farming could introduce greater flexibility into situations where rural job opportunities are limited (Wibberley 1979).

Already the process of loss in farming jobs has gone very far, as the figures for Snowdonia and other national parks quoted in Chapter 4 clearly demonstrate. The question that has to be asked is what will happen, both to the national park communities and to their landscapes (using that term in the broadest sense) if policies and support systems are not devised to sustain small farms and part-time jobs in farming? A study of five parishes in the upland plateau of the White Peak, by Rachel Berger in association with the authors, provides a very clear answer (Berger & MacEwen 1979). Of the 147 farm holdings in the five parishes in 1976, 92 were of 40 ha (100 acres) or less. Most of the 15 farmers interviewed believed that 100 acres were at that time the minimum to support the typical White Peak enterprise, a small single-family dairy farm. The others, to judge by their words or their practice, believed that 100 acres made too small a unit. Of the 147 holdings, MAFF rated only 69 as requiring at least 274 standard man days (smd) of labour or, to put it another way, providing a living for one man full-time. Many of the holdings that MAFF rates below 274 smd, which it regards as 'part-time', are the only source of income for a farmer and his family.

The trend in these parishes is unmistakeable. Between 1963 and 1976 the total number of holdings fell from 224 to 147, the decline being most rapid among the smallest holdings of below 10–12 ha. The number of holdings of 40 ha or more increased from 46 to 55. We concluded that by 1990 or earlier there would probably be no full-time farms of below 40 ha. Should milk continue to be in surplus in the EEC, all the smaller producers could well be forced to drop out or to move into livestock rearing on much larger farms with much less labour. Two farmers in Hartington parish personified two possible trends.

One, a middle-aged bachelor running his farm with his sister, quit dairy farming some five years ago when the estate from which he rented his farm was unwilling to invest in a modern milking parlour. He was persuaded to take a second farm and now runs a 342-acre farm with sheep and suckler cows. The buildings, although listed for their architectural interest, are in disrepair and the whole farm presents a neglected appearance. The stock is grazed in 50-acre blocks and the original stone-walled enclosures, that were fairly well adapted to dairy farming, are falling into ruin. Most of the internal walls are down and even the boundary wall is gapped with wire.

A different path has been followed by the second farmer, a man of substance who owns two farms and rents a third, totalling 970 acres on better lower lying land. While retaining his boundary walls, he has removed most of the field walls to increase fields from 2 acres to nearer 20 acres and more. He is moving away from beef production to dairying, with two herds of 150 cows. He also runs a battery hen unit, employing five women on a part-time basis, and for the last three years has been growing barley to feed the hens. His buildings are large and modern and he makes silage rather than hay. All his pasture has been ploughed and reseeded. Most of his walls and all his herb-rich meadows have gone. He grazes his herds in large fields, using electric fences. He is concerned to keep an attractive landscape, but sees his own well-kept farm as providing one; for him progress *is* attractive. It is apparent that he is well off; the whole family hunts and their style of life differs from all the other farmers interviewed. This, in Keith Dexter's terms, is the 'family farm' of the future, in which one family gives the orders and the other families carry them out. A staff of eight men is employed.

The farmers who are most likely to go to the wall will include many of those who have succeeded until now in climbing up what one of them called 'the slippery slope' of continuous expansion by straining their physical and financial resources to the limit. Those we interviewed were neither lazy nor incompetent. They had kept abreast of technological innovation. Most of them cared deeply both for the land and the landscape and, while they had enlarged some of the smaller fields by removing or neglecting walls, they valued the walls not only for the distinctive landscape pattern they create but functionally as durable and efficient stock barriers and shelter. What they lacked was capital. What they regretted was their inability, with the labour at their disposal, to maintain the walls in as good a state of repair as they would like.

Although the landscape of the White Peak shows few signs of deterioration on a superficial inspection, all the signs of long-term deterioration are there beneath the surface. The clumps of sycamore and beech planted in the 19th century that punctuate the bare plateau are doomed unless grazing is controlled and planting or regeneration encouraged. The labour no longer exists to maintain more than a small part of the 30 000 miles or so of limestone walls that give the landscape its unique chequer-board pattern. As walls and trees go, large new agricultural buildings will become the most prominent features in the scene. Naturalists say that fertilising and reseeding the grassland has removed nearly all their wildlife interest. There are programmes for tree planting, wall building and identifying some of the herb-rich meadows that remain, but the resources are small when compared to the scale of the tasks. The problems of the White Peak are structural and arise from agricultural policies which are powerfully reinforced by other social and economic trends.

It is beyond our capabilities and the scope of this book to devise alternative policies. But there is a wide range of alternative possibilities waiting to be explored, some of which are being tried already in other countries. The first tentative explorations are being made in this country by the Highlands and Islands Development Board, by the Lakes Board in UMEX 3, and in co-operative schemes to enable hill farmers in the Lake District to finish their stock on lower ground. The NFU has secured the co-operation of MAFF, the local authorities, the Tourist Board, the Development Commission and the conservation agencies in the East Fellside and Alston Moor project in the Northern Pennines (CLA 1980). It is exploring ways of reversing the rapid loss of population, jobs, schools, shops, transport and services by tapping local initiative and using the funds of the participating agencies to support specific developments in farming, tourism and small industries. But all these initiatives are up against two basic problems. They have to rely largely on their powers of persuasion and agricultural policy is promoting the very trend they hope to reverse. One of the co-operatives failed early in 1981.

No solution will be found until MAFF decides (or is compelled) to look for one and until it applies some of its money, brains and research capability to this end. MAFF's track record in designing sticks and carrots calculated to entice farmers down the desired road is unequalled. But British farmers and administrators have got to abandon the contemptuous attitudes too many of them express towards the European part-time farmer and begin to see farming as only one component of the upland economy and even of many individuals' incomes. The key to an integrated land use and management policy for the uplands must surely lie in the redistribution and redirection of the very large sums now paid out for afforestation (which is the subject of the next chapter), land drainage and the support of agriculture. The present situation is a complete nonsense. The only way to stop damaging changes in land use or management is to conjure resources out of one government department or agency (usually one with a very small pocket) to compensate landowners or farmers for forgoing the bounty disbursed from the ample pockets of another. MAFF policy, with its narrow focus on productivity and profitability and its heavy bias towards the bigger, highly capitalised enterprises, is on a collision course with the very interests – the conservation of resources and the economic and social wellbeing of upland communities – of which it should be the strongest prop.

In 1981, MAFF is expected to pay out £100 million in LCAs, not counting capital grants in the less favoured areas of England and Wales or the guaranteed sheep prices now paid by the EEC under the new sheepmeat regime. Here is an ample fund from which to support conservation management, the smaller farm units and the more handicapped areas. Appropriate grants could encourage the management of common land. Grants could be graded according to the degree of handicap imposed by nature, or could be designed to encourage farmers to pursue the aims of conservation. They could be tapered, so that the EEC maximum would be paid to the smallest, most handicapped farms and to those adopting conservation regimes, and the least (or nothing at all) to the large ranchers once the sizes of their flocks had reached a ceiling level. Capital grants could be redirected to achieve a range of social and economic objectives, providing holiday accommodation or buildings for light industry or services, encouraging the maintenance of old buildings as well as the construction of new ones and the employment of people as well as their displacement by machines. Payments could be made conditional on keeping rights of way open and providing access to open country. The production of food would cease to be the only objective.

The Hartsop study concluded in 1976 that neither the Lakes Board nor the local authorities could be expected to resolve the problems and conflicts inherent in upland areas generally, and the Lake District National Park in particular, unless the government provided the financial and legislative backing for measures aimed at tackling rural housing shortages, assisting hill farmers and maintaining the landscape (Feist *et al.* 1976). But if present trends are allowed to continue, the statement in the Lake District National Park plan that 'a sustained loss of farmers and farm workers . . . will result in the continued deterioration of the landscape and add to the problems of rural depopulation' (LDSPB 1978, p. 36) will become a self-fulfilling prophecy.

10 *The woods and the trees*

Forest policy

Forests and woodlands are critically important components in the ecology, the landscape, the wildlife and the economies of the national parks. They tend to figure in the literature of conservation (and in the media) as two separate issues. One is the 'threat' of massive coniferous plantation impelled by ambitious planting programmes, grants and tax concessions. The other is the 'problem' of the pervasive, progressive and insidious decline of small deciduous woodlands. But in fact afforestation and passive neglect or mismanagement of woodlands are two aspects of a single forestry policy in which the autonomous government agency, the Forestry Commission, is the dominant force. Since it was established in 1919 to make good losses sustained in the First World War, its overriding concern has been the production of softwood timber.

The Forestry Commission wears two hats. It is the national forest enterprise and as such the largest landowner in Britain as a whole and in the national parks, responsible for continually expanding and planting its estate. It is also the national forest authority, responsible for advising the forestry ministers, for guiding, funding and promoting private forestry and for extending the knowledge of forestry through research and practice. The commissioners are a blend of professional foresters and of people drawn in the main from the forestry and timber industries. Its relations with the private sector are so intimate that they could be described as incestuous. Lord Taylor of Gryfe, on retiring from the chairmanship of the Commission – where he successfully opposed the recommendation of the Sandford Committee (1974) that afforestation should be brought under planning control – became the chairman of the Economic Forestry Group (EFG), the largest of the private forestry companies.

It would be wrong to say that the Forestry Commission is concerned exclusively with commercial afforestation. It can point with legitimate pride to some aspects of its management of the New Forest and the Westonbirt arboretum, for example. It has seven forest parks and its forests are used increasingly for recreation by millions of visitors. It spent £4 million of its £93 million budget on recreation and amenity in 1979–80 (FC 1980a). But it took the Commission 30 years to respond to protests against the consequences of its afforestation policies. Nan Fairbrother articulated the reaction against 'crude and unnatural patterns of straight lines and sharp angles on flow-ing hills, block planting of geometric patches of forest on bare hill-sides, chequer-board arrangements of different species, straight rows of trees ruled up and down slopes and extraction roads like wounds slashed across the hills ... blanket planting in small scale scenery smothering the land-scape in a uniform dark fleece of trees' (Fairbrother 1970, p. 125).

In 1963 the Forestry Commission appointed Dame Sylvia Crowe as its first landscape consultant. In 1967 and 1973 its objectives were modified to place more emphasis on the conservation of the environment, the provision of recreation facilities and the stimulation of the local economy in areas of depopulation (FC 1977a).

But these modifications in its aims and attitudes have left its basic purpose and philosophy largely untouched – 'the production of timber remains the Commission's prime objective and main source of revenue' – and the aim is to be achieved by increasing its productive capacity and earning as much as possible from timber sales (FC 1977a). The same objective guides the Commission as the national forest authority in its relations with private forestry. In 1977 it introduced a small woods scheme to grant aid the plantation of woods between ¼ and 10 ha, and since 1974 it has offered additional grants for planting broadleaved trees. But 90% of the funds it allocates to private forestry are used to grant aid dedication schemes under which owners dedicate their land in perpetuity to timber production. (Planting grants in September 1980 were £100 per hectare for conifers and £225 per hectare for broadleaved trees in dedication schemes exceeding 10 ha.) It has been pro-posed that from October 1981 the small woods and dedication schemes will be replaced by a single simplified scheme for grant-aiding new planting, and that existing dedication schemes will be terminated as the opportunity arises (MAFF 1980b). The new arrangements are designed to simplify administrat-ive arrangements and to withdraw the Commission from continuing involve-ment in the supervision of private forests. They are not intended to change the Commission's overwhelming bias towards conifers. Of the trees planted in 1979–80 by the Commission in Great Britain, or grant-aided by it, 95% were conifers (Table 10.1). One reason, of course, is that much of the newly-planted land was on soils or at altitudes unsuited to broadleaved trees, but another is that the additional grant for broadleaves is insufficient to make afforestation an attractive financial proposition unless conifers constitute the whole or a large part of the plantation.

The proportion of broadleaved trees is, of course, higher in England where most of the lowland woodlands are situated. The figures for Wales, where 96% of the trees planted were conifers (98% on Forestry Commission plantations), shows the extent to which upland planting is almost entirely coniferous. Colin Price, a forest economist, takes the view that the admir-able guidelines on landscape design devised for the Commission by Sylvia Crowe are applied to give aesthetic acceptability to schemes delineated

Table 10.1 Planting and restocking of conifers and broadleaved trees (1979–80) in hectares and as percentages of planted area (from Forestry Commission, *Sixtieth annual report 1979–80*).

	Forestry Commission plantations						Private plantations						Total plantations					
	England		Wales		Great Britain		England		Wales		Great Britain		England		Wales		Great Britain	
	ha	%	ha	%	ha	%	ha	%	ha	%	ha	%	ha	%	ha	%	ha	%
conifer	2882	(94)	1994	(98)	21 181	(99)	1648	(65)	610	(91)	9997	(90)	4530	(81)	2604	(96)	31 178	(95)
broadleaved	184	(6)	44	(2)	318	(1)	897	(35)	58	(9)	1170	(10)	1081	(19)	102	(4)	1488	(5)
total	3066	(100)	2038	(100)	21 499	(100)	2545	(100)	668	(100)	11 167	(100)	5611	(100)	2706	(100)	32 666	(100)

entirely on commercial grounds (Price 1980). The EFG is very frank about the motivation behind private afforestation:

> Forestry is an investment in the commodities of land and timber, both of which merit serious consideration as investment assets. In the past the value of land has outpaced inflation while timber has generally kept pace with it and over the longer term we expect that in future . . . land values will rise at least as fast as inflation, timber prices will increase more rapidly than inflation . . . establishing a plantation is an attractive way of using income which would otherwise be taxed at high rates; and established plantations give real capital growth which is treated sympathetically by current income and capital tax legislation (EFG 1980, p. 1).

Clifford Tandy, Sylvia Crowe's successor, argues persuasively that well-designed forests can bring interest and diversity to hill land, increase the range of wildlife habitats, supplement grazing, increase employment and open up public access (Tandy 1979). So, in theory and to some extent in practice, they do. But the Nature Conservancy Council, as we saw in Chapter 2, is severely critical of forestry practice in the uplands and Tandy admits that only a comparatively small part, even of the Commission's work, receives expert landscape advice. The 'myopic agriculturalist' whom we met in the last chapter is mirrored by the 'single-minded and blinkered forester', to quote Davidson and Wibberley's phrase (*op. cit.* 1977).

The pace of afforestation reached a plateau in 1971–2, dropped steadily between 1972 and 1979, but rose again in 1980 (Table 10.2). A contributory factor to the decline was the white paper on forestry policy (MAFF 1972) which found, on the basis of a crude Treasury cost–benefit analysis, that there was no economic case for afforestation. It justified a reduced afforestation programme entirely on grounds of job creation, amenity, conservation and recreation. But the decline can also be attributed to the setback to the British economy, the steep rise in land prices, changes in the grants for private forestry and fears of a wealth tax.

In response to the decline in afforestation the Forestry Commission, the private Timber Growers' Organisation (TGO) and the Centre for Agricultural

Table 10.2 Land acquired and planted (in hectares) in Great Britain in 1972 and 1980 (from Forestry Commission Annual Reports 1972–3, 1979–80).

Year ended 21 March:	Forestry Commission acquired	new planting	Private owners new planting	Total new planting
1972	17 000	21 758	19 680	41 438
1980	6900	15 830	8302	24 132
1980 as percentage of 1972	41%	73%	42%	58%

Strategy (CAS) began to call from 1977 onwards for an expanded afforesta-tion programme, the justification for which was seen primarily in the need to reduce imports of timber, which cost £2750 million in foreign exchange and took 92% of the home market in 1979 (FC 1977, CAS 1980). But perhaps the most telling argument, the validity of which we return to later, was the fore-cast of a world shortage of timber coupled with rising real costs in the early years of the 21st century. CAS favoured a maximum programme to afforest an additional 1.96 million ha, thereby doubling the woodland area of the UK, by planting 60 000 ha of new land a year. This is three times the 1979 rate of new planting and 50% higher than the rate in 1972 (CAS, ibid.). The Director General of the Forestry Commission spoke of a 'modest' pro-gramme to plant an additional 1.5 million ha by 2025 (Holmes 1979).

In its statement of forestry policy in December 1980 the government accep-ted in general terms the case for reducing imports, but it neither accepted nor rejected the targets of the Commission or the CAS (MAFF 1980). It saw scope, however, for increasing the annual planting rate to 'broadly the rate of the past 25 years in the immediate future' – i.e. to about 35 000 ha or some 75% above the rate achieved in 1979. But its declaration that 'a continuing expansion of forestry is in the national interest' holds the door open for further expansion. The role of the Forestry Commission is to be reduced, by concentrating its activities in 'the more remote and infertile areas where afforestation will help maintain rural employment' and by compelling the Commission to find part of its funds for planting by selling off existing woodlands and land acquired for planting for 'private investment'. The financial institutions, pension funds and commercial forestry companies, whose motivation is financial, are to become the main agents of afforestation. The tax concessions, the effect of which we consider in our study of Cnewr (see p. 221), are to continue as a hidden subsidy to private forestry, the cost of which does not figure in the statistics. The Inland Revenue estimates the loss of revenue from tax conces-sions to high tax-paying woodland owners in 1978–9 at £8–10 million (HC 1980b), or about four times the grants paid to private woodland owners in the same year (FC 1980a). The commitment to private afforestation, in terms of grants and tax reliefs is open ended. The forestry interests can be expected to press ahead with an expanded afforestation programme in the longer term. The questions that concern us in this chapter are the probable impacts on the national parks, the adequacy of the machinery for allocating land uses and for consultation (illustrated by a case study), and the soundness of the assump-tions on which such a programme would rest.

Impact on the national parks

The main focus of afforestation is to be in Scotland, but the FC is looking to England and Wales to provide half a million hectares towards its target of 1.5 million. Its studies show that 570 000 of the 1.2 million ha of technically plantable land in England and Wales are in the national parks (FC 1978).

Table 10.3 Land owned by Forestry Commission and private woodland under dedication schemes in national parks, in hectares and as percentage total of National Park area (from national park statistics, *County Council Gazette*, November 1980, and *Private woodlands*; estimates based on information in national park and structure plans.)

| | Forestry Commission 1980 | | Dedicated woodland | |
	ha	%	ha	%
Snowdonia	33 850	16	3680	2
North York Moors	23 690	16	5126	4
Northumberland	22 379	22	2018	2
Lake District	12 734	6	5200	2
Brecon Beacons	11 122	8	1171	1
Peak District	2600	2	2501	2
Dartmoor	1807	2	2678	3
Exmoor	1340	2	2588	4
Pembrokeshire Coast	720	1	900	1.5
Yorkshire Dales	424	0.2	2600	1.5
total	110 666[a]	8.1	28 462	2

[a] Approximately 75% of land owned by the Forestry Commission is planted.

The Commission has never concealed its view that such designations as national parks and AONBs constitute obstacles in its path and its Director General has urged that 'some accommodation must obviously be found' in these protected areas if a 'reasonable share of forestry expansion is to take place south of the border' (Holmes 1979). Already, over a fifth of the Commission's estate in England and Wales is located in the national parks, although the distribution differs enormously between one park and another (Table 10.3).

Commercial afforestation already has a very strong grip on Northumberland, North York Moors and Snowdonia, and there are extensive commercial plantations in the Lake District and Brecon Beacons – the only parks where they are minimal are Pembrokeshire Coast and the Yorkshire Dales. As long ago as 1974, the Sandford committee reported that Dartmoor was the only national park in which the area under native broadleaved trees substantially exceeded the area under alien conifers (Sandford 1974, Table 8). In the Peak District and Exmoor the broadleaved area marginally exceeded the coniferous plantations. In all the others the coniferous area exceeded the broadleaved area – in Snowdonia by nearly 10 to 1, in Northumberland by nearly 40 to 1. Even in the Lake District, where the broadleaved woodlands are key elements in the valley and lakeside landscapes, there were substantially more coniferous plantations than broadleaved woodlands by 1972. What is now proposed, however it may be disguised by references to integration with agriculture and safeguards for sensitive areas, is a massive afforestation of the rough grazings of the uplands. One authoritative estimate suggests that were an additional 2 million ha to be afforested, without any special protection for national parks, the area of the national parks under forest would be trebled and 35% to 40% of the remaining rough grazings would be taken from the hill farms (Price 1980). The CAS (1980) in its appraisal of plantable land treats national park designation as a constraint, but EFG (1980) publishes a map for the guidance of investors which included all the national park uplands within the areas suitable for afforestation. The national park statistics published in November 1980 showed that the Forestry Commission's holdings increased between March 1979 and March 1980 by 1088 ha in the Lake District and 7520 ha in Snowdonia, an increase of 8% in its holdings in national parks (ACC 1980d).

Plans and controls

It would be reasonable, but mistaken, to assume that the allocation of land for afforestation proceeds within a policy framework laid down by the national park plans. The Forestry Commission relies entirely on the purchase of land on the open market without using its powers of compulsory purchase. So, inevitably, do the private forestry companies. This dictates what the Countryside Commission has criticised as 'a largely opportunistic approach' (Laverack 1979) by which, as Price (1980) puts it, 'the sequence of forest development has remained entirely a function of the market'. One reason why the Forestry Commission dislikes maps identifying areas that are unsuitable for afforestation on grounds of amenity is that it wants to keep its hands free to afforest land that comes on the market, wherever that may be. Land suitable for commercial afforestation often comes onto the market in units that make integration with farming and landscape difficult or impossible. Whole farms may be wiped out and the hill land cut off from the bottom land. The boundaries of individual farms may dictate the form of the plantations, which may clash with the contours of the landscape and the land pattern of adjoining farms. To argue, as the Director General of the Forestry Commission does (Holmes 1979), that the existing consultative procedures do not transfer land to forestry in a haphazard way, is to reject the evidence.

The national park plans express broad intentions to protect the character and accessibility of the open country, but for more specific guidance one has to turn to the forestry maps adopted in most of the parks. The earliest goes back to 1935, long before the national parks existed, when the Forestry Commission yielded to nationwide criticism of its crude plantations in Ennerdale and elsewhere in the Lake District by agreeing with the CPRE not to afforest the central fells. The Commission has honoured the agreement until now and it has been adopted as the policy of the national park board. But the Commission would like it to be amended. Its NW Regional Conservator formally refused to endorse the national park plan on the grounds that it was too restrictive: 'if the Forestry Commission were to give official endorsement to the national park plan in its present form, it could not exercise its proper role in the encouragement of planting in the national interest' (James 1978). He urged the revision of the plan to allow the future to be determined *ad hoc* by decisions on individual cases 'by case law'. The board disagreed.

If the status of the Lake District agreement is in doubt, even less confidence can be placed in the maps agreed (or more or less agreed) in six other parks between the Forestry Commission, the TGO and the National Park Authorities to regulate private afforestation. The former National Parks Commission, faced with the fact that neither it nor the NPAs were able to influence afforestation, agreed with the TGO and the Forestry Commission in 1962 that maps would be voluntarily agreed in each national park (NPC 1962). The maps assign bare land to one of three categories: a) where there is a strong presumption that afforestation will be acceptable, b) where there is a presumption against it but afforestation might be acceptable, and c) where there is a strong presumption against afforestation. But these maps are typical products of the consensus approach. They may take many years to negotiate and are not always complete. They do not necessarily reflect the views or policies of the NPA and they are binding on nobody.

The maps reflect an uneasy compromise that often satisfies neither side. The Forestry Commission thinks the maps are too restrictive. Some of the NPAs (notably Brecon Beacons and Snowdonia) think they are too generous to forestry and would like to renegotiate them, or to substitute maps (as in Brecon) based on different principles. The 1975 Snowdonia map, to take an extreme case, shows a strong presumption in favour of increasing the afforested area of the park from its present proportion of 14% to about 50% (Map 7, Snowdonia National Park Plan). Such a wholesale transformation of the landscape into commercial plantations is patently incompatible with the statutory purposes of conserving natural beauty and promoting recreation. All the NPAs in areas liable to massive afforestation want to be given powers to control afforestation, as the Sandford Committee recommended. This is also the policy of the Association of County Councils. What they have had to accept since the Government rejected the Sandford recommendation in 1976 is an understanding that they (like other local authorities) will be consulted by the Commission on its afforestation proposals (but not necessarily on the land purchases which determine where planting will take place) under the 'consultative' procedure for private afforestation introduced in 1974 and reaffirmed by DOE Circular in 1978 (DOE 1978c).

The 'consultative' procedure

It is hard to conceive a more authoritarian, secretive or biased procedure, compared to which the procedures of town and country planning are models of democracy, openness and fairness. It is open to objection on several grounds. Only a very limited range of people or interests are informed of the proposals to afforest land and even fewer are seriously consulted. The procedure is secret throughout and contains no safeguards to secure natural justice or fair play and, of course, the procedure only determines whether or not grant is paid. It is the policy of the private forestry interests not to proceed with controversial schemes for which grant has been withheld, because to do so might strengthen the hands of the conservation interests and the county councils in pressing for planning control over afforestation. But the investor is legally entitled to proceed without grant and if he does so, he is still entitled to the tax concessions which are the major incentive to afforestation.

When the Forestry Commission receives a proposal from a landowner to enter into a dedication scheme for land not previously used for forestry, it first invites the Nature Conservancy Council, the Countryside Commission and the local planning authority (i.e. the NPA) to comment on the acceptability of converting the land to forestry use. The Countryside Commission has objected that although it is informed, it is not consulted (CC 1980b). The circular (DOE 1978c) strongly urges the local authorities to consult 'local societies' *if they see fit*. The NPAs refer proposals to their own consultative groups on which farming, landowning and some other local interests are represented. But nobody has a right to be informed, let alone consulted even at the local level and national bodies have no place in the procedure. The landowners' proposals are not advertised or published and the entire proceedings are confidential, even to the extent that a NPA is not allowed to see the representations that the Forestry Commission makes to the minister, if a disputed case goes so far. It is extremely difficult, therefore, for individuals or organisations outside a privileged circle to influence decisions.

These difficulties are aggravated by the procedure. Where disagreements cannot be resolved through discussion, the Regional Advisory Committee (RAC) is invited to assist the Forestry Commission. However, the RACs are the creatures of the Commission, which appoints all their nine members, of whom seven are normally picked from the forestry, timber and landowning interests and two are supposed to 'represent' conservation and amenity. We have met no informed observers outside the dominant interests who have confidence in the RACs. The Countryside Commission regards both their terms of reference and their procedures as 'patently unsatisfactory' and denies that the RAC can be regarded as a 'competent and appropriate body objectively to assess the merits of afforestation proposals, or where necessary act as an independent, neutral arbitrator' (CC 1980b).

Where differences of view persist the Forestry Commission 'will seek the views' of the Forestry Minister (i.e. the Minister of Agriculture or the Secretary of State for Wales) who will consult the Secretary of State for the Environment (in England) if there is a 'planning or amenity interest'. The final decision rests with the Forestry Commission, which normally takes the minister's advice although it does not have to do so. In practice the Secretaries of State, or junior ministers from MAFF and the DOE, take decisions on the spot. The Lakes Board has described the procedure as 'a travesty of justice' in a letter to the Secretary of State for the Environment. The Minister of Agriculture, himself a local MP, had given a decision adverse to the Board on a proposal to reclaim Hudson's Allotment, a very sensitive area in the Lake District, after a cursory site inspection. The letter said 'there was no opportunity, except at the site meeting, either in writing or orally for evidence and arguments to be presented by each side and to be rebutted or commented upon by the opposing side. The views of the Forestry Commission remained undisclosed . . . and the Board have had no opportunity to comment on them. Communications between the Ministry of Agriculture and the Department of the Environment have remained behind the curtain, and although it is known that the Countryside Commission was approached in the matter there is no reference in any written documents to their involvement or their views . . . the Minister of Agriculture has not attempted anything in the nature of a judgement accompanied by reasons related to policy, he has simply said that he does not "demur" and the Forestry Commission have not sought to expand on the minister's "non-demurral"' (Himsworth 1976).

The protest was ignored. The procedure gave rise to similar complaints by the Brecon Beacons National Park Officer in 1980 with regard to the Cnewr Estate. For there too the proceedings took place behind closed doors and the park committee was never allowed to see the Forestry Commission's case. The procedure is time consuming and absorbs a lot of professional manpower. The Forestry Commission sees it as a formidable constraint, but in reality the only constraint is the need to assess politically the consequences of disregarding the views of those who are objecting to the proposals. Here the Forestry Commission holds most of the cards. As a result the NPAs rarely carry objections to the Secretary of State. They normally begin by conceding a level of coniferous afforestation that will be 'economic' to the owner and concentrate on trying to extract such concessions over amenity, wildlife, broadleaved content or access as he may concede. The Forestry Commission initiated a review of the procedure in December 1980, but it was aimed at achieving administrative economies, by such means as limiting consultation to the 'more sensitive areas' and requiring those consulted to comment within 21 days (FC 1980). The Commission's consultative paper did not even refer to the criticisms of the Countryside Commission or of the Lakes Board.

A study in compromise

The Cnewr Estate affords an interesting example of the operation of the procedure, the financial forces behind afforestation and the kind of compromise that resulted. The Cnewr Estate, in the words of the Countryside Commission, 'forms part of the wild and open spine of mountains which was the inspiration for the designation of the Brecon Beacons National Park'

(CC 1980f). Clearly its afforestation would be contrary to the intentions both of the Powys structure plan and of the national park plan. It is the policy of the latter that 'tracts of open mountain land' of importance for landscape, recreation or grazing should not be afforested (BBNPC 1977). But this policy conflicts directly with the policies of the Forestry Commission in both its capacities as forest enterprise and forest authority. Neither the Commission, nor the estate, nor the Economic Forestry Group to whom the estate planned to sell land for afforestation, were prepared to accept the NPA's view that the open mountain land should be put in category 'C' of the forestry map, with a strong presumption against afforestation. All subsequent difficulties could have been avoided had the NPA been able to buy the disputed area. The estate was willing to sell, for a period after 1974, but no agreement could be reached on the price because the Powys County Valuer was not prepared to put any value on the land for conservation or recreation. Thereafter, continuing disagreements, first about the Commission's and then about EFG's proposals, led the Secretary of State for Wales to advise the Commission in 1977 not to proceed with any dedication schemes in the absence of overall agreement on forestry development in the area.

However, no agreement had been reached when the estate came forward in 1979 with proposals to plant six blocks totalling 988 acres (400 ha). Four of these were in the very areas where the parties had been deadlocked because the estate refused to accept the committee's insistence that they should be in category C – in effect, no afforestation. The other two were partly in C and partly in B, the area where some afforestation may be acceptable. The initial response of the committee was to oppose all six blocks, on the ground that afforestation of the open mountain was incompatible with its policy. The National Park Officer advised the committee first, that the areas to be planted were in 'locations where the integrity of the characteristic upland landscape would be threatened'; second, that 'an awkward precedent could be created, making it difficult to oppose other erosions of the high open country and thus weakening park plan policy'. The National Park Officer therefore advised the committee not to accept any of the proposed plantations (BBNPC 1979).

However, the committee rapidly agreed to a compromise, accepting the planting of four of the six blocks, with some modifications of the boundaries to soften their impact and to meet an objection from the Nature Conservancy Council. In return for this major concession the committee secured a 25-year agreement with the estate, which had three main points: the remaining disputed areas in the forestry map would be put in category C; permissive paths (not rights of way) would be provided to enable walkers to reach the main summits at most times of the year; and the estate would consult the committee over hill tracks and changes in farming practice that are not subject to development control.

It is characteristic of the secrecy and lack of frankness in the consultation procedure discussed earlier that the Forestry Commission did not disclose the advice it had received from its landscape adviser (Clifford Tandy) to the national park committee, which only learned of it indirectly from the Countryside Commission *after* it had accepted the compromise. For Tandy shared the view of the National Park Officer and the initial view of the committee that Fan Gihirych, perhaps the most controversial of the four blocks, was unsuitable for afforestation 'from the landscape point of view' (CC 1980f). The plantation will occupy a cwm immediately below the sandstone escarpment of Fan Gihirych, which at 725 metres (2323 feet) is the highest point in Fforest Fawr and one of the most prominent landmarks in the entire national park. The Commission no doubt feared that, had the committee known that the Commission was being opposed by its landscape consultant, the committee would not have accepted Fan Gihirych, the omission of which, it later informed the Secretary of State for Wales, clearly would have been desirable in terms of national park policies (BBNPC 1980a). Indeed, the main justification offered by the committee for its acceptance of the compromise was that it was in the unenviable position of having to act effectively with scarcely any powers to do so.

It was a foregone conclusion, once the committee had concluded the deal, that the Secretary of State for Wales would approve it. Had it not been for an objection by the Countryside Commission's Wales Committee, the issue would never have gone to the secretary of state at all. The Commission argued, on the basis of the NPA's policies, that the scheme was incompatible with national park purposes and it drew attention to the large investment of public money involved. But the Secretary of State approved it, with minor boundary adjustments, on the ground that it integrated forestry with hill farming to the advantage of the estate and its employees and achieved a balance between agriculture, forestry and environmental requirements (BBNPC 1980b). It would not, he said, be setting a precedent.

This bland judgement, implying that the compromise was a judicious balance struck between competing claims, obscures the fact that the entire motivation of the scheme was financial, and that the main source of finance was the government itself. The Cnewr Estate wished to raise capital for agricultural development by selling land at the prices prevailing for afforestation and re-investing the proceeds in agricultural development, thereby escaping Capital Gains Tax. The EFG's business, as we have seen, is to buy land on behalf of taxpayers in the upper tax brackets, with the object of using afforestation grants and tax concessions to transmute highly taxed income into tax-free capital gains over a period of years. The EFG calculates that an investor subject to tax at 75% would have to find only £14 963 out of a total capital outlay of £72 550 over ten years on an average upland afforestation site of 100 hectares. Even the 50% taxpayer has to find only £29 925, or 41% of the outlay. At the end of ten years the plantation should be worth £50 000 excluding the value of the land (EFG 1980).

We have calculated the extent of government subvention in a hypothetical case, where 290 ha are sold for coniferous plantation to investors paying

Table 10.4 Government subventions for afforestation and hill farming: hypothetical case 1980–90 (From *Investment in forestry and hill land*, Economic Forestry Group Ltd, April 1980; Agriculture and Horticulture Development Scheme, Explanatory Leaflet, MAFF 1980.)

	£
Afforestation grants under Dedication Basis 111 Scheme, first 10 years, 290 ha	37 000
Tax relief to investor subject to tax at 60%	104 000
Capital grants on farm development scheme, providing 2 additional jobs	65 000
Headage payments, 1000 ewes of hardy breed, at £6.25 over 10 years	62 500
Total	268 500

income tax at 60% and part of the proceeds is re-invested in an Agriculture and Horticulture Development Scheme. It is assumed that capital grants are paid at the higher Less Favoured Area rates and headage payments are made on 1000 additional ewes of a hardy breed at £6.25 per ewe per annum (Table 10.4).

The Brecon Beacons National Park Committee had £500 in its 1980–1 budget for management agreements. One can, therefore, measure very precisely the enormous disparity between the sum of £268 500 of public money offered for forestry and agricultural development and the pittance (£5000 over ten years) on offer to dissuade landowners or investors from forgoing these benefits and incentives. It is not difficult to understand why, in these circumstances, the NPA agreed to compromise. The availability of finance on this scale, in the absence of any power to control afforestation or agricultural development, hampers the search for genuine compromises. For the entire weight of the financial pressure is exerted in favour of one solution, thereby excluding alternatives and producing, at best, a messy compromise.

The Forestry Commission and the private landowners' organisations prefer the consultative procedure we have outlined to planning control. But even the foresters must be frustrated by the absence of clear plans and policies and the waste of time and effort that the procedure involves. National park designation imposes a very limited form of constraint through a war of attrition, in which everybody's patience wears thin. To devise an alternative system will not be easy. Giving the NPAs formal control over afforestation, through a process that would make the Forestry Commission publicly accountable, would be a step forward. A case has been argued for a far more detailed and sophisticated forestry map that would provide a basis for positive programmes of afforestation and woodland management designed to achieve a range of objectives (including timber production) consistent with national park purposes (Price 1980). Implementation might well necessitate some public acquisition of land. The concentration of grants and tax reliefs, to help those who need them and to provide incentives for forestry and woodland projects that harmonise with national park purposes, could release substantial sums for conservation, recreation and job creation. But the starting point of any reformed system must be to question the objectives of current forestry policy and the assumptions on which it rests.

Questionable assumptions

The case for a massive coniferous afforestation programme in the uplands rests on explicit but very questionable assumptions spelt out by the Forestry Commission (1977b) and CAS (1980). For example, the CAS forecast of a world shortage of timber rests on the assumption that the economies of the industrialised nations will grow fourfold over the next 45 years. But the world economic indicators no longer point to growth on this scale. Nor is there any reason to believe that energy or raw materials will be available to support such extravagant levels of consumption in nations that already consume a disproportionate share of the world's resources. The philosophy of growth also leads to the assumption that the demand for timber and timber products in the UK will increase by 45% over the same period. In fact, consumption in the UK fell by 5% between 1965 and 1978 (CAS, ibid.)

The afforestation programmes are focused on the production of pulpwood for conversion into newsprint, paper and board. But the assumptions of growth ignore the implications of the technological changes in information storage and communication that could result in enormous reductions in the consumption of paper and newsprint. They ignore the trend to substitute other materials for paper and board for packaging and the scope for recycling waste. Existing plantations will raise the level of self-sufficiency in the UK to 15% by the next century at present levels of consumption, and to a much higher percentage if demand is reduced by economies in use and the substitution of alternative materials or methods of transmitting information. The forecasts of new jobs in forestry are equally questionable. Forestry is on the same technological treadmill as agriculture and has been shedding labour rapidly as productivity per man is increased by investing in labour-saving machinery for such processes as site preparation and harvesting. The Forestry Commission has claimed (1977b) that planting an additional 1 million hectares would create 1600 'net additional jobs' in forestry by the year 2000 at an undisclosed cost. The jobs are created by statistical sleight-of-hand. When allowance is made for the reduced labour force required to run the existing plantations and the loss of 1000 jobs on hill farms, the result on the Commission's own figures is a net *loss* of 200 jobs between 1975 and 2000. Moreover, the tendency is for more forestry work to be done by contractors employing labour based outside the remoter areas. Allowance must be made, it is true, for the 'multiplier' effect, but the Commission only expects a further 20 jobs to be created locally for every 100 created by expanding timber production – and against this must be set the multiplier working in reverse, by which 20 related jobs are lost for every 100 jobs lost in forestry through further mechanisation and rationalisation.

The investigation of the scientific aspects of forestry by the House of Lords Select Committee on Science and Technology (HL 1980) has exposed, among other things, the very shaky nature of the economic and scientific basis for the afforestation programme. The government requires the Forestry Commission to show an annual return of 3% on its investment, but no account is taken of the losses that the investment may inflict either on other land uses or on the long-term fertility of the soil. In support of its view that 'maximum tree growth is sometimes the enemy of integrated land use', the committee cites the fact that intensive forestry is now known to impair the quantity, flow and quality of water, with the result that 'greater profits to the forestry industry mean greater costs to the water industry'. Commercial forestry assumes that yields of quick-growing species can be sustained indefinitely on the poorer upland soils, but many witnesses referred to the importance of 'ecological sustension' or, in layman's terms, sustaining yield. The Department of Forestry at the University of Oxford considered that this might prove to be the most important limitation to success in forestry. The committee pointed out that while it was possible to reverse many kinds of soil deterioration by various means, including the abandonment of clear felling, the costs were high. It asked but did not answer the question, whether wood was such a valuable commodity as to make intensified management worthwhile. The Institute of Biology suggested that 'the present tenets of forest management may ultimately have to be rethought because of the major risks from pests and pathogens' resulting from planting large even-aged blocks of one or two species and added that 'any extension of forestry along present lines will increase that risk' (ibid., p. 15). Yet the committee had to report that the Forestry Commission, while admitting that 'there is virtually no truly fundamental forestry research in Britain', 'feel no great urge to commission more research' (ibid., p. 33).

Another example of the consequences of foresters' pre-occupation with fast-growing species is the unspoken assumption that Britain will need very few hardwood trees maturing 100 or 150 years from now or reaching the stage of coppicing or thinning in far shorter periods. Within 50 years, unless present trends are drastically reversed, many of the remaining broadleaved woodlands will have gone (NCC 1980b). The CAS and Forestry Commission programmes envisage planting no more than about 5% of broadleaved trees. It is true that at higher altitudes on the poorer soils afforestation means conifers or nothing, at least as a first crop. But for 'economic' reasons conifers are being planted throughout the national parks on soils and at altitudes that could support mixed or broadleaved plantations.

Broadleaved woodlands

The insidious decline of broadleaved woodlands and hedgerow trees is now amply documented. Reports in all the national parks point to the same conclusion. Small woodlands have been written off economically, often management has diminished or ceased, grazing prevents natural regeneration and the inevitable outcome is their ultimate loss. Exceptionally important sites have been acquired by such bodies as the Nature Conservancy Council, the National Trust and the NPAs, but none of them has the resources to acquire more than a small fraction of the threatened woodlands or even to manage all those they already own on sound conservation principles. The Forestry Commission spent £265 000 in 1979–80 on small wood grants, thereby assisting the planting of 377 ha of broadleaved trees (and 365 ha of conifers) in the whole of England and Wales. In 1980 the Countryside Commission had to cut off grants to new applicants under its amenity tree planting scheme for woods up to ¼ ha (on which expenditure had soared from £122 760 in 1975–6 to £807 000 in 1978–9) because government cut back its funds. It seems improbable that new broadleaved planting is even keeping pace with losses from Dutch elm disease, let alone stemming the insidious decline in existing woodlands. There are no grants for the management of existing woodlands or for encouraging natural regeneration.

Conifers have the advantage of growing faster and yielding both a greater mass of timber and a quicker cash return than broadleaved trees. But on the long view broadleaved trees command a higher price, provide a sounder base for local jobs, carry less risk of windblow and fire, have better prospects of natural regeneration, support a richer fauna and flora, often enrich the soil and have a greater potential for recreation and sport. The Forestry Commission has shifted its position in recent years, offering more favourable (although still inadequate) grants for broadleaved planting, and MAFF now offers grants for renewing the hedgerows that, until recently, it was paying farmers to remove. But it is astonishing that forestry 'strategies', designed to be implemented largely by private enterprise, should attach so little importance to the conservation and extension of the existing broadleaved woodlands that are mainly in private ownership. Scientists are now expressing profound concern about both aspects of forestry policy – the monoculture of conifers and the lack of any discernible policy for broadleaved trees, other than that of 'liquidating rather than managing the residual indigenous stock', as one professor of forestry put it to the House of Lords Select Committee.

It is now increasingly recognised, not least by the Select Committee, that one of the keys to the survival of established broadleaved woodlands is to make it possible to manage them economically on a basis that sustains their beauty and wildlife interest. A pilot study of small woodlands on farms in Gwent by the Dartington Amenity Research Trust for the Countryside Commission (DART 1978a) explains the problem and points to a solution dependent on recognising the advantages of small-scale enterprise. The small farmer applies his mind to a five- or six-year farm plan at best. He cannot afford to wait 30 years for a return on the capital invested in trees. He is not in the right tax bracket to benefit from forestry tax reliefs. He is unfamiliar with woodland management and sees no cash in it. The timber contracting industry is geared to large-scale harvesting and selling operations that can yield the £300-a-day turnover (at 1977–8 prices) demanded by a 32-ton truck with integral hoist. Its operators are interested, not in the careful management and replanting of small woodlands, but in 'clear-felling or other operations where they can be quickly in and out'.

A further study of other areas showed that a significant minority of farmers were prepared to look after their own woods if the problems of management, marketing and finance could be overcome (DART 1979). The Forestry Commission has started an experimental advice service in Gwent, but advice cannot solve the structural problems revealed by the studies. The authors summed up their experience after visiting 400 woods: 'our field visits have left us with sadness at such neglect and recent indifference. For at least two generations we have taken everything and (with honourable exceptions) given back nothing. We feel there is a moral responsibility for bringing back these woodlands into health and enhanced beauty which the nation should accept' (DART 1979, p. 85). The DART studies suggest that small woodlands have a serious economic potential for sustained small-scale production and marketing in which the small farmer could play a part, and from which local timber processing industries could develop. The Forestry Commission, however, seems ready to risk a veritable massacre of small woods and copses. An owner can fell 80 cubic metres of timber a quarter without a felling licence, primarily for his own use. He may only sell one sixth of it. The Commission has proposed (FC 1980b) that he should be allowed to sell it all. With timber fetching £3–12 000 an acre, and woodland quadrupling in value if it is converted to farmland, and MAFF improvement grants to be picked up, the financial temptation to fell a quarter of an acre four times a year is enormous. A third of the broadleaf woodlands of England and Wales are of one acre or less.

A new approach

A recent study of the interaction of forestry and farming in Scotland, although focused on the economic, financial and physical factors, concluded that 'small tenanted upland farms integrated with forestry appear to offer the possibility of holding large numbers of people in the countryside' (Mutch & Hutchison 1980). Integration of afforestation with hill or upland farming is now preached universally, and has been one of the formal objectives of the Forestry Commission for many years. But the obstacles (of which land ownership is one of the largest) are rarely faced, and progress has been very small and confined almost entirely to the large farms and estates for which the tax concessions are designed. A member of the Forestry Commission has explained that the Commission envisages 'blocks of forest established in conjunction with agricultural improvement', while looking for 'the coalescence of forests to form large blocks to secure economies of scale' (Stewart 1978). This suggests integration on the scale not of the small farm but of the Cnewr estate and with similar results. Price (1979a) has urged the importance of 'specifying the type of forest that will give the desired environmental and community conditions in the uplands'. But it is precisely this kind of approach that is missing in official contributions to the current debate, a debate in which many of the professional foresters seem to be as blind as the professional agriculturalists to the potential of small-scale production and more sensitive management.

One can begin to see the outline of a new approach to forestry emerging in the DART reports and in the report of the Select Committee. The latter was cautious in its recommendations, particularly on the need for new initiatives in scientific research. But it drew the conclusion from the scientific evidence that the Commission's statutory objectives should be reviewed fundamentally to bring them into harmony with other uses such as water and conservation where 'integration is still in its infancy'. There is a yawning void between the spirit of these reports and the spirit of the government's statement of December 1980 on forest policy which, by coincidence, was made almost on the day on which the Select Committee reported. The government statement seems to have been inspired by three ideological aims: to strip the nation's publicly owned assets of timber and land for the benefit of financial and commercial institutions; to subsidise the latter heavily to enable them to play the leading role in afforestation; and to reduce administrative costs and public involvement in the management of private forestry. The ritual tributes are paid to conservation and the integration of land use, but verbal concern for conservation seems to be focused on the 'sensitive areas' and to have little regard for the countryside as a whole. A former chairman of the Forestry Commission was moved by the statement to tell *The Times* that 'governments never learn' (Mackie 1980).

There can be no doubt of the need for a radically new approach. The big question is whether the Forestry Commission is capable of giving a lead in a new direction or whether its inbuilt obsession with fast-growing species and quick returns makes it the major obstacle to change. A recent study measuring the receptivity of 20 government departments and public agencies to the ideas of some 70 environmental organisations put the Forestry Commission third from the bottom of the list. Only MAFF and the Central Electricity Generating Board were less receptive to their thinking (Lowe & Goyder, forthcoming). There may be a strong case, not for carving up the Commission's estate between the financial and commercial institutions, but for redistributing major parts of it among other public or semi-public bodies (including the NPAs and the National Trust), private agencies and community groups. What the authors object to is not the planting of conifers, which in suitable circumstances can be very beautiful trees and provide very useful timber, but the gross distortions produced by the ideology and objectives of the Forestry Commission and government. Forestry and woodlands have a central role to play in the management of the natural and human resources of the uplands and control over afforestation is a necessary element in any new approach. But controls based on crude forestry maps will not get us very far. There have to be radical changes in government policy and forestry must take its place at the local level in integrated plans for the management of land and resources.

11 *Two explosive issues*

In an increasingly centralised state there is almost no limit to the influence of central government on the physical environment and the social and economic life of the countryside. In selecting the cases of military training and mineral working in national parks for study in this chapter we are very conscious of the wide ramifications of government in the areas that we have had to omit. An outstanding case is water storage and abstraction where the policies applied at local level by regional water authorities have pervasive and sometimes destructive effects on land use, the economy, landscape and recreation.

In the Peak, some 29% of the total area of the park is committed to water catchment. In the Brecon Beacons, 16 reservoirs supply South Wales. The water resources of the Lake District not only give the park its name and international reputation, but have to supply Manchester and other parts of the north-west. A government decision to construct a processing plant for spent uranium at Windscale, coupled with rising demand for water in West Cumbria, led to a prolonged public inquiry in 1980 into proposals to extract more water from Wastwater (the Lake District's wildest and most spectacular lake) and Ennerdale. The Central Electricity Generating Board's policy of relying on pumped storage schemes to provide a reserve of electrical power at times of peak load points inevitably to developments in mountainous areas, where the required drop in level between two storage reservoirs can be obtained. Having completed two pumped storage schemes in Snowdonia, including the remarkable Dinorwic scheme referred to on page 101, the electricity authorities at the moment are investigating two environmentally damaging schemes at sites on Ben Lomond in Scotland and at Longdendale in the heart of the Peak District. Nor are water and power the only areas influenced by central policy making that we have had to leave out. Central government is a major influence in transport and highways, telecommunications, local government services, the storage of nuclear wastes, trade and industry, tourism and other aspects of sport and recreation.

However, our purpose is not to demonstrate the total effect of government policy but to illustrate different ways in which government's influence is felt and the conflicts over policy within government itself. Military training and mineral working are extreme cases, in the sense that no activities do greater violence to the purposes of a national park than bombardment by high explosive or the extraction of minerals by modern (and equally explosive) techniques from large mines or quarries. The government is involved directly in military training, politically through its decisions on defence policy and practically through the operational demands of the armed forces. Its involvement in mineral working is indirect, for mineral extraction is a function of private enterprise within a market economy and government's function is to promote a viable industry, extend geological knowledge and control development. But mineral extraction by private enterprise raises issues very similar to those of the development of water or hydro-electric power by public authorities. Should policies aim to satisfy assumed requirements or to conserve the resource? How are conflicting demands to be resolved?

Mineral working

The changed character of the demand for minerals and the concentration of production in fewer, larger, more capital intensive plants, that we described in Chapter 4, have sharpened the conflicts of interest inherent in mineral extraction. The scale of destructiveness has increased correspondingly, not merely through the ability of modern earth-shifting equipment literally to move mountains, but through the effects of waste disposal, blasting, ancillary works, dust, noise and heavy road traffic. It is hard to conceive of anything more destructive of a rural landscape than such limestone quarries as Tunstead in the Peak or the Swinden or Ribblesdale quarries in the Yorkshire Dales, with working faces up to a mile long, periodical blasting, large noisy industrial processing plants, heavy traffic congesting the roads and dust polluting the villages and countryside for miles around. The china clay workings at Lee Moor in Dartmoor and the vast waste tips are incongruous and unsightly despite recent attempts at landscaping.

Several sets of conflicting and overlapping interests can be identified. There is a clear national interest in providing industry with essential raw materials and, as nature has tended to concentrate Britain's limited resources of valuable minerals in national parks, nobody denies that some mineral working in national parks is inevitable. But the mineral companies are in business in an international market to make money by satisfying demand, which can be grossly inflated by wasteful consumption and extravagant forecasts. The short-term interest of the mineral companies in making profit and of the government in achieving a surplus in its balance of payments conflicts with the long-term national interest in husbanding precious, finite resources by thriftiness in use. The increased demand for fluorspar and limestone between 1951 and 1971 placed such an acute strain on the Peak National Park, where the major resources of both materials are located, that the board's structure plan identified 'the growing scale of mineral working as the most obvious long-term threat to the character of the national park'. The Peak Board sees little justification for the exploitation of the fluorspar resources of the national park by international mineral companies to meet 'general world demands'. It suggests that the national interest may be better served by retaining fluorspar for future use in this country than by exploiting it quickly for short-term gain in export earnings (PPJPB 1980).

The concentration of production in ever larger mines or complexes is in conflict with the national interest in protecting the landscape by locating production in the least sensitive areas and diminishing the scale of the impact. It has been an uphill struggle for many years to modify the industry's tradition of keeping production costs to the rock bottom and abandoning derelict sites without after-treatment or restoration. Also there is a conflict of interest between local working people who want jobs (and get the support of local authorities and trade unions) and those (often outsiders) who place amenity first. But local people too have an interest in protecting their health and the environment in which they live. They also find that as production rises the number of jobs declines.

Neither the scale and destructiveness of modern quarries, nor the need to husband scarce, finite resources were anticipated fully in 1949. But Lewis Silkin, the Minister of Town and Country Planning, spelt out the test of national interest that would have to be satisfied before new mineral workings would be allowed in national parks. This has come to be known as the 'Silkin test' and was as follows:

> It must be demonstrated quite clearly that the exploitation of these minerals is absolutely necessary in the public interest. It must be clear beyond all doubt that there is no possible alternative source of supply, and if those two conditions are satisfied then permission must be subject to the condition that restoration takes place at the earliest possible opportunity (Silkin 1949).

The 'Silkin test' laid the onus of displacing the presumption against mineral exploitation squarely on the developer. Successive governments gave the test verbal endorsement, but they were unwilling to give it statutory force or (as we shall see) to approve its inclusion in structure plans. The test also had an inherent weakness, for it assumed that mineral working inside a national park must be more objectionable in principle than working outside. Unfortunately, some areas outside national parks are as sensitive as areas inside them. Matters have been complicated further by the failure of government to compile inventories of mineral resources or to develop policies for their exploitation related to clearly stated principles.

Divided interests within government itself are reflected in the division of responsibility for minerals between three government departments. The Department of Energy is responsible for the fossil fuels. The Department of Trade is the 'sponsoring department' for a wide range of metallic ores and industrial minerals and as such it is required to promote the viability of the mining industry in ways consistent with the government's wider aims (Stevens 1976). It promotes exploration for minerals by offering 35% grants, only repayable when minerals have been extracted. The Department of the Environment, on the other hand, is responsible for planning land use and for protecting the environment. The Secretary of State imposes government policy, if there is one, by exercising his power to approve or modify county structure plans and by deciding development proposals referred to him on appeal or called in for ministerial decision.

The big mining and chemical companies become heavily committed to the exploitation of a mineral resource long before their proposals are submitted to the local authority in the form of a planning application. Rio Tinto Zinc provoked an explosion of protest when it was discovered accidentally in 1969 that it had been stealthily buying up mineral rights for three years and drilling for copper ore in the Capel Hermon area of Snowdonia National Park without applying for planning permission. Graham Searle has given an illuminating account of RTZ's activities and of the public inquiry that led to the grant of planning permission for test drilling for copper (Searle 1975). Rio Tinto Zinc established the existence of a large body of low-grade copper ore, the extraction of which by open cast working would have totally transformed the landscape. Market uncertainties probably explain RTZ's decision not to proceed with its copper venture, but the issue has been deferred only until the progressive exhaustion of richer ore bodies makes it profitable. The search is now on for oil and gas in the national parks. In 1980 the Secretary of State awarded a license to explore in the Peak District to RTZ (NPN 1980c) and the North York Moors National Park Committee consented to exploratory drilling by Taylor Woodrow Energy Ltd (NPN 1980b). Should oil or gas be found, the test to be applied will no longer be the Silkin test but the criteria that the secretary of state has substituted for it in structure plans for national park areas.

The Peak Structure Plan was the first one affecting a national park to be approved by the secretary of state. It was submitted in 1976 to Peter Shore, the Labour minister, and finally approved by Michael Heseltine, his Tory successor in 1979. Both were agreed in striking out of the plan a more precise version of the Silkin test which the minerals industry had already accepted. This placed the onus of proof on the applicant to show (a) that the proposal is vital to the public interest and (b) that it is clear beyond all doubt that there are no practical alternative sources of supply. If these criteria could be satisfied, the board would nonetheless have to be satisfied on two additional tests: are the environmental and other consequences so adverse as to outweigh the national need for the mineral, and are the detailed methods of working and associated ameliorative measures adequate to minimise the impact of the proposal on the surrounding area? In the event of all four tests being satisfied, the board would then impose conditions to ensure satisfactory control of the various operations and final rehabilitation once operations had ceased.

Shore and Heseltine modified this test in three fundamental ways (PPJPB 1979) and the latter subsequently made similar modifications to the North

Yorkshire Structure Plan which covers the Yorkshire Dales and North York Moors National Parks (NYCC 1980). First, they removed the presumption that new and extended mineral workings would be refused unless the tests could be satisfied and substituted a statement that the authority would 'normally' resist mineral workings that constituted 'a major intrusion' or were 'detrimental on a large scale' to national park purposes. Second, they relieved individual applicants of the need to prove that their proposals were vital to the public interest and that it was clear beyond doubt that there were no practicable alternative sources of supply. The onus of proof was shifted on to the local planning authority. Shore and Heseltine substituted a list of criteria, including the need to conserve the parks but not including the need to husband finite resources, against which proposals would be 'vigorously examined'. Third, they deleted policies designed to reserve the highest grade chemical limestone – which is now widely used for aggregates in construction or for road surfacing – for uses which require its unique chemical properties. They substituted a statement that the authority would 'have particular regard to the need for high purity limestone for industrial purposes'.

The implications of the revised wording can be appreciated by studying successive ministerial decisions by Shore and Heseltine on ICI's appeal against the Peak Board's refusal to permit the extension of its Tunstead limestone quarry (DOE 1978b, 1980a). Tunstead is the largest limestone quarry in Europe, an immense integrated plant whose primary function is the production of high quality limestone products from the highest grade chemical limestone. Its development enabled ICI to close smaller quarries. The proposal was to drive a new mile-long face more than half a mile into the national park so as nearly to double its annual output from 5.5 to 10 million tonnes. As the quarry straddles the national park boundary, planning permission was required both from Derbyshire County Council and from the Peak Board. The former gave planning approval in 1974 but the latter refused – the decisions reflecting the county council's concern about jobs and the board's concern about environment. ICI appealed and the appeal was heard at a protracted public inquiry in 1976. The Inspector reported in favour of ICI in 1977 and the minister decided in ICI's favour in 1978. The board appealed to the High Court, which ruled in favour of the board on certain points of law. The minister gave his modified decision in favour of ICI in 1980. Few cases illustrate more clearly the protracted, wasteful and costly nature of the adversarial process as a device for determining policy.

The case raised at least three important questions. The first was whether it was in the national interest to double the quarry's capacity to meet the demand anticipated by ICI, whose 'experts' submitted grossly exaggerated forecasts. Demand for industrial purposes was based on the assumed growth of the British economy at between 2.2% and 3% annually into the 21st century. The technical assessor calculated that ICI was assuming a 5% compound annual growth in steel production, a rate 'unparalleled in modern times' by an industry whose production had been almost static for 15 years (and has since fallen by more than half). The head of ICI's Chlorine Alkaline Product Group anticipated that the demand for alkali (mainly used in glass manufacture) would expand by 3.25% a year 'into the indefinite future'. The inspector found that 'the evidence for this vast postulated expansion in the lime demand is meagre and unconvincing'. Nevertheless, he accepted ICI's estimate of future demand on the ground that 'it is better to be on the over-generous side'. The minister concurred and granted a 60-year permission to satisfy a demand for which no convincing evidence had been produced.

The second question was whether limestone of chemical grade should be extracted and used for purposes for which lower-grade rock would serve equally well. The industry has been concentrating production in large complexes where economies of scale can be achieved by extracting chemical grade limestone and using it to meet the demand for aggregates as well as for chemical uses. This has led to production expanding more rapidly in national parks, where some of the highest quality limestone is located, than in areas outside. The volume of limestone produced for aggregate in Derbyshire (including the Peak) increased by 715% between 1954 and 1971. Tunstead is primarily designed to produce limestone for chemical purposes and ICI has undertaken that aggregates will only be produced as a byproduct. But a roadstone coating plant and additional crushing capacity have been installed specifically to meet the rising demand for aggregates. The inspector concluded that 'an over-optimistic resource plan might tempt ICI to increase aggregate sales to take up any slack that might occur in chemical demand'.

Nevertheless, the secretary of state upheld ICI's appeal against a condition restricting the use of high-grade limestone for aggregates, on the legal ground that planning legislation did not enable planning authorities to say for what use a mineral should be sold. The board appealed and the High Court upheld the board's view that it had such a power. However, when robbed of his legal pretext, the secretary of state declined to change his policy saying that he preferred to rely on voluntary undertakings.

The third question was whether ICI should have to demonstrate that there were no practicable alternative sources of supply. The technical assessor found that ICI's submission on alternatives was 'far too sketchy to serve the purpose for which it was designed'. Both the inspector and the minister decided that the onus of proving that suitable alternative sources of supply did not exist rested on the board. The absence of a national inventory of mineral resources or any national plans for their exploitation thus became a factor favouring the developer, for the board clearly has neither the resources nor the status to remedy the omissions of central government.

Many years of protest led the government to appoint a committee to inquire into planning control over mineral development. Its report (Stevens 1976) confirmed many of the difficulties. These included problems of enforcement, the lack of recognised procedures to secure satisfactory after-use or restoration of the site (through insurance bonds or otherwise), the existence of many earlier permissions without time limits or with insufficiently tough conditions and the prohibitive cost of buying out earlier permissions. As we write, legislation to implement some of the recommendations on these matters is in preparation. But there is no indication that the government will respond to the Stevens recommendation that the government should formulate national policies for individual minerals or groups of minerals, against which planning authorities could test applications and assess alternative sources of supply.

However, it is incorrect to say, as some of the government's critics do, that it has no minerals policy. The decisions on the Peak and North Yorkshire structure plans and the Tunstead appeal show that the policy is to allow market forces and considerations to be the main generators of the programmes for extracting minerals. Ministers have reversed the presumptions against mineral working in national parks, rejected policies that would husband a finite resource and accepted without question the need to meet whatever demand the market throws up. The secretary of state, in modifying the North Yorkshire Structure Plan, accepted the conclusions of the report made to him by the inspectors on the public examination of the plan. This criticised the plan for giving insufficient weight to the 'commercial security' of operators and expressed the fear that in a national or international market undue restrictions in the national parks could lead to excess pressure in areas where less restrictive policies operated. This point of view is incompatible with the Silkin test, but it puts nothing constructive in its place.

In the absence of a national plan or strategy, the NPAs are compelled to compromise with the mineral companies, or to engage in a gladiatorial contest at public inquiries. Not only are the results hard to predict, but the adversaries are very unevenly matched. On the one side is a huge multinational company, able to spend virtually unlimited sums on technical and legal advice and knowing the business of minerals inside out. On the other is a small local authority, which lacks comparable skills, knowledge and resources. The Tunstead inquiry lasted for five months and placed such a strain on the Peak staff that, we were told, all but essential office work was brought to a standstill. Stevens identified the local authorities' lack of professional and technical skills when faced by the mineral companies as a major weakness and recommended that they should have more, qualified staff at their disposal. But the cutbacks in local government staff and finance can only further weaken the authorities.

The secretary of state's rejection in 1979 of an appeal by Whitby Potash Ltd, a subsidiary of Consolidated Goldfields, is said to point to a firmer conservation policy. The company had asked the North York Moors National Park Committee to renew an earlier permission to mine and refine potash on a site near Whitby that had lapsed through non-use. The secretary of state's refusal was based on two grounds (DOE 1979b). The first was that the extraction technique to be adopted would have sterilised a vast amount of ore; the second was that the industrial complex with a chimney 80 metres high discharging 12 to 14 tonnes of sulphur dioxide and soot into the atmosphere every day, a processing building 30 metres high and a loading tower 41 metres high would be a 'massive intrusion into the rural scene'. However, it is not unfair to point out that the secretary of state was under no pressure to find in the company's favour. The company was clearly in no hurry to proceed with the development in the prevailing market conditions and withdrew its application shortly before the decision to reject it was made. The decision letter holds the door open for a future application to be granted if the design were less brutal and the exploitation of the resource more efficient.

The Peak Board has succeeded over a quarter of a century, by sheer persistence and in the face of unhelpful decisions by successive ministers, in progressively tightening up the conditions imposed on mineral companies. In 1979 it made a breakthrough in the restoration of old workings by making the grant of permission to Dresser Industries Inc. to extract a million tonnes of fluorspar from Lathkill Dale conditional on the deposit of a bond for £175 000. The need for such a bond was evident from the fact that the adjoining site had previously been exploited and abandoned by an Italian company. The board secured the bond by refusing planning permission in the first place. But the price paid by the board was also a heavy one. Lathkill Dale, one of the most beautiful in the park, will be despoiled for many years – and Lathkill Dale is just the beginning as far as Dresser's are concerned. Its general manager was reported as saying 'we are aiming to dig out 400 000 tonnes a year, and to be around for 20 years, so I suppose you could say one new site for each year. But we think it will get easier as time goes by' (*The Guardian* 25 September 1978). It is a verdict that, in our view, is supported by the evidence. Resource conservation plays little or no part in government policy and the mineral companies can sense which way the wind is blowing.

The *ad hoc*, demand-oriented market approach and the gladiatorial combat between unequal parties are the wrong way to settle these conflicts between competing interests. Plans for the management of resources at the local level should be prepared by local planning authorities within the framework of national mineral policies. The frugal use of minerals and the conservation of the environment should be built into the policies and plans at both levels. The experience gained with coal and oil suggests that full control over exploitation and after-use is unlikely to be achieved unless mineral rights are publicly owned and their exploitation regulated by the terms of licenses granted by the state.

Military training

The use of national parks for artillery ranges and other forms of military training was established many years before the national parks were designated.

It cannot have come as a surprise to anybody that Lady Sharp concluded, in her report on military training in Dartmoor (Sharp 1977), that it was 'exceedingly damaging'. But it struck her as odd that when the park was designated in 1954 no reference seems to have been made to the established military use. Yet it was as obvious then as it is now that, in Lady Sharp's words, 'military training and a national park are discordant, incongruous and inconsistent'. The question that has to be faced is whether the designation of a 'national park' has any validity if such a manifestly destructive and incompatible use is tolerated within it.

The Ministry of Defence is established in every national park except Exmoor. It owns or leases 44 000 ha in the National Parks (see Table 7.1), or more than four times the holdings of the NPAs. The MOD land holdings are concentrated in three main areas, in each of which it is one of the largest employers. In Northumberland the ranges and dry training areas occupy 22 700 ha, or about a fifth of the national park. In the Pembrokeshire Coast, the Castlemartin tank range of 2700 ha occupies one of the most spectacular stretches of the coast and prevents the public use of the long-distance coastal path when firing is taking place. But Dartmoor, where the military own or lease about 13 369 ha, mainly for firing ranges, has for long been the scene of the greatest controversy and presents the conflicts generated by military use in the sharpest form.

Military training is dangerous, damaging, intimidating and obtrusive. The noise and disturbance caused by firing live ammunition are aggravated by the use of helicopters and low-flying aircraft. The ground is scarred by shell and mortar fire. In Dartmoor the widespread archaeological sites and tors are particularly vulnerable. The public is allowed access to the ranges when firing is not taking place, on a more generous scale in Dartmoor, where firing is suspended at holiday periods, than in Northumberland. The Ministry of Defence has advised the authors that in the 12 months from November 1979 to October 1980 firing took place on 106 days on the Okehampton range, 114 days on Willsworthy range and 50 days on Merrivale range, peaking in June. Firing took place in every month except August. But the ominous red lettered 'danger zone' markings on OS maps, the difficulty of knowing when firing will take place and the widely advertised existence of unexploded ammunition deter the walker. Controlling public access necessitates a vast apparatus of warning signs, flags, notices, huts and prominent observation points. Even 'dry training', in which no live ammunition is fired, can bring large numbers of men into quiet areas firing blank ammunition, using pyrotechnics, supported by helicopters and vehicles, digging in and fencing. Military roads penetrate some of the remotest areas of both Northumberland and Dartmoor National Parks. Lady Sharp found that the invasion of the heart of Dartmoor's northern moorland plateau by military and civilian cars, using the military road and tracks, was perhaps the worst aspect of the military presence.

It has been argued, for example, by the Nature Conservancy Council at the Sharp inquiry, that the military presence causes no significant damage to flora or fauna and benefits them indirectly by maintaining the traditional grazing regime and reducing recreational use. Not all scientists share this view. The Conservation Officer for Dartmoor National Park has expressed concern at the possibility of erosion caused by the Army's new howitzer, which is reported to have made craters 3–4 ft deep and up to 20 ft across at 10-ft intervals on Great Knesset Tor (WMN 1980). One theme of the conference of NPAs, held in Northumberland in 1979, was the value of military occupation in protecting wildlife from human beings, preventing the Forestry Commission from planting conifers and providing jobs for local people. We were reminded of the town planning professor who gave evidence on behalf of the Snowdonia National Park Joint Advisory Committee at the inquiry into the Trawsfynnydd nuclear power station in 1959. Such was his enthusiasm for the project that the inspector, Colin Buchanan, who advised the Minister to reject the project, summarised the professor's view as being that 'no national park is really complete without a nuclear power station'. No national park, it seemed at the Northumberland conference, was really complete without an artillery range, although the Northumberland NPA has opposed the storage of nuclear wastes in the Cheviots.

In a similar spirit the Pembrokeshire Coast National Park Committee suggests in the National Park Plan that military use has probably prevented the spread of the kind of 'development' that the committee's predecessors allowed to disfigure long stretches of the coastline. But these arguments only highlight the weakness of NPAs and the failure of national park designation to protect the environment or to manage recreation. They do not justify the use of national parks for artillery ranges or the exclusion of the public from some of their wildest and most beautiful parts.

The positions adopted by the NPAs tend to be ambivalent. The Countryside Commission, in its review of national park plans, rebuked authorities with major military installations for failing to press for their removal (CC 1980d). The Dartmoor plan does in fact call for the termination of live firing, and the Brecon Beacons plan would like to see the small arms range at Cwm Gwdi, in the heart of the park, removed 'as soon as possible'. But established military bases provide jobs that would not be replaced easily and there is strong emotional and political support for the military presence. In practice, the desire to accommodate the military is stronger than the desire to exclude it. The position of the Ministry of Defence, on the other hand, is crystal clear. It is prepared to make marginal adjustments to its military training areas and programmes in the interests of public relations and has become positively keen about wildlife conservation. It is determined to hang on to all its major training areas, including those in national parks, and to retain some scope for their expanded use. One reason for this determination is that firing ranges fall into the same category as prisons and borstals. Public opinion is for them, provided they are located somewhere else. It is almost impossible for the MOD to open new ranges without facing a public outcry and resorting to its ultimate civilian weapon (which it tries not to use) of compulsory purchase.

The running controversy over the use of Dartmoor illustrates these tendencies very clearly. Dartmoor is a small, very heavily used and accessible park. It was designated largely because it contained the most extensive area of high moorland in southern Britain, covering 48 000 ha (118 500 acres) or over half the area of the park. The MOD occupies 13 369 ha (33 021 acres) or over a quarter of the high moorland (Fig. 11.1). Its firing ranges extend over 11 380 ha (28 109 acres) and occupy 78% of the 'wilderness' area that the NPA has identified in the northern moorland plateau (DNPC 1981), as well as the lovely upper Tavy and Cowsic valleys. The MOD owns the Willsworthy range, but operates the other ranges and dry training areas under leases or licenses from other landowners. The Duchy of Cornwall, which owns most of the high moorland, licenses the Okehampton and Merrivale ranges, extending to 10 000 ha (24 700 acres) (Table 7.1). The acuteness of the conflict provoked by military use on this scale can be judged from the fact that Lord Nugent's Defence Lands Committee received more representations about Dartmoor than about any other site (Nugent 1973). But the Nugent Committee also started its review of military land holdings on the

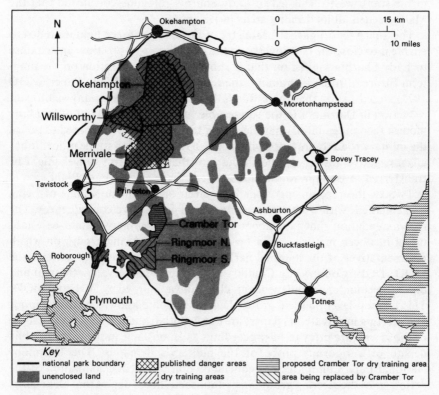

Figure 11.1 Military training areas of Dartmoor. Crown copyright reserved.

assumption that no new sites to which training could be transferred from Dartmoor would be available. As a result, the Nugent recommendations only led to marginal reductions in the military holdings on Dartmoor from about 53 square miles to 51 square miles (Sharp 1977). John Cripps, the chairman of the Countryside Commission, complained in a note of dissent that the Nugent Committee had made no real effort to find alternatives to Dartmoor, as was in fact the case.

Once more the MOD went through the motions of an inquiry, this time in partnership with the Department of the Environment whose former Permanent Secretary, Lady Sharp, was appointed to inquire into the continued use of Dartmoor for military training. But again no genuine investigation either of the military's needs or of alternative sites was made. That there is scope for relieving pressure on England and Wales is suggested by the fact that 91% of the MOD's land holdings are in these countries and only 9% in Scotland (CC 1979c, Table 111 A9). Lady Sharp was required to have regard to the needs of the Army and the Royal Marines to retain their bases in the south-west and to have training facilities in the area. She interpreted her terms of reference – 'to consider whether military training needs could, without unacceptable loss of efficiency, be met elsewhere' – to mean 'elsewhere in the south-west'. This led to Lady Sharp's foregone conclusion that the MOD needed all its training areas in Dartmoor.

The Sharp report gave the Ministry of Defence the green light it needed to enable it to close the controversy and to consolidate its position. In response to Lady Sharp's suggestion that it should declare its position on the long-term future of military training, the joint MOD/DOE White Paper (MOD 1977) stated firmly that there was no possibility of making any significant reduction in Dartmoor in the foreseeable future. It rejected out of hand the modest recommendation that the armed forces should be prepared to police the military road to prevent civilian cars driving off it on to the moor. It has given negative answers to the suggestions that small arms ranges might be transferred to Bodmin Moor, and artillery firing to Salisbury Plain.

Two of the recommendations have been or are in the course of being implemented, with what we can only regard as negative consequences. The recommendation that permanent consultative machinery should be established has been met by setting up a consultative steering group, on which representatives of the national park committee, the army and marines, the MOD, DOE, Countryside Commission, Nature Conservancy Council and others meet under an 'independent' chairman appointed by DOE and MOD. This is a top-level political group, lacking intimate knowledge of the moor and meeting in private. Its papers are confidential, and it is regarded by some of those who are privy to its proceedings as an obstacle in the way of public debate or a rigorous probe of the military's demands. The Dartmoor National Park Committee has concluded that a critical examination of the period since the steering group was established 'does suggest that all benefits have accrued to military training interests' (DNPC 1981).

The recommendation that dry training should be transferred from 473 ha of National Trust land at Ringmoor to some other place or places within the park is in the process of being implemented. The National Trust decided to terminate its license to the MOD because it believed that the permanent use of its land for military training was inconsistent with the Trust's obligations to the public and incompatible with the purposes of a national park (Sharp 1977). The unique 'inalienable' status of Trust land meant that only an Act of Parliament could have overridden the Trust's decision. As a result, dry training is to be moved from the Trust's land even deeper into the southern moorland to Cramber Tor, an area that had not suffered in this way before. The decisive factor in the decision was the readiness of the South West Regional Water Authority (SWRWA), which owns Cramber Tor as part of its catchment area for Burrator reservoir, to allow dry training on its land. The MOD came to an understanding with the SWRWA before formally presenting its proposals to the national park committee and to the steering group in 1980. The committee and the group then accepted the advice of the National Park Officer that Cramber Tor was the 'least damaging' alternative. Both he and the Countryside Commission took the view that it would have been less damaging to continue training at Ringmoor and the Countryside Commission entered a formal objection to training at Cramber Tor on the ground that the need to use publicly owned land for this purpose had not been made out (CC 1980e).

The policy of the landowner is clearly of far greater significance than the policy of the NPA. If any part of Dartmoor is crying out for 'relief' it is the northern 'wilderness' on Duchy of Cornwall land, much of it a grade 1 SSSI, that has been taken over lock, stock and barrel for firing practice with high explosive. Since the Sharp report, the military has been consolidating its hold and intensifying its activities, laying new land lines, erecting prominent look-out huts and trying out its new howitzer. The Prince of Wales Council, unlike the National Trust, feels bound by government and has agreed to license the Duchy's moorland for military training so long as this is government policy. Lady Sayer, a Dartmoor commoner married to a retired admiral, who has for years been the main thorn in the military's flesh, regards the Duchy as a complaisant landowner which can be relied on not to be too fussy about enforcing the conditions of its license. Lady Sayer has not been contradicted in her assertions that the military has repeatedly ignored conditions designed to protect the natural and archaeological features (Sayer 1977, 1980).

The Dartmoor National Park Committee, which is chaired by another retired admiral and is far from unsympathetic to military needs, approved the following basic policy objectives in January 1981:

'military training in Dartmoor as a National Park is inappropriate. The objective must be its ultimate withdrawal, and thus all decisions of the National Park Authority with regard to military matters in the meantime

must take this into account, and seek to minimise the impact of training'
(DNPC 1981, p. 6).

On this basis the NPC has asserted that it may reasonably scrutinise the
Services' proposals for improvements in its training facilities 'upon the
simple basis that the more money is sunk in Dartmoor the more difficult it
will be to bring about the ultimate removal of military training . . . small
improvements may have to be opposed not so much for what they are but for
the way in which they, when taken with other improvements, may frustrate
the long term objective'. The NPA therefore decided 'to resist investment in
military facilities which might consolidate the present position: to discourage all training that could not be done elsewhere, and not to approve the
licensing of new land for military use in the National Park'.

Military training presents in its starkest form the contrast not merely
between conflicting government policies, but between conflicting aspects of
human nature and society. The supreme irony of Dartmoor is to go there in
search of freedom and to find its centre dominated by a jail, or to go there in
search of peace and natural beauty and to find them blasted to pieces by men
being systematically trained in violence. The vast 'golf balls' of the Fylingdales missile radar stations on the North York Moors, jointly operated with
the US, remind those who would get away from it all that there is no escape
from nuclear war, of which Fylingdales would probably be a 'first strike'
victim. The US's largest underwater surveillance station, monitoring Soviet
submarine movements, is at Brawdy in the Pembrokeshire Coast National
Park and is a prime candidate for a nuclear strike aimed at disabling the US
information network. There is no room for compromise between those who
believe that this training ensures peace and those who believe as we do, on
the basis of historical experience, that it makes war more likely. There are no
easy solutions and no one solution need have a universal application. But
three possible approaches suggest themselves.

One would be to exclude the military area from the national park on the
ground that military training, and live firing in particular, totally negates its
purpose. This would reveal the true position but would eliminate the protection given to the areas to be excluded and would consolidate the military
presence in them. Another would be to continue the present policy, which is
to accept military training even in its most violent forms, while using designation as a lever to extract some concessions from the military. Experience
suggests that designation has secured some minor concessions, such as
improved public access and marginal boundary changes. But acceptance in
principle of military training relieves the MOD of all serious pressures and
probably guarantees the permanent presence of the military on whatever
scale it chooses. A third strategy is to continue protective designations on the
clear understanding that the MOD will progressively withdraw and ultimately terminate military training. Every military claim would then be ruth-
lessly probed. Had the policy approved by the Dartmoor National Park

Committee in January 1981 been operative in 1979–80 no alternative would have been provided when the military were obliged to withdraw from Ringmoor. This strategy cannot be very successful without a fundamental change in MOD policy, at least as regards national parks and probably as regards the level of military preparedness. But if it were adopted by the Countryside Commission, the NPAs and their individual members and the voluntary conservation and recreation groups, continuous pressure could be exerted for the reduction and ultimate elimination of the military presence. The objectives of management are the critical issues, and the land management policies of the public land-holding agencies are at the heart of the problem. Dartmoor offers the clearest evidence of this. Military training is shifting from Ringmoor to Cramber Tor solely because the National Trust, fortified by its statutory position, denied the use of Ringmoor to the MOD. The NPA, not being the owner of the land and having no legal powers, was little more than a passive observer while decisions were being made elsewhere in the light of the management policies of the public and semi-public bodies concerned.

Part 5   *Change of direction*

Introduction

We have travelled a long way from our point of departure, which was to ask
whether there is a place for national parks in the peculiarly British meaning
of the term in our system for conservation and enjoyment of the countryside.
It should come as no surprise to those readers who have accompanied us on
our journey to learn that we do not think this question can be answered in a
meaningful way unless we do so in a context that is far broader than the
national parks themselves. The future of the national parks is inseparable
from the future of the countryside as a whole. We have, therefore, divided
the final part of this book into two chapters. The first draws some conclusions concerning the national parks, their purposes, the criteria for their
selection, the meaning of designation and how the system could be strengthened, given a sounder social and economic base and extended to some additional areas. The final chapter discusses the meaning of conservation and the
contrasting approaches favoured by government and by some conservationists – the cosmetic approach on the one hand and the integrated approach on
the other. This in turn leads into a debate on the purposes of protective designation, the roles of persuasion and compulsion, the division of responsibility
for conservation between the Countryside Commission and the Nature
Conservancy Council, and the political obstacles standing in the way of
effective policies for the conservation and enjoyment of the countryside.

12 *A place for national parks*

Lessons of a misunderstood system

A visit to national parks in the Canadian Rocky Mountains and to Yellowstone in the United States brought home to us the richness and the variety of the scenery and the experiences offered by our own national parks. The extraordinary profiles and textures of the Canadian Rockies, sculptured by geological processes, time and weather, are unforgettable. But one can drive for hundreds of miles without any change in the essential elements of the landscape – snow-capped peaks, glaciers, glaciated valleys, rivers and waterfalls and, on the lower slopes, seemingly endless blankets of natural forest consisting mainly of spruce and lodgepole pine. The visitors who have the time, the interest and the enterprise – a tiny fraction of the whole – to venture deep into the natural wilderness on foot, horseback or ski are richly rewarded. But from the tarmac corridor, where most visitors spend most of their time, the natural environment is seen as a dramatic spectacle – and even the most spectacular scenery can pall.

Our national parks are not in the same class for grandeur, natural phenomena or the extent of wilderness. But a lifetime is not long enough to explore their diversity, where the scenery changes every mile, the semi-wild is within easy reach and man's continuing relationship with nature has added another dimension to the experience of most visitors. We are blind neither to the beauty of the lowlands and other upland areas nor to the fact that landscapes in the lowlands are exposed to threats at least as serious as those faced by the national parks. Nor are we indifferent to the recreational potential of other areas, or to the recreational needs of urban areas remote from the national parks. The point about the national parks is not that they are more beautiful than other areas, but that they have unique combinations of specific qualities. These vary from park to park and from place to place, but common to them all are extensive areas of relatively wild country. Taken together they constitute a precious national resource of international significance. In an exploitative, consumer society equipped with modern technology, special measures are required for the protection and management of such areas if they are to be handed down to future generations with their essential qualities intact and if reasonable provision is to be made for the conflicting needs of the present generation of inhabitants and visitors.

Our study of the national park system in Part 3 and of the impact of central government policies in Part 4 has shown that the system is still essentially a cosmetic one. Its ability to constrain the government policies and the economic forces that are reshaping the economic and social structure of the countryside, and literally changing the face of nature, is marginal and superficial. Radical changes in the direction of government policies and economic trends (to which we return in Chapter 13) are of greater import-ance to the long-term future of the national parks than tactical adjustments to the national park system, essential as these may be.

But even tactical adjustments are difficult to achieve. The national park system is now held in a state of inertia by a balance of mutually antagonistic forces, the reasons for which must be understood before considering what changes to the system are needed and how they might be brought about. On the one side, any threat to the existence of the national parks generates a powerful political and emotional response. The Countryside Review Committee's report on Conservation and the Countryside Heritage (CRC 1979) proposed to split the national parks and Areas of Outstanding Natural Beauty (AONBs) into two tiers. The upper tier, consisting of virtually unin-habited, small areas of 'superlative landscape quality' to which public access could be controlled, would have been managed by a central agency (presum-ably the Countryside Commission). Any 'development' likely to conflict with the conservation of the environment would have required the approval of parliament. The lower tier would have been administered by local authori-ties, with a specific government grant, through executive committees on which there would have been no appointed members. The Lake District and Peak national park boards would have been abolished. Afforestation and agricultural improvements were to remain outside the scope of controls. So far as we know, the Forestry Commission was the only national organisation to support the CRC recommendations. Because the county councils combined with the conservation and recreation interests in defence of the *status quo*, the Secretary of State for the Environment was provided with the perfect excuse for deciding, as he did in November 1980, not to proceed with the review of national park administration that his Labour predecessor had virtually promised for 1981.

But on the other side, any movement to designate new national parks or to extend national park-type administration to other areas generates, if anything, a stronger political and emotional response in the opposite direc-tion. In 1965 the National Parks Commission initiated consultations about a Cambrian Mountains National Park in central Wales, and the Countryside Commission designated it after reducing its area in deference to objections (CC 1972). It did so in the teeth of what the Commission itself called 'the vociferous opposition' of the local authorities, landowners and farmers and, as it turned out, even of such amenity bodies as the Council for the Protection of Rural Wales. The Secretary of State for Wales, going back on a pledge to hold a public inquiry, rejected the designation out of hand in 1973. (The story can be traced in the Commission's annual reports from 1965 to 1973.)

In 1978, the Commission issued a discussion statement on the future of the AONBs. It concentrated on the idea that the AONBs should be given a recreational purpose and put on an organisational and financial basis similar to that for national parks (CC 1978). The model set up for discussion was a local authority executive committee, without appointed members but with a Treasury block grant, a duty to produce a management plan for the whole AONB and an AONB officer and staff. The response from local authorities and others was almost unanimously hostile to this suggestion, although they gave some support to the establishment of joint advisory committees (JACs) in AONBs located in more than one local authority area (CC 1980a). These would be not unlike the JACs whose impotence in the national parks had led to their replacement in 1974 by national park authorities. The Commission then announced its decision to rely on JACs and its abandonment of any intention to secure more effective protection of AONBs except by voluntary arrangements and by increasing grants to AONBs at the expense of grants elsewhere in the countryside (CC 1981a). The Commission's statement and an independent review of AONBs (Himsworth 1980) both showed, however, that there was little enthusiasm in any quarter for extending the national park administrative model into any of the AONBs. The question is 'why?'.

The short answer is that the national park system as it now stands satisfies nobody, except perhaps the Association of County Councils. National parks are part of the land-use planning and development control system, which no longer commands the confidence reposed in it in the 1940s or 1950s. The voluntary bodies primarily concerned with national parks, such as the CPRE and the Council for National Parks, have lost ground within the conservation movement over the past 30 years by comparison with bodies such as the RSPB or the county trusts for nature conservation which engage in practical conservation work. If the Council for National Parks or the CPRE want to strengthen the national park system, landowning, farming and other local interests see it as the thin end of a wedge leading to more controls, higher costs, government interference and (the ultimate bogey) even land nationalisation. Local people, faced with all the problems of depopulation, reduced services and shrinking farm incomes, can easily see the national parks as direct competitors for scarce local resources, spending money on services for visitors while inhibiting local initiative through development control and offering little or nothing in the way of support for local services or enterprises.

The county councils now hold the balance of power, but are prepared to accept only minor changes that leave their control of the national park system undisturbed, as the Hurley report on national park administration (see p. 119) and the ACC response to it clearly showed (ACC 1980a). The national parks are in a 'no win' situation. If the national park system is to be strengthened, two things have got to happen more or less simultaneously. One is to promote the economic and social revival of the uplands. The other is to loosen the grip of the county councils on national park administration while at the same time giving people who live and work in the parks a greater say in it. The problem is how to combine, within the national park authorities, elements of both central and local government in ways that will secure better representation of local communities and the strengthening of the national interest in conservation and recreation. If the inertia is to be overcome, a package must be devised that has something in it for the majority of farmers, other residents in rural areas, conservationists and townspeople who want to take their leisure in the countryside.

Strengthening the system

Purposes and criteria

National parks should serve three specific purposes. The first two are already expressed in the statutes as the conservation and enhancement of their natural beauty and the promotion of their enjoyment by the public. The first purpose should be amended to place the emphasis on the conservation of nature (to include natural systems and resources) and of beauty (whether 'natural' or the result of man's interaction with nature). To the two existing purposes a third should be added – the improvement of the social and economic conditions of the area. Both the socio-economic and the recreational purposes must be achieved in ways that are congenial to the long-term aim of conservation, but this will not happen without the new approach to conservation that is discussed later in this chapter and the next.

The 'duty' imposed on national park and other authorities by Section 37 of the 1968 Countryside Act, 'to have due regard' to the needs of agriculture and forestry and to the economic and social interests of rural areas, does not enable them positively to promote economic and social wellbeing. Section 11 of the 1949 National Parks and Access to the Countryside Act confers a general power on the national park authorities 'to take all such action as appears to them to be expedient' for the accomplishment of national park purposes. But this section is interpreted very narrowly (LDSPB 1976) and does not, in any case, enable the NPA to take any action primarily intended to benefit local people. Transport services or visitor accommodation may be assisted if the primary purpose is to benefit visitors, but not if it is to benefit residents. Counsel has advised the Lakes Board that it is not permissible for the NPA to provide a fence or to re-route a path under Section 11 of the 1949 Act if the purpose is to benefit the farmer or landowner, or to repair a wall that is not in the public's line of vision (Ryan 1978). All national park authorities require some social and economic powers. But when the park has a fairly clear geographical, cultural or political identity, as in the Peak, the Lake District or Snowdonia, the NPA has a stronger capability than elsewhere for assuming broader rural development functions. These could include the provision of small factories or workshops with assistance from the Development Commission.

The word 'national' implies two things – national significance in terms of the quality and extensiveness of the predominantly semi-wild landscape and national commitment in terms of priorities, powers and resources to the management of land for national park purposes. The word 'park' implies recreational use and 'national park' suggests that this is of such a kind and on such a scale that it should be a national responsibility. The word 'park' does not mean that the public can go anywhere. On the contrary, it is precisely because our national parks are lived-in landscapes that management is essential to minimise the inevitable conflicts. The designated area should be an integrated unit, not one that cuts artificially across the upland profile, separating the management of the access land from the cultivated land or the hills from the valleys as the CRC unwisely proposed. But 'park' does mean that the public should have a legal right to walk in open country and to use a comprehensive network of footpaths and bridleways giving access to the most beautiful and interesting landscapes. The extensive estates in public or semi-public ownership (now a quarter of the land in national parks) could form the nucleus of a large public estate managed for national park purposes. But public ownership is not essential if the public has rights of access to privately owned open country and if the NPA has the resources and the powers to ensure that the land is managed in ways that are consistent with national park purposes.

The designation 'national park' is appropriate, therefore (a) if the area includes tracts of beautiful, semi-wild open country* of national significance sufficiently extensive to dominate the landscape; (b) the recreational or other uses are such as to require special measures to achieve the three national park purposes, and (c) parliament, central government and all its departments and agencies are committed in the management of their land, and in the direction of their policies, to the achievement of national park purposes. To these criteria should be added a fourth – that the public should have legal rights of access to open country and to common land, subject to necessary exceptions in the interests of wildlife conservation and subject also to byelaws and management arrangements. But this is a wider problem and calls for legislation on the lines recommended by the Dower and Hobhouse reports and the Royal Commission on Common Land (see pp. 19, 206) to secure these rights for the public throughout the countryside.

Like many others who have wrestled with the problem of what to call these areas, we have concluded that the name 'national park' should be retained

---

* 'Open country' is defined by Section 59(2) of the 1949 National Parks and Access to the Countryside Act to mean mountain, moor, heath, down, cliff, foreshore (including any bank, barrier, dune, beach, flat or other land adjacent to the foreshore). Section 16 of the 1968 Countryside Act extends the definition to include woodlands, rivers, canals, expanses of water through which a river runs, together with banks, towpaths and strips of land affording access and launching points or picnic places.

despite its patent incompatibility with the IUCN national park category (see p. 5). The British national parks legislation came 20 years before the IUCN definition, and to abandon the term now could only be interpreted as downgrading the status of the parks. The only alternative IUCN category, 'the protected landscape', is appropriate to 'cultural landscapes' influenced by man. But it is excessively tourist orientated, giving a higher priority to recreation and tourism than it does to the conservation of nature or natural systems. There are also substantial departures in many national parks on the IUCN list from IUCN principles. There is no need to apologise, therefore, for applying the term to landscapes that are used and influenced by man, if semi-wildness is the dominant characteristic and management is directed to the conservation of natural and human resources. The mistake that was made in 1949 was to use the name 'national park' without giving it sufficient meaning or credibility.

Designation

All the existing national parks except Northumberland and Pembrokeshire Coast could satisfy the suggested criteria, subject to boundary adjustments which raise questions of judgement rather than of principle. Dartmoor's future as a national park is dependent on a firm commitment to eliminate the military ranges. The Northumberland and Pembrokeshire Coast National Parks raise more fundamental issues.

The Northumberland National Park consists of three parts. Hadrian's Wall on its southern border is linked to the Cheviot Hills in the north by moorland and fell country, of which two-thirds is occupied by military ranges or commercial forestry plantations. The time has long passed, we suggest, when the entire Hadrian's Wall, with its related structures, farms, access land and sites of exceptional wildlife interest, should be recognised as a major national monument. It is not a national park in our interpretation of the term, but it should be owned and managed for the nation for the purposes of conservation, archeological research, education and recreation. The present national park committee plays a minor role, being concerned primarily with development control, public transport and public relations. Parts of the wall lie outside the park in Cumbria and Northumberland. Ownership, management and custodianship are divided between the National Trust, the Department of the Environment, as the custodian of ancient monuments, and private owners including the Vinlandia Trust. The interested bodies, including the Cumbria, Northumberland and Tyne—Wear county councils and the NCC, are linked by a consultative committee serviced by the NW regional office of the Countryside Commission and an officers' working party. The setting up of a committee was recommended by a study (DART 1976) which did not explore any more radical ideas for solving the considerable problems it identified. Yet there is a strong case for a special trust to be constituted by Act of Parliament to acquire and manage the Wall for the nation. The national park committee model is hopelessly inappropriate. The remainder of the Northumberland National Park would not satisfy our criteria for national park status. But there is a case for designating a Cheviot National Park on both sides of the Scottish border, excluding the military ranges.

In the Pembrokeshire Coast National Park the inseparability of scenic beauty from nature and the inadequacy of the existing powers or machinery to protect either are glaringly obvious. Legislation to protect the marine environment and to co-ordinate a multiplicity of coastal agencies is urgently required. An amendment to the Wildlife and Countryside Bill to enable the NCC to designate marine nature reserves was resisted by the government but was carried by 98 votes to 54 in the House of Lords on 17 February 1981. The designated area should be extended seawards to protect marine habitats and to integrate the management of the foreshore and the marine environment with that of the land. It should be extended landwards to relate to landscape and settlements and to give the NPA enough elbow room to combine coastal rehabilitation with a workable recreational management policy. The tank range at Castlemartin would have to go. The landward extension could include the establishment of a peripheral zone within which the NPA would be able to influence land use decisions without being directly involved in management. But it was forcefully presented to us in the Pembrokeshire Coast that the management of the coast itself required some form of public ownership, and the national park authority should clearly include people representing maritime and nature conservation interests. The Pembrokeshire Coast fully justifies national park status, but there is an acute mismatch between the problems of a coastal park and the present concept of a national park.

Two of the most obvious candidates for national park status are the New Forest and the Broads. Neither is an AONB (although a strip of the New Forest is within the South Hampshire Coast AONB) and each is a 'special case'. But the more closely one looks at existing or potential national parks the more evident it becomes that they are all, in some degree, special cases that do not precisely fit any standard model.

The New Forest probably approximates more closely to the concept of a national park than any other lowland area in England and Wales. As long ago as 1889, Sir William Harcourt summarised the purpose of the 1877 New Forest Act by saying that it 'was not to be treated simply as a place of profit, but regard has to be had to its ornamental character as a National Park' (Hand 1979b). The Nature Conservancy Council believes the ancient and ornamental woodlands to be the finest relics of undisturbed forest in western Europe. About three-quarters of its 145 square miles (375 square kilometres) are publicly owned, being Crown land managed by the Forestry Commission. The public has access to more than 80% of the area, attracted by the beauty of its scenery, the interest of its wildlife and domestic animals (including the deer and the ponies) and its superb walks and rides. It owes its survival mainly to the status of the extensive areas of common land, which is regulated by the Court of Verderers primarily in the interests of the commoners. This leads to overgrazing, but the Court of Verderers imposes an essential check on the activities of the Forestry Commission and the local authorities, particularly within the Open Forest and the forest Inclosures. The Court enjoys 'a degree of control over the Forest which is remarkable by any standards' (Pasmore 1977, p. 250), and illustrates the benefits of establishing an external control over afforestation.

In the post-war years the natural qualities of the Forest were brought to the verge of disaster by the combined effects of motor vehicles invading the open land and the Forestry Commission adopting a secret and illegal plan to fell broadleaved trees, of which the Court of Verderers was not informed. 'In less than a decade, close on a thousand acres of hardwood were clear felled, in flagrant violation of the 1877 Act and with irreparable damage to the Forest' (p. 236 ibid.). The public exposure of this policy led the government to suspend all hardwood felling in 1970, and to the adoption of a more conservationist approach to woodland management in the following year. In association with Hampshire County Council, the Commission implemented a conservation plan which cleared parked cars out of the Open Forest between 1971 and 1978. The Countryside Commission appoints one member of the Court of Verderers, but the Nature Conservancy Council does not appoint any. Despite the international importance of the New Forest, the NCC has only an advisory role in the management of Crown land. There are no National Nature Reserves or SSSIs, only informal understandings as regards management. The Forestry Commission exercises what it no doubt regards as a benevolent dictatorship over the greater part of the New Forest subject to the constraints imposed by the Court of Verderers.

The New Forest is under severe continuing pressure, the latest manifestation of which is a proposal by Shell UK Ltd to drill for oil near Lyndhurst (*The Times*, 5 February 1981). The case is clear for giving the New Forest the title, the purposes, the funding and the protection appropriate to a national park. But nobody we consulted in the New Forest wants to see the establishment of a national park committee of Hampshire County Council, which would only complicate matters without contributing to the solution of problems. The Forestry Commission may be the best management on offer, but no lasting confidence can be placed in it until it is given a new statutory direction and develops a new breed of forester who is better attuned to the needs of woodland conservation. It should, in any event, be made to share its authority not only with the Court of Verderers but with the Nature Conservancy Council, which has a wider range of interests, knowledge and skills than is normally found in the Forestry Commission.

The Norfolk Broads, which have been considered on and off for national park status since the Dower report (*op. cit.* 1945), are another case where nature and scenic beauty are inseparable, and the protective designations available to the Countryside Commission or the NCC are largely irrelevant to the problems. The Broads are an inland system of rivers and lakes in the Yare basin, created in mediaeval times by peat extraction. They satisfy the suggested national park criteria. A national water park in the Broads would contain a unique pastoral landscape, one of the country's most important wetlands (embracing a tremendous range of aquatic plants) and a centre of national significance for sailing, boating, fishing and nature study. But the ecology of the Broads is seriously threatened by eutrophication and water pollution from domestic sewage and agricultural fertilisers, over-exploitation of the waterways by unlimited numbers of commercial and private power boats, land drainage grant-aided by MAFF and by the Yare barrage proposed by the Anglian Water Authority. The barrage is intended to prevent the sea flooding the Yare basin, at a cost with associated land drainage works of £20 million (O'Riordan 1980). But it would do so, in the view of nature conservationists, at the cost of destroying much of the Broads' remaining wildlife interest. The main beneficiaries would be 300 farmers, who would make enormous capital gains by reclaiming the marshlands (Caufield 1981).

In 1977 the Countryside Commission had recommended the establishment of a Broads National Park Authority and the passing of legislation to give it powers to control navigation and to maintain and improve the rivers and broads (CC 1977b). The conservation and amenity interests would have preferred a special Broads Authority to be set up by legislation to take over the responsibilities of the local planning, water and navigation authorities (Hand 1979a). Faced with intense opposition from the farming, commercial boating and other interests, the Commission agreed to give a trial to a new Broads Authority proposed by the six district and county councils. The authority was set up in 1978 as a joint committee under Sections 101–102 of the 1972 Local Government Act without any of the special powers the Commission had been pressing for. Its constitution was, however, acceptable to the water, navigation and commercial recreation interests and to the local authorities. Of its 26 members, 12 are district councillors, seven county councillors, three are appointed by the Countryside Commission and two each by the Anglian Water Authority and the Great Yarmouth Port and Haven Commissioners. The NCC, which played the leading role in identifying the Broads' ecological problems, has no formal role. The Broads Authority exercises planning and countryside powers, delegated to it by the local authorities, within a tightly defined area enclosing the broads, rivers and marshland, and it has a consultative role within the catchment area of the river system. No powers have been, or can be, delegated to it by the water or navigation authorities.

Like the NPAs, the Broads Authority will probably turn out to be better than nothing. One of the Countryside Commission's appointees on the authority has affirmed that there is sufficient common ground between the agricultural and conservation interests in Broadland to lend optimism to the view that a workable management plan could be devised (O'Riordan 1980). It would involve purchasing critical ecological habitats, compensating landowners for maintaining rough pasture, maintaining the dykes and not squandering money on the barrage and land drainage. But the author also said that the dice are loaded against a realistic scale and degree of protection. 'The blunt truth is that the ethos of land drainage and agricultural improvement generally does not take adequately into account the conservation and amenity value. Neither the law nor the deployment of financial resources favours a proper balancing of these demands' (ibid. p. 13). He concluded that without reforms in agricultural and land drainage policies and in the legal and financial framework no realistic and long-lasting solution could be achieved. Yet the Countryside Commission ignored these fundamental problems when it issued a statement in February 1981 announcing that the Broads Authority 'has proved that it has the potential of achieving substantial environmental improvements in the Broads and is the agency best fitted to address the landscape, conservation and recreational management problems of the area' (CC 1981b). There should be a Broads National Park, but it would have no chance of lasting success, even if differently constituted to give proper representation to conservation interests, unless the reforms O'Riordan has postulated are carried out. The Broads illustrate more clearly than any other area we have studied that the critical factor in conservation is not so much the constitution or powers of the special authority, as the wider financial, legal and ethical framework in which it operates.

The next question to ask is whether there are other areas of beautiful, semi-wild open country of national significance in England and Wales, the use of which for recreational or other purposes *requires* special measures to achieve national park purposes. Identifying national parks is not a scenic beauty competition, in which the 'national park' label is stuck on the winners and a less prestigious label (such as AONB) is stuck on the rest. Nor does the question imply that areas which fail to satisfy national park criteria are less in need of protection or management. There are other parts of the country, particularly in the lowlands, equally beautiful in their own way, that are exposed to greater pressures than some of the national parks.

Several upland areas, such as the Forest of Bowland AONB and the proposed Northern Pennines AONB, have the physical characteristics and the scale of a national park. But, quite apart from the political problems that designation within the present system would raise, they seem to have an essentially regional role and significance. Only a deliberate decision to promote their enjoyment on a national scale as a major element in a programme for upland regeneration could justify national park designation.

The scope for national parks in the lowlands, limited by geography in the first place, has been severely reduced over the past 30 years as heath and downland have been ploughed, fenced and afforested, wetlands have been drained and woodland felled or planted with conifers. We question whether the extent of open, accessible country with semi-wild vegetation in such areas as the North, South or Wessex Downs, the Chilterns or the Wye Valley, where national parks have recently been proposed (Shoard 1980), could satisfy either existing national park criteria or those we have suggested. The Dorset heaths, the scene of Thomas Hardy's Wessex novels, had been reduced by 1960 to a third of the area they had occupied in 1811, and were halved again by 1979 (Goode 1981). A more detailed study might establish that one or two more national parks are still feasible in the lowlands. But other ways must be found for conserving what is left of the natural world in the lowlands or for extending the opportunities for public access to 'open country' or to what is now private parkland or woodland. National parks are an important element in the systems for countryside conservation and recreation, and they provide immensely valuable opportunities for testing techniques for countryside management that can be applied elsewhere. But they are not a panacea to be applied to areas that do not satisfy the criteria.

If the suggested criteria for national park designations are accepted, the next place to which one should turn when considering any extension of the national park system must be Scotland. Here are by far the largest expanses of open, semi-wild landscapes in the British Isles, the only ones in fact where an IUCN-type national park could be seriously considered. The North-West Highlands and Islands are identified by the IUCN in its World Conservation Strategy as a priority area for the establishment of protected areas with 'mixed mountain and highland systems' (IUCN 1980). But Scotland has taken a different path from the rest of the United Kingdom and the political support for national parks either in the IUCN or the Anglo-Welsh meaning of the term seems to be weak.

The five 'national park direction areas', which were all that remained by 1948 of the national parks recommended by the Ramsay report (1947), were finally extinguished by the Secretary of State for Scotland in 1980 (SDD 1980a). The government also decided not to proceed with legislation to establish 'special parks' in such areas as the Cairngorms, Glen Nevis/ Glencoe and Loch Lomond/Trossachs – all of which were on the Ramsay list. These would have been, in all but name, national parks on the Anglo-Welsh model administered by authorities similar to the Peak and Lake District Boards, with one-third of their members appointed by the secretary of state. The 'special parks' were to have been the top tier of a recreational 'park system for Scotland' proposed by the Countryside Commission for Scotland (CCS 1974). Scotland is left, therefore, without any special machinery for managing and protecting such valuable areas as the Cairngorms or for dealing with the acute problems created by intensive development for winter sports and tourism eagerly promoted by the regional councils and the tourist boards.

The Secretary of State has, however, designated 40 'national scenic areas' (SDD 1980b), which were identified by the Countryside Commission for Scotland on a subjective assessment of their beauty (CCS 1978). The national scenic area concept, which relies entirely on development control to conserve natural beauty, is a strange reversal of the ideas of the 1940s. Designation as a national scenic area has only two practical consequences. The

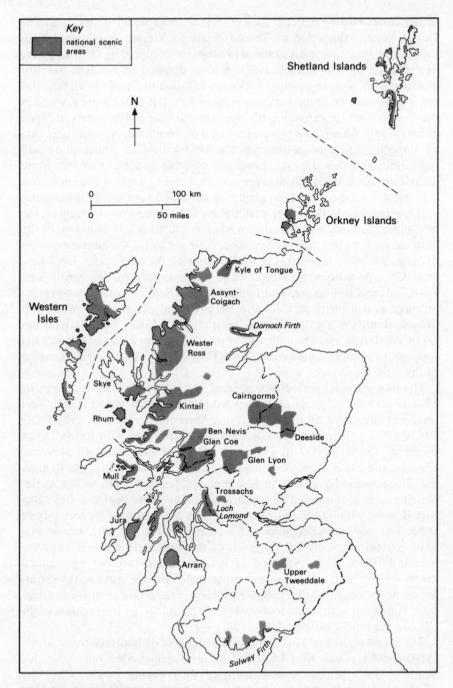

Figure 12.1 Scotland's national scenic areas. Source: *Scotland's scenic heritage*, Countryside Commission for Scotland 1978. Crown copyright reserved.

first is that if the local planning authority intends to grant planning permission for any substantial developments to which the Countryside Commission for Scotland objects, the Secretary of State is given 28 days within which to call in the application for his own decision. The second is that within these areas development control is marginally extended to cover all buildings and structures over 12 metres high, including agricultural and forestry developments, vehicle tracks above 300 metres altitude and local highway authority roadworks costing more than £100 000. But the 'national scenic areas' have no significance either for nature conservation or for recreation and the NCC has no formal status in the system.

The course that has been taken in Scotland can only be explained by the specific economic, political and cultural features of Scotland's development. The factors behind the rejection of the national park idea include the strength of the landowning interest, the extreme lengths to which depopulation has gone in the Scottish countryside and the overriding concern for jobs and tourist development in an acutely depressed economy. But the decisive factor was the determination of the new regional authorities not to surrender any part of their responsibility for development control. The Scottish system, as it has evolved, contains some interesting features such as the regional parks, and the secretary of state's more direct involvement in development control. But Scotland, in our judgement, has taken the wrong turning. There is a gaping hole in its protective and recreational systems where national parks that satisfied our suggested criteria could have been. And the national scenic area is a negative, cosmetic device that widens the split in conservation between nature and scenic beauty.

Administration

Scanning the existing national parks and other areas where national parks might be designated has brought out the difficulty of fitting every national park into the conventional administrative model. It ought to be possible to transform national park committees into national park boards, or to develop different administrative models to suit particular cases. As things now stand, however, Schedule 17 of the 1972 Local Government Act gives the Secretary of State no power to constitute a national park board anywhere outside the Lake District and the Peak, nor does it allow the title of national park to be used, or the National Park Supplementary Grant or any special national park powers to be provided elsewhere unless the area is administered by a county council committee or a joint committee. The *status quo* satisfies the present (1981) government and the Association of County Councils. The decision of Cumbria County Council to deny two of the district councils in the Lake District any representation on the Lakes Board (see p. 117) has persuaded the government to give the district councils a statutory right of representation (Heseltine 1980). But this is a very minor modification of the system. It seems unlikely to alter the balance of representation significantly in any national parks. Nor would it be right to suppose that giving a district council a statutory right to appoint one member will necessarily satisfy the demand for representation by the district councils, the parishes or local residents on the NPAs.

The defects in the present administrative model emerged clearly in Part 3 of this book. The composition of the present NPAs is strongly skewed to the benefit of the larger farmers and landowners and the county councils, and to the disadvantage of conservation and recreation interests, the urban users, the working class and lower income groups and women, and not least to the disadvantage of the residents of national parks. The county councils are able to control finance, staffing and policy, particularly in parks run by county council committees. And the national parks, as we saw in Chapter 5, are now forced to compete for capital funds with essential local services. We conclude that there is a need to relate the administrative model more closely to the needs of specific areas. The Pembrokeshire Coast, the Broads, the New Forest and the Roman Wall all point to the need for some flexibility in the composition of the authority. Legislation would certainly be required to set up a Broads National Park Authority with effective powers over water, land drainage and navigation, or to give the Nature Conservancy Council statutory rights to participate as a partner in the management of the New Forest.

The basic model, replacing the existing national park committees, should be autonomous boards, which we would prefer to call councils. They would be hybrid bodies combining elements of both central and local government. Like the present Lake District and Peak Boards, they would be independent of the county councils in such matters as policy, finance and staffing. They would be free to use (or not to use) the services of the county or district councils. The county councils would be strongly represented with at least a quarter of the seats, but they would be in no position to impose their policies. Another quarter could be split between representatives of district councils and members elected directly by the residents of the national park. Local interests would, therefore, be better represented than they are now. The county councils pose as the guardians of rural interests. But since the reorganisation of 1974, they are far more representative of such urban areas as Plymouth, Scarborough, Carlisle, Llandudno or Taunton than they are of the rural areas. They are remote from the uplands. If it is argued that it would be undemocratic to allow an authority that is only half elected to levy a rate, we would reply that the ratepayers only contribute 12% of the gross income and that it is even more undemocratic to give the county councils control in return for a 12% contribution (see Table 5.5).

A 50–50 split between elected and non-elected members would increase the scope for securing a good mix of national, regional and local interests, and would make it easier for ministers to rectify the imbalances in the membership to which we have drawn attention. Ministers should be required to appoint members with the requisite skills, knowledge or commitment to national park purposes, although whether ministers do so or not will depend on their attitudes and that of their civil servants. We do not agree with the Countryside Commission's view that it should appoint all the non-elected members. But it is essential to establish close links between the NPAs and both the conservation agencies not only through their officers, but also at the membership level. Both the NCC and the Countryside Commission (or a unified conservation and countryside recreation agency, should one be established) should be directly represented on the NPAs by their own appointees who would be fully informed of the agencies' policies and of the situation in the national park. Places could also be found for representatives of major urban authorities, or at some future date of regional authorities, that might be prepared or required to contribute financially to the national park.

We are fully aware of the strength of the interests which are attached to the administrative *status quo*, and of the difficulty of shifting them. Whether politicians are prepared to face up to these interests must depend, in the end, on the political support that can be developed for reforming the national park system and, more widely, for conserving the resources of the countryside.

Putting muscle into management

The solutions to the problems we have discussed do not lie exclusively, or even mainly, in strengthening and extending controls or other compulsory powers. But designation of an area means little unless the responsible authority has adequate powers to resolve conflicts of interest and to deal with greedy, incompetent, ignorant or lazy people. There is an urgent, immediate need to put some teeth into the system of control and some muscle into the emerging system of land management, not only in the national parks but (as we will argue in the next chapter) throughout the countryside. It is true that even the best-intentioned public authority can be as foolish or as selfish as any individual. But the need to have safeguards and democratic accountability in the exercise of powers should not be used as an excuse to allow private interests to destroy the national heritage or to prevent its enjoyment by the public.

The government has elevated its objections to legal controls over land management to the level of a principle and has vigorously resisted amendments designed to put some teeth into the 1980–1 Wildlife and Countryside Bill even in national parks or SSSIs. But there is a clear case, for which the evidence has been provided in earlier chapters, for bringing building and civil engineering works (including roads) associated with forestry or agriculture, and land drainage, within the scope of development control. The privilege, that farmers and foresters now enjoy, of being able to claim compensation (under Section 169 of the Town and Country Planning Act 1969) where the value of their interests is reduced by the refusal of planning permission or the imposition of conditions, should be withdrawn. If the planning authority requires owners to incur extra expense, for example by building in slate or stone, those who cannot afford to do so should be given financial help whether they are farmers or not. The problems of small or part-time farmers should not be solved by giving them a privileged position within the development control system.

The extension of development control from buildings to living systems raises very difficult issues. It is a negative process that delivers the answer 'yes', 'no' or 'subject to conditions' but it cannot provide positive or continuing management. 'Conservationists...are looking for a *long-term* commitment to specific and often quite complex systems of management. We could hardly impose a coppice rotation on a wood by statutory planning controls, or legislate against the effects of windfall and disease in an ancient deer park' (Mabey 1980, p. 236). Experience has taught us that listing does not save historic buildings for which no use can be found, nor does a Tree Preservation Order protect a tree from anything except the axe. There is nothing in the record of development control to suggest that it is easily extended from the built to the living environment, or that if it were applied to living systems it would be as successful as its advocates think. Nevertheless, the advantages of bringing all afforestation proposals under development controls, before an accountable local planning authority meeting in public, with power to grant, refuse or amend proposals without paying compensation would on balance be substantial.

In general, however, the aim of protecting and managing the living landscape is best pursued outside the planning system. An alternative system of land management and control is beginning to take shape in the national parks, run by people who are in closer contact with the farming population than the professional planners and are skilled in such matters as land management, farming, forestry and the natural sciences. But goodwill, co-operation and technical skills have to be backed up by powers of control and intervention. The tools the NPAs lack are (a) a statutory notification system, (b) the power to define or 'list' landscape features that are or may be in need of protection, (c) the power to make countryside conservation orders, (d) the power to acquire land compulsorily for any national park purpose, and (e) access to capital for land acquisition. The present arrangements by which proposals to make grant-aided agricultural improvements have to be notified to the NPA should be extended to proposals for which no grant is claimed. But it is also necessary to protect specific features in the landscape against a wider range of operations. These might be defined as any operation likely to damage or destroy their fauna, flora, physiographical features or ecosystems or to affect their character or appearance. Notification of these operations would be required only in so far as they affect specific landscape features listed by the NPA or in SSSIs. Decisions on proposed improvements or other operations would be guided by the national park plan and any local or subject plans and by policy maps, of which the Exmoor moorland maps are a prototype. The NPAs should have a power – as would a minister in default – to make Countryside Conservation Orders (CCOs) to prohibit specified operations within specified areas and where appropriate to impose positive management duties as Porchester advised in the case of Moorland Conservation Orders in Exmoor. The existence of a power to make a CCO would stop the proliferation of separate orders for the protection of moorland, limestone pavements, woodlands, historic field boundaries or other listed features. It would simplify life for farmers and landowners if all notifications were made to the NPA, which would in turn notify and consult the NCC.

The normal outcome of notification, should the proposed operation be unacceptable to the NPA, would be to modify it or to conclude a formal or informal agreement to manage the land in ways that would be acceptable. Whether an agreement that is consistent with conservative land management is possible will depend mainly on the degree to which the technical advice and the incentives on offer from MAFF and other sources favour such an agreement. The power to make a CCO would at least enable the NPA (or the NCC in the case of an SSSI) to put an immediate stop to operations to which it objected, and to secure the *status quo* for the time being. But where a farmer or landowner is unwilling or unable, even with the incentives and encouragement offered, to manage the land to the satisfaction of the NPA, it needs to have the power (which the NCC has already) to buy land compulsorily and thus to ensure its future either by managing it directly or by leasing it under appropriate conditions to a suitable tenant. Compensation should be paid at existing use value, disregarding any increase in value that might have resulted from agricultural improvement or afforestation.

The procedures we have described would impose a smaller administrative load on farmers or NPAs than might appear at first sight. All grant-aided agricultural improvements are already notified to the NPA. NPAs are consulted now on grant-aided afforestation proposals and on applications for tree felling licences. No estimate can be made of the number of significant agricultural or forestry schemes that go ahead without grant-aid, but the additional number that would have to be notified under the suggested procedure seems unlikely to be very large. The main difference would be that the NPA (or in some cases the NCC) would be able to negotiate from a position of strength instead of from one of palpable weakness. It would have the ability to intervene effectively should negotiations fail. We learned in the Peak that access agreements could not have been negotiated in many cases without the power to make access orders, but no orders have in fact been made. Experience with compulsory purchase powers points to the same conclusion, that the existence of a back-up power encourages agreement.

A new deal for the uplands

Where the NPA approaches the farmer in a spirit of helpful co-operation, as in the Lake District's upland management service, the farmer will usually make a positive response. We do not see the National Park Officer approaching the farmhouse door wielding the big stick and threatening the use of compulsory powers. We see him, on the contrary, as the farmer's friend and counsellor, offering technical advice and resources and armed with knowledge of other sources from which know-how or financial help could be obtained. There should no longer be any question of paying or haggling over compensation for the loss of profit that could have been made by destroying a valued landscape feature under some scheme grant-aided by MAFF or the Forestry Commission. But the NPA should be in a position to offer incentives towards conservative land management. Loans and grants should be available for appropriate developments, whether related to agriculture or not, together with opportunities for full-time or part-time jobs in upland management or under other programmes. The NPO should be in a position to co-ordinate the resources available from all the agencies or authorities operating in the area in an agreed programme of benefit both to the farmer and to the national park. The emphasis should be on sustaining the local life and economy as well as the landscape, through support of the small and part-time farmers and maintaining or creating employment on the land. The national park's policies should be an integral part of a 'new deal' for the uplands.

One of the keys to the revival of the uplands is held by MAFF and its advisory service ADAS. MAFF, as we saw in Chapter 9, remains on a collision course with the very interests – the economic and social wellbeing of upland communities and the conservation of nature and resources – of which it should be the strongest support. It has been suggested authoritatively that MAFF might take over responsibility for the NCC if not for the Countryside Commission, and that ADAS should become the main source of conservation advice for farmers (Strutt 1978). We saw enough when visiting French regional and national parks to appreciate the advantages that France enjoys through having a Ministry of Agriculture with broader responsibilities for the management of countryside resources such as timber and water, and for the social wellbeing of rural areas. But it would be a mistake to entrust rural affairs or the protection of the landscape to MAFF as things are now or seem likely to be in the near future. ADAS officers should be trained and knowledgeable in conservation and able to give farmers the necessary advice or to put them in touch with those who can. But MAFF's ideology is not going to change overnight, nor are its officers likely to undergo an instantaneous spiritual (or technological) conversion. However sympathetic the individual ADAS officer may be to a different approach, he remains bound by MAFF's policies. Both Labour and Tory governments accepted Strutt's recommendation that MAFF should be the main source of conservation advice for farmers, but neither has given ADAS the money, the people or the training they would need for this purpose. By allowing farmers to proceed with grant-aided capital projects without the prior consent of

ADAS, the Minister of Agriculture has effectively prevented ADAS from developing a conservation capability.

Fortunately, there is no need to wait for the reform of the Common Agricultural Policy to give a new direction to the UK's agricultural policies in the uplands. For the EEC Less Favoured Area Directive was designed, as we have seen (p. 198), not to raise productivity but to sustain the population and the economic and social wellbeing of the uplands and to conserve their landscapes. The package of reforms that we suggested in Chapter 9 (see p. 211) would redirect LFA funds towards the smaller and the part-time farmers and the more handicapped areas. It would encourage the conservative management of land (including commons), create more jobs, enhance recreational opportunities and increase income from benign forms of tourism. It could be done now, within EEC directives, by using existing funds differently. As and when MAFF changes direction, it will become easier for ADAS to work in partnership with the NPA and the NCC, and collisions will be less frequent. Here and now the NPAs and the NCC are the main sources of advice on conservation in the national parks and the SSSIs. But neither of them has the resources of money or skilled people they need, nor the strength to do more than bend agricultural and forestry policies that are in opposition to their interests. We return, therefore, in the final chapter to the need for a radical change in the direction of government policies and of social attitudes towards conservation.

13 Conservation and the countryside

The official attitude

Successive governments have left the policies that are threatening the rural environment essentially unchanged. They seem to regard conservation as a separate land use to be confined to special reserves or to land that can be spared from modern agriculture and forestry, or as a desirable extra to be paid for out of a minuscule financial allocation. The present government (1981) is concentrating such resources as it spares for environmental conservation on the 'sensitive areas', by which it means national parks and SSSIs but not AONBs. Within them, as we have seen, farmers are now required by MAFF to notify grant-aided improvements to the NPA or the NCC, but if no grant-aid is sought there need be no notification. Even within the 'sensitive areas', conservation is dependent in the event of conflict on the farmer voluntarily negotiating management agreements. The Wildlife and Countryside Bill (1980–1) introduced a compulsory procedure for the notification of any changes, whether grant-aided or not, likely to damage or destroy selected 'super SSSIs', probably no more than 40 or 50 out of 3900 SSSIs, of which 3000 are of 'biological interest'. Despite the evidence that the rate of damage to SSSIs in 1980 was nearer 10% a year than the 4% previously estimated (NCC 1981, and see p. 70) the government initially resisted amendments that would have extended notification to all SSSIs (but see Postscript, p. 284). The 'super' procedure only protects a site for a maximum of 12 months, unless the NCC has the resources to pay compensation or to acquire the site. The obligation to pay compensation for loss of future profits or subsidies, presumably on the Exmoor model, raises the price of 'good will' to very high levels. But the government is not prepared to provide funds that begin to match the scale required – hence its decision to protect only a handful of sites. Nor is any government ever likely to provide the money to protect even the SSSIs, let alone national parks, AONBs or the rest of the countryside on these terms. This approach is fundamentally hostile to conservation and it is matched by the government's totally negative attitude towards opening up more of the countryside for active, but quiet, enjoyment.

A classic statement of the government's attitude towards conservation was made by Michael Heseltine, the Secretary of State for the Environment, in November 1980:

I get concerned by glib talk of 'farming versus conservation' . . . The fact is that unless farming is in good shape the countryside can't be – and in this high cost industry high output and profitability are crucial. I don't deny that from time to time points of controversy arise. But these are the exception, not the rule. Less publicised are the excellent working relationships which are the norm between farmers and other countryside interests. Let no one think that I regard conservation lightly. But I recognise that conservation is rarely achieved without cost. My job is to balance the two (Heseltine 1980, pp. 23–4).

In short, farmers can be trusted to conserve the countryside, while putting profits and production first, because there is no real conflict between farming and conservation. But here Heseltine has himself resorted to a glib half truth, for few people argue that there is a straightforward confrontation between farming and conservation. It is not farming but the application of modern agricultural technology to the limited objectives of productivity and profitability that has been identified as the enemy of conservation. The government's own advisers, including MAFF and the NCC, have said that 'the really significant new dimension' of recent changes in *modern agricultural technology* 'is that virtually all of them have been unfavourable to wildlife and landscape' (CRC 1978, p. 13, our italics). They have also been depriving rural areas of the human resources required for their maintenance and severely reducing the opportunities for people to experience nature and to enjoy the countryside. The assistant chief scientist to the NCC has said that

we are now in danger of losing a substantial proportion of *all* our wildlife. If current trends continue many species of plants and animals will become extinct in Britain before the end of this century . . . SSSIs occupy less than 6% of the land of Britain: even their complete protection is not enough. What we really need is a national policy for rural land use which takes full account of the requirements for wildlife (Goode 1981).

An integrated approach

Conservation, properly understood, is not in opposition to farming or to the exploitation of natural resources for the benefit of man. Nor is it a separate activity. Its object (to paraphrase the World Conservation Strategy) should be to ensure Earth's capacity to sustain development and to support all life, by maintaining essential ecological processes and life-support systems, by preserving genetic diversity and by ensuring the sustainable utilization of species and ecosystems (IUCN 1980). According to this view the conservation of living resources (and of non-living resources such as minerals or fossil fuels) is a process that should run through every aspect of economic development and every decision affecting the use and management of land. It has no geographical or political limits. The advanced economies, of which Britain is one, are now facing a period of relative scarcity of materials as well as the progressive loss of natural or semi-natural environments. To the conventional economic objectives of profitability, full employment, maintenance of essential goods and services and export earnings must be added resource thrift, the concept of sustainability and the conservation of nature itself. As this book has shown, in the national parks, where the integration of conservation with economic and social development has been the implicit aim since their inception, it has not been possible to achieve such integration in the face of economic forces and government policies pulling the other way.

Protection of the rural environment must begin, therefore, with radical changes in agricultural and other policies as they affect the entire countryside and a different approach to compensation and controls. MAFF, of course, works within the framework of the Common Agricultural Policy (CAP) which 'puts emphasis on technological advance, high productivity, reduction of labour force, economies of scale and greater capitalisation' (EEB, 1978a). The CAP has to be reformed, not merely to reduce its cost and to eliminate unwanted surpluses, but to imbue it with the spirit of conserving both natural and human resources. A more appropriate agricultural strategy for a world that should be husbanding finite resources and promoting ecological diversity and stability has been suggested by the European Environmental Bureau, which is recognised by the EEC as the collective voice of more than 40 voluntary organisations concerned with conservation. This strategy would include: a careful selection of appropriate uses for every area of land, a reduction in the dependence on non-renewable resources (especially artificial fertilisers) and conversely the encouragement of sustained-yield systems and in general the development of varied and stable agricultural ecologies. An integral part of this objective would be the protection and enhancement of the rural environment (including its human communities) and the conservation also, as a matter of urgency, of traditional rural skills and of the endangered gene pool of domesticated plants and animals (EEB 1978b). Before MAFF could make such a radical change in direction, it would have to go through a process not merely of re-education but of unlearning much of what is accepted as the conventional wisdom.

Policies in all the primary industries should be re-assessed to determine how they can be redirected away from the narrowest of financial or production objectives, towards a positive role in the conservation of resources and the development of associated industries, trades and crafts. We raised the question in Chapter 10 of whether the Forestry Commission's inbuilt obsession with fast-growing species and quick returns had not made it a major obstacle to change. Even the House of Lords Select Committee on Science and Technology, on which foresters were strongly represented, recommended that its statutory purposes should be fundamentally reviewed to bring them into harmony with other uses, including nature conservation. But a fundamental review would have to question the treatment of private forestry as a tax haven for high taxpayers and the failure of the Commission to integrate forestry with farming on the small scale, or to increase employment in rural areas. The Commission's failure to devise any effective schemes for the care of existing woodlands or large-scale hardwood planting re-inforces our view that the Commission, given its traditional orientation and composition, is not the best custodian of the nation's woodlands.

We saw in Chapter 11 that the mineral companies' extractive policies are guided primarily by a desire to achieve economies of scale in production, and are not governed by national policies for the conservation of the minerals or of the environment. Water management still seems to be dominated by the need to satisfy demand forecasts rather than by the need to eliminate waste and conserve the resource. The English and Welsh regional water authorities and the farmer-dominated land drainage boards seem to regard themselves as being under a statutory duty to go on draining until the last wetland disappears, and they appear to have access to very large capital sums for this purpose. One does not need to accept in every detail Marion Shoard's estimate (*op. cit.* 1980) that British farmers benefited to the extent of £5000 million in 1979–80 from the CAP and the British taxpayer, to recognise that very large sums are going into the support of current agricultural trends. The more closely one looks at the public funds being invested in agriculture, forestry and land drainage, the stronger becomes the case for rechannelling a substantial part of them into rural development programmes of which conservation is an integral part.

The future of the countryside in general, and of the uplands in particular, depends on breaking out of the cycle of intensification and decline described in Chapter 4 by integrating conservation with development. Low input, resource-conserving, more labour-intensive, smaller-scale technologies, particularly in the primary sector and its associated industries and trades, could be the saving of the countryside. The conventional objection to this approach is that the country cannot afford it. But the real question is whether the country can afford what Heseltine calls 'high cost' agriculture if the total costs to society are added up – population decline, landscape deterioration and other environmental costs in addition to the very high direct costs of farming. As we write, it is reported that the number of registered unemployed may soon reach 3 million or more, and the cost of maintaining an unemployed man with a wife and two children is put at £6006 a year (*The Times*, 7 February 1981). It would not cost more to provide satisfying work for large numbers of people, full or part-time, in the positive tasks of land management for the purposes of production, recreation and conservation. The countryside is starved of the labour it needs to give it the care and maintenance it deserves. More people, skilled and unskilled, are needed on the farms and in the woodlands, to maintain a comprehensive network of footpaths and bridleways at high standards, and in locally based trades and industries and in services of many kinds. The national parks should be generating jobs of this kind, which could be shared between local tradesmen and NPA ground staff. The great merit of integrating conservation with development is that far from placing a dead hand on change it can offer benefits and opportunities to the great majority of those who earn their living in the countryside, or would like to do so.

MAFF, backed by the Agricultural Research Council, should encourage conservative farming through its research, its advisory service and its incentives. Were it to do so, many conflicts – such as that over moorland reclamation in Exmoor – would probably disappear. Similar changes of direction in policies for forestry, land drainage and water management and a conservative policy for mineral extraction would defuse many other confrontations. The occasions for pitched battles between entrepreneurs, backed by large amounts of public money, and conservationists, lacking both money and powers to resist them, would become fewer. It would be to the financial advantage of farmers to practise, not 'dog-and-stick' farming, but technologically advanced conservative farming based on appropriate research. Goodwill and co-operation would then come more easily. The objection to effective controls over the indifferent, the greedy or the ignorant farmer or landowner would then be seen in its true colours – as a defence of the absolute rights of property owners to do as they please whatever the public interest may be. Controls might not be welcomed, but they would have a far better chance of acceptance.

It is now possible to discern the beginning of a shift in public and even farming opinion away from the capital-intensive, labour-extensive economies-of-scale approach to rural needs that has given such devastating impulsion to the cycle of intensification and decline described in Chapter 4. The South West Region of the NFU, for example, announced 'a significant change in direction' in its agricultural policy in July 1980 in a widely circulated leaflet:

> Essentially, what we are saying is that Britain's well established post-war agricultural policy of replacing manpower by machines and by oil-based chemicals and fertilisers and of moving towards ever larger farms, is being overtaken by events and that agricultural policy in the future must take into account the need to keep people working on the land and living in the villages and also the need to conserve our traditional farming pattern, based on small or medium sized family farms, and landscape. Obviously this is particularly important in a region like the South-West (NFU 1980).

A coalition of eight rural organisations called Rural Voice (the constituent bodies were the National Federation of Women's Institutes, NFU, National Union of Agricultural and Allied Workers, CLA, CPRE, National Association of Local Councils, Standing Conference of Rural Community Councils, National Council for Voluntary Organisations) was launched at a major conference in November 1980 to call for a comprehensive strategy for rural areas. The very breadth of its representation testified to the feeling that had built up throughout the 1970s that post-war policies had produced a profound malaise in the social and economic life of the countryside. Many of the points made in their initial statement, *Towards a rural strategy* (NCVO 1980), find an echo in our own assessment of the rural scene – the attack on 'the damaging sectoral approach whereby different agencies each pursue their own independent policies'; the plea to MAFF (supported, on this occasion, by the NFU) to recognise the benefits of small and part-time farming; the emphasis on small-scale industry housed in converted barns or workshops and local authority housing for local needs; and the call to reverse the trend that is wiping out local schools and services or concentrating them in distant 'key centres'.

Increasing interest is now being taken in the rural policies of other countries in the EEC, where positive policies are being promoted to slow down rural depopulation by sustaining the single family and the part-time farmers. A report on Bavarian dairy farms, sponsored by the Milk Marketing Board, observed that the UK 'has the largest farms in Europe, employing the least labour per hectare and present policies are pushing still further in this direction'. But in Germany farm policies 'are primarily designed to prevent the large and intensive farmer receiving aid to further increase the size of his business' (Arlington 1981, pp. 33–4). Moreover, 'major government assistance has been required in Germany to move industry into the remote rural areas' to provide supplementary jobs for part-time farmers. It is true, as the SW Regional NFU says, that 'there is nothing very revolutionary' about the agricultural policies of France and Western Germany. But under British conditions, where the cycle of rural decline has gone so much further, a renascence of the kind that Rural Voice seeks can hardly be achieved without intervention in the economy, and in the land and property markets, that would be strongly resisted by many of those who are calling for a new approach. More small or part-time farmers means fewer big farmers. It is not surprising that the first conference of the Smallfarmers Association should have been unable to agree on the issue of government intervention in the land market (Tranter 1981). If we are serious about changing direction, we cannot take refuge in generalities about consensus. We must recognise deep-seated conflicts of interest and be prepared to upset some of those who benefit from the current trend.

Designation and control

There can be no geographical limits to our (by now familiar) conclusion that the lasting conservation of the countryside involves the radical redirection of government policies affecting the land, and channelling resources that are now being misused into conservative land management. The measures necessary for protecting the national parks are but one part of a national system for the conservation and enjoyment of the countryside. It is not too much to say that, in the long run, unless the entire countryside is managed in the spirit of conserving its living and non-living resources, the specially protected 'sensitive areas' will be unlikely to survive. The idea that islands of nature and of scenic beauty can prosper in a sea of destructive practices and a climate of ignorance, greed and philistinism is fatally flawed. Even the immensely greater and better protected national parks of the US cannot be isolated from the wider ecological systems within which they function (Herbst 1980). Moreover, there are places abounding in beauty, wildlife and local history in every type of landscape, including those of industrialised agriculture and the urban fringe, that will never qualify for designation as SSSIs or AONBs. National parks are indeed part of the national heritage, but so are countless meadows, lakes, rivers, ponds, copses, hedgerows, woodlands, walks and rides, many of which are only known to and loved by local people. It is in its way as important to prevent the disappearance of the places that local people cherish in the everyday countryside as it is to protect the outstanding landscapes and special sites. The system for landscape conservation must extend its reach to provide a protective and a helping hand throughout the countryside, to conserve the continuity and diversity of nature and the irreplaceable record of natural and human history, as well as scenic beauty.

The pace and scale of technological change driven by economic forces and official policies have created what amounts to an emergency. The first priority is to hold the situation by hanging on to what is left. The countryside as a whole needs a system for the conservation of landscape – using the term in its ecological and scenic meaning – based on the twin principles of control and designation and broadly similar to that suggested for national parks in Chapter 12. Development control should, therefore, be extended to include agricultural and forestry buildings and engineering works, land drainage and afforestation. The arrangements for notifying grant-aided agricultural improvements should be extended from national parks and SSSIs to other statutorily designated areas, and to all landscape features listed by the appropriate authorities as worthy of conservation wherever they may be located. The local authorities (and in SSSIs the NCC) should have powers to make Countryside Conservation Orders to protect any landscape or feature, and local authorities should also have compulsory powers to buy, manage or lease land for the purposes of conservation. But, as in national parks, negative controls are secondary to the positive aims of management. All rural authorities should have land management committees.

Designation has an essential role to play wherever the quality and extensiveness of the landscape (again using the term in its broadest sense) and the recreational and other pressures call for the comprehensive planning of land use, special administrative arrangements and powers of intervention and control. Designation, however, can be a trap for the unwary and can lead to an unnecessary proliferation of lines on the map, unless it carries with it a commitment to conservative land management and the necessary resources and powers. The Department of the Environment publishes a map showing that 44.5% of the land surface of England and Wales is 'protected land' (DOE 1974a). The designations shown include national parks, AONBs, Forest Parks and the New Forest, Areas of Great Landscape Value (indicated in development or structure plans) and National Nature Reserves. The figure of 44.5% excludes such designations as Heritage Coasts, SSSIs and the huge 'nature conservation zones' now creeping into county structure plans (the whole of Dartmoor is such a conservation zone), which overlap other designations. To some people it seems eminently satisfactory that so large an area is 'protected'. To others it seems absurd to demand a special degree of protection for half the land surface and for more than half of the rural area. The figure is too big if designation implies a special degree of protection or management, but too small if it implies that the undesignated areas contain nothing much that is worth conserving. The term 'protected land' is, in truth, thoroughly misleading. A recent study of the East Sussex AONB showed that 'little distinction is made between the AONB and other rural areas' and that the designation is mainly used as a reason for refusing applications for new housing (Anderson 1981).

We reject entirely the 'sensitive area' approach in which a small degree of protection for some designated areas (currently national parks and SSSIs) becomes a substitute for a national policy for the conservation and enjoyment of the countryside, or a cover for the absence of such a policy. We see designation very differently. Its primary purpose should be to promote conservative land management with all the special arrangements for administration and management that the characteristics and uses of the area require. The designation of 'outstanding' landscapes also facilitates resistance to destructive trends, because central and local government have had to acknowledge their special characteristics and to give lip service at least to the need to protect them. Designated areas provide a more favourable ground on which to do battle for conservation, because they enjoy a special place in the affections of the public or in the minds of scientists. They also provide better opportunities than elsewhere to develop ideas or techniques for conservative land management and to promote better human relations. They are, to mix the metaphors, redoubts to be held at all costs against the day when the whole countryside is managed on the basis of conservation principles, they are bridgeheads from which to advance into wider territory and they are laboratories for research and development.

The Countryside Commission missed a great opportunity to reconsider the whole question of designation when it initiated its review of AONBs (CC 1978). The Commission was so obsessed at the time by the notion that it had found the answer to countryside management in the reorganised national park system, with its single authority, its officers, its statutory 75% grant

and its management plan, that it failed to open up a debate on more fundamental issues, such as the purpose of the designation. It concluded its review
by accommodating its position to the known views of those with a vested
interest in the *status quo* and of the government of the day. This meant that
the AONB designation was given a recreational function but not a clear
purpose or effective powers (CC 1981a). We suspect that, if the purposes and
functions of AONBs were re-examined, not from the standpoint of the
Countryside Commission but from a standpoint embracing that of the
Nature Conservancy Council as well, it might be thought desirable to clarify
and to limit the existing designations. We ask whether the designations
AONB, Area of Great Landscape Value, Heritage Coast, 'nature conservation zone' and some of the larger SSSIs might not be replaced by a single
designation, the Countryside Conservation Area (CCA), designed primarily
to promote conservative land management.

We do not see such areas as the exclusive concern either of the NCC or the
Countryside Commission, for the designation would be designed to protect
both scenic beauty and natural systems or features. A classic example of the
need for such a designation is provided by the Berwyn Mountains, where the
NCC and the Countryside Commission have each stirred up confusion and
resentment by proceeding with separate SSSI and AONB designations for
much the same areas. The powers available in CCAs to list features, to
require notification, to make Countryside Conservation Orders and to buy
land compulsorily would be precisely the same as those available to national
park authorities. Where the CCA is intensively used for recreation, but does
not satisfy the criteria for a national park, there would be a case for managing it as a regional park, with an authority constituted by urban and rural
authorities. But fully developed ideas on the administration and management of CCAs are unlikely to emerge so long as the conservation of nature
and the conservation of scenic beauty are regarded as two separate functions
to be discharged by two separate national agencies.

Bridging the divide

If one takes the ecological view, that scenery is the visual expression of the
living landscape, the 'great divide' between the Nature Conservancy Council
and the Countryside Commission, that we described in Chapters 1 and 2,
seems distinctly odd. Whatever justification there was for this division in
1949, the argument today surely favours their merger into a single conservation agency, at least in England and Wales. The NCC stated in evidence to
the House of Lords (NCC 1976) that the differences between itself and the
Commission were 'fundamental and inevitable'. Yet the only reason it
offered was that the NCC had to adopt a more cautious attitude towards
public access. The NCC itself has cited the Malvern Hills AONB as 'a
wonderful example of how scenic beauty, wildlife and landforms are

inter-related and indivisible' (NCC 1975). In 1970, reviewing its first 21 years, the Conservancy said that it had *begun* to see its task as caring for the environment as a whole (NCC 1970; our italics). In its response to the NCC's consultation paper on forestry, the Countryside Commission spelt out the fact that the requirements for nature conservation, as stated by the NCC, were almost identical to the requirements for 'landscape' conservation as stated by the Commission (CC 1980g).

In our view, the existence of two agencies, one run by scientists and the other by generalists or planners, has institutionalised the differences between two sets of professionals, each of which would be encouraged by closer association to broaden and illuminate what is too often a restricted point of view. It has delayed the movement that is visibly taking place towards the common ground, as the NCC has moved outwards from nature reserves and SSSIs and the Commission has moved outwards from national parks and AONBs towards the care of the environment as a whole. A spectrum of interests has emerged with sectional interests at either end – the NCC's interest in species conservation, for example, or the Commission's research on leisure and visitor management. But both are increasingly concerned with an ever-growing area of common interest in between (Swanwick 1980). Dr Bryn Green, a former Regional Director of the Nature Conservancy, has argued that 'a united organisation structure is essential if amenity land planning and management is to be effective' (Green 1976).

There are difficulties in effecting a merger of this kind, not the least of which is the resistance from the professionals on either side. But the arguments that have been put to the authors in defence of the continued separation of the agencies have been singularly unconvincing. The scientists fear that scientific work would be held back, and the planners or generalists fear that narrow-minded scientists would lack a broad perspective on the countryside. Both fears confirm, we suggest, the need to bring the agencies closer together. We are not suggesting a shotgun marriage, of the kind designed to raise a cheer when the minister announces that he has reduced the number of government agencies by one or the number of bureaucrats by a dozen. A united agency should employ more people, not fewer. The government rejected a merger, conceived as an economy, in 1979–80 and decided to concede to the Commission the independence from the civil service that the NCC has enjoyed since 1949. The Commission's newfound autonomy could drive the two agencies further apart, but the fact that both now have independent status and neither is within the civil service could facilitate the formation of a strong, united countryside conservation agency.

We would expect such a united agency to play a very positive role in promoting legislation and programmes designed to improve the public's opportunities for enjoying the countryside – the management of commons, access rights to commons and open country and the proper maintenance of an extensive network of footpaths and bridleways adapted to modern usage. Its overriding concern, however, would be the active, and authoritative,

promotion of the conservation of the natural environment at central government and local level. Whether it would do so in practice would be largely a
political question, as the agency would be no better than the members
appointed by the government, and it would require resources of money and
manpower on a different scale. A mere reshuffle of the old packs would not
of itself bring the countryside the protection and support it needs. But the
case for unification should be given urgent and serious consideration.

The rights of landownership

We have left the most contentious issue of all, the rights of landownership
and the sanctity of market forces, to the last. The prevailing view that
conservation can only be achieved through the goodwill and co-operation of
landowners and farmers is a dangerous half-truth. But once we enter the
arena of land and property rights we are entering a political and emotional
minefield. Behind all the publicly proclaimed ideals of the NFU and the
CLA, who describe farmers and landowners as the custodians of the
countryside or the stewards of the nation's heritage (NFU/CLA 1977, CLA
1975) are the harsh facts of self-interest and sectional interest. We all think
of the land as 'our country' and it is one of the basic resources on which life
depends. But land is also private capital, an investment that is specially
prized in times of inflation, a commodity to be bought and sold, a source of
political, economic and social power and influence, and a resource to be
exploited for profit. The expansionist farmer is locked into a relentless
process of capital accumulation.

The NFU and the CLA are essentially trade associations or political
lobbies whose primary purpose is to protect the material interests of their
members. The NFU is perhaps the most effective political lobby in this
country and it is dominated by the bigger farmers. Farmers and landowners
permeate every level of central and local government. They constitute, as we
have seen, about a third of the membership of national park authorities.
Farming is the only industry guaranteed a seat in the Cabinet. Farmers and
landowners are strongly represented in the House of Lords and the Countryside Commission. The links between the Nature Conservancy Council and
private forestry interests have been described as 'strong if not incestuous'
(Rose 1980). This all-pervading influence is used to resist controls over agriculture and forestry, and to ensure that such powers of control or intervention as do exist are exercised very sparingly or not at all. The farming and
landowning lobby has exercised what amounts to a veto on legislation to give
the authorities powers to protect such threatened areas as Exmoor and the
SSSIs.

The ideology of landownership and farming is a tangle of mutually
contradictory ideas, combining the assertion of an absolute right 'to do as I
think fit with my land' with the view that landowners are stewards holding

land in trust for future generations (CLA 1975). But this is a double-edged argument, for a steward is defined as the manager of another's property (OED). The concept implies that the land belongs to the people. As interpreted by the CLA, it concedes the public interest in theory, but reserves to the private owner the exclusive right to determine where the public interest lies. It has been observed that the realities of capitalist enterprise would seem to contradict the validity of the ideology of 'stewardship' with embarrassing vividness (Newby *et al.* 1978). 'The only significant legal obligations regarding property ownership today fall, not on the owner, but on the non-owner – those who do not own land are obliged not to trespass, but those who do are not obliged to distribute the benefits' (ibid. p. 337).

Priddy (1979) has pointed out that the farmer's self-image of the independent, individualistic, straight-talking Conservative dedicated to competition and free enterprise clashes glaringly with the reality of his constant demands for help, protection and legislative support. Farmers have given the authors catalogues of the iniquities of the market; how viable farms are broken up by selling them off in lots to achieve a higher price; how farming, landscape and the community are damaged when an absentee businessman buys a hill farm for afforestation; how high land prices place impossible barriers in the way of the farmer who lacks the capital to expand, or the farm worker who wants to become his own boss, or the young man from agricultural college who wants to get a foothold on the farming ladder. But they overlook the fact, clearly established by the Northfield report on the ownership of agricultural land (1979), that the main cause of rising land prices in the 1970s was not so much buying by financial institutions as buying by farmers for agricultural expansion and investment.

Yet most farmers retreat from any measures that might interfere with the so-called 'free market' which, they complain, is so destructive of the values they cherish and the interests they represent. Almost any kind of public intervention or control is denounced as the thin end of the wedge of land nationalisation. Landowners are quick to spot the fallacy of relying on market forces when their own interests are threatened. John Quicke, a former chairman of the CLA, told a land conference that 'market forces cannot be allowed to determine whether developers use farmland or sites in inner cities' (*Farmers' Weekly*, 2 November 1979). But he went on to reject the idea of greater control over farmland.

When the crunch comes, farmers' and landowners' spokesmen want controls – but only over others. As we have seen, there is a growing minority of farmers (NFU 1980, Tranter 1981) that recognises the contradictions in orthodox farming attitudes. The correspondence columns of *Farmers' Weekly* bear continuous witness to the fact that some small farmers, in particular, recognise the damage that a totally free market in farmland does to their interests. But small farmers do not get appointed to such bodies as the Northfield Committee which inquired into the ownership of agricultural land. Raven Frankland, a Conservative member of Cumbria County Council, a landowner and a member of the Yorkshire Dales National Park Committee, told the authors 'we can't allow a free-for-all with such a valuable commodity as land. We actually need more regimentation. The landowners may not like it, but I'm not concerned with what the landowners like. They'll have to like it in 20 years time. Controls over the land market have been largely accepted in Europe, where the need to keep the local farming population on the land is recognised'. In Wales and the North of England, in particular, we sensed a growing concern among small and part-time farmers about the effects of the 'free for all' in land both on them personally and on the landscape.

Recent evidence suggests that the number of farmers who appreciate their responsibility to the environment is increasing (Fitton 1981) and this is one of the hopeful factors in the situation. But the assumption that all farmers and landowners, or even a majority, have the commitment and the skill to care for the environment flies in the face of the evidence. Some of those who have the commitment and skill are forced into damaging practices by the trend in costs and prices encouraged by current policies. Derek Barber, chairman of the Countryside Commission since 1981, is an expert consultant in agriculture, a former MAFF adviser and one of the nation's leading figures in wildlife conservation. He has said that 'as someone who spends half his time in agriculture, I blush frequently with embarrassment when reading of farmers and landowners who talk the most appalling and elementary nonsense about wildlife conservation' (*Farmers' Weekly*, 4 April 1980). He offered his own 'highly subjective estimate' that 'about 15% of farmers are committed conservationists; 15% are philistines in a conservation sense and will never do anything about it; and the middle 70% would do more if they knew how and their interests are gently stimulated'. A study for the Countryside Commission, which compared farm management by institutional landowners with management by individual farmers, traditional landowners and estate agents found that in all classes of tenure the existing practices fell very far short of the aims of conservation (Worthington 1980). Farmers, agents and owners had an extremely superficial understanding of landscape quality. There was no evidence that the presence of the owner exerted a positive influence on conservation, unless he was interested in game. The majority of land agents clearly felt their prime duty was to manage their clients' investments for maximum or near maximum profit, and any consideration which reduced this was not very welcome. Most tenancy agreements gave little real protection to landscape features which owners might wish to conserve. Not only were most of the changes taking place in farmed landscape 'detrimental to its character, amenity and historical interest, and to the conservation of landscape' but landowners and their agents were 'sceptical that such objectives could be implemented effectively on any wide scale' (ibid. p. 32).

Studies by Newby and others in East Anglia (1978, and Newby 1979a) suggest that, although individual attitudes vary enormously within the different categories of farmers and landowners, those who are most responsive to the needs of conservation are the 'traditional' landowners – to many of whom landownership has an element of social responsibility in addition to being a business – and the smaller farmers who lack the capital and sometimes the motivation to go in for the most advanced technologies. But these are precisely the sectors of landownership that are declining. The sectors that are growing are those within which owners are most likely to regard the land simply as a means of production, or to have predominantly financial objectives (Massey & Catalano 1978).

Any serious attack on the problems presented by conflicting demands on the countryside must therefore face the basic issue of property rights. Farmers themselves should accept the fact that Britain needs a land reform, not least in the interests of the majority of farmers themselves. Britain has gone further down the road towards agribusiness than any other European country, but it has been the slowest to recognise the problems that this has created. It still has the free-est land market in Europe. In other western European countries there is a wide range of powers designed to enable public authorities to control land sales and to acquire land for restructuring fragmented holdings, creating viable units, supporting small farms, starting young farmers, limiting the size of holdings, excluding institutional or absentee buyers and so on (Davidson & Lloyd 1977, Carty 1978, Arlington 1981).

Our 1967 Agriculture Act enables the Minister of Agriculture to set up rural development boards with powers to control the sales of agricultural land over 10 acres, to restructure farms, to control afforestation and to support rural services and farm tourism. The well-founded fears of Welsh farmers that the powers would be used to accelerate the process of concentrating farms into large units forced the government to abandon its intention to set up a board in Wales. A board was set up in the Northern Pennines, and terminated after eighteen months by the incoming Tory government on the ground that it was inconsistent with Tory philosophy. The powers remain on the statute book, and they could have been used to promote a diversified, small-scale rural economy. But the concept was fatally flawed both by the use to which it was put and because the powers were entrusted to an agricultural board appointed by MAFF and in no way answerable to the communities affected (Capstick 1978, 1980).

It is one of Britain's tragedies that very little thinking or research has gone into the problems of rural land tenure. The Tory Party identifies itself with landowners and big farmers. The Labour Party has never had a serious policy for rural land. It has been obsessed by the need to assemble land for urban development and to recover development value for the community (Edwards 1981). Land nationalisation has never been more than a barren slogan, and one that ignores the basic truth that large public bureaucracies can be more destructive physically and socially than private owners if given the wrong directives.

A government determined to take a new course could start by giving new directives to the present landholding agencies. A majority of the Northfield Committee recommended, at a time when many county councils were selling off their smallholdings, that the government should consider a limited extension of publicly owned agricultural land as the only way in which young farmers without capital could get a foothold in farming (Northfield 1979). The committee rejected a statutory limitation on farm size but conceded that this could help to prevent rural depopulation and would slow down the process of farm amalgamation. It advised the government to reconsider the case for reviving rural development boards, particularly in the hills and uplands.

It is beyond the scope of this book and our capabilities to say what form powers to intervene in the land and housing market, to restructure holdings and to extend the public estate should take. Rural development should be a job for elected local authorities, provided and helped from the centre. We have no doubt that unless such powers are provided and used, the purposes of countryside conservation and rural regeneration will be frustrated. But land policies, however radical, will achieve little unless they form part of the larger package of social, economic and environmental measures to which we have already referred in this chapter. Allocating land to small or part-time farmers within the present framework of agricultural policies and economic incentives would be self-defeating.

The politics of change

What began as a study of national parks in England and Wales has broadened out into a re-assessment of national policies for the conservation of the countryside and the social and economic life of rural areas. Growing familiarity with the national parks and exasperation over many aspects of their administration has diminished neither our affection for them nor our belief that they constitute a precious national resource. Tactical adjustments to the national park system are necessary, but the achievement of the broader national park purposes we have suggested is dependent above all on radical changes in the direction of government policies and economic trends. There is potential within the national park system, despite its defects, for the emergence of a far more positive approach to conservative land management. But the present system is essentially cosmetic and there are very severe limits to what can be achieved by surface treatment if the underlying causes are neither diagnosed nor dealt with. If we as a nation are serious about continuing to enjoy our national parks, and about conserving the natural and human resources of the countryside, we will have to choose between cosmetics and conservation. But conservation, in the sense in which we use the term, combines a conservative approach to land management with a revolutionary challenge to the established habits of thought and the entrenched interests of contemporary society.

Max Nicholson, for many years the director of the Nature Conservancy and perhaps Britain's best-known conservationist, has compared conservationists to people who are 'trying to extinguish and prevent fires amid a community of arsonists, who start four more fires for every one we bring under control'. Most of the problems arise, he argues, through the ill-advised application of modern technology by industry, often acting at the behest of governments or international agencies, bankers and insurance funds and many kinds of public and private concerns. 'Few people in these worlds know or care anything about the natural environment and they are advised by economists, accountants, engineers and other professionals who if anything are even more ignorant' (Nicholson 1981). He sees the problem, therefore, as being essentially one of establishing lines of communication between the conservationists and the decision-makers, so that the latter will become sufficiently educated to see the error of their ways. Great improvements in communications, in education, in field work and research are all indispensable. It is equally important to expand the opportunities for the people of the towns, who are cut off from the natural world, to enjoy nature and to understand it through direct experience. Urban voters may have the final say in determining the future of the countryside.

But ignorance is not the main issue. Education seems unlikely to be successful so long as 'arson' is richly rewarded and the penalties are mild, rarely enforced or non-existent. Experience suggests, on the one hand, that fundamental changes of attitude cannot be brought about simply by giving orders and issuing decrees and, on the other, that deeply entrenched interests and attitudes cannot be overcome by persuasion and education alone. The issues are ideological, economic and ultimately political, and will be resolved only when politicians are well enough informed and subjected to sufficient pressure to make conservation a politically and economically attractive course. Political and other interests are already persuaded that it is wise to make verbal gestures towards conservation and to apply the cosmetics more freely. The problem is how to shift the balance of political forces so that politicians will begin to confront the real issues.

We do not present the many suggestions made in this book for the reform of the national park system, or for a more radical approach to countryside problems generally, as cut-and-dried-solutions to a very complex set of inter-related issues. We offer them as a contribution to a debate in which they should be critically examined. It will be objected that, at a time when the nation is going through the most severe economic depression for half a century or more, we are asking for substantial expenditures for purposes that are only marginal to national prosperity, or even irrelevant to it. There are two answers to that objection. The first is that we are proposing to transfer resources now spent on supporting the unemployed or on high-cost, resource and capital intensive farming or forestry, into low input, more labour intensive jobs both in agriculture and in other rural activities. High costs, once thought to be the secret of Britain's success in agriculture, are now emerging as one of the causes of falling real farm incomes (MAFF 1981, Curry 1981). Economics are already beginning to modify the trend. If less capital was diverted into high-cost agriculture, yielding a very low return, capital would be released for other purposes. The second is that, although the conservation of nature and natural resources may be irrelevant to the outmoded economics of a society whose goal is ever-increasing material consumption, it is central to the economics of sustained continuous yield.

It will also be objected that many of our ideas and even the general direction of our thinking are unrealistic in the light of current political and economic trends and the strength of the interests to which they present a challenge. We live in an unstable and unpredictable world, within which the movement for conservation will have to struggle very hard if it is to influence events. But the conservation movement will never achieve its objectives if it tries to rely entirely on goodwill and persuasion, evades the conflicts of interest and denies the political nature of the issues it is raising. Conflict raised to the level of violence is destructive. But conflict within the limits of democratic debate and decision-making is a creative force without which society ossifies. The future of the countryside may ultimately depend on whether it remains a political backwater in which the ideology and interests of the rural establishment go unchallenged, or whether it becomes a focus of political debate and action.

Postscript

The prolonged and controversial committee stages of the Wildlife and Countryside Bill in both Houses of Parliament delayed the passage of the Bill and inflated it into a document of more than 100 pages, 70 odd clauses and more than 15 schedules. But the length and complexity of an Act of Parliament are no guide to its value as a piece of constructive legislation. The value of this Bill, or Act as it will soon become, is in inverse proportion to its length. The Director of the Council for the Protection of Rural England was speaking for many people and organisations when he described the Bill as 'a missed chance to save Britain's wild places' (*The Times*, 10 July 1981). Its significance may ultimately prove to lie in the fact that the Conservative government's doctrinaire resistance to any effective controls over farming or forestry operations in the interests of conservation strained the traditional non-party, consensus approach to conservation to breaking point. Conservation and agriculture were brought into the political arena, and the real issues raised by agricultural policy were discussed. The Labour Party, after extracting some minor concessions, agreed in the end not to oppose the Bill's final stages in the House of Commons. But it frequently divided the House, and committed itself to the principle of bringing agricultural and forestry operations within the scope of development control.

Under pressure from the conservation and amenity bodies, and from MPs and peers of all parties, the government amended the Bill in an attempt to give more credibility to the voluntary approach on which it relied. It yielded in the end to the demand that farmers should be required to notify potentially damaging operations, not merely in a handful of 'super' SSSIs (as the government originally intended) but in all of them. The Bill, while retaining the 'super' SSSIs, introduces a system of 'reciprocal notification' in all SSSIs by which the Nature Conservancy Council has to notify farmers of the features that it wishes to protect, and to specify the operations that might damage them. The farmer has to give three months notice of his intention to undertake any of the operations specified by the NCC, whether grant-aided or not. The penalty for not giving notice is a maximum fine of £500 – a derisory sum when compared to the increased values that can be obtained by woodland clearance or land drainage. Ministers are also to publish a code for the management of SSSIs, to be approved by both Houses of Parliament but having no legal force. The scheme introduced in 1980 for notifying grant-aided agricultural improvements in national parks remains unchanged, and the Bill (as we saw on p. 244) retains the reserve power to introduce a statutory notification system for moorland reclamation. Limestone pavements in national parks can now be protected by orders made by the NPA or the secretary of state. But, otherwise, farmers remain free to do as they please throughout the countryside, provided that they give the statutory notice in SSSIs. Areas of Outstanding Natural Beauty and the remainder of the countryside are unaffected by the new notification procedures unless ministers apply them to other areas.

The success of the Bill depends, therefore, on the readiness of farmers voluntarily to conserve the countryside, and on the value of the inducements that can be offered to them to do so. Here the Bill breaks new ground. Where the NCC or a national park authority object to agricultural operations of which they have been notified, the Minister of Agriculture (or the Secretary of State for Wales) is required to consult them and (in England) the Secretary of State for the Environment before deciding whether or not to withhold the grant. If he decides to withhold the grant, the NCC or the national park authority is required to offer the farmer a management agreement that will impose restrictions on the proposed operations, and pay compensation 'calculated in accordance with guidance given by the Ministers'. The 'voluntary' nature of the system has therefore become one-sided. The farmer is free from all constraints, and has acquired a statutory right to be compensated for losing his grant and the profit he might have made by damaging the environment. The NCC and the national park authorities are given no powers to control him, but are under a statutory duty to pay compensation. Our fears that the Exmoor guidelines will become the model for compensation elsewhere have been accentuated by Ministers' repeated reference to the success of management agreements in Exmoor.

The obvious question, how much money will the NCC and the national park authorities be given to pay the compensation, has received a dusty answer. Tom King, the Minister of State for the Environment, promised that the government will meet its commitment to conservation 'as far as possible, within such resources as are available' (HC 13 July 1981). The prospect of finance on the scale required by the Exmoor guidelines is poor in national parks and SSSIs, and dismal or non-existent elsewhere. The high cost of compensation and the lack of money to pay it are bound to make the NCC and the national park authorities far more cautious in objecting to agricultural operations; successful objection brings with it a legal demand for compensation. Farmers will be tempted to put up damaging schemes, in the knowledge that the more damaging the scheme the greater will be their chances of picking up compensation. The Wildlife and Countryside Bill suffers from the very defect that torpedoed the 1932 Town and Country Planning Act. The latter failed because local authorities were required to pay compensation for restricting development, but had neither the means nor the inclination to do so. The failure of the Wildlife and Countryside Bill outside the 'sensitive' national parks and SSSIs could be even more disastrous. For in the wider countryside the Bill provides no system of any kind for notification, for withholding grants or for paying compensation, and there will be even less money there for conservation.

Readers of this book will be aware of the crucial importance of agricultural policy for conservation. Significantly, this was widely recognised in both Lords and Commons. But the government rejected the chance to reconsider agricultural policies that was given to it by an amendment, moved by Lord Sandford and carried against the government in the Lords by 47 votes to 45. The Sandford amendment reflected widespread concern in rural areas. It was the outcome of consultation with the county and district councils, the Countryside and Development Commissions, the NFU and the CLA. It amended Section 29 of the Agriculture Act 1970, which restricts agricultural grants to the purposes of 'an agricultural business'. It was limited to national parks and such other areas as ministers might specify, and extended the narrow purpose of Section 29 to embrace the conservation of natural beauty, the public's enjoyment of it, the maintenance of a minimum population, the development of tourism and craft industry and other measures to benefit the rural economy. The Sandford amendment was, therefore, an attempt to give the purposes of the EEC Less Favoured Area Directive the force of law, but it was seen by the Ministry of Agriculture as a direct threat to its traditional policies.

The government's response was to accept 'the spirit of Sandford', but in deference to the Ministry of Agriculture it destroyed the substance. The Sandford amendment was replaced by a new clause that spelt out more clearly the existing responsibility of ADAS to advise farmers on conservation and socio-economic matters. It also required the Minister, when making capital grants for farm development schemes, to further the conservation of the countryside and the public's enjoyment of it – but *only* 'so far as may be consistent with the purposes of the scheme and with the said Section 29'. Section 29 itself remained unchanged, and the new clause firmly subordinated conservation to the primary purpose of promoting 'agricultural business'.

Bibliography

ACC (Association of County Councils) 1980a. *The national park system of England and Wales*, memorandum of views.

ACC 1980b. *Report of a study week-end*. National Parks Sub-Committee. April (unpublished).

ACC 1980c. Personal communication from *Treasurer*.

ACC 1980d. Statistics, National Parks. *County Council Gazette*, vol. 73, no. 8, November.

Addison, C. (chairman) 1931. *Report of the National Park Committee*. Cmnd 3851. London: HMSO.

Agriculture Act 1970. London: HMSO.

Aldous, T. 1980. The natives are getting restless. *The Countryman* vol. 55, no. 2.

Anderson, M. A. 1980. The land pattern of areas of outstanding natural beauty in England and Wales. *Landscape Planning* no. 7.

Anderson, M. A. 1981. Planning policies and development control in the Sussex Downs AONB. *Town Planning Review* vol. 52, no. 1.

Arlington, M. 1981. *A comparison of dairy farming in Bavaria and England and Wales*. Report no. 25. Reading: Milk Marketing Board.

Avery, B. W., D. C. Findlay and D. Mackney 1975. *Soil map of England and Wales*. Southampton: HM Ordnance Survey.

Barbier, C. P. 1963. *William Gilpin: his drawings, teaching and theory of the picturesque*. Oxford: Clarendon Press.

Barrett, J. 1978. A walk on the wildside. *Vole* no. 10.

BBNPC (Brecon Beacons National Park Committee) 1977. *National park plan*. Policy B2.34C.

BBNPC 1979. *Proposals for afforestation of the Cnewr Estate*. Report by National Park Officer, July.

BBNPC 1980a. *Submission to Secretary of State for Wales on proposals to afforest Cnewr Estate*. April.

BBNPC 1980b. Cnewr afforestation. *BBNPC Newsletter* no. 24.

Beresford, T. 1975. *We plough the fields*. Harmondsworth: Pelican.

Berger, R., and A. M. and M. MacEwen 1979. *The White Peak, a study in landscape conservation*. Bartlett School of Architecture and Planning, University College London.

Berry, G., and G. Beard 1980. *The Lake District: a century of conservation*. Edinburgh: Bartholomew.

Blacksell, M., and A. W. Gilg 1981. *The countryside: planning and change*. London: George Allen and Unwin.

Bonham-Carter, V. 1971. *Land and environment*. London: Hodder and Stoughton.

Brotherton, I., O. Maurice, G. Barrow and A. Fishwick 1977. *Tarn Hows, CCP 106*. Cheltenham: Countryside Commission.

Buchanan, C. *et al*. 1963. *Traffic in towns*. London: HMSO.

Burton, S. 1970. Introduction to *Exmoor National Park guide*. London: HMSO.

Campbell, D. 1980. Target Britain. *New Statesman* 31 October.

Capstick, M. 1972. *Economic effects of tourism in the Lake District*. Economics Department, University of Lancaster.

Capstick, M. 1978. Economic, social and political structures in the uplands of Cumbria. In *The future of upland Britain*, vol. 2, R. B. Tranter (ed.). Reading: CAS.

Capstick, M. 1980. *A critical appraisal of three* ad hoc *planning authorities in upland Cumbria and Yorkshire 1951 to 1974*. Centre for North-West Regional Studies, University of Lancaster.

Carty, J. A. 1978. Appendix to *Proposals for changes in the Highlands and Islands Development (Scotland) Act to allow more effective powers over rural land use*. Inverness: Highlands and Islands Development Board.

CAS (Centre for Agricultural Strategy) 1980. *Strategy for the UK forest industry*. Reading: CAS.

Caufield, C. 1981. What can we save of Broadlands? *New Scientist* vol. 89, no. 1234.

CC (Countryside Commission) 1970a. *The coastal heritage*. London: HMSO.

CC 1970b. *The planning of the coastline*. London: HMSO.

CC 1972. *The proposed Cambrian Mountains National Park*. PC/13. The Committee for Wales. Newtown: Countryside Commission (CC).

CC 1974. *The Upland Management Experiment*. CCP 82. London: CC.

CC 1976. *The Lake District Upland Management Experiment*. CCP 93. Cheltenham: CC.

CC 1977a. *Handling of Stowey Allotment by Exmoor National Park Committee*. Report to Secretary of State for the Environment. 10th annual report CC: London: HMSO.

CC 1977b. *The Broads, possible course of action*. CCP 104. Cheltenham: CC.

CC 1977c. *Submission to the Strutt Committee, statement 22 November 1977*. Cheltenham: CC.

CC 1978. *Areas of Outstanding Natural Beauty*, discussion paper, CCP 116. Cheltenham: CC.

CC 1979a. *Countryside rangers and related staff*. Advisory series no. 7. Cheltenham: CC.

CC 1979b. *Dales rail*. CCP 120. Cheltenham: CC.

CC 1979c. *Digest of countryside recreation statistics*. CCP 86. Cheltenham: CC.

CC 1979d. *National parks census data 1971*. WP 15. Cheltenham: CC.

CC 1979e. Public holding of land in national parks, Appendix 1. In *Eleventh report 1977–8*. London: HMSO.

CC 1979f. *The Snowdonia upland management experiment*. CCP 122. Cheltenham: CC.

CC 1980a. *Areas of Outstanding Natural Beauty*. Response to the discussion paper, CCP 137. Cheltenham: CC.

CC 1980b. *Forestry policy*. Paper 80/286. Cheltenham: CC.

CC 1980c. *Guided walks*. CCP 130. Cheltenham: CC.

CC 1980d. National park plans, comments by CC. In *Twelfth report CC, 1978–9*, Appendices 1a–1e. London: HMSO.

CC 1980e. *No military training on Camber Tor*. Statement 10 April 1980. Cheltenham: CC.

CC 1980f. *Proposals to afforest parts of the Cnewr Estate*. Submission to Secretary of State for Wales, 18 March. Newtown: CC.

CC 1980g. Response to the NCC consultation paper on forestry. Cheltenham: CC.

CC 1981a. *Areas of Outstanding Natural Beauty*. A policy statement, CCP 141. Cheltenham: CC.

CC 1981b. *The Broads*. Statement by the CC, 17 February. Cheltenham: CC.

CCS (Countryside Commission for Scotland) 1974. *A park system for Scotland*. Perth: CCS.

CCS 1978. *Scotland's scenic heritage*. Perth: CCS.

Cherry, G. 1975. *National parks and recreation in the countryside*. Vol. II: *Peacetime history, environmental planning*. London: HMSO.

CIS (Counter Information Services) 1980. *Hardship hotel*. London: CIS.

CLA (Country Landowners Association) 1975. *Your land*. London: CLA.

CLA 1980. *Employment in rural areas*. London: CLA.

Clouston, E. 1980. Plot and counter plot. *Guardian* 23 January.

Coleman, A., and I. Feaver 1980. Farm vandalism – who carries the can? *Farmers' Weekly* 4 July.

Common Land in England and Wales 1958. *Report of the Royal Commission*, Cmnd 462. London: HMSO.

CRC (Countryside Review Committee) 1976. *The countryside – problems and policies*. London: HMSO.

CRC 1977. *Leisure and the countryside*. Topic paper 2. London: HMSO.

CRC 1978. *Food production and the countryside*. Topic paper 3. London: HMSO.

CRC 1979. *Conservation and the countryside heritage*. Topic paper 4. London: HMSO.

Cripps, J. 1977. *Letter to chairman, Exmoor National Park Committee, 18th February*. Cheltenham: CC.

Cripps, Sir J. 1979. *The Countryside Commission: government agency or pressure group?* Town Planning discussion paper No. 31. University College London.

Cundale, G. C. 1979. Llangorse Lake is dying; fact or fantasy? *Breconshire Naturalist* no. 29, Spring 1979.

Curry, D. 1981. To save our farms. *Observer* 15 February.

Curtis, L. F., F. M. Courtney and S. Trudgill 1976. *Soils in the British Isles*. London: Longman.

Curtis, L. F., and E. Maltby 1980. Conserve or concede? *Farmers' Weekly* 27 June.

Daniels, Sir G. 1979. Public will turn from meat and milk. *Farmers' Weekly* 9 November.

DART (Dartington Amenity Research Trust) 1973. *Llangorse Lake, a recreation survey 1972*. Totnes: DART.

DART 1976. *Hadrian's Wall, a strategy for conservation and visitor services*. CCP 98. Cheltenham: CC.

DART 1978a. *Small woodlands on farms*. Report to Countryside Commission. Totnes: DART.

DART 1978b. *Visitor centres*. In association with Department of Psychology, University of Surrey. Totnes: DART.

DART 1979. *Small woodlands on farms*. Pilot study, further report to Countryside Commission. Totnes: DART.

Davidson, J., and R. Lloyd 1977. *Conservation and agriculture*. London: Willy.

Davidson, J., and G. P. Wibberley 1977. *Planning and the rural environment*. Oxford: Pergamon.

Davies, E. T. 1977. *Dartmoor and Exmoor National Parks: changes in farming structure. 1952–72*. University of Exeter.

Dennier, A. 1978. National park plans. *Town Planning Review* vol. 49, April.

Dexter, K. 1978. *Farm size in relation to technology and competition*. Cirencester: Royal Agricultural College.

Dimbleby, G. W. 1962. *The development of British heathlands and their soils*. Oxford Forestry Memoirs 23. Oxford: Oxford University Press.

DNPC (Dartmoor National Park Committee) (undated). Working Party report: *Conservation of ancient monuments*.

DNPC 1977. *Dartmoor National Park plan*.

DNPC 1981. *Military use of Dartmoor*. Report 9 January.

DOE (Department of the Environment) 1971. *Local government in England*. Cmnd 4584. London: HMSO.

DOE 1972. *Heritage coasts*. Circular 12/72. London: HMSO.

DOE 1974a. *Conservation of the countryside*. Desk atlas no. 20, fifth rev. London: DOE.

DOE [and WO (Welsh Office)] 1974b. *Local Government Act 1972: National Parks*. Circular DOE 65/74, WO 103/74. London: HMSO.

DOE 1975. *Sport and recreation*. Cmnd 6200. London: HMSO.

DOE 1976a. *Regional councils for sport and recreation*. Circular 47/6. London: HMSO.

DOE [and WO] 1976b. *Report of the National Park Policies Review Committee*. Circular DOE 4/76, WO 7/76. London: HMSO.

DOE [and WO and DOT (Department of Transport)] 1977. *Roads and traffic – National Parks*. Circular DOE 125/77, WO 182/77, DOT 8/77. London: HMSO.

DOE 1978a. *Common land: preparations for comprehensive legislation*. Report of an interdepartmental working party. London: DOE.

DOE 1978b. *Limestone quarrying at Old Moor, Wormhill*. Decision letter 8 May.

DOE [and WO] 1978c. *Trees and forestry*. Circular DOE 36/78, WO 64/78. London: HMSO.

DOE 1979a. *Proposed wildlife and countryside bill*. Consultation paper.

DOE 1979b. *Solution mining of potash in Whitby area*. Decision letter 8 October.

DOE 1980a. *Limestone quarrying at Old Moor, Wormhill*. Decision letter 31 January.

DOE [and WO] 1980b. *Touring, caravanning and tent camping*. Ministers' conclusion, 5 November.

Dower, J. 1945. *National parks in England and Wales*. Cmnd 6378. London: HMSO.

Dower, M. 1965. *The challenge of leisure: the fourth wave*. London: Architectural Press.

Edwards, J. 1978. Report of NFU annual meeting. *West Somerset Free Press* 3 February. *NFU Insight* 20 February.

Edwards, M. 1981. Does land matter? *Built Environment*.

EEB (European Environmental Bureau) 1978a. *One Europe one environment – a manifesto*. Brussels: EEB.

EEB 1978b. Common Agricultural Policy: conclusions drawn by the EEB from a seminar on the CAP. Brussels: EEB.

EEC (European Economic Community) 1972a. Directive 72/159/EEC. The modernisation of farms. *Official Journal, L-96*. Brussels: EEC.

EEC 1972b. Directive 72/161/EEEC. Socio-economic guidance. *Official Journal, L-96*. Brussels: EEC.

EEC 1975. Directive 75/268/EEC. Mountain and hill farming in certain less-favoured areas. *Official Journal L-128*. Brussels: EEC.

EFG (Economic Forestry Group) 1980. *Investment in forestry and hill land*. London: EFG.

ENPC (Exmoor National Park Committee) 1977a. *National park plan*.

ENPC 1977b. *National park plan supplement*.

ENPC 1980. *Policy for Porchester, Maps 1 and 2*, 4 November.

ENPC 1981a. *Management agreements for Exmoor National Park*. Dulverton: ENPC.

ENPC 1981b. *Porchester maps of moorland, Maps 1 and 2*.

ETB (English Tourist Board) and Trades Union Congress 1976. *Holidays, the social need*. London: ETB.

Fairbrother, N. 1970. *New lives, new landscapes*. London: Architectural Press.

FC (Forestry Commission) 1977a. *The Forestry Commission's objectives, policy and procedure*. Paper no. 1. Edinburgh: Forestry Commission.

FC 1977b. *The wood production outlook in Britain*. Edinburgh: Forestry Commission.

FC 1978. The place of forestry in England and Wales (draft paper), quoted in *Strategy for the UK forest industry*, CAS report no. 6. Reading: CAS.

FC 1980a. *59th annual report*. Table 2. Edinburgh: HMSO.

FC 1980b. *60th annual report*. Table 1, Appendix VII and statement 2 of 1979–80 accounts. Edinburgh: HMSO.

FC 1980. *Private forestry*, consultative paper on the administration of felling control and grant aid. Edinburgh: Forestry Commission.

Feist, M. J. 1978. *A study of management agreements*. CCP 114. Cheltenham: CC.

Feist, M. J., A. M. K. Leat and G. P. Wibberley 1976. *A study of the Hartsop Valley*. CCP 92. Cheltenham: CC.

Fitton, M. 1978. *Snowdonia UMEX, the farmers' attitudes*. Countryside Commission internal paper. Cheltenham: CC.

Fitton, M. 1979. Countryside recreation – the problems of opportunity. *Local Government Studies*, July/August.

Fitton, M. 1981. The farmer and the landscape. *ECOS* vol. 2, no. 1.

Fletcher, J. T. 1975. *Letter to chairman and members of the Yorkshire Dales National Park Committee, 14 October*. North Yorkshire County Council.

Gasson, R. 1979. *Labour sharing in agriculture*. Wye College, University of London.

Gemmell, A. 1978. Comments to Department of the Environment on CRC. Topic paper 2, *Leisure and the countryside*, unpublished.

Gemmell, A. 1980. Personal communication.

Gibbs, R. S., and M. C. Whitby 1975. *Local authority expenditure on access land*. M6, Agricultural Adjustment Unit, University of Newcastle-upon-Tyne.

Gilder, I. 1980. Do we need key settlement policies? *The Planner* vol. 66, no. 4.

Goode, D. 1981. The threat to wildlife. *New Scientist* vol. 89, no. 2347.

Green, B. H. 1976. Changes in the countryside, Appendix 55, sixth report Session 1975–6, House of Commons Expenditure Committee, *National parks and the countryside*. London: HMSO.

Guimet, L., and N. Martin 1978. *Some aspects of the Scottish mountain economy*. Grenoble: Institut National d'Etudes Rurales Montagnardes.

Gwynedd County Council 1976. *The impact of a power station on Gwynedd*.

Haines, A. L. 1977. *The Yellowstone story*, vol. 2. Yellowstone Library and Museum Association and Colorado Associated University Press.

Hall, C. 1978. Oh for a closer walk with glee. *Vole* vol. 1, no. 8.

Halliday, B. 1980. Landowners reject policy document. *West Somerset Free Press* 6 June.

Hand, M. 1979a. *The Broads*. Working paper for authors.

Hand, M. 1979b. *The New Forest*. Working paper for authors.

Harland, H. 1980. *Letter from SW Regional Surveyor, MAFF, to Exmoor National Park Officer, 22 August*.

HC 1980a. *Eighth report of the Committee of Public Accounts, session 1979–80*, vol. 3, paras 111–6. London: HMSO.

HC (House of Commons) 1980b. *Official report*, 15 July.

Herbst, R. L. 1980. Assistant secretary for wildlife and parks. *Courier* vol. 3, no. 8. Washington: US National Park Service.

Heseltine, M. 1980. *Speech to Rural Voice conference*, 14 November. London: DOE.

Hill, H. 1980. *Freedom to roam*. Ashbourne: Moorland Publishing.

Himsworth, K. H. 1976. Lake District National Park Officer, *Letter to Secretary of State for the Environment, 26 July*. LDSPB.

Himsworth, K. H. 1980. *A review of areas of Outstanding Natural Beauty*. CCP 140. Cheltenham: CC.

Hobhouse, Sir Arthur (chairman) 1947a. *Report of the National Park Committee (England and Wales)*. Cmnd 6628. London: HMSO.

Hobhouse, Sir Arthur (chairman) 1974b. *Report of the Special Committee on footpaths and access to the countryside*. Cmnd 7207. London: HMSO.

Holmes, G. D. 1979. *Relating forestry to farming*. British Association Annual Meeting, Forestry Section.

Hookway, R. J. S. 1967. *The management of Britain's rural land*. Proceedings of the Town and Country Planning School, RTPI.

Hookway, R. J. S. 1975a. *Conflicts and opportunities*. Report of the annual conference of National Park Authorities. North Yorkshire County Council.

Hookway, R. J. S. 1975b. *Letter to North Yorkshire County Council*. Minutes of Yorkshire Dales National Park Committee.

Hookway, R. J. S. 1977. *Countryside management, the development of techniques*. Proceedings of the Town and Country Planning School, RTPI.

Hookway, R. J. S. 1978. National park plans: a milestone in the development of planning. *The Planner* vol. 64, no. 1.

HL (House of Lords) 1968. *Official Report*, 20 May. London: HMSO.

HL 1979. *Policies for rural areas in the European Community*. Report of Select Committee on European Communities. London: HMSO.

HL 1980. *Scientific aspects of forestry*. Report of Select Committee on Science and Technology. London: HMSO.

HL 1981. *Official report*, 16 March. London: HMSO.

Howell, D. 1974. *National parks – the challenge to the new authorities*. Report of the annual conference of National Park Authorities, CCP 74. Cheltenham: CC.

Hurley, C. W. 1979. *A study in the administration of national parks*. London: Association of County Councils.

Huxley, Sir Julian (chairman) 1947. *Report of the committee on the conservation of nature in England and Wales*. Cmnd 7122. London: HMSO.

ITE (Institute of Terrestrial Ecology) 1979. *Exmoor moorland management study* draft report (unpublished).

IUCN (International Union for the Conservation of Nature and Natural Resources) 1975. *World directory of national parks and other protected areas*. Morges, Switzerland: IUCN.

IUCN 1980. *World conservation strategy*. Morges, Switzerland: IUCN.

James, J. H. 1978. *Letter from conservator, NW Conservancy of the Forestry Commission to Lake District National Park Officer*, 7 July.

Jones, Sir W. Emrys 1972. *The future of the uplands*. DINAS Conference report. London: MAFF.

Laverack, M. D. 1979. *The Countryside Commission's view of forestry policy*. Society of Arts Conference. Cheltenham: CC.

LDSPB (Lake District Special Planning Board) 1976. *The law and upland management*. Report to Board.

LDSPB 1978. *Lake District National Park plan*.

LDSPB 1980. *Proposed caravan and camping legislation*. Report to Board.

Leonard, P. 1979. *Agriculture in the National Parks of England and Wales*. Unpublished paper. Cheltenham: CC.

Local Government, Royal Commission on, 1969. Cmnd 4040. London: HMSO.

Longland, J. 1972. *Reform of local government in England and Wales; National Parks, recommendations by the Countryside Commission*. London: CC.

Lord, R. 1979. Small farmers left out in the cold. *Farmers' Weekly* 9 November.

Lowe, P., and J. Clifford 1979. *The countryside in 1970 conference; issues, ideology and impact*. Bartlett School of Architecture and Planning, University College London.

Lowe, P., S. Buchanan and J. Clifford 1979. *Patrician preservationists*. Bartlett School of Architecture and Planning, University College London.

Lowe, P., and J. Goyder, forthcoming. *Environmental groups in British politics*. London: George Allen & Unwin.

Mabey, R. 1980. *The common ground*. London: Hutchinson, in association with NCC.

Mackie, J. 1980. Seeing the wood. Letter to *The Times* 18 December.

MAFF (Ministry of Agriculture, Fisheries and Food), SO (Scottish Office), WO (Welsh Office) 1972. *Forestry policy*. Statement. London: HMSO.

MAFF 1979a. *The agricultural development and advisory service*. Policy review: London: MAFF.

MAFF 1979b. *Farming and the nation*. Cmnd 7458. London: HMSO.

MAFF 1980a. *Agriculture and horticulture development scheme*. Explanatory booklet AHS5. London: MAFF.

MAFF 1980b, SO, WO and FC (Forestry Commission) 1980b. *Review of forestry policy*. Statement, 10 December. London: MAFF.

MAFF 1980c. *Breakdown of livestock compensatory allowances*. Supplied by MAFF information office, London.

MAFF 1981. *Annual review of agriculture 1981*. Cmnd 8132. London: HMSO.

Massey, D., and A. Catalano 1978. *Capital and land*. London: Edward Arnold.

Miller, G. R., and A. Watson 1976. Heather moorland: a man-made ecosystem. In *Conservation in practice*. A. Warren & F. B. Goldsmith (eds). London: Wiley.

MLNR (Ministry of Land and Natural Resources) and Welsh Office 1966. *Leisure in the countryside England and Wales*. Cmnd 2928. London: HMSO.

MOD (Ministry of Defence) 1977. *Statement on the continued use of Dartmoor for military training*. Cmnd 6837. London: HMSO.

Monkhouse, P. 1975. *Introduction, Peak District National Park guide*, 2nd edn. London: HMSO.

Morris-Jones, H. 1973. The people and their language. In *Snowdonia National Park guide*, 2nd edn. London: HMSO.

Mutch, W. E. S., and A. R. Hutchinson 1980. The interaction of forestry and farming. *Economics and management*. Series no 2, Department of Forestry and Natural Resources, University of Edinburgh.

Nabarro, R. 1973. Do public works help the uplands? *New Society* 29 November.

NC (Nature Conservancy) 1970. *Twenty-one years of conservation*. London: HMSO.

NCC 1975. *Nature conservation in the Malvern Hills AONB*. London: NCC.

NCC 1976. Memorandum in *National parks and the countryside*. Sixth report, House of Commons Expenditure Committee, Session 1975−6. London: HMSO.

NCC 1977. *Nature conservation and agriculture*. London: NCC.

NCC 1980a. *Fifth report 1978−9*. London: HMSO.

NCC 1980b. *Evidence to House of Lords, Forestry sub-committee*, 11 June. London: HMSO.

NCC 1980c. *NCC calls for further measures to protect wildlife habitats*. Statement, 12 December. London: NCC.

NCC 1980d. *Agricultural improvement grants*. Statement. London: NCC.

NCC 1980e. *Moorland conservation in Exmoor National Park*. Statement by SW Regional Office, and *Submission to Exmoor National Park Committee on Porchester Map 2*. Taunton: NCC.

NCC 1981. *New evidence of increasing destruction of wildlife habitats*. Statement, 11 February. London: NCC.

NCVO (National Council for Voluntary Organisations) 1980. *Towards a rural strategy*. London: NCVO.

NDDC (North Devon District Council) 1977. *Letter reporting decision of ordinary meeting of 16 August, Porchester study file*. London: DOE.

Newby, H. 1979a. *Green and pleasant land*. London: Hutchinson. Paperback edn 1981. Harmondsworth: Pelican.

Newby, H. 1979b. *Urban fringe management, the farmers' response*. Internal paper. Cheltenham: CC.

Newby, H., C. Bell, D. Rose and P. Saunders 1978. *Property, paternalism and power*. London: Hutchinson.

NFU (National Farmers' Union) 1980. *Agricultural policy*, statement by SW Regional Office, 28 July. Taunton: NFU.

NFU and CLA (Country Landowners' Association) 1966. *The reclamation of Exmoor*. Taunton: NFU.

NFU and CLA 1977. *Caring for the countryside*. A statement of intent for farmers and landowners. London: NFU and CLA.

Nicholson, M. 1972. *The environmental revolution*. Harmondsworth: Pelican.

Nicholson, M. 1980. Interviewed by C. Pye-Smith and P. Lower. *ECOS* vol. 1, no. 1.

Nicholson, M. 1981. Rallying to the call of the wild. *The Guardian* 4 March.

Nicholson, N. 1975. Looking at the Lakes. In *Lake District National Park guide*, 2nd edn. London: HMSO.

Northfield, Lord (chairman) 1979. *The acquisition and ownership of agricultural land*. Report of the committee on, Cmnd 7599. London: HMSO.

NPC (National Parks Commission) 1962. Private afforestation in National Parks, Appendix I. *Thirteenth annual report*. London: HMSO.

NPN (National Park News) 1979–80. Minister supports park policies. *NPN* Winter 79–80. Cheltenham: CC.

NPN 1980a. Park buys the Roaches. *NPN* Spring 1980. Cheltenham: CC.

NPN 1980b. Oil and gas exploration, *NPN* Summer 1980. Cheltenham: CC.

NPN 1980c. Will RTZ strike it rich in the Peak District? *NPN* Summer 1980. Cheltenham: CC.

NT (National Trust) 1979. *Egremont Estate, press release*, 8 May. London: NT.

Nugent, Lord (chairman) 1973. *Report of the defence lands committee*. Cmnd 5714. London: HMSO.

NYCC (North Yorkshire County Council) 1980. *Secretary of state's proposed modification to Structure Plan*. Report, September.

NYMNPC (North York Moors National Park Committee) 1978. *Nawton Tower Estate*. Report, September.

O'Connor, F. B. 1976. The ecological basis for conservation. In *Conservation in practice*, A. Warren & F. B. Goldsmith (eds). London: Wiley.

O'Riordan, T. 1980. The Yare barrier proposals. *ECOS* vol. 1, no. 2.

Parry, M., A. Bruce and C. Harkness 1981. The plight of British moorland. *New Scientist* 28 May.

Pasmore, A. 1977. *Verderers of the New Forest*. Pioneer Publications.

PCNPC (Pembrokeshire Coast National Park Committee) 1977. *National park plan*.

PCNPC 1980. *Minutes 17 March*.

Pearsall, W. H. 1965. *Mountains and moorlands*. Glasgow: Collins (third impression).

PFA (Public Finance and Accountancy) 1981. Recent developments. January.

Pharaoh, C., and R. Anderson 1980. Non structure plans – and the logic of expedience. *The Planner* vol. 66, no. 5.

Phillips, J. 1977. Certain aspects of Exmoor (report dated October 1976). In *Supplement to Exmoor National Park plan*. ENPC.

Porchester, Lord 1977. *A study of Exmoor*. London: HMSO.

PPJPB (Peak Park Joint Planning Board) 1974. *Structure plan report of Survey.*
PPJPB 1978a. *National park plan.*
PPJPB 1978b. Secretary of State for the Environment's *Proposed modifications to the Peak structure plan.*
PPJPB 1979. National Park Officer's report on *Secretary of State's modifications to structure plan.*
PPJPB 1980. *Peak District National Park structure plan.*
Price, C. 1979a. *Forestry and regional development.* Paper. Bangor: Forestry Department, University College of North Wales.
Price, C. 1979b. Public preference and the management of recreational congestion. *Regional Studies* vol. 13, no. 2.
Price, C. 1980. Afforestation and the fate of the national parks. *Town and Country Planning* vol. 48, no. 6.
Priddy, S. 1979. The unknown farmer. *Farmers' Weekly* 13 April.
Pugsley, J. 1977. Porchester would tie the farmers' hands, interview. *West Somerset Free Press* 12 December.

Quicke, J. 1979. Report of land decade conference. *Farmers' Weekly* 2 Nov.

RA (Ramblers' Association) 1980. *Footpath statistics.* Press statement, 29 March. London: Ramblers' Association.
Ramsay, Sir J. D. (chairman) 1945. *National parks: a Scottish survey.* Cmnd 6631. Edinburgh: HMSO.
Ramsay, Sir J. D. (chairman) 1947. *National parks and the conservation of nature in Scotland.* Cmnd 7235. Edinburgh: HMSO.
Redcliffe-Maud, Lord (chairman) 1969. *Report of the Royal Commission on local government.* Cmnd 4040. London: HMSO.
Ridley, Viscount 1979. *Report of National Park Authorities conference.* Northumberland County Council.
Roaches, the 1977–1980. Reports to PPJPB 1977–79. Personal communications; and *National Park News* Winter 1979–80.
Roper, L. W. 1973. *FLO, a biography of Frederick Law Olmsted.* Baltimore: Johns Hopkins University Press.
Rose, C. 1980. *Expert advice. ECOS* vol. 1, no. 2.
Runte, A. 1979. *National parks, the American experiment.* Lincoln, Nebraska: University of Nebraska Press.
Ryan, G. 1978. *Upland Management Service.* Counsel's opinion to Lake District Special Planning Board, 12 March. LDSPB.
Ryle, Sir M. 1980. *Sunday Times* 5 October.

Sandford, Lord (chairman) 1974. *Report of the National Park Policy Review Committee.* London: HMSO.
Sax, J. L. 1976. America's national parks, *Natural History,* special suppl., vol. LXXXV, no. 8.
Sayce, R. B. 1978. *Agriculture in the hills.* Report of the Conference of National Park Authorities, Exmoor National Park Committee.
Sayce, R. B. 1980. Evidence to House of Lords Select Committee on European Communities, 1979–1980. 27th Report. *Policies for rural areas in the European community.* London: HMSO.
Sayer, Lady 1977. *The exceedingly damaging military use of Dartmoor.* Published privately.
Sayer, Lady 1980. The scandal of Camber Tor. *Great Outdoors* August.
Scott, Mr Justice (chairman) 1942. *Report of the Committee on land utilisation in rural areas.* Cmnd 6378. London: HMSO.

SDD (Scottish Development Department) 1980a. *The Town and Country Planning (Notification of applications) (Scotland) Direction*. Edinburgh: HMSO.

SDD 1980b. *The Town and Country Planning (Restriction of Permitted Development) (National Scenic Areas) (Scotland) Direction*. Edinburgh: HMSO.

Searle, G. 1975. Copper in Snowdonia National Park. In *The politics of physical resources*, P. J. Smith (ed.). Harmondsworth: Penguin, in association with the Open University Press.

Sharp, Lady 1977. *Dartmoor: a report into the continued use of Dartmoor by the Ministry of Defence for training purposes*. London: HMSO.

Sheail, J. 1976. *Nature in trust*. Glasgow and London: Blackie.

Shoard, M. 1978. Access: can present opportunities be widened? *Countryside for all?* Conference proceedings, Countryside Recreation Research Advisory Group (CRRAG), CCP 117. Cheltenham: CC.

Shoard, M. 1980. *The theft of the countryside*. London: Temple Smith.

Silkin, L. 1949. House of Commons *Official report*, 31 May.

Sinclair, G. and V. Bonham-Carter 1966. *Can Exmoor survive?* Dulverton: Exmoor Press.

Sinclair, G. 1979. *The semi-natural vegetation of the national parks*. Report to the authors.

Smart, G. 1980. *Strategies in decline*. Bartlett School of Architecture and Planning, University College London.

Smith, I. 1976. *Architecture: a celebration*. Inaugural lecture, Department of Architecture, University of Bristol.

SNPC (Snowdonia National Park Committee) 1975. *Rural land use management*. Discussion paper.

SNPC 1977. *Snowdonia National Park plan*.

SNPC 1979. *Snowdon management scheme*.

SNPC 1981. *Minutes of January meeting*, incorporating report of Yr Wyddfa sub-committee, 19 December 1980.

Spedding, C. R. W. 1981. The role of small scale farming. In *Small farming and the nation*. R. B. Tranter (ed.), CAS paper no. 9. Reading: Centre for Agricultural Strategy.

Stevens, Sir R. (chairman) 1976. *Planning control over mineral working*, report of Committee on. London: HMSO.

Stewart, G. G. 1978. *Inter-relations between agriculture and forestry*. Edinburgh: Forestry Commission.

Strang, Lord 1963. *13th Annual Report of the National Parks Commission, 1961–62*. London: HMSO.

Strutt, Sir N. (chairman) 1978. *Agriculture and the countryside*. Report of the Advisory Council for Agriculture and Horticulture in England and Wales. London: MAFF.

Swanwick, C. 1980. *Nature conservation and landscape conservation*. Working paper for authors, University College London.

Symonds, H. H. 1949. *Report and Newsletter*. Friends of the Lake District, September.

Tandy, C. R. V. 1979. *Landscape design of hill forests*. British Association Annual Meeting, Forestry Section.

Tranter, R. B. (ed.) 1981. *Small farming and the nation*, CAS paper 9. Reading: Centre for Agricultural Strategy.

Tudor. J. E. 1980. Report of *Annual Conference of National Park Authorities*. Brecon Beacons National Park Committee.

Wager, J. 1976. *Management agreements in principle and practice*; a case study of Monsal Dale. Bakewell: Peak Park Joint Planning Board.

Warren, A., and F. B. Goldsmith (ed.) 1976. *Conservation in practice*. London: Wiley.

WMN (Western Morning News) 1980. *Fury over army's guns*. 26 September.

Westmacott, R. and T. Worthington 1976. *New agricultural landscapes*. CCP 76. Cheltenham: CC.

Wheeler, N. 1980. The coastline: the last frontier. *The Planner* vol. 66, no. 6.

Wibberley, G. P. 1979. *The maintenance of a stable rural population*. Paper given to European Confederation of Agriculture 31st assembly. Wye College, University of London.

Wildlife and Countryside Act 1981. London: HMSO.

Williams, R. 1973. *The city and the country*. London: Chatto and Windus.

WO (Welsh Office) 1967. *Snowdonia, purchase of 13 000 acres*, Press release, 7 November. Cardiff: WO.

WO 1971. *Vaynol Estate*. Statement to House of Commons by David Gibson-Watt MP, 10 July. Cardiff: WO.

WO 1973. Decision letter by Secretary of State on *Appeal by PGL Voyages Ltd*, 22 June, and report by the inspector, 8 February. Cardiff: WO.

WO 1976. Decision letter by Secretary of State on *Appeal by PGL Voyages Ltd and PGL Young Adventurers Ltd*, 13 December, and report by the inspector, 25 July. Cardiff: WO.

WO 1979. *Briefing paper for Parliamentary answer on Vaynol Estate*. 5 February (PUS/TAJ/17/79). Cardiff: WO.

Wordsworth, W. 1977. *Guide to the Lakes*. E. de Sélincourt (ed.). Oxford: Oxford University Press.

Worthington, T. R. 1980. *The landscapes of institutional landowners*. A study for the Countryside Commission. Cheltenham: CC.

WSC (Windermere Steering Committee) 1980. *Windermere, a management plan for the lake*. Consultation document. Kendal: S. Lakeland District Council.

WTB (Wales Tourist Board) 1974. *Tourism in Gwynedd, an economic study*. Cardiff: WTB.

Yapp, B. 1969. *The week-end motorist in the Lake District*. London: CC.

YDNPC (Yorkshire Dales National Park Committee) 1977. *National park plan*.

Index

Matters and place names specific to a national park are indexed under that national park. References applying to the economic, historical, physical, recreational or social characteristics of national parks generally, and comparative descriptions, are indexed under national parks, general characteristics. Other references applying generally to national parks and national park authorities are indexed under national park administration, national park authorities, national park management plans, national park policies or national park system, or under the appropriate subject heading, e.g. public landownership. Figure page numbers are in italics, e.g. *15*; table page numbers are in bold, e.g. **14**.

Abrahams, H. 21
access
  agreements 17, 19, 23, 139, 146, 148, 156, 162, 163, 169, 176, 253, 265; **132**
  compulsory purchase for 113, 169, 176
  to commons 87, 205
  de facto 20, 87, 148, 156, 166
  expenditure 132
  under National Parks and Access to the Countryside Act 1949 13, 20, 114
  to open, wild country 8, 19, 75, 93, 144, 146, 175, 253
  network/systems 87–9, 149, 253
  orders 20, 114, 169, 175, 265
  right to 19, 67, 87, 149, 205, 253
Access to Mountains Act 1939 7
accommodation, holiday, *see* holidays
Addison committee/report 6
Advisory Council for Agriculture and Horticulture 204, 207
affluent, consumer society, impact of 22, 249
afforestation, *see* forestry and afforestation
age and sex structure 105; *106*
Agricultural Development and Advisory Service (ADAS) 103, 153, 174, 182, 197, 200, 204, 207, 266, 286
agricultural land classification map 59
Agricultural Research Council 201, 270
agricultural supports
  Agriculture and Horticulture Grants Scheme (AHGS) 200, 205, 210
  Agriculture and Horticulture Development Scheme (AHDS) 178, 199, 200, 205, 210, 234, 286; **224**
  case for redirection 210, 271, 283-4
  confidentiality of 177, 182, 187
  cost of 103, 192, 199–201, 210–11, 271; **224**
  duty to withhold 177, 182, 186, 191–2
  in Europe 200, 273
  in Exmoor 174, 176–7, 182, 185, 190, 191–2, 204

agricultural supports (*cont.*)
  grant-aided improvements 64, 142, 166, 169, 205, 258, 264, 265, 266, 285–6
  headage payments 101, 174, 190, 199, 202, 211; **224**
  land drainage 257, 262, 271
  Livestock Compensatory Allowances, *see* headage payments, above
agriculture, *see* farming, farms
agriculture and forestry, needs of, statutory duty 24, 138
Agriculture Acts, 1947, 1967, 1970 24, 103, 281, 286
Agriculture, Fisheries and Food, Ministry/Minister of (MAFF)
  and conservation 139, 165–6, 177, 181, 191, 203, 266 passim, 285–6
  and Countryside Commission/Nature Conservancy Council 204, 266
  and Countryside Review Committee 138
  and development control 154
  and EEC directives 192, 199
  farm development plans 166, 200; **214**
  Farming and the Nation, white paper 204, 207
  and forestry 197, 220
  grant aid, *see under* agricultural supports
  and hill farming 101, 197
  key to upland revival 266
  and land drainage 257, 272
  and management agreements 190, 191, 193
  need to change direction 210, 267, 270
  notification of 'improvements', *see under* farming
  policies, policies criticised 23, 101–3, 139, 141, 173–4, 182, 191–2, 197–201, 203–5, 206–7, 210, 229, 268, 270, 272, 284–6
  and Porchester inquiry 180, 182
  and reclamation of moorland, *see under* Exmoor National Park

Agriculture, Fisheries and Food, Ministry/ Minister of (MAFF) (*cont.*)
and rural affairs, development 23–4, 163– 4, 204, 210, 266, 281
and small, part-time farms 207
socio/economic role 201, 266
and upland management 163, 165, 210
see also Agricultural Development and Advisory Service (ADAS), agricultural supports, Exmoor National Park, farming
Agriculture and Horticulture Development Scheme (AHDS), *see under* agricultural supports
Aldous, T. 108
Anderson, M. A. 11, 197, 275
Anglian Water Authority 257
Areas of Great Landscape Value 275, 276
Areas of Outstanding Natural Beauty (AONBs) 16, 23, 153, 164, 250, 258, 268, 274, 285
Arlington, M. 200, 273
Article 4 Directions 83, 174
Assisted Areas 84, 97; **98**
Association of County Councils (ACC) 104, 119, 120, 128, 135, 137, 142, 218, 219, 251; **128, 129, 130–1, 132, 151, 158**
Atomic Energy Authority 34
Avery, B. W., D. C. Findlay and D. Macney 59

Barber, D. 280
Barbier, C. P. 68
Barrett, J. 57, 87
Bavaria, agricultural policy 103, 200, 273
Berchtesgaden National Park 95
Beresford, T. 197
Berger, R. and A. M. and M. MacEwen 208
Berry, G. and G. Beard 90
Biology, Institute of 226
Birkett, Sir N. 7
Blacksell, M. and A. W. Gilg 28, 149, 150
Blaenau Ffestiniog 14; *48*
Blenkinsop, A. 149
boards and committees, *see under* national park authorities
Bodmin Moor 242
bogs, bog-trotting 57, 58n, 59; *39, 41, 43, 45, 47, 49, 51, 53, 55, 57*
Bonham-Carter, V. 68
bracken and gorse 59; *39, 41, 43, 45, 47, 49, 51, 53, 55, 57*
Brecon Beacons National Park *50–1, 106*; **14**
afforestation, woodlands 142, 217, 221; **217**
characteristics, general, *see under* national parks, general characteristics
Cnewr estate 168, 216, 221, 229
common land 205

Brecon Beacons National Park (*cont.*)
Craig-y-Nos country park 75
Fan Gihyrich 223
Fforest Fawr 223; *50*
forestry map 219, 222
Great Forest of Brecknock 66
landscape policy 142
limestone 57
Llangorse Lake 95, 170
management agreements 224
moorland, heather and grass 59, 193
Mountain Centre 157
pony-trekking 85, 170
reservoirs 231
tree planting 167
Welsh language 107
Brecon Beacons National Park Committee 22, 25, 117n, 129, 142, 167–8, 170, 171– 2, 218–19, 221–4, 240; **116, 123, 124, 125, 130–1, 133, 151, 158–9**
see also under national park management plans
Brecon County Council 170
bridleways, *see* footpaths and bridleways
British Ecological Society 8
Broadleaved woodlands 59, 62–3, 142, 167– 8, 173, 191, 212–13, 216–18, 224, 226– 8, 271; *39, 41, 43, 45, 47, 49, 51, 53, 55, 57*; **132**
Broads, the, and Broads Authority 14, 77, 170, 255, 256–7, 262
Brown, 'Capability' 68
Buchanan, C. 240
Buchanan, C. *et al.* 91
Burton, (Tim) S. H. 60

Cambrian Mountains, proposed national park 250; *15*
camping and caravans 81
Capital Gains Tax 215, 223
Capital Transfer Tax (CTT) 12, 160, 167
Capstick, M. 203, 281
Caravan Club 81, 82
Caravan Sites and Control of Development Act, 1960 82
caravans, *see* camping and caravans
cars, car ownership, car parks 4, 23, 73–4, 77, 85–6, 90–3, 101, 111–12, 144–7, 148– 9, 239, 256
see also roads and highways, vehicle penetration
Carty, J. A. 182
Caufield, C. 257
caves, caving 85, 112, 119, 146
Central Electricity Generating Board (CEGB) 101, 160, 229, 231; **158–9**
central government
change in direction needed 70, 93, 165–6, 229–30, 249–50, 267, 270–2, 281–2, 283–4

central government (*cont.*)
  and conservation 22–3, 268
  cuts in local services 108, 134, 191, 237
  duties, responsibilities of 4, 166, 193
  financial control by 134
  'interference' by 120
  internal policy conflicts 231–2, 233, 243–4
  policies, *see under* Agriculture, Ministry of; conservation; Defence, Ministry of; Environment, Department of; forestry; Conservative and Labour governments
Centre for Agricultural Strategy (CAS) 104, 215, 218, 225, 226
change, the politics of 282
Cherry, G. 7, 18
Cheshire County Council **116**
Cheviot Hills 57, 80, 240, 254; *38*
Chilterns, the 258; *14*
china clay 57, 99, 232; *56*
circulars, government
  consultative procedures for forestry 219
  national park plans 68, 136, 138
  national parks 11, 29, 90, 143, 146
  sport and recreation 143, 146
  traffic and highways in national parks 29, 90, 114
Clark, D. 149
Cleveland County Council **116**
climate, *see under* national parks, general characteristics
climbing, climbers 85, 89, 112, 169
Clouston, E. 152
coalition government (1940–45) 7–8
coast, coastal management 57–8, 59–60, 86, 255
  see also heritage coasts
Coleman, A. and I. Feaver 89
Common Agricultural Policy (CAP) 101, 270
  see also under European Economic Community
common land, rights of common 67, 68, 142–3, 148–9, 178–9, 205–7, 210–11, 255–6, 266–7
Commons, Open Spaces and Footpaths Preservation Society 205
Commons Registration Act 1965 206
compensation, *see under* management agreements
compulsion, compulsory powers, compulsory purchase 26, 113, 142, 169, 172, 174, 177, 183, 184, 186–7, 218, 247, 266, 274, 275–6
  see also access orders, control, development control, Moorland Conservation Orders
conflicts of interest xi-xii, 23, 26, 28–9, 62–3, 115, 138–9, 139–40, 141, 142–3, 166–8, 169, 172–93 passim, 204–5, 210–11, 232–3, 237–45, 271–2, 273,

conflicts of interest (*cont.*)
  283–4
coniferous plantations 59–63, 70–1, 212–18, 221, 229–30; *39, 41, 43, 45, 47, 49, 51, 53, 55, 57;* **214**
consensus approach, *see under* management of land, *see also* goodwill
conservation
  agreements 167, 183, 185
  and Agriculture, Ministry of 166, 177, 182–3, 191–3, 203–5, 268–72 passim
  'amenity clause', Section 11 Countryside Act 1968 24, 177
  of broadleaved woodlands 227
  central government attitude, policies 22, 70, 268–9, 270–2, 273–4, 282–4
  and cosmetics 70, 247, 249, 259–61, 282–3
  and the countryside 268–84
  definitions, meaning of 23, 70, 269–70, 282–3
  divided responsibility for xi–xii, 8, 16–19, 111, 247, 276–8
  ecological approach to 140–2, 274–5, 276–7
  economics of 269–70, 283–4
  expenditure on 128–9; **129, 130–1**
  and farming 9–10, 26, 69–70, 103, 107, 141–2, 175, 181–3, 192, 204–5, 207, 264–5, 268–72 passim, 280–1, 283–6
  and forestry 23, 26, 70, 212, 219, 224, 229, 271, 284
  integrated approach to xi–xii, 247, 269–70, 271–2, 273–4, 282–4
  of landscape, natural beauty, scenery, scenic beauty xi–xii, 8, 10, 16–19, 68–73 passim, 111, 140, 141–3, 160–1, 169–70, 178, 204, 252, 264–5, 266–7, 273–5, 276–7, 280–1
  local authorities, proposed powers 274
  and military training 239, 240–1, 243–5
  and minerals 232–3, 234–5, 236–8, 271
  movement for 8, 283–4
  national policies/systems for 269–70, 271, 273–5, 282
  in national park and structure plans 139–43
  and national park authorities 143, 251–2
  new approach to 252
  official attitude to 252, 268–70
  and open country 13
  options for land management 70, 283
  politics of 70
  of resources (human and natural) 29, 64, 69, 105, 111, 139, 232, 235, 237, 238, 266, 269, 273, 282
  resources for 22, 268, 286
  statutory duty, purpose 5, 13, 16, 24, 177, 252
  voluntary approach to 70, 176, 178, 185, 186, 268, 284, 286

conservation (*cont.*)
  see also under Agriculture, Ministry of (MAFF); Exmoor National Park: management of land; nature conservation; Sites of Special Scientific Interest
Conservation Areas 16, 113
Conservation and the Countryside Heritage (CRC) 250
Conservation of Nature in England and Wales (Huxley report) 9, 17
conservationists xi, 72, 90, 283
Conservative government, ministers 12, 22, 25, 185, 191, 193, 205, 216, 229, 266–9, 284, 285–6
Conservative Party, conservatives 115–17, 122, 125, 185, 279, 281; **125**
Consolidated Goldfields 99, 237
consultation, consultative procedures 70, 139, 142, 162, 218, 222, 265
control, xi, 26, 85, 86, 136, 142, 143, 170, 175, 183, 197, 256, 263, 272, 274, 278, 284–6
  see also compulsion, development control
copper, 57, 234
Cornish Coast, proposed national park 14
Cornwall, Duchy of 66, 160, 241, 243; **158–9**
cosmetics 70, 247, 250, 261, 282
Council for National Parks 251
Council for the Protection (formerly Preservation) of Rural England (CPRE) 6, 122, 178, 218, 251, 284
Council for Small Industries in Rural Areas (CoSIRA) 108
Country Landowners' Association (CLA) 124, 175, 176, 183, 187, 189, 193, 204, 210, 278, 286
country parks 24, 74
countryside, the
  custodians, stewards of 204, 278
  functions of NPAs 113
  management/planning of 11, 26, 137, 156, 276
  policies for, problems of 23, 26, 270, 273, 274, 275, 282
  see also depopulation, farming, forestry, hill farming, recreation, rural areas, uplands
Countryside Act 1968 13, 16, 23, 27, 81, 114, 175, 187
Countryside Bill 1978–9 185
Countryside Commission
  agreement with County Councils Association 25, 115, 119
  and AONBs 251, 275
  and appointed members 115n, 121, 263
  and the Broads 256
  and Cambrian Mountains National Park 250
  Dales rail 92
  and designations 275
  establishment of 22–3, 24

Countryside Commission (*cont.*)
  and Exmoor 179, 184, 187, 190, 193
  and farming 203, 204, 207, 280
  and forestry, tree planting 212, 218, 220, 228
  grants 23, 103, 127, 142, 227; **128**
  and Hadrian's Wall 254
  and landscape 68, 203, 204, 207
  long distance paths 87; **128**
  and MAFF 266
  management agreements/projects 24, 163–6 passim, 168, 180, 190, 193, 204, 210
  and military training 240, 243, 245
  and national parks, national park plans 25, 68, 119, 121, 136, 138, 161, 240, 286
  and the Nature Conservancy Council xii, 16, 72, 276
  and the New Forest 255
  and public land management 161–2
  rangers 156
  recreation 24, 74, 89, 145, 171
  and Sandford Committee 26
  status, powers, duties 18, 24, 25, 277
  see also National Parks Commission
Countryside Commission for Scotland 68, 259
Countryside Conservation Area (proposed) 276
Countryside Conservation Orders (proposed) 265, 274, 276
Countryside in 1970 Conferences 23
Countryside Review Committee (CRC) 87, 121, 126, 138, 138n, 144, 204, 250, 269
county councils
  access, rights of way 19, 88
  AONBs 16
  finance 127, 131, 191, 262; **128**
  local/structure planning 10, 136, 145
  national parks xi, 11, 12, 21–2, 113, 115–21, 124–7, 129–31, 134, 191, 251–2, 261–3; **116, 128**
  and staffing 118, 120, 132, 262
County Councils Association 8, 25, 119, 181
  see also Association of County Councils
Cousins, J. 27
Creech-Jones, A. 7
Cripps, (Sir) J. 26, 179, 242
Cripps, Sir S. 12
Crowe, Dame S. 213
Cumbria (County Council) 25, 68, 115, 254; **116**
Cundale, G. C. 170, 172
Curry, D. 184
Curtis, L. H. (and others) 58, 174, 186
cycle of intensification and decline 99, 105, 112, 271, 272; *100*
cycling, plan for 148

Dalton, H. 8, 12, 21

Daniels, Sir G. 208
Dartington Amenity Research Trust (DART) 87, 171, 227, 254
Dartmoor Commons Bill 206
Dartmoor National Park 56, 57, 106; **14**
  afforestation, woodlands 216; **217**
  ancient monuments, archaeological sites 65, 239
  characteristics, general, *see under* national parks, general characteristics
  china clay 57, 99, 232; *56*
  common land 205, 206
  Cornwall, Duchy of 66, 160, 241, 243; **158–9**
  Cramber Tor 243, 245
  Cranmere Pool 92
  Dartmeet 79
  Deeper Marsh management plan 167
  designation 238
  development control in 150, 155
  farm employment, holdings 103, 160
  military use, road, 14, 92, 239, 254; *241*
  moorland, 59, 146, 173, 193, 239, 241
  'nature conservation zone' 141, 275
  prison 79, 244
  recreational use 75
  vehicle penetration 92
  wilderness 241, 243
Dartmoor National Park Committee 22, 74, 119, 129, 132, 155, 160, 167, 241, 243 passim; **116, 123, 124, 125, 128, 129, 130–1, 133, 151, 158–9**
  see also under national park management plans
Davidson, J. and R. Lloyd 281
Davidson, J. and G. P. Wibberley 76, 99, 108, 215
Davies, E. T. 103
day-trips, trippers, *see also* holidays, holiday makers 79, 80
defence lands/report/white paper 29, 160, 239, 242; **158–9**; *241*
Defence, Ministry of 34, 92, 139, 146, 160, 239; **116**
  see also military training
Dennier, A. 143
Dennison, S. R. 10, 23
depopulation, rural 9–10, 23, 33, 99, 103, 152, 198, 203, 207, 211, 213, 251, 271, 273; *100*
Derbyshire County Council 22, 116, 118n, 235; **116**
designation, designated areas 12, 27, 247, 254, 274; *15, 38–57, 260*; **14, 116**
development areas 97; *98*
Development Board for Rural Wales 108; *109*
Development Commission 108, 137, 210, 253; *109*
development control 11–12, 113, 114, 134, 136, 137, 249–55, 251–2, 284, 286; **151**

development control (*cont.*)
  applications, calling-in 118
  Article 4 Directives 83, 174
  building design 150, 152, 153–5
  caravans, camping, holiday accommodation 82
  county matters 118
  enforcement 171
  extension of, proposed 264, 274–5
  and farming 11, 150, 152, 153–4, 261, 263–4, 274–5, 284
  and forestry 11, 26, 142, 150, 153, 212, 219–20, 224, 229–30, 261, 263–4, 274, 284
  and key centres, settlements 150
  and living systems 264
  mineral workings 234–8
  policy framework 113, 136
  powers of national park authorities 11, 113–14, 117
  pre-1974 11, 27, 150
  and social and economic needs 96, 152
development plans, *see* structure plans
Devon (County Council) 96, 118, 135, 140, 174, 175, 189; **116**
Dexter, K. 207, 209
Dimbleby, G. 71
Dinorwic pumped storage scheme 101, 231
district councils, councillors 25, 82, 117, 122, 125, 134, 153, 181, 192–3; **116**
Dorset heaths 258
Dower, J. 8, 18, 23, 93
  report on National Parks in England and Wales 7–18 passim, 19–20, 25, 80–1, 253–4, 256
Dower, M. 23
Dresser Industries, Inc. 238
du Cann, E. 191
Duff, Sir P. 21, 22
Dyfed County Council 119, 120; **116**

East Fellside and Alston Project 210
ecology, ecologists, ecosystems, ecological view 3, 4–5, 8, 9, 63–4, 68–9, 71–2, 140–1, 146, 148, 162, 170, 172, 182, 185–6, 225–6, 269–70, 274–5, 276–7; *38*
Economic Forestry Group (EFG) 212, 213, 218, 222, 223; **224**
economic and social development, *see under* rural areas
economic and social interests of rural areas, statutory duty towards 24, 29, 96, 138
economic growth/ideology of 70, 225, 235, 284
Edinburgh, Duke of 23
Edwards, J. 187
Edwards, M. 281
electricity authorities 58
  see also Central Electricity Generating Board

elitism and democracy 93
Emerson, R. W. 3
employment, unemployment, job creation 96, 105, 108, 164, 225, 233, 239, 240, 271–3
enclosures, the 66
energy, 64, 70, 73, 91, 92, 104, 140, 208, 225
Energy, Department of 233
English Tourist Board 80
enjoyment, *see under* recreation
Environment, Department of the
  camping, caravanning 83
  common land 206
  defence 242–3
  Exmoor reclamation 175, 180, 184, 189, 192, 193; **188**
  forestry 220
  highways/traffic 28, 90, 114
  minerals policy 233, 237
    see also under minerals
  national parks/grants/plans 11, 26, 29, 68, 90, 121, 136, 138, 143, 146
  sport and recreation 144, 146
Environment, Secretary of State, Minister of State for the 26, 83, 115, 121, 136, 141, 146, 152, 180, 189, 191, 220, 234, 236, 250, 268, 285–6
erosion, of footpaths and soils 62, 85, 89
European Economic Community (EEC)
  agricultural policies within 103, 190, 198, 198–201, 210–11, 270, 273, 280–1
  farm modernisation directive 101, 198–9, 200–1
  less favoured area directive 84, 101, 103–4, 192–3, 198–200, 266–7, 286; *102*
  socio-economic directive/policy 199, 201
  UK membership 197
European Environmental Bureau 270
Exmoor National Park *54–5, 106;* **14**
  access agreements 175
  afforestation and woodlands 173, 191, 216–17; **217**
  and Agriculture, Ministry of 174, 175, 176–7, 181, 182–3, 189–90, 191–3
  beech hedges 62
  Bye Common 189, 206
  the Chains 60
  characteristics, general 173, 181
    see also under national parks, general characteristics
  critical amenity area map 142, 175, 176, 178, 180, 181, 187
  Dunster 60
  farm employment, holdings 103, 207
  farm holidays 83
  Forest of Exmoor 59, 66, 174
  Fortescue estate 169
  Glenthorne, North Common, Yenworthy 168, 178, 182, 183, 184, 189; *179;* **188**
  grants/90% grant 135, 170, 185, 189, 191, 193

Exmoor National Park (*cont.*)
  Haddon Hill 168, 183; *179;* **188**
  Larkbarrow 135, 169, 189, 191; *179;* **159n; 188**
  management agreements/compensation guidelines 167, 178, 183, 189, 268, 286; **188**
  moorland conservation, reclamation 64, 167, 169, 172–93 passim, 278; *179*
  moorland conservation maps 142, 182, 185, 187, 264; *179*
    see also critical amenity area map *above*
  Moorland Conservation Orders (MCO) 183, 186, 265
  moorland loss 175, 176–7, 181
  moorland management, report on 62, 64, 177–8
  nature and scenic conservation 140–1, 182, 185–6
  Porchester, Lord, report on Land Use in Exmoor 142, 173–5 passim, 177, 181–9, 191, 193, 203, 265; *179;* **188**
  soils and vegetation 58–60, 62–3, 174–5, 199; *55, 179*
  Stowey Allotment 168, 179, 182, 183; *179*
  upland profile in 62
  see also Countryside Commission, Nature Conservancy Council
Exmoor National Park Committee(s) 22, 25, 64, 75, 126, 132, 135, 160, 169, 174–5, 176–93 passim; **116, 123, 124, 125, 130–1, 133, 151, 158–9**
  see also under national park management plans
Exmoor People's Association 191
Exmoor Society 175, 178

Fairbrother, Nan 71, 104, 212
farmers/landowners, *see* landowners/farmers
farming/farms
  and access 144, 148
  alternative policies for 209–11, 270, 271–3
  capital-intensive/labour extensive 10, 101–4, 140, 177–8, 198–9, 202–3, 206–8, 210–11, 269, 270, 271–2, 283–4
  and controls 224, 263–5, 278–82, 284
  derating of 131
  employment/unemployment 96, 101–3, 165, 198–9, 203, 207–8, 210–11, 271–2; *100*
  family farms 202, 207, 209, 272
  farm size, structure 103, 198, 201, 208, 218, 281
  impact on nature/landscape 64, 69, 71, 203, 208
  labour shortage 62, 142, 165, 201–3, 210–11, 269
  low-input, conservative, labour intensive, traditional 10, 64, 104, 177, 201, 270, 271, 283

farming/farms (*cont.*)
 moorland reclamation 63, 183–93 passim
 in national park and structure plans 138,
  141, 178
 notification of 'improvements' 70, 142,
  176–7, 183, 186–9, 192, 264–5, 268,
  274–5, 285–6
 policies, *see under* Agriculture, Ministry
  of
 production 101, 183, 192, 197, 198–9, 204,
  207, 208, 269
 sacred cow of agriculture 26
 small, part-time farms, farmers 99, 101–3,
  199, 201–2, 207–8, 210–11, 266, 271–
  2, 279; *100*
 statutory duty towards 24, 138
 and technology 62, 103–5, 174, 197, 201,
  203–5, 206–8, 209, 269, 270, 271–2,
  280–1
 visitor impact 89, 165
 wages 134
 young farmers 203, 282
 see also agricultural supports, CAP, conflicts of interest, conservation, development control, EEC, forestry, hill
  farmers, holidays, less favoured areas,
  rural areas, upland management
Feist, M. J. (and others) 165, 166, 211
field study centres 85, 156–7
finance, *see under* national park authorities
Fitton, M. 74, 76, 89, 157, 280
Fletcher, J. T. 119
Florida Everglades 3
fluorspar 57, 99, 232, 238
Foot, Lord 176
footpaths, footpath system, bridle ways 19–
  21, 75–6, 85–6, 87–9, 113, 144, 148,
  162–3, 164, 166, 252–3, 277
 see also access, long distance paths, right
  of way
Footpaths and Access to the Countryside,
  Special Committee 9
forestry, and afforestation 212–30; *39, 41,
  43, 45, 47, 49, 51, 53, 55, 57*; **214, 215,
  217, 224**
 assumptions questioned 225–6
 capital intensive, labour extensive 104–5,
  225–6, 227–8
 Cnewr estate 168, 216, 221–5, 229
 commercial forestry plantations/foresters
  34, 63, 71, 216–18
 consultation/procedure 142, 218, 219–25
 control over 26–7, 142, 212, 224, 264–5,
  278–82, 284
  see also under development control
 employment 104–5, 216, 225–6
 expansion programmes 104, 212, 215–18,
  225–6
 farming, integration with 11, 223–4, 228–
  9

forestry, and afforestation (*cont.*)
 grants and tax concessions 141–2, 167,
  212–13, 216, 223–5, 227–8, 265–6; **224**
 impact on nature/landscape 64, 69–70,
  71–2, 212–13, 225–6
 maps 166, 218–19, 221–3, 224, 229–30,
  264–5
 Ministers 197, 212, 220
 a new approach 228–30
 in national park and structure plans 138–
  9, 141–3, 218
 planting, *see under* Forestry Commission
 policy 23, 71–2, 139, 216, 227, 229
 private forestry, role and motivation 212–
  15, 216, 218, 223–4, 229; **217, 224**
 research 63, 226, 229
 scientific aspects, technology 62, 104–5,
  225–8, 270–1
 statutory duty towards 24, 138
 threat to countryside, uplands 63, 212
 timber, timber merchants 212–15, 225
 and water abstraction 226
 see also broadleaved woodlands, Cnewr
  Estate, coniferous plantations, conservation, Countryside Commission, Department of the Environment
Forestry Commission
 attitudes/ideology 143, 212–15, 216–17,
  218, 229–30, 271
 and conservation 212–13, 229, 271
 consultation procedures 218, 219–21
 and Countryside Review Committee 138,
  250
 dedication schemes 212–13, 220, 221–2;
  217, 224
 and employment 216, 225–6
 expansion, campaign/programme 104,
  215–16, 225
 felling licences 228
 forest parks 88–9, 212, 274
 grants, tax concessions, *see under* forestry
 integration of farming and forestry 228
 Lake District agreement 218–19
 and landscape/nature 138–9, 212–15, 219,
  222–3, 266
 land ownership/acquisition/disposal 89,
  160–2, 212, 216, 217–18, 224, 229–30;
  158–9, 217
 national forest authority, enterprise 212–
  13
 and New Forest 215, 156
 objectives 161–2, 212–13, 224–5, 228,
  229–30, 271
 planting 212–18; **214, 289**
 policy 139, 212
 recreation role 80–1, 84, 88–9, 212–13
 Regional Advisory Committees 220
 and research 63, 226
 small woods scheme 212–13, 227
Forest of Bowland 258

France, agricultural policies 200, 266, 273
France, national and regional parks 6, 84, 126, 266
Frankland, R. 279
Fylingdales radar station 244

Gasson, R. 202
Gemmell, A. 76, 88, 148
General Development Order (Town and Country Planning) 1977, amendment to 114
General Household Survey 1977 75
geology, geological processes 36
Gibbs, R. S. and M. C. Whitby 20, 169
Gilder, I. 152
Gilpin, W. 68
Glamorgan-Mid 97; **116**
gliding, hang-gliding 85
Goode, E. 64, 259, 269
goodwill (and consensus) 70, 139, 143, 167, 204, 219, 264, 268, 273, 278, 284
government, *see* central government
Gower Peninsula 83
Goyt Valley 92
granite 36
grants, grant-aid, *see under* agricultural supports, Countryside Commission, forestry, *see also* National Park Supplementary Grant, Rate Support Grant
grasslands 59–60; *39, 41, 43, 45, 47, 49, 51, 53, 55, 57*
grazing 58, 60, 64, 217
Great Yarmouth Port and Haven Commissioners 257
Green, B. H. 277
grouse moors/shooting 7, 34, 60, 62, 148
Guimet, L. and N. Martin 200
Gwynedd (County Council) 96, 101, 107, 163; **116**

habitats, habitat, destruction 33, 60, 63, 64, 71
Hadrian's Wall 65, 79, 232, 254, 262; *38*
Hall, C. 94
Halliday, B. 178, 190
Hampshire County Council 256
Hardy, Thomas 73, 259
heather, heather moors 59–60, 62–3, 64, 148, 177; *39, 41, 43, 45, 47, 49, 51, 53, 55, 57*
see also moorland
hedges, hedgerows 62, 203
heritage coasts 24, 164, 275, 276
Heseltine, M. 108, 152, 234, 268–9, 271
Highlands and Islands Development Board 210
highways, *see* roads
Hill, H. 7
hill farmers, farming, farms 60, 64, 99, 101–4, 141, 163–6, 173–4, 197–203, 218, 225

Hill Farming Act 1946 198
Himsworth, K. H. 221, 251
history of man in national parks 64–8
history of national parks 3–29
Hobhouse, Sir A.
report on footpaths and access to the countryside 8, 9, 17, 19, 253
report on national parks in England and Wales 8–9, 11–12, 13–14, 17, 18, 19–20, 80–1, 120–1, 253–4
Holmes, G. D. 216–17, 218
holidays, holidaymakers 79–84
accommodation 80–3, 149, 252
farm holidays 83–4, 97
'honeypot' areas 75, 79, 94, 145
Hookway, R. J. S. 27, 119, 138, 145, 161–2, 168–9, 180
hostels 81
housing, Housing Act, 1980 105, 117, 150–3
Howell, D. 127, 161, 181
Hurley, C., report on national park administration 119–20, 251
Huxley, Sir J., report on nature conservation in England and Wales 9, 17, 18

Iddesleigh, Lord 193
Imperial Chemical Industries (ICI) 99, 235–6
Industry, Department of 139, 161
information/interpretive services 86–7, 127–8, 156–7, 162, 249–50; **128, 129, 130–1, 133**
see also visitor centres
installations in national parks 22, 231–45
Institute of Terrestrial Ecology 19, 63, 140, 177
International Union for the Conservation of Nature and Natural Resources (IUCN) 4–5, 254, 259, 269
issues xi–xii, 95, 212, 283–4

Jackson, P. 118n
James, T. H. 219
Jefferson, T. 3
jobs, *see* employment
Joint Advisory Committees (JAC) 21–2, 174, 175, 176, 251
joint national park committees 25, 117n
joint planning boards 21, 25
Joint Standing Committee for National Parks 7–8
Jones, Sir E. 198

Kendal to Windermere Railway 6
Kennet, Lord 176
King, T. 170, 185, 284
Königsee 95

Labour Party, Labour 21–2, 118n, 122, 126, 281, 284; **125**

Labour governments, ministers 6, 8, 23, 24, 144, 185, 204, 250, 266
Lake District National Park *44–5, 106*; **14**
  afforestation and woodlands 142, 216–17, 218–19, 220–1; **217**
  Brockhole visitor centre 87, 157
  'capacity' of 146
  caravans 81–4
  characteristics general, *see* national park general characteristics
  common land 205–6
  development control in 149–50, 152, 154
  Ennerdale 218–19, 231
  farm employment, holdings 201–3, 207, 210–11
  Friends of the Lake District 6–7
  Grasmere 83, 203
  Hartsop valley/study 165, 211
  holiday accommodation 81
  housing 105, 150, 152, 211
  Hudson's Allotment 221
  Kendal to Windermere railway 6
  land acquisition/ownership 12, 160, 264; **158–9**
  Landscape Areas Special Development Order 1950 (LASDO) 11, 114
  Langdale 84
  as a national park/property 5, 6–7
  National Trust 6, 160
  power boating, water-ski-ing 86
  recreation survey 74–5
  roads/traffic 90, 117
  Seafell and Derwent Fells 160
  slate quarries 56, 99
  Tarn Hows 71, 79, 94–5
  Troutbeck caravan site, valley 82, 203
  Ullswater 83
  Upland Management Experiment/Service 87, 163–6, 167, 210, 265–6
  vandalism 89
  Wastwater 231
  Watendlath 92
  water management, resources 86, 231
  Windermere 75, 85–6, 95, 157
  Windscale 231
  and Wordsworth 6, 73
Lake District Special Planning Board 11, 22, 25, 27–8, 71, 83, 115–17, 129–30, 132, 142, 146–7, 149–50, 152, 153–4, 160, 164–6, 210–11, 218–19, 220, 250, 252, 262; **116, 123, 124, 125, 130–1, 133, 151, 158–9**
  see also under national park management plans
Lancaster, Duchy of 66; **158–9**
land
  agents 280–1
  as capital 278
  drainage 210, 257–8, 262, 271–2, 274–5
  management, *see* management, of land

land (*cont.*)
  market/intervention in 142, 218, 273, 278–82
  nationalisation 251, 279, 281–2
  prices 278–9
  'protected' 274–5
  public land, *see* public landownership
  reform, policy for rural land 273–4, 280–2
  speculation 11, 169–70
  valuation 169, 178–9, 221–2
land, acquisition by public bodies 11–12, 18, 26–7, 113–14, 129–30, 134–5, 142, 157–8, 169–70, 172, 178, 180, 189–90, 191, 218, 222, 224, 227, 265, 268, 276; **215**
  expenditure on in national parks 129–30, 134–5, 169; **129, 130–1, 132**
  see also compulsion, compulsory purchase powers
Land and Natural Resources, Minister/Ministry of 23, 24
land use(s), land use planning xi–xii, 6, 8, 10, 11, 34, 59–60, 63, 69, 120, 136–7, 138, 141, 143, 197, 224, 229, 268, 269–70
Land Use in Exmoor, Porchester report, *see under* Exmoor National Park
Land Utilisation in Rural Areas, the Scott report 9–11, 19, 206
landowners/farmers
  attitudes, ideology, motivation of 19–20, 73–4, 77, 83–4, 89–90, 142, 148, 163–4, 173, 187, 190, 198–9, 201–2, 208, 278–81, 286
  interests/lobby 11, 12–13, 20, 126, 173, 175–6, 178, 187, 193, 251, 261–2, 278–9, 283–4
  as members of national park authorities 122–5; **124**
  power, influence of 96, 124–5, 142–3, 175, 192, 278–9
  rights of 168, 175, 184, 192, 272, 278–82
landownership 11–12
  see also land, public landownership
landscape(s)
  and agricultural technology 203, 269
  capacity for recreation 146–8
  conservation of, *see under* conservation
  cultural/man-made xi, 6, 9, 71, 253
  degraded 14
  and depopulation 105, 203
  and hill farming 104
  incremental changes in, deterioration of 70, 111, 138–9, 141, 203–4, 206–7, 209, 211
  living landscape 68–9, 71, 75, 86, 111
  and management 253, 280
  and mineral workings 232–3, 237–8
  of the national parks 33–64
  and natural beauty, scenery, scenic beauty xii, 5–6, 16, 68–9, 70–1, 111, 182, 274

landscape(s) (*cont.*)
  and nature, *see under* nature, natural world
  outstanding 16, 274, 275
  'protected', vulnerable 6, 142, 150, 254, 275
    see also land, protected
  semi-wild 69–70, 71–2, 93, 253
  and socio-economic trends/policies xi, 70, 266
  threats, pressures 22–3, 26–7, 139, 212
  understanding of 280
  and urban experience 91
  see also lowlands
Landscape Areas Special Development Order 1950 (LASDO) 11, 27, 29, 114
Laverack, M. D. 218
leisure 23, 73, 76, 277
Leisure and the Countryside (CRC) 144
Leisure in the Countryside, White Paper 1966 23
Leonard, P. 103
less favoured areas (LFAs) 101, 103, 192, 198–200, 210, 267; *102*
Liberal Party, Liberals 122, 125–6; **125**
limestone, limestone dales, quarries 14, 36–57, 99, 232, 235–6
  pavements 36, 265, 285
Livestock Compensatory Allowances, *see under* agricultural supports
local authorities 73, 75, 80–1, 83, 87, 108, 129–30, 134, 274
Local Government Act 1972 25, 113–14, 118, 119, 257
Local Government (Finance) Act 1974 25, 127
Local Government Planning and Land Act 1980 114, 134
local government reorganisation, 1974 22, 24–5, 28, 111, 120, 177–8
local interests, people in national parks 125–6, 251–2, 261–2
local plans, planning, 113, 116, 136–7
Londoners 77–8
long distance paths 20–1, 87, 239
Longland, Sir J., report 25
Lord, B. 208
Lords, House of, reports of select committees
  European communities' policies for rural areas 103, 166
  scientific aspects of forestry 63, 225–6, 270–1
  sport and leisure 74
Lowe, P. (and others) 19, 23, 161
lowlands, lowland landscapes 69–70, 77, 93, 249, 259

Mabey, R. 10, 69, 264
MacDonald, J. Ramsay 6
Mackie, J. 229
Macmillan, Harold 22

MAFF, *see* Agriculture, Fisheries and Food, Ministry of
Malvern Hills 276
man and nature 3, 34, 58, 69, 70–2, 140–1
management agreements 26–7, 113, 142–3, 156–7, 162, 166–70, 178–80, 182–4, 187–93, 268
  compensation for 143, 167–8, 180, 183–4, 189–93 passim, 268, 285–6
  definitions of 166
  expenditure **132**
  financial guidelines 190–3 passim
  limitations of 165–6, 168–9
  resources for 223–4
  voluntary approach 142–3, 187–92, 268
  see also under Exmoor
management, concept of, approach xi–xii, 26, 136
management, of land
  alternative system 264
  back-up powers, 182–3
    see also controls
  coastal 255
  code for in SSSIs 285
  of common land 205–6
  by consensus 26–7, 138–9, 142–3, 204, 218, 273
  conservative land management 210, 265, 266–7, 274, 275, 282–3
  expenditure 128; **129, 130–1, 132**
  integrated approach 228–30, 269–73
  options 71
  plans and policies for 169, 171–2, 238
  projects 156, 157, 162–6
  of public land 156, 157–62, 245
  quality of 280–1
  see also under countryside, national park management plans, recreation, upland management
Manchester, 36, 90, 131, 231; **116**
Manpower Services Commission 97, 132, 163, 167
maps, policy 193, 264–5
  see also under Exmoor National Park
marine nature reserves 255
Massey, D. and A. Catalano 281
membership of national park authorities, *see under* National Park Authorities
Milford Haven 101; *52*
military training/use 63, 92, 231–2, 238–45, 254–5; *241*
  'dry training' 239, 241, 242–3
  employment 240–2
  impact/conflict with other interests 62–3, 231–2, 239–40, 243
  live firing/ranges 14, 238–41, 242–3, 255
  policy options 244–5
  Sharp report, military training in Dartmoor 239–40, 242–3
  see also Defence, Ministry of

Miller, G. R. and A. Watson 62
mineral/mining companies 34, 99, 232–3, 237–8, 271
mineral rights 238
minerals and rocks/mineral workings 99, 140, 232–8, 243
Monkhouse, P. 80
moorland/moorland conservation, reclamation 58–63 passim, 70–2, 142, 173–93 passim, 241, 285; *179, 241;* **188**
see also under Exmoor National Park
Moorland Change Project 193
Moorland Conservation Orders 183–5, 186
Morris-Jones, H. 66
motor bikes 92
motorcar/motorists, *see* car
motorway and trunk road system 77, 90; *78*
Mutch, W. E. S. and A. R. Hutchinson 228

Nabarro, R. 101
National Council for Voluntary Organisations 272–3
National Farmers' Union (NFU) 124, 174–5, 176, 181, 183, 186–7, 190, 193, 203–4, 210, 272–3, 278, 279, 286
National Heritage Memorial Fund 129–30, 191
National Land Fund 12, 129
national park administration
    appraised, post 1974 120, 261–3
    Countryside Review Committee proposals 250
    and county councils 8, 115–21, 125–7, 130–1, 134–5, 251, 261–2; **116**
    and district councils 53, 115–17, 125–7, 134, 261–2; **116**
    Hurley report on 119–20, 251
    Longland report on 25
    pre 1974 21–3, 25, 27–8, 251
    see also national park system
national park authorities
    appointed members 11, 18, 115, 118–19, 121–7, 136, 251; **123**
    boards and committees 11, 18, 21–2, 25, 27–8, 113–21, 134–5, 251, 262
    democratic accountability 115–17, 263
    duty to offer management agreements 285
    finances of 25, 28, 86, 93, 117–18, 119–20, 127–31, 134–5, 164, 169–70, 266; **128, 129, 130–1, 132**
    future role of 251–2, 264–6
    land acquisition, attitude to 157–60
    landownership 157–60; **158–9**
    see also public landownership
    local representation 125–7, 261–2
    membership composition 11, 17–18, 24–5, 115–16, 115n, 250, 261–3; **116**
    members' characteristics/attitudes 121–7; **123, 124, 125**
    policies of, *see* national park policies

national park authorities (*cont.*)
    powers 11, 22, 81, 86, 113–14, 115–19, 139, 142–3, 177–8, 183, 186–7, 223, 224, 252–3, 264–5, 286
    purposes, statutory, *see under* national park system
    socio-economic role 252–3, 265–6
    staff, staffing 115, 117n, 117–18, 120, 128–9, 132–4, 140, 164; **133**
    see also national park administration, system
National Park Direction Areas, Scotland 12, 259
national park lobby, movement xi, 6–9, 18, 93, 251
national park management plans 25, 113–14, 136, 137–41, 142–8, 162, 240
    Brecon Beacons 142, 219, 221–2, 240
    Dartmoor 146, 155, 240
    Exmoor 178, 185–6
    Lake District 140, 141–2, 146–7, 157, 210–11, 218–19
    North York Moors 140
    Peak District 140–1, 146, 147–8
    Pembrokeshire Coast 139
    Snowdonia 147, 219
    Yorkshire Dales 68, 140
National Park Officer(s) 21–2, 25, 115, 118, 119–20, 131, 178, 243, 266
national park policies
    analysis of 138–9
    conservation 139–43
    farming/forestry 141–2, 218–19
    management 145–9, 162–4, 170, 172, 238, 265
    military 240–3
    minerals 140, 218–19, 232–4, 237, 238
    recreation/transport 143–9
    social and economic 96, 107, 152–3, 252
National Park Policy Review Committee 11, 25–6
    see also Sandford report
National Park Supplementary Grant (NPSG) 25, 117, 127–8; **128**
national park system
    appraisal of 27–8, 29, 70, 111–12, 249–52, 282
    boundaries, designated areas 13–14, 96, 254–61; *15, 260;* **14**
    concept, criteria, definitions 3–6, 13, 253–4, 256
    purposes and duties xi–xii, 5–6, 13, 16, 24, 29, 73, 96, 111, 222–3, 252–3
    reform of, strengthening of 252–4, 282–3
    see also Addison, Cherry, Dower, Longland and Sandford
National Parks and Access to the Countryside Act 1949 xi, 5, 9–23 passim, 25, 27, 73–4, 77, 114–15, 128–9, 156, 170, 252,

National Parks (later Countryside) Commission 6, 13, 16−19, 21, 22−3, 77, 121, 219, 250

National Parks Committee, report, *see under* Hobhouse, A.

National Parks in England and Wales, report, *see* Dower report

national parks, general characteristics of
  archaeological, ancient monuments 64−5, 140, 239
  areas designated and population *15*; **14**
  Assisted Area status 97; *98*
  climate 33, 57−8, 60, 63
  demographic 96−7, 105; *106*
  ecological 63−4, 69; *61*
  employment, activities 96−105
  geological 33−57
  historical 64−8
  landform 34−6
  landscape and scenery 5−6, 9, 33−64, 68−9, 96, 111, 249−50
  Less Favoured Area status 101; *102*
  local life and culture 105−8
  natural life and resources 33−64, 69, 231
  physical features 33−56, 59−60; *35, 38, 40, 42, 44, 46, 48, 50, 52, 54, 56*
  recreational role, use 74−80; *78*
  social and economic 95−7, 97−9, 105−7, 108−10; *100*
  soils and vegetation 33−4, 57−64, 71−2, 175, 182, 186, 226; *39, 41, 43, 45, 47, 49, 51, 53, 55, 57, 61, 179*
  Special Investment Area status 108; *109*
  unique qualities 249
  upland profile 59−64; *61*
  see also depopulation, farming, forestry, public landownership

National Parks and Conservation of Nature in Scotland, report 12, 259−61

national parks in USA 3−4, 91, 274

National Scenic Areas (Scotland) 261

National Union of Agricultural and Allied Workers 124, 272

National Trust, The 6, 11, 74, 81, 84, 87, 160−1, 178, 227, 243, 254; **158−9, 188**

natural beauty xii, 4, 5−6, 13, 16, 24, 26, 68−9, 73−4, 93, 111, 177, 252, 285−6
  see also under conservation, landscape

natural (and human) resources, conservation of, *see under* conservation

nature, natural world/environment/systems
  ascendancy of 69, 111−12
  conservation of, *see* nature conservation
  changes/damage losses to 62, 63−4, 89, 111, 203, 205, 269
  demands on, exploitation of 71−2, 89, 94−5, 269−70, 273−4
  hill-farming and 64
  and landscape, natural and scenic beauty 5−6, 16−19, 33, 68−9, 185, 193, 255, 256−7

nature, natural world/environment/systems (*cont.*)
  man and 3, 34, 58, 69−70, 71, 140−1
  natural features, processes 60, 69
  significance of for townspeople, urban man 74, 75−6, 112, 283
  significance of in uplands 58
  trails 89
  unity of 71
  see also wildlife

Nature Conservancy (1949−73) 16−19, 170

Nature Conservancy Council
  and Agriculture, Ministry of (MAFF) 204, 266
  AONBs 275−6
  and the Broads 257
  consultations, notification 69−70, 268
  and the Countryside (National Parks) Commission 16, 19, 71, 72, 276−8
  and the Countryside Review Committee 138n
  damage to sites, wildlife 70, 205, 268
  and Exmoor 173−4, 182, 189
  and farming 24, 70, 203, 205, 266, 268−9, 285−6
  and forestry 24, 63, 220, 222
  Hadrian's Wall 254
  landownership and management 168; **158−9**
  Llangorse Lake 170−1, 172
  membership 278−9
  military use of Dartmoor 239, 342
  and national parks 68
  and the New Forest 255−6, 262
  research 63
  role/status 19, 277
  and rural land use policy 269−70
  and Sandford Committee 27
  and scenic beauty 68
  woodlands 62
  see also Nature Conservancy

nature conservation xi, 8−9, 16−19, 63, 68−72 passim, 74, 111, 139−40, 141−2, 148, 204, 252, 253, 266, 269−70, 271, 274, 276−8

nature conservation zones 274−5, 176

nature reserves/national nature reserves (NNRs) 7, 8, 17, 18, 69, 140, 160, 162−3, 168, 256

Nature Reserves Investigation Committee 8

New Forest, New Forest Act 1877 66, 212, 255−6, 262, 175

Newby, H. (and others) 20, 209, 279, 280

Niagara Falls 94

Nicholson, M. 8, 18, 283

Nicholson, N. 75

Norfolk Broads, *see* Broads

North Devon District Council 181

North Downs 258

North York Moors National Park *46, 47, 106;* **14**
   afforestation 216–17; **217**
   caravans 81
   characteristics, general, *see* national park general characteristics
   common land 205
   farm employment, holdings 207
   Fylingdales, radar station 244
   grouse-shooting 62
   Lancaster, Duchy of 66; **158–9**
   Lyke Wake walk 85
   moorland, heather 59, 176, 191, 193; *47*
   oil and gas exploration 234
   potash (mining) 57, 118, 237–8
   Rievaulx Abbey 66
North York Moors National Park Committee 25, 118, 130, 160, 167, 234, 237; **116, 123, 124, 125, 130, 133, 151, 158–9**
   see also under national park management plans
North Yorkshire County Council 118–19, 125, 145, 235, 237; **116**
Northern Pennines Rural Development Board 281
Northfield, Lord, report 279, 282
Northumberland County Council 254; **116**
Northumberland National Park *38, 39, 106;* **14**
   afforestation and woodlands 142, 216–17; **217**
   characteristics, general, *see* national park general characteristics
   Cheviot Hills 36, 56, 80, 240, 254–5
   farm employment, holdings 203, 207
   future of 254
   Hadrian's Wall 65, 79, 254
   Kielder forest park 88
   military training 238–40
   nuclear wastes 240
   Vinlandia Trust 254
   Whin Sill 65
Northumberland National Park Committee 22, 142, 150; **116, 123, 124, 125, 130–1, 133, 151, 158–9**
   see also under national park management plans
notification of 'improvements', *see under* farming/farms
nuclear power, waste 231, 240
Nugent, Lord, Committee and report 241–2

O'Connor, F. B. 63
O'Riordan, T. 257–8
oil and gas, exploration 234, 256
Olmsted, F. L. 3–4, 74, 76, 80, 94
open country 13–14, 19–20, 21, 73–4, 77–9, 93, 112, 149, 150–2, 173, 218, 222, 253–4, 258–9
   definition of 13, 253n

outdoor centres 81
Oxford University, Department of Forestry 226

Parcs Naturels et Régionaux 6
Parry, M. (and others) 193
Pasmore, A. 256
Peak District National Park *42, 43, 106;* **14**
   access agreements 19–20
   afforestation 142, 216–17; **217**
   agricultural production, value of 101
   bus and rail timetables 148
   'capacity' of 146–7
   characteristics, general, *see under* national park general characteristics
   Chatsworth 60
   country parks 75
   day visitors 79, 101
   Dovedale 79, 147
   farm employment, holdings 208–9
   fluorspar 232–3, 238
   Goyt Valley 92–3
   grouse shooting, moors 62, 148
   holiday accommodation 81
   landscapes, contrasting 36
   Landscape Areas Special Development Order 1950 (LASDO) 11
   limestone, limestone dales 36, 56–7, 147, 232–3, 235–7
   Longdendale pumped storage scheme 231
   minerals, mineral workings 56–7, 99, 232–8
   Monsal Dale 36, 168
   natural and rural zones 140–2
   oil and gas exploration 234
   Pennine Way 21, 36
   recreation survey 74
   the Roaches 169
   Tunstead quarry 232, 235–7
   water resources 231
   White Peak 36, 208–9
Peak Park Joint Planning Board 11, 22, 25, 28, 84, 90, 99, 116–17, 118n, 134, 140–2, 148, 152, 154, 160, 167, 169, 232–3, 234–7, 238, 250, 262; **116, 123, 124, 125, 130–1, 133, 151, 158–9**
   see also under national park management plans
Peak Park Structure Plan/Report of Survey 84, 99–101, 113, 116n, 140–1, 146–7, 232, 234
Pearsall, W. H. 58, 68, 71
Pembrokeshire Coast National Park *52, 53, 106;* **14**
   afforestation 216–17; **217**
   Brawdy underwater surveillance station (US) 244
   Castlemartin tank range 239
   characteristics, general, *see under* national park general characteristics

Pembrokeshire Coast National Park (*cont.*)
  coastal landscape, management 36, 60, 86, 101, 255
  coastal path 87
  construction schemes and employment 101
  farm holidays 83
  future of 254, 262
  holiday accommodation 81–2
  military training, land, installations 160, 238–9, 240, 244
  oil development 101
  tourism 104–5
  Upton castle 167
  Welsh language 107
Pembrokeshire Coast National Park Committee 101, 115, 119, 120, 134, 139, 240; **116, 123, 124, 125, 130–1, 133, 151, 158–9**
  see also under national park management plans
PGL Voyages Ltd, PGL Young Adventurers Ltd 171
Pennine Way 21, 36
Pharaoh, C. and R. Anderson 137
Phillips, J., report 63, 64, 177–8
Phillips, Mrs P. 181
picnic sites, picnicking 86, 89, 145, 166
Plaid Cymru 107; **125**
plans, planning, planning system 11, 136–49, 251, 264; **129, 130–1, 133**
  see also development control, land use(s), national park management plans, structure plans
plant succession 63; *61*
pony trekking 85, 170–1
population, demographic characteristics 105; *106*
Porchester, Lord; study, report, *see under* Exmoor National Park
potash (mining) 57, 99, 118, 237–8
Powys, county of, county council, structure plan 64, 97, 103, 222; **116**
Preseli hills 14; *52*
Price, C. 213, 219, 224, 229
Priddy, S. 279
property rights, *see under* landowners/farmers
'protected land' 275
protected landscapes, IUCN definition 6
public conveniences 86, 145
Public Expenditure, white paper 1980 134
public inquiries 118–19, 173, 181–4, 231, 235
public landownership 5, 11, 129–30, 174–5, 181, 217, 229, 240–1, 245, 253, 255–6, 281–2; **158–9**
public transport, *see* transport services
Pugsley, J. 186

Quicke, J. 279

Raistrick, A. 107

Ramblers' Association, the 7–8, 87–8, 148
Ramsay, Sir J. D., report on National Parks and the Conservation of Nature in Scotland 12, 259
rangers, *see* wardens
rates/ratepayers, contribution to national parks 28, 120, 127, 131; **128**
Rate Support Grant 127–8, 134–5; **128**
recreation, countryside
  active and informal recreation 85–7
  central government approach 184, 269
  and conservation 26, 29, 145–8, 170–1, 252
  demand for 73–7, 145
  and elitism 93–5
  enjoyment xi–xii, 4–5, 26–7, 73, 74, 75–6, 80, 94–5, 111, 252, 258, 269, 274, 275, 277, 283
  expenditure 128–9; **129, 130–1**
  facilities and services 86–7, 156–7
  Forestry Commission, role 81, 88–9, 212–13
  impact of 89–90, 165
  management, projects 23–4, 86, 93–5, 145–9
  motorised sports 86, 145–6
  national parks, role in 77–80, 84–5, 143–4, 249; *78*
  and national park authorities 84–6, 251–2
  policies and strategies 143–9, 255
  post-war changes in 73–4, 77
  public sector, role 87, 89–90, 111–12
  and social class 73–5, 93, 111–12
  social recreation 80, 149
  statutory purpose 4–6, 13, 16, 252
  and townspeople, urban areas, needs of 74–6, 80, 249, 251–2
  water authorities' role 88
  see also access, Countryside Commission, footpaths, holidays, information, open country, tourism, transport, visitors, walking
Redcliffe-Maude, report 24
regional councils for sport and recreation 144
regional parks 6, 84, 261, 275–6
Reith, Lord 8
reservoirs 170, 231
resources, conservation of, *see under* conservation
Ridley, Lord 128, 135
rights of way 20, 87–8, 148–9
  see also footpaths and bridleways
Rio Tinto Zinc 99, 234
Rocky Mountains, the Canadian 249
roads and highways, traffic 28, 29, 77–8, 90–3, 112, 114, 117, 118, 145–6, 162–3, 239, 249; *78*
  see also, tarmac corridor, traffic management, transport services
Roman Wall, *see* Hadrian's Wall
Roper, L. W. 3–4, 74

Rose, C. 278
Royal Commission on Common Land, report 67, 205
Royal Commission on Local Government, report 24
royal forests 66, 174
Runte, A. 3, 4
rural areas
    communities 10–11, 201, 206–7, 270
    countryside policy in the 1960's 23–4
    development functions, programmes 252–3, 271, 282
    development boards 24, 164, 281–2
    European Communities, policies for 103, 166
    land policy 274, 278–82
    local services, and decline of 23, 97–8, 104–5, 108, 134, 136–7, 273; *100*
    need for change in policies 266–7, 270
    Scott report on land utilisation in 9–11, 19, 206
    social and economic conditions, problems, trends xi–xii, 9, 26, 96–110, 112, 165, 204
    strategies, policies for the future 270–3, 274, 275, 282–4
    see also countryside, depopulation, employment, farming, forestry, hill-farming, uplands
Rural Voice 108, 272–3
Ryan, G. 252

Sandford, Lord 26, 287
    amendment to Wildlife and Countryside Bill 287
    report on national park policies, 11, 25–8, 127–8, 150, 161, 176, 212, 216–17, 219
Sax, J. L. 76, 80, 94
Sayce, R. B. 103, 201
Sayer, Lady 243
scenery, scenic beauty xi–xii, 3, 33, 68–9, 70–2, 111, 182, 189, 190, 255, 258–9, 274, 276–7
science, scientists, scientific view 8, 16, 19, 226, 276–7
Scotland 12, 108, 199, 200, 216, 228, 231, 242, 259–61
    a park system for, report 259
    Secretary of State for 259
    see also Countryside Commission for Scotland
Scotland's Scenic Heritage, report 68, 259–61
Scott, Mr Justice, report 9–11, 19, 206
Scottish Development Department 259–61
Searle, G. 234
second homes 66, 81, 107, 152
Second Land Utilisation Survey 175
semi-wild, semi-wildness 69, 71, 93, 253–4, 258
    see also open country, wildness

'sensitive areas', and approach 82, 144, 221, 229, 232, 233, 268, 274, 275–6, 286
services, local, *see under* rural areas
Sharp, Lady, report 239–40, 242–3
Sheail, J. 17
Shell (UK) Ltd 99, 256
shepherding 62, 64, 202–3
Shetland County Council 108
Shoard, M. 93, 258, 271
Shore, P. 152, 234–5
Silkin, L. 8, 19, 21, 140, 233
Silkin test 140, 233–4, 237
Sinclair, G. 59, 175
Sinclair, G. and V. Bonham-Carter 175
Sites of Special Scientific Interest (SSSIs) 69–70, 141–2, 170, 256, 267–8, 269–70, 274–5, 276–7, 284, 285
    damage or destruction to 70–1, 170, 268
slate (quarries) 14, 36, 99
small woodlands 142, 167, 213, 227–8
    see also broadleaved woodlands
Smallfarmers Association 208, 273
Smart, G. 138
Smith, I. 155
Snowdonia National Park *48, 49, 106;* **14**
    afforestation and woodlands 142, 216–17, 218–19; **217**
    The Arans 147–8
    Cadair Idris 147, 163
    Central Electricity Generating Board (CEGB) 160
    characteristics, general, *see under* national park general characteristics
    construction schemes and employment 99–101
    copper and copper exploration 57–8, 234
    Dinorwic pumped storage 101, 231
    farm employment, holdings 103, 165, 202
    forest park 88
    Forestry Commission holdings 160, 218
    forestry map 219
    the Glyders 147
    holiday accommodation 81–2
    Landscape Areas Special Development Order 1950 (LASDO) 11
    moorland, heather 59, 193
    nature trails 88–9
    nuclear power station 240
    recreation management 147–8
    second homes 107
    slate and slate-quarrying 36, 56
    Snowdon, Snowdon Management project 147–8, 162–3
    Swallow Falls 79
    Upland Management Experiment and Service 87, 164–5
    Vaynol estate 163; **158–9**
    wardening study 156–7
    Welsh language 65–6, 107
Snowdonia National Park Committee 22, 103,

Snowdonia National Park Committee (*cont.*) 130, 132, 142, 162–3, 165, 219, 240; **116, 123, 124, 125, 130–1, 133, 151, 158–9**
see also under national park management plans
social and economic conditions, problems, trends, *see under* rural areas
Society for the Promotion of Nature Reserves 8
soils, upland 57–60, 62–4, 71, 226; *61*
Somerset (County Council) 96, 108, 135, 174, 175, 177, 179–81, 184, 189; **116**
South Downs 14, 77, 258
South-West Regional Water Authority 167, 243
South Yorkshire County Council **116**
Special Parks, in Scotland 259
Spedding, C. R. W. 201
Sport and Leisure, report on, 1973 73–4
Sport and Recreation, White paper on, 1975 144
Sports Council 171
staffing, *see under* national park authorities
Staffordshire County Council **116**
Standing Committee for National Parks 7–8
Stevens, Sir R., report 233, 237
Stewart, C. G. 229
Strang, Lord 22
structure plans 11, 113, 116, 118, 136–9, 141, 144, 152, 233–5, 236–7, 274–5
Strutt committee/report 204, 207, 266
Swanwick, C. 17, 277
Symonds, H. H. 18

Tandy, C. 215, 223
Tansley, Sir A. 18
tarmac corridor 91–2, 112, 249
Tarmac Ltd 99
Taylor of Gryfe, Lord 212
Taylor Woodrow Energy Ltd 234
technological change, fix 91, 274, 282–3
see also under farming, forestry
Tory, *see* Conservative
tourism, Tourist Boards 4, 80–1, 84, 97, 99, 104–5, 107, 117, 145, 165–6, 267
social tourism 80
town and country 73–7, 108–10
Town and Country Planning Acts, 1932, 1947, 1971 7, 10, 21, 82, 113, 152, 286
towns and villages (settlements) 60–2
Trade, Department of 233
Trades Union Congress 8
traffic management and environment 90, 112, 145, 162–3
see also cars, roads and highways
transport services, policies 76, 80, 91, 92–3, 105, 117, 145–6, 148–9, 162–3, 252
Transport, Ministry of 90, 139
Tranter, R. B. 207, 273, 279
Trawsfynnydd, nuclear power station 240

tree planting 162, 167–8, 212–13, 226–7
Tree Preservation Orders 113, 169
trunk-roads, *see* motorway and trunkroad system
Tudor, J. E. 202
Tyne-Wear County Council 254

upland management service/experiments 87, 162, 163–6, 167, 210, 266
uplands, the 33–72 passim, 96–112, 197, 198–9, 205, 210–11
characteristics, significance of 58, 69
communities 197, 210
cycle of intensification and decline 99, 105, 271; *100*
economy and independence of 67
new deal for 265–7
paradox of 105
profile 59–63, 104; *61*
value of, threats to 34, 64–5, 104
see also depopulation, forestry, hill farming, national parks general characteristics

vandalism 89–90
vegetation, semi-natural 34, 56–64, 71, 175, 182, 185–6, 258–9; *39, 41, 43, 45, 47, 49, 51, 53, 55, 57, 61, 179*
deterioration, changes in 62–4
vehicles, penetration by 91–2, 256
Vercors Regional Park 84
Verderers, Court of 256
visitor centres 86, 156, 249; **133**
visitor use, visitors 62, 74, 79, 86, 89, 144, 249, 252
see also recreation, tourism
volunteers 90, 132

Wager, J. 168
Wales, Welsh language, culture 36, 56–8, 107, 162, 170, 197, 202, 223, 250, 281
Secretary of State for/Welsh Office 163–4, 171, 197, 222, 223, 250; **158–9**
Walker, P. 26, 199
walking, walkers, walks, 75–6, 85, 86, 90, 112, 146, 148–9, 253
walls, maintenance of 208–9
wardens (and rangers) 20, 89, 131–4, 145, 156–7, 162, 164; **133**
Warren, A. and F. B. Goldsmith 70
water abstraction, management, storage 85–6, 88, 95, 170–2, 231, 271
water authorities, industry 34, 167, 226, 231, 257, 271; **158–9**
waterways 114, 257
Welsh Development Agency 163
Welsh Office, *see under* Wales
Welsh Tourist Board 84
Welsh Water Authority 170
Wessex Downs 258
West Yorkshire County Council **116**

Western Morning News 240
Westmacott, R. and I. Worthington 203
wetlands 257, 271
Wheeler, N. 86
Whitby Potash Ltd 237
White Peak, the 36, 56−9, 208−9
Wibberley, G. P. 97, 108, 208
wilderness, wild country, wildness 3, 6, 13, 69, 92, 93, 146, 173, 249
    see also open country
wildlife, wildlife resources 58, 60, 63, 69, 70, 89, 139, 156, 170, 182, 204, 205, 240, 253, 257, 269, 274, 280
    see also nature, nature conservation
Wildlife Biological Service 17
Wildlife Conservation Council 16
Wildlife and Countryside Bill (Act) 1980−81 x, 70, 88, 113, 148, 156, 186, 193, 255, 263, 268, 284
Wildlife Special Conservation Committee 9
    see also Huxley report
Willey, F. 23
Williams, R. 73, 108
Windermere 75, 85, 95, 157
women 122, 126, 262; **133**
woodlands, *see* broadleaved woodlands, small woodlands
Wordsworth, W. 4, 6, 73
workers/working class 6−7, 73−4, 76, 93, 122, 124, 126, 263
World Conservation Strategy 72, 259, 269
Worthington, T. R. 280

Wye Valley 258

Yapp, B. 80
Yare basin, barrage 257
Yellowstone National Park 3, 79, 91
Yorkshire Dales National Park *40, 41, 106;* **15**
    afforestation 216; **217**
    Aysgarth Falls 79
    caravans, static 81
    characteristics, general, *see* national parks, general characteristics
    Dales Rail 92
    farm employment, holdings 207
    Ingleborough 88
    Joint Advisory Committee 22
    limestone, limestone quarrying 57, 232, 235
    Semer Water 95
    Shunner Fell 88
    Swinden, Ribblesdale quarries 232
    Three Peaks walk 85
    walkers' maps 148
    Whernside Manor Cave and Fell Centre 85, 119
Yorkshire Dales National Park Committee 22, 25, 68, 115, 119, 126, 140, 148, 160; **116, 123, 124, 125, 130−1, 133, 151, 158−9**
    see also under national park management plans
Yosemite National Park 3
Youth Hostels Association 81